BANG
HANDBOOK

กรุงเทพฯ

BANGKOK HANDBOOK

MICHAEL BUCKLEY

MOON
PUBLICATIONS INC.

**BANGKOK
HANDBOOK**

Please send all comments,
corrections, additions, amend-
ments, and critiques to:

**MICHAEL BUCKLEY
c/o MOON PUBLICATIONS, INC.
CHICO, CA 95928 USA**

Published by
Moon Publications, Inc.
722 Wall Street
Chico, California 95928, USA

Printing History
1st edition January 1992

Printed by
Colorcraft Ltd.

Front Cover: Kinnaree statue at the Grand Palace, Bangkok. Photo by Michael Buckley.

Library of Congress Cataloging in Publication Data
Buckley, Michael, 1950-
     Bangkok Handbook / Michael Buckley. — 1st ed.
       p.   cm.
     Includes bibliographical references and index.
     ISBN 0-918373-67-0 : 10.95
     1. Bangkok (Thailand)—Description—Guide-books. I. Title.
DS589.B2B8   1992
915.93—dc20
                              91-33445
                              CIP

Printed in Hong Kong

"Krung Tep" they call this place of contradictions . . .
—H.W. Smyth, FIVE YEARS IN SIAM

❧ ❧ ❧

The City of Angels has its problems, but to many Thais it still remains the city of dreams, the place that draws thousands each year in the search for fortune, or glamour, or just a decent living. As the repository of so many hopes, Bangkok has an extraordinarily vibrant atmosphere, and is by turns racy and refined, full of both poise and intrigue. The sheer intensity of life here is enough to empower the city with its own myth, its own destiny.
—Alistair Shearer, THAILAND: THE LOTUS KINGDOM

IS THIS BOOK OUT OF DATE?

Most of this book was written on the spot—the material was fed into a wordprocessor in Bangkok, and was current as of mid-1991. No stone has been left unturned in the interests of accuracy and being bang-up-to-date. However, guidebooks are rather like extended newspapers: the prices, phone numbers, and other details will invariably change (although the logistics and the background material should remain the same). Can you help me keep this book up to date? I would really appreciate hearing from you in Bangkok, and welcome suggestions, map-alterations, comments, corrections, ideas for new things to see or do, beefs, bones of contention, anecdotes . . . Drop a postcard or a letter to:

Michael Buckley
c/o Moon Publications
722 Wall Street
Chico, CA 95928, USA

CONTENTS

CHARTS

ABBREVIATIONS

air-con—air conditioned
ATM—automatic teller machine
d—double occupancy
GH—guest house

pp—per person
s—single occupancy
SRT—State Railways of Thailand
TAT—Tourism Authority of Thailand

MAPS

MAP SYMBOLS

═══ EXPRESSWAY	◯ NATIONAL ROUTE
── MAJOR ROAD	● CITY/TOWN
── OTHER ROAD	▲ WAT
─ ─ TRAIL	◆ LONGTAIL BOAT LANDING
══ BRIDGE	★ ATTRACTION
••••••• FERRY ROUTE	▲ ACCOMMODATION
─ ─ ─ UNPAVED ROAD	+ DINNER CRUISE
～～ WATER	□ EXPRESS BOAT LANDING
••••••• RAILROAD	■ POINT OF INTEREST
	◯ CROSS RIVER FERRY

ACKNOWLEDGEMENTS

In Bangkok: Special thanks to John Gibson, who generously provided a stable base, gave me access to a word processor—and thus enabled this project to get under way. A long-time Bangkok resident, John was able to steer me through the labyrinth of the city, and gave loads of good advice. My thanks also to: Ketnapa Siri and Eddie Buddhani of TAT for help with research and illustration; Sawang Attavirojnkul for generous hospitality, for great stories, and for showing me around Chinatown and the Sao Ching Cha neighborhood; Pra Opart Piyawannakul, the wandering monk, for insights; Jeffrey Alford for his contributions on Thai food; Diethard Ande of White Lotus for tracking down books; John Everingham for assistance with illustration; and John Hoskin and William Klausner for inspiration.

In Vancouver: Gratitude to Geoff Flack for his valuable ideas, contacts, help with background material, and for his contribution on driving in Bangkok; and thanks to Ju Flack, Peter Sevcik and Irene Holman, Patsie Lamarre, Tom Quinn, Allison Norman, Jackie Parsons, Dwight Elliott of the Travel Bug, Sandra Frost, and Tony McCurdy of Wanderlust Books.

In Chico: A big debt to Bill Dalton and the Moon crew for their patience and perseverance— Mark Morris for liaison, suggestions, and for laying the groundwork for this venture; Taran March for her superb editing and direction; Dave Hurst for art direction; Anne Hikido for layout; Bob Race for illustrations and cartography; Brian Bardwell for cartography; Mark Arends for indexing and proofing; and thanks to Carl Parkes, author of the upcoming *Thailand Handbook*, for information exchange.

ACKNOWLEDGMENTS

INTRODUCTION

BEING THERE

The only major city in Thailand, Bangkok is the undisputed political, cultural, religious, administrative, industrial, and commercial nerve center of the kingdom. Visitors arrive in Bangkok hoping to see everything in three or four days: in fact, there is enough in this city to keep you busy for several months, and a further month can easily be spent in the immediate vicinity of Bangkok. Those on group tours often decide to spend some extra time on their own in Bangkok at the end of a tour.

The Thai name for the city, *Krung Thep,* City of Angels, underscores the importance of Bangkok for the Thais. It is where the king resides—the Divine City. First impressions of Bangkok for today's visitor are anything but angelic—arrival is rather like being dropped into a battle zone. Yes, Bangkok is very polluted; yes, Bangkok is noisy and dirty, and congested with traffic. And yes, it is hot, chaotic, and confusing. But it is a very human place, too: though it is

large and sprawling, Bangkok does not support people with a big-city mentality—many of the residents in this boomtown are fortune seekers who come from villages in rural Thailand, particularly the northeast. If you're lost or need a hand, cheerful Thais will go out of their way to help. In addition to being a royal city, Bangkok is a Buddhist city—a strange concept, but Buddha teaches humility and moderation, and Buddhist values permeate this society. But it is another value called *sanuk* that makes Bangkok—and Thailand—very different from any other place in Asia. *Sanuk* can be roughly translated as "fun and games," but it is much more than that: it is a very positive attitude—laughing in the face of adversity, and downplaying negative values.

Lingering in Bangkok's air is a certain smell—a combination of curry, incense, open sewers, durian, gasoline, jasmine, ginger, lemongrass, charcoal, and diesel fumes. If you can see past the traffic problems and the concrete and the heat, you will find a vibrant city with sumptuous food, the best shopping in Asia, bright markets, and sidewalks bristling with life and energy. Due to Bangkok's ugly exterior, a sudden encounter with something of great beauty appears nothing short of miraculous—as when you find an exquisite array of freshly carved fruit on a street-vendor's stand, or when you chance across a longtail boat loaded to the gunwales with fresh-cut roses and orchids, on its way to the markets.

Some of Bangkok's most dazzling sights are not the standard ones—rather, they're fleeting visions. These visions last for a few seconds, or maybe a minute, but they stay with you a long time. You go into a temple, turn around, and there's a man about to release an entire cage of birds. Not just one cage—he releases *three*

cages to earn merit. Then he buys a stack of turtles and eels and puts those in the trunk of his car (a Mercedes, as it turns out) to be released in a canal somewhere. Or you're whizzing along in a *tuk-tuk,* and a motorcyclist overtakes you. Riding sidesaddle on the back of the machine is his girlfriend—somehow *balanced* there, suspended in space (is there Krazy Glue on the seat?), dressed in immaculate skirt and blouse, with sandals dangling carelessly. And she's calmly paring her nails as the bike weaves through the traffic at breakneck speed.

Bangkok may be crazy—Bangkok may be chaotic—but Bangkok is life at its most intense. Get into the spirit of *sanuk*—and have a great time in Bangkok!

HISTORY

EARLY HISTORY

The origins of the Thais are obscure. According to one theory, over the centuries Thais migrated into northern and upper central Thailand, possibly from Yunnan in southwest China. This, however, has come under question since the discovery in the 1960s and '70s of prehistoric artifacts in Ban Chiang, a village near Udon Thani in the northeast. It is thought that Ban Chiang's metal tools may date to 3500 B.C.; the pottery fragments found there are much older.

Dvaravati And Khmer Kingdoms
From the 6th to 11th centuries A.D., an independent state, the Dvaravati Kingdom, arose in central Thailand. Linked by cultural and family ties were a group of towns clustered around Nakhon Pathom, Lopburi, and U Thong. The people of the Dvaravati period were Mon, a mysterious race whose religion appears to have been Mahayana Buddhist. To the east, in Cambodia, a powerful Hindu empire centered at Angkor was developing—the Khmers. The Khmers gradually absorbed the Mons, took over large portions of Thailand, and held sway from the 11th to 13th centuries. They ruled from Angkor, with a secondary capital at Lopburi. At this time, the boundaries of Thailand were not defined: to the south,

the Srivijaya empire from Indonesia controlled the southern peninsula up until the 13th century. In the north, a series of kingdoms was based around the Chiang Mai area, culminating in the powerful Lanna Kingdom, which ruled from the 13th to 16th centuries.

Sukothai Period
In 1238 two Thai chieftains in Central Thailand joined forces to oust the Khmers and establish the first Thai kingdom of Sukothai. Though the Sukothai period lasted less than 200 years, it ushered in a uniquely Thai style of architecture and sculpture, and numerous Thai traditions. The zenith of the period was the reign of King Ramkamheng the Great (1275-1317), who is credited with devising the Thai alphabet. The Buddhist faith gave impetus to the new civilization, although elements of Khmer Hindu belief were retained. The Sukothai preoccupation with religion in fact led to its political decline—the kingdom waned after Ramkamheng and was finally taken over by a younger state to the south, called Ayuthaya.

Rise And Fall Of Ayuthaya
Ayuthaya was the base of Thai kings for four centuries, from 1350 to 1767—and one of the richest and most opulent cities of Asia. The kingdom was established in 1350 by King U Thong;

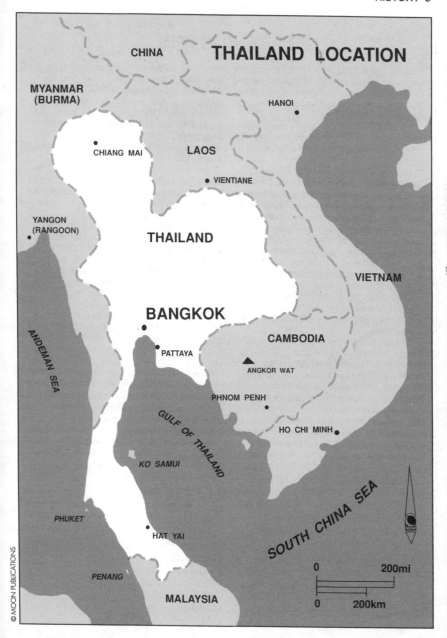

THAILAND IN BRIEF

Thailand means "Land of the Free." The country's name was altered from "Siam" to "Thailand" (Muang Thai) in 1939, in proud recognition of the fact that Thailand is the only nation in Asia that has not been colonized by a foreign power.

The Land: Thailand is roughly the size of France —with an area of 513,115 square kilometers. On the map, the country is shaped like the head of an elephant, with a "trunk" stretching toward Malaysia. Thailand is bordered by Malaysia to the south, Burma to the west, Laos to the north, and Cambodia to the east—3,700 km of borders in all, and subject to ongoing military activity. There are 73 provinces in the kingdom, with a governor administrating each.

Geographically, the country can be roughly divided into four regions: the mountainous north where winter temperatures are cool enough to permit cultivation of temperate fruit like peaches and strawberries; the semiarid and drought-prone northeast plateau, bordered by the Mekong River; the fertile central plains, which are dotted with rice paddies and orchards; and the diverse terrain of the southern peninsula, comprising mountains, swamps, jungle, and fine beaches.

Climate: Tropical, with a year-round humidity. Average annual temperature is 28°C; average humidity is 75%. There are three distinct seasons: hot (March-May), rainy (June-October, with monsoons in the south), and "cool" (November-February). The "cool" season averages 25°C in Bangkok, but in the mountain areas to the north of Thailand (Chiang Mai), temperatures can drop to 8°C overnight. The best time to visit Thailand is the November to February "cool" season; the early rainy season (June to August) is the next best choice. The hot season (March-May) is extremely hot, but has a number of festivals, including Thai New Year. Avoid the late rainy season (September-October).

People: Population is estimated at 56 million, of which roughly 80% live in rural areas and 20% in urban areas. Largest cities: Bangkok, Nakhon Ratchasima, Ubon Ratchathani, Udon Thani, Khon Kaen, and Chiang Mai. Ethnic groups: Thai (78%), Chinese (14%), Malays (four percent), other minority groups, including Indians, Hmongs and hilltribe groups, and refugees from Laos, Cambodia, Burma and Vietnam (four percent). Life expectancy in Thailand: 61.

Language: Thai is a tonal language with a written form derived from Mon and Khmer scripts (in turn derived from Sanskrit). There are four main Thai dialects; other minority languages are spoken in the kingdom. Literacy rate is around 85%. English is the main language used for international communication and is widely used in Bangkok.

Religion: Buddhist (94%); Muslim (four percent); the remaining two percent comprises minority religions—Christian, Hindu, Sikh, other. According to legend, Buddhism first appeared in Thailand during the 3rd century B.C. after the Indian Emperor Asoka sent missionaries to Southeast Asia. There are about 30,000 temples in Thailand, most of them Theravada Buddhist.

Head of State: The present king, His Majesty King Bhumibol Adulyadej, was crowned in 1950. He is the ninth ruler (Rama IX) in a dynasty that dates back to 1782, and the longest-reigning monarch in Thai history.

Government: Constitutional monarchy, headed by King Bhumibol Adulyadej, and dominated by the military. Since the switch from absolute monarchy to constitutional monarchy in 1932, there have been 17 coups or attempted coups in Thailand.

Economy: Agricultural and industrial economy based on free enterprise. Main export earners: textile products, rice, rubber, tin, foodstuffs, precious stones, manufactured goods. Main source of foreign income: tourism, with over five million Asian and foreign visitors in 1990. Currency unit is the baht (US$1 = B25). Minimum daily wage (Bangkok, 1991) is B100 (US$4).

---

by the 15th century, Ayuthaya had conquered vast territories, and overrun the Khmer capital of Angkor Wat. In the 16th century, Ayuthaya itself was overrun by the Burmese, who were envious of the city's wealth, particularly the king's stable-full of white elephants. The fiercely independent Thais rallied under King Naresuan the Great and ousted the Burmese in 1584. At its height, Ayuthaya was said to have a population of one million—larger than London at the time. Thai royalty traveled through the waters in processions of as many as 450 sumptuous teak barges, elaborately carved and gilded. The wealth of the kingdom derived from its conquests and from the export of rice, teak, salt, spices, hides, and other goods. Europeans made contact with the court of Siam, seeking trading privileges and secure bases for trading ships—particularly during the reign of King Narai (1656-1688), when the French established a settlement in Lopburi. Traders from China, Japan, and the Middle East came to Ayuthaya too, making this a truly cosmopolitan city.

In 1767, Ayuthaya fell to the Burmese after a 15-month siege. The city was completely razed, its treasures looted, and its libraries and historical records burned.

THE BANGKOK ERA

Founding Of Bangkok
After the fall of Ayuthaya, the remnants of the Thai forces regrouped to the south under a Thai general called Phya Taksin. Taksin managed to rally the Thai factions and established a new capital in Thonburi, the west bank of present-day Bangkok, in 1769. Thonburi and Bangkok had formerly guarded the approaches to Ayuthaya—there were French-built fortresses on both sides of the river. Thonburi was a customs port, being the furthest point north on the Chao Phraya that European and Chinese ships could reach before cargo was transferred to smaller vessels for the trip north. Bangkok was a simple fishing village.

By 1770 Taksin had reestablished the Thai nation, and proclaimed himself king. Taksin was a brilliant technician. He recaptured Ayuthaya from the Burmese and conducted successful campaigns in Laos, Cambodia, and Vietnam. Over the years, Taksin became deranged and unpredictable—some say because of the stress he was under to establish a new Thai identity and power. He was deposed in a coup in 1781, and executed the following year.

Taksin's leading general, Phya Chakri, became king. As a fresh start, and because of strategic reasons, he relocated the capital to the right bank. He ordered a canal dug to create an artificial island, named Rattanakosin ("Indra's Precious Jewel," an oblique reference to the Emerald Buddha, the magical Buddha which

Phya Chakri had brought back from a campaign in Laos). On Rattanakosin, General Chakri set out to realize his dream: to reconstruct the glory that once was Ayuthaya. In fact, some of Ayuthaya's original architects and artisans were employed to build the new palaces, monasteries, and fortifications of Bangkok—and red-brick rubble transported from Ayuthaya on barges was used in the foundations. Cornerstone of the new city was Wat Pra Keo, completed in 1785 to house the Emerald Buddha. Using captive Cambodian and Laotian laborers, Chakri fortified the city by digging a second defensive canal further east, and by walling the entire area enclosed by this canal and the Chao Phraya River.

Growth Of Bangkok
The Chakri dynasty kings continued to shape Phya Chakri's dream—enthusiastically building and adding monasteries to this Ayuthaya-in-progress. King Rama II set about restoring the literary heritage lost at Ayuthaya. King Rama III added nine new temples, restored 60 other edifices, and raised the *prang* of Wat Arun to its present height. The Chakri kings were remarkable diplomats and shrewd leaders—King Mongkut (Rama IV) managed to steer clear of the foreign domination that was plaguing other parts of Asia. King Mongkut spent 27 years in a monastery before assuming the throne in 1851; he spoke English and Latin, and was well versed in Western history, mathematics, and science. Mongkut kept up a correspondence with Western leaders, fostered relations with foreign powers, signed trading agreements, overhauled the legal system, and laid the groundwork for the transformation of Thailand into a modern state.

Modernization
In 1868, King Mongkut died of malaria, and his son, King Chulalongkorn (Rama V) ascended the throne. Chulalongkorn introduced radical reforms. Modernization saw the abolition of slavery, the building of schools and the first hospital (Siriraj, opened 1888), and the introduction of electric lighting (1884), electric trams (1893), the first rail lines, and imported automobiles. King Rama V was the first Thai monarch to visit Europe—he sent his many sons to study in European capitals, and employed

RIVER CITY

Bangkok was dubbed "City of Temples" by early visitors. Its other characteristic feature was water—there were many floating rafthouses, and almost all transport and communication was based on boats, in a labyrinthine network of canals. John Crawford, an English ambassador to the Court of Siam, was unsuccessful in his attempts to establish trade relations with Thailand, but he left a detailed picture of the capital as it appeared in 1822:

> The morning presented to us a very novel spectacle—the capital of Siam, situated on both sides of the Menam. Numerous temples of Buddha, with tall spires attached to them, frequently glittering with gilding, were conspicuous among the mean huts and hovels of the natives, throughout which were interspersed a profusion of palms, ordinary fruit trees, and the sacred fig. On each side of the river there was a row of floating habitations, resting on rafts of bamboo, moored to the shore. These appeared the neatest and best description of dwellings; they were occupied by good Chinese shops. Close to these aquatic habitations were anchored the largest description of native vessels, among which were many junks of great size, just arrived from China. The face of the river presented a busy scene, from the number of boats and canoes of every size and description which were passing to and fro. The number of these struck us as very great at the time, for we were not aware that there are few or no roads at

Bangkok, and that the river and canals form the common highways, not only for goods, but for passengers of every description . . . The right bank of the Menam, where our residence was, had only a narrow strip of dwellings along the river-side. Behind these, the country, which is inconvenient foot-paths, and frequent canals, over which there are no other bridges than single narrow planks or trunks of trees.

Thirty-three years later, Sir John Bowring, envoy of Queen Victoria, arrived, and was this time successful in concluding a far-reaching treaty with King Mongkut that opened Thailand to British trade. Bangkok's canal system at this time was greatly expanded. Bowring wrote:

> The highways of Bangkok are not streets and roads, but the rivers and canals. Boats are the universal means of conveyance and communication. Except about the palaces of the Kings, horses or carriages are rarely seen . . . There are a few houses in Bangkok built of stone and brick; but those of the middle classes are of wood, while the habitations of the poor are constructed of light bamboos, and roofed with leaves of the atap palm.

In 1862, King Mongkut ordered Bangkok's first major road—New Road—to be laid out along a former elephant track. By the 1880s, road-building got under way in earnest, and canal traffic was on the decline; by the 1930s, the houseboats had disappeared.

European advisers. He introduced a European-style cabinet, established a standing army, revised the legal code according to Western standards, and set up a modern civil service. Through skillful diplomacy he kept colonial powers at bay. To ensure Thailand's independence, however, a large tract of territory (equivalent to what is now Laos and Cambodia combined) was ceded to the French in various stages between 1867 and 1907; a minor tract near the Malaysian border was ceded to the British in 1909.

The 20th Century

King Chulalongkorn's forty-year reign saw the building of many of Bangkok's major roads, buildings and monuments. By the time of his death in 1910, Bangkok had a population of 600,000 and was one of the largest and most imposing cities in Southeast Asia. The 20th century brought a swift rise in educational standards in Thailand, and a desire for greater freedom. This process started under Chulalongkorn, when students sent to Europe were exposed to revolutionary ideas. In 1917 Chulalongkorn University was

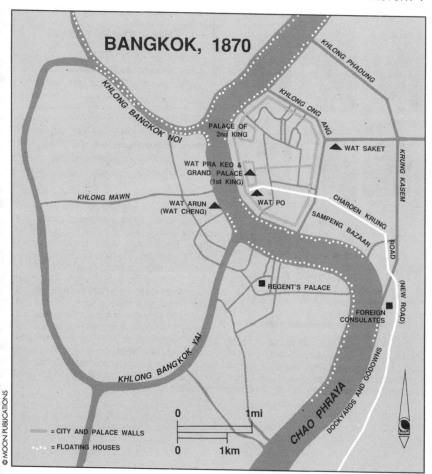

BANGKOK, 1870

KHLONG PHADUNG

KHLONG BANGKOK NOI

KHLONG ONG ANG

PALACE OF
2nd KING

WAT SAKET

KRUNG KASEM

WAT PRA KEO &
GRAND PALACE
(1st KING)

KHLONG MAWN

CHAROEN KRUNG

WAT PO

WAT ARUN
(WAT CHENG)

SAMPENG BAZAAR

REGENT'S PALACE

(NEW ROAD)

FOREIGN
CONSULATES

KHLONG BANGKOK YAI

CHAO PHRAYA

DOCKYARDS AND GODOWNS

0   1mi

0   1km

= CITY AND PALACE WALLS
= FLOATING HOUSES

© MOON PUBLICATIONS

established in Bangkok, and in 1921 compulsory elementary education was introduced by Oxford-educated King Rama VI. The king encouraged criticism of government policies, which set the stage for a bloodless coup against his successor, Rama VII, in 1932. Absolute monarchy came to an end (King Rama VII opted for a constitutional monarchy), but military dictatorship soon filled the vacuum of power.

Since 1932, Thailand has been governed by an uneasy alliance between military and civilian leaders, with the emphasis on "military." In 1935, King Rama VII abdicated while on a visit to England; he was succeeded by a ten-year-old prince, Ananda Mahidol, who left to study in Switzerland. During WW II, the military government of Thailand found it expedient to side with the Japanese. After King Ananda returned to Bangkok, in 1946, he was found shot dead at the Grand Palace—the murder has never been solved. Four years later, his younger brother, Bhumibol Adulyadej, was crowned King Rama IX.

Rattanakosin Bicentennial, 1982

CHAKRI DYNASTY KINGS

Rama I (Phya Chakri) 1782-1809
Rama II (Phuttha Lertlah) 1809-1824
Rama III (Pra Nangklao) 1824-1851
Rama IV (Mongkut) 1851-1868
Rama V (Chulalongkorn) 1868-1910
Rama VI (Vajiravudh) 1910-1925
Rama VII (Prajadhipok) 1925-1935
Rama VIII (Ananda Mahidol) 1935-1946
Rama IX (Bhumibol Adulyadej) crowned 1950

The 1950s, '60s, and '70s were periods of great upheaval in Thailand—a succession of coups, military governments, and an economic boom in the 1960s with an influx of U.S. troops involved in the Vietnam war. In 1973 a student uprising ushered in a brief period of democratic government, which was brought down in a bloody countercoup in 1976. Prime Minister Prem Tinsulanonda, a former general, managed to hold onto the reins of civilian government for an unprecedented eight years (1980 to 1988), surviving two coup attempts. An elected government ruled from 1988 to 1991, when it was ousted by a military coup. Despite the coups and changes of government, Thailand seems like Utopia when compared with its Asian neighbors—in particular Burma, Cambodia, and Laos, where economies have been on a downward spiral, where freedom of speech is severely restricted, and where human rights is a pressing issue.

KAREN WHITE

sema

MODERN BANGKOK

GOVERNMENT

Thailand is a constitutional monarchy with the trappings of parliamentary democracy. The government has been variously described as a military dictatorship, a quasi-democracy, and a military regime masquerading as a democracy. Parliament is composed of a 261-member senate appointed by the king and dominated by the military; there is a 347-member house of representatives elected by the people. To effectively function, the prime minister must have the support of the army: civilian attempts to gain more power and military resistance to those efforts have been a major source of tension in Thailand since the 1932 abolition of absolute monarchy. Since that time, there have been 17 coups or attempted coups, and the country's "permanent constitution" has been revised more than a dozen times.

In 1991, a bloodless coup ousted civilian prime minister Chatichai Choonhaven (who left the country), and key ministers were detained. Martial law was imposed; the press was subjected to tough censorship; and the junta appointed a caretaker prime minister, Anand Panyarachun, promising to hold free elections. The main reason cited for the 1991 coup was corruption among members of Chatichai's government. The new junta froze the bank accounts of more than two dozen senior politicians and civil servants pending investigation. Corruption is nothing new in Thai politics—buying of votes is a regular practice. One party leader suggested that leaders of political parties should take an oath at the Emerald Buddha Temple not to engage in illegal practices.

MONARCHY

The king is revered as a deity in Thailand: Thais will brook no criticism of royalty, past or present. The monarchy endures despite frequent changes of government—many Thais see the monarchy as a perpetual symbol. The present king is His Majesty King Bhumibol Adulyadej, the longest reigning of the monarchs in the Chakri lineage. His image is found on all bank notes and coins, many stamps, and on countless posters and calendars. In Thai cinemas, every show starts with the royal anthem, and the king's portrait is projected on the screen.

The royal family consists of King Bhumibol, Queen Sirikit, their son, and their three daughters. King Bhumibol was born in 1927, a nephew of King Rama VI; on the death of his brother in 1946, he was to ascend the throne but court astrologers recommended a delay. In 1949, he was involved in a serious automobile accident in Switzerland. However, he recovered, married Princess Sirikit, and was crowned King Rama IX in 1950. In 1955 King Bhumibol toured the northeastern provinces, which sparked a lifelong quest to improve the lot of those in impoverished rural areas and of hill tribespeople. He spends a great deal of time in the rural areas and oversees development of agricultural schemes, and educational and health programs. In addition to his official roles, the king is a talented saxophonist and painter, and an expert yachtsman.

ECONOMY

Up until the 1950s, the Thai economy was almost exclusively based on its land and sea resources. In the early 1960s the industrial sector became a force in Thailand's economy: although most of the Thai population is rural, manufacturing now accounts for over 25% of the gross domestic product. In 1990, agriculture accounted for 15% of the GDP, down from 23% a decade earlier.

In recent years, Thailand has enjoyed one of the highest growth rates in Asia. At the center of this boom is greater Bangkok, where over 30,000 industrial plants and workshops turn out goods ranging from foodstuffs to furniture, textiles to computer components. Back in the 1970s, toy-making was unknown in Thailand; today it's a thriving business. The ready-made clothing industry is a similar story. Foreign in-

H.M. King Bhumibol Adulyadej and H.M. Queen Sirikit light candles to pay respects to Buddha during preliminaries to an award ceremony.

JOHN EVERINGHAM

vestors, drawn by cheap labor, have backed up new enterprises such as the manufacture of videocassettes, microwave ovens and electrical appliances, and assembly of motor vehicles. Main trading partners and foreign investors are Japan, the U.S.A., Singapore, and Taiwan.

Bangkok is the fastest growing economic sector in Thailand because manufacturing, exporting, tourist services, and financial services are concentrated there. Per capita income in Bangkok is estimated to be US$3000, which is just over twice the national average, and several times the per capita income in poor up-country areas.

Thailand's major exports include textile products, rice, rubber, tin, foodstuffs, and precious stones. Manufactured goods now account for a large proportion of exports, but the phenomenal exchange-earner for Thailand in recent years has been tourism. The tourist service industry is the success story of the 1980s. Over five million tourists visited Thailand in 1990, as compared with two million visitors a decade earlier. The rapid expansion in tourism and exports has placed severe strains on Thailand's infrastructure. In Bangkok, there is great pressure on the port facilities, airport facilities, telephone system, electrical supply and other utilities, mass transit, and hotel facilities.

PEOPLE

Ethnically, Thais comprise 80% of the population of Thailand, and are bound by common religious beliefs, language, and a fierce sense of nationalism. Over its long history, Thailand has absorbed many ethnic groups—Mon, Khmer, Burmese, Vietnamese, Laotian, Chinese, Malay, Persian, and Indian. A 1927 guidebook to Bangkok described passengers on a tram thus: "There will be found sitting together yellow-robed Siamese monks, long-bearded Arabs, sarong-clad Malays, voluble Chinese . . . dark-skinned Tamils, Burmese, Mon, the *panung*-clad Thais and members of a host of other races." In the last few decades, large numbers of refugees fleeing from conflicts in Vietnam, Cambodia, and Laos have crossed into northern and eastern Thailand.

A result of Thailand's absorption of these different races is that there are no typically Thai features: there are round-faced Thais, Thais with angular faces, dark-skinned Thais, light-skinned Thais, and even Thais with Caucasian features. Out of this melting pot there has arisen, however, a character that is still distinctly Thai (in the same way that Khmer architecture, Indian mythology, and Chinese food have all been absorbed and converted into something distinctly Thai). Thais are renowned for their gentle, hospitable, and fun-loving nature; their politeness, deference to superiors, and respect for elders; and for their tolerant live-and-let-live approach.

Bangkok is a young city—probably half the population is under 30. As a boomtown of the last few decades, it has also seen a meteoric rise of a wealthy middle class—referred to by some as "Thai yuppies." Bangkok has a heavy Chinese influence in its ethnic makeup. About 14% of the population of Thailand is Chinese—determined by language, ethnic origin, and culture. The largest Chinese community is in Bangkok, where it is estimated that up to half the population is ethnically Chinese. Statistics are difficult to work out since second and third generation Chinese often do not speak Chinese and have assumed Thai names—they consider themselves Thai.

During the 17th and 18th centuries, Chinese traders found a niche as middlemen in the rice trade between Thailand and southern China. Chinese immigration to Thailand picked up during the 19th century, when there was a series of crop failures and disasters in southern China. King Mongkut, himself of Chinese lineage, encouraged Chinese immigrants (mostly single males) to intermarry with Thais, hoping that they would pass on the qualities of thrift and industry to their children. Indeed, much of the banking and trading in Bangkok is today dominated by Thai nationals of Chinese descent. In the past, occasional anti-Chinese sentiment has surfaced, particularly after the 1949 Communist takeover of China. But for the most part, relations with the Chinese have been harmonious—to a large extent due to intermarriage and similar religious beliefs.

Minority groups in Bangkok include Malays and Indians. The Malays are virtually indistinguishable from the Thais apart from their religion, which is Muslim. The Indians, by contrast, are easily distinguished—they are mostly Punjabis and Sikhs, and rarely mix with the Thais, maintaining their culture intact, although they speak Thai.

URBAN PROBLEMS

The metropolis of Bangkok covers an area of 1,537 square km, of which the built-up area comprises possibly 400 square km. Though early visitors dubbed Bangkok the "Venice of the East," a more appropriate term now would be "The Urban Nightmare" or "City of a Thousand Decibels." The place is a boomtown with no apparent zoning laws—gleaming towers of glass overlooking decrepit stilt housing on ancient canals; glittering temples juxtaposed with conglomerations of cement; and cheerfully sprinkled throughout all this are steamy bars and massage parlors. The lack of planning and zoning has a lot to do with greedy developers and corrupt officialdom. Bangkok has experienced rapid growth since 1960, backed by massive Japanese and Western investment. The economic boom has disfigured Bangkok, and caused severe pollution problems and a chronic lack of facilities.

That Sinking Feeling

Since 1960, the city of Bangkok has been slowly sinking. This is due to several factors, the main one being that more than a million cubic meters of water are pumped out of ground wells daily to supply residents. Bangkok is as flat as a pancake, and built on layers of soft clay and sand sediment that contain large amounts of water. As the water supply close to the surface dwindled, drillers started to go deeper—down to 20, 60, even 200 meters—and the underground layers, depleted of water, started to shrink. In the monsoon season, at high tide, the river invades the city streets; and because many canals on the Bangkok side have been filled in and paved over, there are few channels to carry off floodwater. The most severe flooding was in 1983, lasting four months.

Population Explosion

Officially, the head count in Bangkok relies on voting records. That figure gave almost six million residents with a density of 3,755 people per square km (1990 census). Unofficially, the figure is probably over eight million—there are many Bangkokians who are registered in their hometowns to the north, and not in Bangkok, because changing the registration is too much of a headache and too expensive. A figure of eight million means that 14% of Thailand's population lives in greater Bangkok. A large number of new residents come from the impoverished northeast seeking better wages and conditions. Bangkok's population was estimated at just over 1.5 million in 1960, which means there has been a minimum four-fold increase in residents over the last 30 years.

Traffic And Pollution

People don't discuss the weather in Bangkok—they discuss hydrocarbons in the atmosphere. In 1988 there were 40% more cars and trucks on the streets of Bangkok than in the previous two years—by the time you read this, add 30% more. In 1990, there were 300,000 new vehicles registered, half of them motorcycles. This has led to notorious congestion and to a thick pall of exhaust fumes, which, combined with Bangkok's heat, are deadly. The traffic, the pollution, and the noise are so bad in Bangkok that many residents suffer from respiratory problems and impaired hearing. Trucks, buses, *tuk-tuks,* and two-stroke motorcycles well exceed acceptable noise and emission control levels and would never be allowed on the streets of any Western nation (Japanese companies manufacture vehicles in Thailand that would never be allowed to operate in Japan itself). So far very little has been done about traffic and pollution: overpasses have been built at heavily trafficked intersections to try and improve the "flow"; an elevated expressway system has been built (with

a sinking Bangkok in mind?), but that, too, is choked with traffic. A huge volume of toxic pollutants is released into the air by vehicles and by about 19,000 factories.

A major part of the problem is that traffic is big business. There is a lot of money to be made from the manufacture and sale of vehicles, the sale of rights for taxi license plates and other permissions, and the very high luxury tax on imported vehicles. Solutions have been suggested, including introducing a Skytrain (overhead train on track—non-polluting as it relies on magnetic fields); imposing stricter emission control systems for vehicles; switching buses from leaded gas to propane and vehicles to unleaded gas; limiting the use of private cars to certain days (dictated by license plate number), but none of these plans has been implemented. The powers that be, it seems, will wait for the inevitable to occur before taking any steps.

The Environment

Thailand has a poor environmental management record. In Bangkok, though some attempt has been made to educate people against littering, the Chao Phraya River continues to double as sewer and garbage dump. Untreated sewage is dumped into the river at an alarming rate, exacerbated by the new condominium towers and hotels constructed along the banks. A wastewater treat-

homeless boy looking for handouts

THE MECHAI CRUSADE

Statistics on AIDS in Thailand are tricky to pin down, since official agencies tend to underestimate the figures. What is clear is that the number of HIV-positive cases has dramatically increased since 1988, amounting to a national crisis. Around Bangkok the HIV virus spread rapidly among heroin users; around Chiang Mai, meanwhile, researchers found that AIDS was spreading among prostitutes in cheap brothels and their clients. AIDS has moved from homosexuals and bisexuals to drug-users and female prostitutes—and on to the rest of the population.

By early 1991, while there were fewer than 100 reported cases of full-blown AIDS, the official number of HIV-carriers was put at 25,000. Unofficially there may be ten to twenty times that number of cases. The World Health Organization's projection is 1.6 million HIV-carriers in Thailand by 1995. If all those infected with HIV come down with AIDS symptoms, Thailand's health-care system will not be able to cope with the crisis.

In 1988, a national anti-AIDS program was inaugurated under the auspices of WHO's Global Program on AIDS, with funding from the Thai government and from a dozen international sources. In 1989 the campaign got under way in earnest with the distribution of 43 million condoms by the U.S. Agency for International Development. The turning point in the campaign occurred when Thailand's army chief pledged full support for the anti-AIDS campaign, allowing free advertising time on army-controlled TV and radio stations, and initiating testing of all soldiers. Simultaneously, the king's third daughter, Princess Chulabhorn, came out strongly for a public campaign against AIDS.

Spearheading the anti-AIDS campaign is outspoken critic and crusader Mechai Viravaidya. In 1974, Mechai founded the Population and Community Development Association (PDA), which is privately funded and was set up to deal with Thailand's runaway population growth. Mechai used showman skills and a keen administrative flair to bring home the message to Thailand's rural poor that a large family was no longer the sign of prowess it once was. His main weapons were education, promotion of vasectomy, and the use of condoms. In 1970, Thailand had 3.3% annual population growth; by 1986, the rate had dropped to 1.6%—one of the most dramatic declines in birth rates ever recorded.

One of the problems Mechai faced was breaking down public associations of condoms with promiscuity and prostitution. Mechai has a wacky sense of humor—he arranged condom-inflating contests in bars and shops, and had condoms handed out in rural areas by pretty assistants. He distributed condoms at weddings, and even funerals. Condoms were frequently advertised in the media and widely available in shops and supermarkets. So successful was the campaign that "Mechai" has entered the Thai language as slang for a condom.

In 1987, with family planning a spectacular success story, the "Condom Man" turned his attention to another battlefield: the threat of AIDS. The PDA launched an educational campaign on AIDS using an informative cassette—at a time when few spoke out on the subject for fear of damaging the tourist trade. Mechai has since used a mixture of hard facts, humor, and horror in his campaign, with his experience in promoting condoms laying the groundwork. He has taken his campaign into classrooms and offices, and has urged the business community to become involved in the fight. He has enlisted the help of Avon door-to-door saleswomen to distribute AIDS information along with lipstick and face creams. He has organized anti-AIDS rallies in Bangkok's red-light districts—with assistants dressed in head-to-toe cloth condoms distributing brochures, condoms, and tapes to bargirls and passers-by.

A highly controversial AIDS bill proposes sweeping measures to counter AIDS: these include health officials forcibly testing anyone suspected of carrying the virus (prostitutes, homosexuals, drug addicts, and "promiscuous people"), and confinement of people with AIDS in "therapeutic centers." Critics say the authoritarian measures gravely violate human rights and will simply drive AIDS victims underground. Similar Draconian laws have been tried (and utterly failed to prevent the spread of AIDS) in Sweden, Great Britain, and Australia.

ment plant is being built, but will not be in operation till 1994. Increased tourist traffic on the Chao Phraya has taken its toll too—boat-tour operators (particularly floating restaurants) dump their wastes straight into the water.

There is very little regulation of hazardous chemicals in Thailand. In September 1990, a truck loaded with LPG (liquefied petroleum gas) overturned on New Petchburi Road in Bangkok and exploded, sending out a fireball that killed 89 people, seriously injured 33 people, and destroyed 64 vehicles, 40 houses, and 50 shops. It was only then that the authorities made a move to restrict transport of LPG and ban its use in sukiyaki restaurants. In early 1991, a fire broke out in Bangkok's port area of Klong Toey, and warehouses full of highly toxic chemicals went up in the blaze. The Duang Prateep Foundation, the main relief organization in the area, estimated that upward of half of the slum's 70,000 residents fell ill from the resulting contamination. The homeless continued to live in makeshift shelters in the highly toxic area for weeks after the disaster.

Heroin And AIDS

Klong Toey is the largest of Bangkok's slum areas. The homeless rate is quite high around Bangkok—over a million live in mat housing or run-down shacks, or sleep where they can. A significant problem in Bangkok's slums is heroin use. There are an estimated 150,000 to 350,000 heroin addicts in Thailand, mostly in urban areas—and Bangkok is the largest urban area. Heroin addiction is cited in connection with crime and prostitution, but since 1988 it has been dramatically associated with AIDS. Heroin dealers operate "shooting galleries," going down lines of addicts and giving them all a fix with the same needle. Intravenous drug users and prostitutes (male, female, bisexual) are most frequently found in slum areas, leading to rapid transmission of the HIV virus.

The first AIDS cases reported in Thailand in the mid-1980s were restricted to homosexuals. However, a second wave of HIV-positive cases swiftly followed—mostly involving heterosexual drug addicts. In 1987, one percent of Bangkok addicts who sought medical treatment were infected with HIV; figures from 1989 showed over 40% infected. A brisk anti-AIDS campaign was launched in 1988, with information centers in slum areas seeking to distribute condoms and raise awareness of risks involved. In the city's drug rehabilitation centers, bleach is provided to addicts to sterilize needles.

WHAT'S IN A NAME

The full official name of Bangkok is *Krungthep Mahanakhon Bovorn Rattanakosin Mahintharayutthaya Mahadilokpop Noparatratchatathani Burirom Udomratchanivetmahasathan Amornpiman Avatarnsathit Sakkathattiyaavisnukarmprasit*, which comes out to 167 letters, and earns it longest place name in the world in the *Guinness Book of Records*. The scholarly transliteration is even longer—175 letters—but fortunately, this tongue-twister boils down to a short form, *Krungthep Mahanakhon*. A rough translation of the full name: Great City of Angels, Abode of the Emerald Buddha, The Invincible Realm, Grand Capital of the World Endowed with Nine Precious Gems, Delightful City Abounding in Royal Palaces Which Resemble the Divine Living Places of the Reincarnated Gods, City of the God Indra . . .

As befitting the Heavenly City of the Gods and Kings, many of Bangkok's streets and features are named after kings or legendary figures. Rama I Road, Rama IV Road, and Rama IX Bridge are named after kings. Chulalongkorn University was named after King Rama V; Ramkamheng after a 13th century Sukothai king; Pra Arthit after the sun-god.

"Bangkok" is a term that appeared in the 17th century and that has been picked up and perpetuated by foreigners. There is some contention over what Bangkok means: earlier spellings rendered it "Bancok" or "Bancock." The most popular theory is that Bangkok means the "village of the wild plum": *ban* means village, and *kok* or *makok* is the name of a species of wild plum tree (sometimes translated as bitter olive) that once grew in profusion along the banks here. Wat Arun, in fact, was once called Wat Makok. Another theory is that Bangkok comes from a Malay term meaning "river bend": there were large numbers of Malays resident in early Bangkok, and Bangkok lies right in a big bend of the Chao Phraya River.

BUDDHISM

Buddhism originated in India but has not survived there because of a revival of Hinduism, and because of widespread destruction during Moslem invasions from the 8th to 13th centuries. Hinduism predominated in India, but Buddhism continued to flourish in other parts of Asia, with two main schools—Theravada Buddhism (southern Asia—Thailand, Burma, Cambodia, and Sri Lanka), and Mahayana Buddhism (northern Asia—Tibet, China, Japan, Mongolia and Korea). Stated simply, Theravada Buddhists believe in a personal quest for enlightenment, while Mahayana Buddhists work toward the enlightenment (and salvation from suffering) of all beings. Theravada Buddhists claim to adhere to the original teachings of Buddha, while Mahayana Buddhists have, in addition to faith in Buddha, belief in a vast array of bodhisattvas or enlightened beings.

Buddhism focuses on suffering—its causes and eradication. Buddha taught that suffering ends only when nirvana (enlightenment, attainment of ultimate truth, gaining of wisdom) is obtained. While Buddha utilized ideas current in India at the time (the concepts of rebirth and karma), Buddha's teachings diverged from Hindu beliefs in that he did not believe in a superhuman god or power, or in the concept of "soul." He promised that the answers to life's mysteries were to be found within oneself, and he taught that a person leading a worthy life (avoiding extremes, doing right actions) could carry over karmic energy into a later existence.

Buddhism is an easygoing religion: it has few rules, no fixed place of worship, no dogma. Buddha recommended that lay people try to follow the "path" as best they can—he never dictated an absolute commitment. Thus Buddhism is remarkably tolerant. It respects all other religions, and places few limitations on beliefs. Some Buddhists, for instance, do not believe in reincarnation. It is possible to be Christian and Buddhist, or Jewish and Buddhist, or atheist and Buddhist (not as strange as it sounds: in Buddhism there is no Creator). It follows that it is possible to be Communist and Buddhist—but in the Communist parts of Asia these two creeds have been at odds because of Communist intolerance of Buddhism.

The Enlightened One

The founder of Buddhism was Prince Siddhartha Gautama, born around 560 B.C. in Lumbini, on the border of present-day Nepal and India. He grew up in a luxuriant palace setting, married a princess, and fathered a child. In his twenties, Prince Siddhartha ventured outside the palace walls and saw a poor man, a sick man, a dead man, and a Brahman monk. Seeking to understand the causes of suffering and the riddle of existence, he decided to leave his family and become a wandering ascetic. He spent six years as a solitary forest-dweller, at first studying under two Hindu masters and later joining a band of ascetics. He remained dissatisfied with what he'd been taught and struck out on his own "path" through meditation. He sat cross-legged under a fig tree at Bodhgaya, India, and went into deep meditation for 49 days—formulating a body of wisdom that was to spark a new religion. In the final stages of meditation, he was tempted by the demon Mara. On the night of the full moon in May, at the age of 35, he became The Enlightened One—the Buddha.

Shortly afterward, Buddha delivered his first sermon, "Setting in Motion the Wheel of the Law," at Deer Park in Sarnath. Buddha later founded a monastic community and codified the principles according to which followers should live; he continued to preach and travel until his death at the age of 80. Buddhists believe that he is one of the many Buddhas who appeared in the past—and that more will appear in the future.

Iconography

In Buddhist statuary and art there is a system, derived from Pali texts, of 32 special physical features of the Buddha and 80 secondary features. There are four poses for Buddhas (called *asanas),* and a variety of hand gestures, called *mudras.* The *asanas* and *mudras* illustrate key events in the Enlightened One's life: many fine examples of Buddhist iconography are found in Bangkok's National Museum. There are four main poses for the Buddha: seated (meditation position); standing and walking (preaching); and reclining (this position represents Buddha's entrance into nirvana at the moment of his physical death). In the 19th century, King Rama III attempted to systematize the *mudras,* and came up with a list of 40 gestures, but most are uncommon. The common gestures are the following six:

Dispelling Fear: Standing or Walking Buddha—right hand extended upward, palm out (a Thai variant is both palms out). This "don't panic" gesture relates to various stories—one about subduing a rampaging elephant, another about forbidding relatives to dispute, and another about calming flood waters.

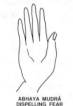

ABHAYA MUDRÀ
DISPELLING FEAR

DHARMACHAKRA MUDRÀ
TURNING THE WHEEL OF THE LAW

DHYÀNA MUDRÀ
MEDITATION

VARADA MUDRÀ
BESTOWING BLESSINGS

BHUMISPARSHA MUDRÀ
CALLING THE EARTH TO WITNESS

VITARKA MUDRÀ
PREACHING

mudras

Bestowing Blessings: Standing Buddha—position is similar to dispelling fear, except that the hands are extended downward, palms out.

Meditation: Seated Buddha in lotus position—hands cupped in lap, serene smile, eyes slightly downcast.

Calling the Earth to Witness: Seated Buddha—right hand draped over knee. This is the most common pose seen in Thai statuary and symbolizes the exact moment of enlightenment. The meditating Gautama (the Buddha-to-be) was tempted by the demon Mara and her sensual dancing girls. Gautama resisted; when asked by Mara to prove his perfect state of virtue, he reached forward to touch the ground, and replied, "The earth shall be my witness." The earth-goddess Torani rose up, and wringing the water out of her hair, drowned Mara's armies —and washed away the demons of delusion, ignorance, and attachment.

Preaching: Standing Buddha or Walking Buddha, with right hand held at chest height, palm out, thumb and forefinger joined.

Turning the Wheel of the Law: Seated Buddha—hands held together at chest height, each hand with thumb and forefinger joined, right palm outward, left palm inward, forming circular gestures. This symbolizes Buddha's first sermon, "Setting in Motion the Wheel of the Law."

Buddhism In Thailand

Buddhism permeates every facet of life in Thailand—to the extent that monks are called upon to consecrate a new building or even a new Boeing 727. Thailand has some 30,000 Buddhist temples—mainly Theravada Buddhist, plus a handful of Mahayana Buddhist (deriving from Chinese or Vietnamese sects). There are an estimated 250,000 monks and 25,000 novices throughout the kingdom. A Thai temple or *wat* is a bit like a community center—it can function as a school, hospital, dispensary, meeting hall, information and employment agency, or village hostelry. Monasteries handle their own finances and are supported entirely by donations—fairs are often held in the grounds as fund-raising ventures. Temples are sanctuaries—in the case of Wat Pailom, north of Bangkok, a wildlife sanctuary (rare open-billed storks find a place to nest there, having been chased away from other sites).

BOB RACE

The concept of sanctuary may extend to housing the aged, the bankrupt, or the abandoned.

Theravada Buddhism in Thailand is divided into the majority Mahanikaya order and the stricter Thammayut order (founded by King Mongkut, and presently followed by about 10% of the population). The most respected figure in Thai Buddhism is the Supreme Patriarch, currently Somdej Phra Yannasangvorn. He is the Thai equivalent of the Pope, with administrative power over the entire Thai *sangha* (Buddhist community or brotherhood). Bangkok's Wat Bovornivet, Wat Mahathat, and Wat Paknam are important centers of learning, with renowned meditation masters.

Among the problems facing the Buddhist brotherhood is a declining interest in Buddhism among the younger generation, and negative publicity generated by a string of scandals involving monks (peccadillos of certain monks and irregular practices such as predicting the outcome of lotteries). A reformist movement, operating out of Wat Santi Asoke (in the Bundkapi district on the outskirts of Bangkok), claims that Thai Buddhism has been corrupted and seeks to get back "on track." Santi Asoke monks are vegetarian, are allowed only two personal possessions (saffron robe and alms-bowl), and must not use motorized transport.

Temple Offerings

Temple offerings in Thailand consist of three objects placed in front of the Buddha image— candle, lotus bud, and incense sticks. The candle symbolizes the light of understanding. The lotus bud has long been associated as a special symbol of the Buddha—signifying the purity of Buddha's thoughts (a lotus flowers with great beauty in the dark swamps). Incense sticks (there must be three of them) stand for the "Triple Gem" —Buddha, *dhamma* (teachings) and *sangha* (brotherhood). Offerings of floral wreaths and bowls of food are also made—the food is usually collected and redistributed to the needy.

Other temple offerings and practices are related to gaining merit. Creating or maintaining temple decoration is considered meritorious for lay people, and thus the act of gilding Buddha statues is also considered meritorious. Paper-thin gold leaf, which is sold in tiny squares, is pressed onto Buddha images. The gold leaf is usually placed on the chest of the image (in the belief of ensuring a good heart); on the head (to ensure wisdom); or on the mouth (to ensure right speech). The act of buying and then releasing captive animals is considered meritorious—at a number of *wats* and shrines around Bangkok there are birds, tortoises, and fish on sale for this purpose.

Accruing Merit

The ultimate goal in Buddhism is the attainment of nirvana—or the cessation of suffering. Classical Buddhism interprets this as breaking a long cycle of birth, death, and rebirth; contemporary Buddhism also sees nirvana as enlightenment attainable during one's lifetime.

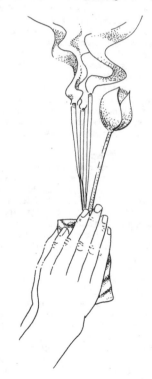

BOB RACE

temple offerings

AMONG THE BELIEVERS

Shrines

Thais place extraordinary faith in Brahmanic and animist shrines, amulets, and other talismans for protection. These beliefs come from a mixture of sources: from Buddhism, Brahmanism, and a belief in spirits, astrology, ghosts, and supernatural forces. The Thai mania for guardian shrines and amulets is perhaps no more bizarre than the Western mania for insurance, which affords protection from accident, theft, or other misfortune.

Each Thai house is protected by a shrine or a spirit-house to keep ghosts out. The most feared ghosts are those thought to arise from the bodies of violent death victims—as in a hit-and-run accident, or murder (or in the old days, being eaten by a tiger). If such a ghost appears in a residence or business building, it can wreak havoc by causing fire, sickness, or worse. Hospitals and police stations have shrines outside to deflect evil forces. Hotels and department stores invariably have a resident guardian spirit to oversee fortunes. The most famous of these is Erawan Shrine on Ploenchit Road. Spirits are said to reside in trees, which is why certain older specimens around Bangkok are garlanded with flowers. Cities need protection too: for Bangkok, there is Lak Muang shrine, which houses the city pillar.

Amulets And Talismans

To keep the person protected from harm at all times, portable charms are required. A Thai could be wearing a cloth undervest with prayers printed on it, or a Thai male might have a string around his waist with some wooden penises dangling off it—to ensure potency. Men involved in high-risk professions (army officers, gangsters) believe that magical tattoos can protect them from bullets and knives—which may explain why some are tattooed from head to toe. But the most common protector is a small Buddha image (usually produced in clay from a mold) which is set in a metal case and hung on a pendant around the neck. These charms come in a great range of forms and functions: from an eye-covering Buddha (general protection) to a ten-eyed deity (said to be good against accidents) to an ivory image (good against ghosts).

Amulets are said to be ineffective if the owner has a malevolent mind, or if the wearer does not believe absolutely in their power. The "power" comes from having been blessed by a famous abbot or monk, or a king. Miraculous stories about the supernatural powers of amulets grace the pages of half a dozen magazines in Thailand devoted solely to these charms. Some are connected with winning the lottery (as when a man got an amulet from Wat Rakang and won six lottery prizes in a row); surviving accidents intact (man in car accident survives unscathed, but his friends are seriously injured—after the accident, he finds all his amulets have disappeared, but their gold frames remain); and other paranormal phenomena.

One story from an amulet magazine shows a pick-up truck riddled with bullets, the body of a man riddled with bullets, and an amulet from Wat Paknam (Bangkok). The amulet was a gift from husband to wife: he was killed in an attack with high-powered weapons; she escaped with bruise marks where she was supposedly hit by bullets which did not pierce the skin. After the attack she recovered and drove her husband to the hospital, where he died. Different issues of Wat Paknam amulets are said to be very powerful—and though these might start out at B100 each, they could go up to B30,000.

Prices for the super-amulets—those said to have special powers—are in the one-million-baht range. Among these is a clay Buddha image called Pra Somdet Wat Rakang, made in 1867 by the highly revered monk Somdet Putthajarn Toh. This amulet, which was originally produced in several molds, is believed to confer invulnerability—its power is said to come from the monk's blessing. Originals are worth over one million baht (US$40,000), and some are in the hands of collectors, who, regardless of the powers of such a piece, regard it as a financial investment, similar to buying a famous artwork. Herein is a quandary: if an amulet is worth a million baht, would not a thug kill the owner in order to get it? There have been a number of cases where this has happened—instead of the amulet protecting the owner, the owner may have to protect the amulet. Even spiritual leaders are not immune. In 1991, *The Nation* reported the case of an abbot in Samut Prakarn province who was stabbed to death and robbed of six highly prized Buddha amulets.

Pra Rawd is another amulet in the million-baht range. Also thought to confer invulnerability, it is believed to be the oldest amulet whose history can still be traced—images date to the 12th century Haripunchai Kingdom. Popular among women is Pra Somdet Nang Paya (which means "queen"), a tri-angular-shaped amulet from Wat Nang Paya in Phit-sanulok. Believed to bring prosperity is Pra Soumkor from Kamphaeng Phet. It is said that in its under-ground storage place was the inscription, "Those who have these amulets will not fall into poverty."

Not all the high-priced amulets are old: one called Pra Somdet Chitrlada was produced by the present king for those working closely under him, or those working in border areas where there was a lot of fighting going on at the time. Military personnel, as can be imagined, are greatly interested in the powers of amulets, and an officer may wear half a dozen of them in the field, just in case. The weight of these is a bit of a liability—they could add up to half a kilo

dangling round the neck. During the Vietnam War days, GIs on leave in Thailand became engrossed with amulets and their powers.

Buddha himself preached a doctrine of nonat-tachment to material things, and most certainly, Bud-dha would have condemned this trade in amulets. But there are a few explanations as to why the trade continues. Most of the amulets are produced in tem-ples and then blessed by an important spiritual lead-er. This is a simple fund-raising venture; the practice brings in high revenues for temple-building.

Naturally, faking the more highly regarded im-ages is a roaring trade. Examining the small clay images through a magnifying loupe—checking fea-tures, age, texture, and other factors—is a favorite pastime at amulet markets around Bangkok. This is rather like stamp-collecting: if a clay image has been "misprinted" from a mold, the value goes up.

☞ พระวัดปากน้ำ รุ่น ๖ เนื้อสีเทา

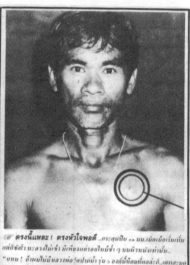

☞ ตรงนี้แหละ ! ตรงหัวใจพอดี ...กระสุนปืน .. มม.เม็ดเนื้อเริ่มเกิด แต่ผิวยังไม่ช้ำ มีเพียงแค่รอยไหม้ช้ำ ๆ บนผิวหนังเท่านั้น..
"แหน ! ถ้าผมไม่มีหลวงพ่อวัดปากน้ำ รุ่น ๖ องค์นี้ห้อยที่คอละก็..เทศะมอ เรไปหัวร์เมืองผีชะแล้ว"

(right) This man, a taxi driver operating near Bangkok, was shot by a high-powered handgun at close range, but the bullet did not pierce his skin. The circle shows mark left by the bullet—a burn mark and a bruise. The driver says that if he didn't have this amulet, he would now be having a holiday in hell.

(left) The Wat Paknam amulet that saved his life: the amulet cost B100, but if someone offered him a million baht for it now, the taxi driver says he wouldn't sell it.

—taken from an amulet magazine

Many Thai males spend some time as monks in order to accrue merit.

Many Buddhist practices in Thailand hinge on accruing merit (doing good deeds). By following the right path in this life, it is believed that a person will be able to carry over karma into the next life. Karma is cause and effect: good deeds have good effects; bad deeds have bad effects. Many Buddhists believe that they may have inherited some bad karma from previous lives—a situation that must be corrected by doing good deeds in the present life.

Women accrue merit by giving food to monks who go around with alms-bowls in the morning. The monks' bowls are sometimes referred to as "begging bowls," which is erroneous as the monks are not begging at all—it is a privilege to feed them, thereby gaining merit. Merit can be accrued by making donations to the temples; by assisting in the building or repair of *wats,* Buddha images, religious schools, and shrines; or by going on pilgrimage to Buddhist shrines.

The ultimate form of merit-making for males is to become a monk. A very high percentage of Thai males become monks at some time or another—for perhaps a week, perhaps a month, or three months. They usually can get paid leave from a company for such a retreat. The initiate leaves behind his worldly possessions, has his head and eyebrows shaved, and dons saffron robes. The family expects this of their sons as a form of merit-making, bringing honor to their parents. Since women cannot be ordained as monks, a monk can accrue merit for his mother and sisters as well as for himself. A son may also enter a monastery for a short period if there is a death in the family. People going through a period of hardship make a vow that they will do a seven-day retreat to calm themselves down, and to remind themselves that nothing in this world is permanent. Most young men will enter the monastery during the rainy season, a three-month period when all monks forgo travel and stay at their monasteries.

A contentious issue in Thai Buddhism (and in other forms of Buddhism) involves the role of women. Because the ordination lineage for females died out in medieval times, nuns are not recognized as full members of the monastic community, and mainly perform menial tasks in the *wats.* In Thailand, females cannot be ordained as monks, and therefore cannot attain complete spiritual fulfillment. There are white-robed nuns in Thailand, but no separate nunneries (the nuns must study under a monk). To get around the problem of nonadmission to monkhood, some Thai nuns have studied in Korea or Taiwan, where it is possible for women to become ordained monks.

MYTHOLOGY AND THE ARTS

Thai artforms derive from Hindu and Buddhist legends—from the Indian *Ramayana* epic and the *Jataka Tales* (former lives of Buddha). Other stories come from Thai folk tales, from Ayuthayan "soap operas," and from the Javanese romantic epic, *Inao*. Major art patrons in the past have been larger temples and the monarchy.

Hindu Legends

Hindu legends most likely filtered through to Thailand by way of Cambodia. In Hinduism there are three important gods: Brahma, the Creator of the universe, Vishnu the Preserver, and Shiva the Destroyer (and Reproducer). The mount of Brahma is Erawan, the three-headed elephant. The mount of Vishnu is Garuda, a giant mythical

ceramic-studded Yaksha

bird with a human body, but the wings, legs, and beak of a bird. As the king of Thailand is considered an incarnation of Vishnu, the *garuda* (also known as *krut*) is a royal emblem, and symbol of the Chakri dynasty. You'll see the *garuda* figure with the red torso mounted on the outside of a number of government buildings and offices (particularly the post office and banks), or on the outside of those businesses fortunate enough to have obtained royal approval in the past (this practice is no longer followed). All Thai bank notes carry the emblem, and the *garuda* stamp is also on your visa.

Garuda's enemy is his half brother Naga, the king of serpents, who dwells in subterranean regions. *Garuda* and multiheaded *nagas* are often seen locked in battle in murals and in sculpture. The motif is believed to have the power to chase away evil spirits. Lengthy seven-headed *nagas* are sometimes found on balustrades lining steps leading up to a temple; five-headed versions are also found on banisters. In a modified form, the *naga* appears on the rooftops of temple buildings: at the peak of a roof-end is a stylized *garuda* (called a *chofa*—a slender bird head and neck), and sliding down from this point are *nagas*. The *naga* somehow crossed over into Buddhist statuary: the serpent is considered a protector of Buddhism. Lopburi-Khmer statues of Buddha show seven-headed, cobra-like *naga*-hoods behind the statue. Vishnu is shown in a similar pose in Hindu legends, and, according to the Hindus, Buddha is a reincarnation of Vishnu (Buddhists do not accept this version of things).

The *Ramakien*

The seventh avatar (descent to earth in human form) of the god Vishnu was Prince Rama. A Sanskrit epic poem, the *Ramayana,* first written by Valmiki over 2,000 years ago, tells the story of Prince Rama, who set out in quest of his princess, Sita, and to destroy Ravana, a powerful demon intent on world domination. The *Ramayana* is the most important myth in south-

masked drama—
mythology in motion

TAT

east Asia, with varying forms in India, Thailand, Laos, Burma, Indonesia, and wherever the sphere of Indian influence extended. The story parallels Western myths—from the story of Helen of Troy in the *Iliad* to the *Star Wars* saga—in focusing on the struggle between good and evil. The *Ramayana* probably reached Thailand by way of Cambodia or Indonesia.

The *Ramakien* is the Thai version of the epic, recounting the tale of lovers Rama and Sita. The beautiful Sita is abducted by the wicked King Tosakan (ten-headed, ten-armed), who imprisons her in his palace on the island of Longka. Prince Rama sets off to rescue Sita—in this endeavour he is assisted by his brother Luxaman, and by a simian army under a mischievous albino monkey-god, Hanuman. Overcoming impossible obstacles, the rescuers build a causeway to Longka. After a pitched battle, Tosakan is killed by an arrow from the magic bow of Rama, and Sita is rescued. The allies of Tosakan include an array of demons—*asuras, rakshas,* and *yakshas. Yakshas,* giants with fierce expressions and long pointed teeth, are found in six-meter-high statues in the Grand Palace and at Wat Arun in Bangkok, although their role at the palace is guardians against evil.

The *Ramakien* was adapted by the kings of Thailand themselves: the most complete version was written by King Rama I. King Rama II worked on the legend, and King Rama VI conferred the name "Rama" retroactively on the kings of the Chakri line—thus royalty, deity, and legend have become intermingled.

PERFORMING ARTS

Khon

The *Ramakien* legend is the basis for the Thai performing arts. *Khon*—classical masked dance-drama—was originally limited to the royal palace (in Ayuthaya and in Bangkok), and performances would go on for several nights, taking about 20 hours. The story is told through stylized (and strenuous) gestures and postures, which take years of training to perfect. At one time all the parts were performed by men. Today only excerpts from *khon* are performed—by both men and women. There is no shortage of material—it is calculated that a performance of the entire epic would take more than a month, with 725 hours of continuous dance-drama involving 311 characters. *Khon* is called masked drama because all of the characters (except Rama, Sita, and Luxaman) wear intricate papier-mâché masks.

Lakhon And Likay

Two derivatives of *khon* are *lakhon* and *likay*. These use similar costumes and movements, but no masks. *Lakhon* is mostly danced by women—you can see a form of *lakhon* dancing at Erawan shrine in Bangkok, where performers are hired by supplicants. One form of *lakhon* is based on the Manora folktales of southern Thailand. As opposed to court entertainment, *likay* is village-fair entertainment—burlesque, social satire and comedy of classical themes. It is usually seen at festivals or temple fairs—performances at Lak Muang shrine in Bangkok are paid for by supplicants. A bizarre variant of *likay* is a simian theater, where all the parts are played by monkeys.

Pipat

Accompaniment for *khon, lakhon,* and *likay* is provided by the *pipat*, an orchestra of five to fifteen musicians, playing drums, cymbals, gongs, bamboo-bar xylophones, flutes, and fiddles. Similar to the Balinese gamelan orchestra, *pipat* percussion eludes the Western ear, seeming to lack harmony or melody. The music is, however, attuned to the emotions portrayed on the stage—of the classical repertoire of about 1,200 compositions, there are 13 specifically for anger, 21 for sorrow, and eight to convey excitement. The same emotional pitch is conveyed by woodwind instruments, cymbals, and drums at Thai boxing matches. Music is essential to all kinds of occasions—festivals, marriages, ceremonies, folk dancing.

Nang

Rarely seen in Thailand today is another form of court entertainment—*nang* (shadow play), in which oxhide puppets with moveable parts are manipulated behind a translucent screen, onto which shadows are cast by candlelight. Songs and comic dialogue are used to recount stories. *Nang* shadow play is a very old form of court entertainment—it is thought that Thai dance movements evolved from the actions of the puppeteers as they shifted around huge buffalo-hide characters behind a screen, and provided missing emotions and gestures. *Hun krabok* is straightforward puppetry (no screen) reenacting a story about an 18th-century rebellious Ayuthayan prince.

The royal court has been replaced, it seems, by a tourist audience—puppetry performances are sometimes given at dinner-dance tourist venues. *Khon* excerpts are performed at these places, along with folk dances from the northeast—the candle dance, the fingernail dance—and displays of *krabi krabong,* a traditional martial art involving sword-fighting practice.

FINE ARTS

Murals And Sculpture

Early Thai fine art forms—mural painting and sculpture—were religious in basis, as in medieval Europe. Major sources for mural painting in temples are the *Jataka Tales,* Buddhist and Hindu cosmology, the life of Buddha, and the *Ramakien.* The *Jataka Tales* describe the 550 lives of Buddha before he attained enlightenment—the most important of these are the last ten lives, during each of which a particular virtue was perfected. These stories have evolved into folk legends.

Thai temple murals were conceived as tools for teaching both monks and lay people through graphic narrative scenes. *Jataka* fables, for instance, can be retold by following the mural sequence. The murals have a total lack of perspective—the hallmark of classical Thai style. Of interest to historians are the fine details in the murals: while many show demons and celestial beings, they also show ordinary people going about their daily business, and even occasional Western subjects (French soldiers on horses from the Ayuthaya period, American ships with missionaries). In temple interiors, the back wall behind the main Buddha image usually shows scenes from Buddhist cosmology; the side walls show scenes from Buddha's life or the *Jataka;* the front wall above the main entrance shows Buddha's temptation by the demon Mara. In Buddhist cosmology there are three worlds—the world of desire, the world of form, and the world of nonexistence. In mural painting, the first two stages are usually represented by rather Dantesque versions of hell, earth, and heaven.

Thai temple decoration was done anonymously by lay people to gain merit. The amount of decoration in a Thai temple is staggering when all the woodcarving, panelling, ceramic work, glass mosaic, and other detailed work is taken into account. But it is temple doorways and window shutters that dazzle—they have transcended the limits of craft and become works of art. Some doorways and windows are carved out of teak, others lacquered, others inlaid with mother-of-pearl. A Thai specialty is flaming mother-of-pearl, which derives from the shell of the turbo snail, found in the Gulf of Thailand. When it catches the light, this shell radiates deep pinks and luminescent greens. The craft was first developed for decorating ceremonial vessels and scripture boxes, and later wooden panels and shutters. Magnificent gold-leaf lacquer decoration adorns temple doors and shutters—although found on a wide variety of household objects and furniture, the finest craftsmanship was reserved for objects intended for religious or royal use.

As with figures depicted on temple doors, exterior Thai statuary mainly consists of guardian figures or protectors of Buddhism—which could be a pair of *norasinghs* (bronze Khmer-style lions), stone Chinese warriors with flowing beards and long swords, huge ceramic-studded *yakshas* with clubs, mosaic-covered demon figures from the *Ramakien*, or deities from Brahman legend such as the seven-headed *nagas* found on the balustrades of steps leading up to a temple. Interior temple sculpture is almost exclusively devoted to images of Buddha and follows strict guidelines: the sculptors did not intend to be original. Even so, the "formula" could be stretched, and there is a great range of sculptural styles depending on the period: from squat, chunky Dvaravati Buddha images to realistic-looking Lopburi-Khmer Buddhas; from flowing, graceful Sukothai-style Buddhas to regally dressed Ayuthayan-style images.

Temple Architecture

Bangkok has a crazy mix of architectural styles —French, Gothic, Greek, Chinese, Portuguese— but its most striking feature is its temple architecture, which reflects centuries of influence from India, China, Burma, Cambodia and other parts of Asia. Toward the end of the 19th century, Western styles began to influence temple design and royal architecture. The Buddhist *wat,* or temple, supports a complex community and consists of a bewildering array of structures. A good way of identifying structures is to visit Wat Pra Keo in Bangkok. This temple serves as an awesome three-dimensional textbook of the architectural styles briefly described here:

Bot: Also known as the *ubosot,* this is the main chapel or assembly hall, containing the principal Buddha image and surrounded by eight sacred boundary stones. It is used for meditation, ordination, and other rituals. The *bot* is usually rectangular, with multitiered roofing covered in glazed tiles. Architecturally, the *bot* absorbed many influences—initially from Burma, Cambodia, and China. The Sukothai period saw an enlarged front door; Ayuthaya-period *bots* used concave foundations, with a curved base.

doorway detail from Rakang, Bangkok

TAT

*Wat Pra Keo,
illuminated at night to
mark a special occasion*

Later Ayuthaya-period *bots* featured Gothic-style roofs and rococo decorations, and windows cut into the walls—features adapted by King Narai, who employed French architects.

Viharn: The prayer hall or secondary hall containing a large image of Buddha. The *viharn* is virtually identical to the *bot,* except it has no sacred boundary stones and is used for different functions—for merit-making ceremonies, and sermons delivered to lay people. The tallest *viharns* in Bangkok are at Wat Kalayanimit (a landmark along the Chao Phraya River), and at Wat Suthat.

Chedi: A bell-shaped monument or pagoda (in India called a *stupa*) which emulates the original mound of earth containing the ashes and relics of Buddha. *Chedis* usually contains the ashes of royalty or wealthy donors. The world's largest *chedi* is at Nakhon Pathom, to the west of Bangkok.

Prang: A chunky tower deriving from the Khmers of Angkor, and originally of Hindu origin—with features and statuary dedicated to Vishnu, Shiva, and Brahma. It is symbolic of Mount Meru, the mythical mountain abode of the gods. The Khmers built in stone; the Thais built in brick and stucco. The finest example in Thailand is Wat Arun.

KAREN WHITE

prang

Mondop: An elaborately decorated square structure with a pyramidal pointed roof, containing sacred texts or holy relics. Wat Pra Keo has a fine *mondop.* Up-country near Lopburi is the famed Pra Puttabat *mondop,* enshrining a sacred footprint of the Buddha.

Ho Trai: A quite different style of library is the *ho trai*—consisting of traditional teak housing raised on stilts. This was designed to keep at bay rats, ants, and tropical insects which find the library books quite tasty—Buddhist texts were traditionally made from palm-leaf paper. Wat Rakang in Thonburi has a very fine *ho trai.*

Prasat: A ceremonial building with an elegant cruciform shape. Religious *prasats* are topped by *prangs* (as at Wat Pra Keo); royal *prasats* are topped with Thai-style spires. Both styles can be found at the Grand Palace, where Amporn Pimok Prasat pavilion is regarded as the finest example in Thailand.

Other Features: *Sala*—an open-sided pavilion, used for meetings or lectures, and as shelters by overnight guests or pilgrims; *guttis*—monks' living quarters; *ho rakang*—a bell or drum tower used to summon monks to services and meals; *sala kanprien*—a congregation hall, used for religious instruction.

FESTIVALS AND HOLIDAYS

National Holidays

January 1: New Year's Day
Jan/Feb: Maha Puja*
April 6: Chakri Day
April 12-14: Songkran
May 5: Coronation Day
Early May: Plowing Ceremony*
May/June: Visakha Puja*
July/August: Asalha Puja*
August 12: Queen Sirikit's Birthday
October 23: Chulalongkorn Day
December 5: King Bhumibol's Birthday
December 10: Constitution Day
December 31: New Year's Eve

determined by lunar cycle

Thai holidays and festivals are connected with good harvests, or with Buddhism or royalty. Most are moveable: those marked with an asterisk are based on the Buddhist lunar calendar; celebrations usually take place on full moon days. Holidays connected with royalty are based on the Western calendar and are largely private affairs—the exact date can move if the holiday falls on a weekend. There is always some kind of festivity going on somewhere in Thailand—TAT puts out a color brochure with major events featured for the current year so you can keep track.

Two periods in Bangkok when things come to a virtual stand-still (shops or offices closed, trains fully booked) are between December 25th and January 2nd (Christmas to New Year), and at Chinese New Year (late January or early February—many businesses close for four to five days). Neither of the occasions are official holidays, but everybody takes time out regardless. To make sure the new year is properly ushered in, there are three separate celebrations—Western New Year, Chinese New Year, and Songkran (Buddhist New Year). Holidays and festivities present special opportunities for photography—bring a tripod, as some of the action takes place after dusk. The following holidays and festivals are celebrated in Bangkok.

January/February

Maha Puja: Important Buddhist holy day, usually in February, celebrating an occasion of impromptu preaching by Buddha. Merit-making ceremonies take place during the day at temples throughout the country, and at dusk, candlelit processions walk three times around the monastery chapel as the full moon rises.

Chinese New Year: Thai Chinese make temple offerings and exchange gifts at family reunions. Similar to Western Christmas: a family occasion with no big public festivities. Usually in February; many shops closed in Bangkok.

March/April

Kite-fighting: Takes place in Sanam Luang, a large field opposite the Grand Palace—usually in March. There are tournaments involving other traditional sports such as *takraw*.

Chakri Day: April 6, commemorating the founding of the Chakri Dynasty in 1782. This is the only day of the year that the Royal Pantheon at Wat Pra Keo is open to the public.

Songkran: April 12-15 marks the Buddhist New Year—originally water was sprinkled on Buddha images in temples; today, Songkran is an excuse to throw buckets of water over all and sundry in the streets—a couple of days of crazy fun at the peak of the hot season. Subdued celebrations in Bangkok (you'll get doused if you venture along the canals), but riotous celebrating by the Mon community in Pra Padaeng, in Samut Prakarn, just south of Bangkok.

May/June

Coronation Day: May 5th anniversary of the king's coronation with a private ceremony at Wat Pra Keo.

Plowing Ceremony: Takes place at Sanam Luang opposite the Grand Palace. An ancient Brahman ritual, presided over by the king and celebrating the official start of the rice-planting season—with sacred oxen pulling a plough, and various ceremonies predicting harvest success.

*Visakha Puja: Marking the birth, death, and enlightenment of Buddha. As on Maha Puja, an evening candlelit procession circles the main monastery building under the full moon.

July/August

*Asa.ha Puja: In July or August, this occasion is celebrated in the same manner as the other *pujas:* it commemorates Buddha's first sermon and marks the start of Buddhist Lent *(Khao Phansa),* or rainy season, when all monks are expected to remain in their temples and when ordination of novice monks takes place.

Queen Sirikit's Birthday: August 12th. Public buildings are decorated to honor H.M. Queen Sirikit, and at night buildings in and around the Grand Palace are strung with lights.

September/October

Ok Pansa: In October, at the end of Buddhist Lent and the Rains Retreat, lay people present monks with new robes and other items for the forthcoming year.

Chulalongkorn Day: October 23rd—in memory of highly revered King Rama V. Wreath-laying ceremony at equestrian statue near National Assembly Building.

November/December

Longboat Racing: The end of the rainy season is celebrated with boat racing and regattas in various parts of Thailand. In Bangkok, racing takes place on the Chao Phraya River, close to the Sheraton Hotel. Longboat races also take place at other times of the year—the newspapers have details.

Golden Mount Fair: A lively temple-fair held at Wat Saket in the first week of November, with folk drama, carnival rides, product stalls, foodstalls, and candlelit processions around the temple.

*Loy Krathong: This festival takes place on the full moon night in November. Thais everywhere launch *krathongs,* small banana-leaf boats containing a lighted candle, incense, flowers, and a small coin, onto rivers and canals. This offering is said to honor the water spirits and cleanse the previous year's sins. Best viewed on the banks of the Chao Phraya.

Deepavali: Held in November, the Festival of Lights centers around a small Hindu temple on Silom Road.

Trooping of the Colors: On December 3rd, several days before the king's birthday, the elite Royal Guards march past members of the royal family, and swear allegiance. This event is held in the Royal Plaza near the National Assembly Building.

King Bhumibol's Birthday: December 5th. Festivities occur throughout Thailand, with houses and buildings lit up at night. Spectacular illumination by night of Grand Palace area and Rajadamnern Avenue.

Royal guards show their form at a "Trooping of the Colors" parade, a few days before the king's party in early December.

BANGKOK BASICS
VISAS, MONEY, SERVICES

VISAS

The 15-Day Transit Visa: You can get this visa stamped at the point of entry (usually Don Muang Airport). Proof of onward ticketing must be shown, and the 15-day period is nonextendable.

The 30-Day Tourist Visa: Thai diplomatic missions abroad issue a cheap 30-day nonextendable visa. It runs from the date of entry, and there is a three-month leeway period to get there.

The 60-Day Tourist Visa: Issued by Thai diplomatic missions abroad, this visa must be used within three months; it can be extended another 30 days in Bangkok at the discretion of immigration officials. A more expensive visa obtainable outside Thailand is a dual-entry tourist visa (two periods of 60 days; you have to leave the country and reenter after the first 60-day period).

The 90-Day Non-immigrant Visa: If you can offer a good reason for a longer visit—business,

working purposes, study, or research—you may be able to get this visa. The complication here is that you will need a tax clearance certificate to leave the country. There is also a dual-entry non-immigrant visa, which will give you 180 days (two periods of 90 days; you have to leave the country and reenter after the first 90-day period).

Visa Extensions: Apply to the Immigration Division, Soi Suan Plu, South Sathorn Road, Bangkok, tel. 286-9230. There are other immigration offices in places like Pattaya. You need two photos and two copies each of the initial and visa pages of your passport; cost is B500, and there are long queues. You can have one of the legal consultation offices around Bangkok and Pattaya handle the extension for you. Besides visa extensions, they can help with tax clearance, work permits, business registration, marriage registration, construction permits, and contracts. Or you can take a quick ride out of the country—say to Penang in Malaysia—and pick up another Thai visa there. Thai embassies are located in most Asian capitals.

Overstaying: A fine of B100 per day for each day beyond the duration of the visa is levied at Don Muang Airport by immigration officials. Foreigners staying in Thailand over 90 days in a calendar year or who derived income while staying in Thailand must obtain a tax clearance certificate from the Revenue Department before being allowed to leave the country.

BEFORE YOU GO

Paperwork
It's a good idea to carry photocopies of initial and visa pages of your passport. As a security measure, type up all important numbers (passport, credit cards, and so on), along with important addresses, on a single page; then have reduction photocopies run off and distribute them about your person and in your baggage. Thais love business cards—these can be made up on the spot in Bangkok if necessary (laser printing on ground floor of Siam Center).

Ticketing And Logistics
Book your airline ticket well in advance (two months or more). Even during the off-season, planes can be packed because Bangkok is a stepping-stone to other points in Asia and India. It's difficult to get airline bookings in the high season (Nov.-Feb.), and hotel bookings can be tricky then, too.

Unless arriving from an infected area, no vaccinations are required. However, it's advisable to have standard shots or boosters for tetanus, polio, and typhoid, and to carry malaria pills if going up-country.

The thought of landing in Bangkok is intimidating for most travelers, though it's really no different from landing anywhere else in Asia. The best way to counter fear of the unknown is to read up as much as you can on Bangkok and Thailand, and to tune your ear to the Thai language (even listening to a language tape will be of benefit—see "The Thai Language" at back). If it makes you feel more comfortable,

have a hotel reserved for the first night or two. See the Arrival in Bangkok section (under "Transport") for customs regulations and arrival details.

What To Pack
Pack as little as you can. Halve the baggage and double the money—leave lots of space for shopping in Thailand! Just about everything you need can be found in Bangkok, including things you haven't even thought of. Electrical goods and appliances (foreign-brand radios, videos, camera equipment, computers) are much more expensive because of high import taxes; other items may be in short supply or difficult to find (it's the lack of small items that you take for granted, like good ballpoint pens, that annoy).

Because of hot weather, concentrate on packing loose cotton or linen clothing; at night, when it's cooler, you can wear synthetics or even a light jacket (useful to counter fierce air-conditioning in restaurants). There is lots of cheap clothing available in Bangkok—large sizes are difficult to find, but this problem is solved by having custom cotton clothing made up (just hand over an item of clothing and the tailor will copy it within 24 hours). Socks, underwear, swimsuits, and shoes are hard to find in larger sizes—although swimsuits and shoes can be custom-made quickly. Loose or easily removed footwear is a good idea in Bangkok because your feet will swell in the hot climate, and you will need to remove shoes to enter temples or Thai homes.

Pack any prescription drugs you may need—you can most likely find the same drugs in Bangkok, but it may take time. International brand cosmetics are expensive. Bring your own supply of sunscreen and insect repellent for out-of-town trips. If you're planning on snorkeling, bring your own mask and snorkel since larger sizes are not always available for rental.

MONEY

Thailand has a free money market, with few restrictions on import and export of foreign funds. Thus banking is very easy, and facilities in Bangkok are excellent.

EMBASSIES AND CONSULATES

Some 50 countries maintain embassies or consulates in Bangkok—from the Asia/Pacific region, Europe, Eastern Europe, the Middle East, North America, and South America. The English edition of the Yellow Pages gives a full list of embassies with current addresses. Phone ahead to check address, opening hours, and visa requirements—the best time to go visa shopping is in the morning from 0800 to 1200. Most embassies are concentrated in the Ploenchit Road-Wireless Road area, the Sukhumvit area, or the Sathorn Road-Silom Road area.

Australia tel. 286-0411
37 South Sathorn Rd.

Austria tel. 286-3011
14 Soi Nandha, Soi Attakarnprasit

Bangladesh tel. 235-3639
Soi 63, Sukhumvit

Belgium tel. 391-8067
44 Soi Pipat, off Silom Rd.

Brunei tel. 251-6984
26/50 Chidlom Rd., Ploenchit

Burma (Myanmar) tel. 233-2237
132 N. Sathorn Rd.

Canada tel. 234-1561/9
Boonmitr Bldg. 11F, 138 Silom Rd.

China tel. 245-7030/49
57 Rajadapisek Rd., Din Daeng

Denmark tel. 213-2021
10 Soi Attakarnprasit (off Sathorn)

Finland tel. 256-9306
Amarin Plaza 16F, Ploenchit Rd.

France tel. 213-2201/5
29 South Sathorn Rd.

Germany tel. 213-2331/6
9 South Sathorn Rd.

India tel. 258-0300/6
46 Soi 23, Sukhumvit Rd.

Indonesia tel. 252-3135/40
600 Petchburi Rd.

Ireland tel. 223-0876
Thaniya Bldg, 62 Silom Rd.

Italy tel. 287-2054/7
399 Nang Linchee, Tungmahamek

Japan tel. 252-6151/9
1674 New Petchburi Rd.

Korea tel. 236-7999
Sathorn Bldg 10F, 90 N. Sathorn

Laos tel. 286-9244
193 South Sathorn Rd.

Malaysia tel. 286-1390/2
35 South Sathorn Rd.

Nepal tel. 391-7240
189 Soi 71, Sukhumvit Rd.

Netherlands tel. 254-7701/5
106 Wireless Rd.

New Zealand tel. 251-8165
93 Wireless Rd.

Norway tel. 253-0390
Bank of America Bldg, 2/2 Wireless Rd.

Pakistan tel. 253-0288/90
31 Soi 3, Sukhumvit Rd.

Philippines tel. 259-0139/40
760 Sukhumvit Rd.

Portugal tel. 234-0372
26 Bush Lane (off New Rd.)

Singapore tel. 286-2111
129 South Sathorn Rd.

Sri Lanka tel. 251-2789
48 Soi 1, Sukhumvit Rd.

Sweden tel. 236-7156
Boonmitr Bldg, 138 Silom Rd.

Switzerland tel. 253-0156/60
35 Wireless Rd.

U.S.S.R. tel. 234-9824
108 North Sathorn Rd.

United Kingdom tel. 253-0191/9
1031 Wireless Rd.

U.S.A. tel. 252-5040
95 Wireless Rd.

Vietnam tel. 251-5835/8
83/1 Wireless Rd.

Costs

For 1991, Thai government figures showed that tourists stayed an average of seven days in the kingdom and spent B3000 (US$120) a day. Highest expenses were shopping and accommodations, followed by food and drink, and touring and transport. Bangkok allows you considerable leeway on expenses—for an Asian capital it is cheap (compared to Singapore, Manila, or Hong Kong). Watching every penny, you can survive on US$9 a day if you stay in a guesthouse and eat at streetstalls or basic restaurants; or you can spend US$9000 a day with no trouble at all—stay in a luxury suite at the Oriental Hotel for B45,000, and hire a Daimler (B7000) for the day's shopping spree. An American firm specializing in business travel and living costs ranked Bangkok in the mid-range for expenses, with a 1990 per-diem rate of US$186—about the same as Boston or Los Angeles. The rate was based on three meals a day and a standard room at a first-class hotel.

Currency Exchange

The Thai currency unit is the baht—approximate exchange rate is B25 to the U.S. dollar, and B45 to the UK pound. Banks generally charge B8 commission on each traveler's check converted. Cashing checks or exchanging foreign cash is never a problem in Bangkok. Rates are much the same around Bangkok—marginally better for traveler's checks than for cash; the hotels give worse rates for both. Major Thai banks with currency exchange facilities are Bangkok Bank, Thai Danu Bank, Thai Farmers Bank and Siam Commercial Bank. Banking hours are 0830-1530 Mon.-Fri., with currency exchange centers and mobile units open in key tourist areas (Khao San Road, Oriental Hotel area, Patpong Road) from 0700-2100 seven days a week. Foreign-owned banks are well represented in Bangkok, with branches of Bank of America, Chase Manhattan Bank, Bank of Nova Scotia, ANZ Bank, and National Australia Bank. American dollars are widely available—you can convert U.S. traveler's checks into U.S. cash at most banks, or any amount of Thai baht back into U.S. dollars, or open a bank account in U.S. dollars.

Credit Cards

These are widely used and accepted by major banks (for cash advances), restaurants, shops, and hotels. Thailand has a high incidence of credit card fraud—be careful with your cards. There have been cases in Chiang Mai of hotel staff removing credit cards from stored luggage and running up illicit bills. For inquiries concerning credit cards: Visa and Master Charge, Bank of America Bldg, tel. 251-6333, or Thai Farmers Bank HQ, tel. 273-1199; Diners Club, 11F, Dusit Thai Bldg., Rama IV Road, tel. 238-3660; American Express, 388 Paholyothin Road, tel. 273-0033.

Garuda is a royal emblem: appearing on banks, it signifies "By Royal Appointment."

Change

Thai bills come in denominations of B500 (purple), B100 (red), B50 (blue), B20 (green) and B10 (brown). Change is a perennial problem as no one ever seems to have any of it. The best notes are B50 (ideal for taxis), but even the banks can't seem to supply these. There are B10, B5, and B1 coins. The larger B10 coin is easy to identify—it has a copper center and a silver border. There are four varieties of the one-baht coin and three varieties of the five-baht coin. To tell the difference, look at the side of the coin: if the edge is copper, it's five baht. The baht is further divided into 100 *satang*—the 25-*satang* and 50-*satang* coins are tiny and copper-colored.

Taxes And Tipping

It is not necessary to tip taxi drivers or theater ushers, but it is customary to give hairdressers a small tip. Tipping is not a Thai custom, but in increasingly commercialized Bangkok, it's catching on. In restaurants, 11% government tax and a 10% service charge are often added to the bill; if not, a 10% tip is appreciated. In most situations, leaving B5 or B10 (or if generous, B20) on the tray is polite—this applies to restaurants where a service charge has already been applied, or to bars. Leaving one baht is considered an insult. For hotel and airport porters, B5 to B10 a bag is sufficient.

ATMs

Major banks have ATM service (Automatic Teller Machines). These machines are at street level—open all day (some until 2100 or 2200). If the ATM says "All Visa And Master Charge Cards Accepted," you can use your card to draw on your account back home, using your regular four-digit secret code (make sure the ATM says *all* Visa Cards—some ATMs will only accept local cards). Follow the instructions that appear on the screen (in Thai and English), and you can withdraw B1000, B5000, or B7500—whatever your daily limit is back home, converted into baht. Through the wonders of international banking, the transaction appears on your next Visa billing back home converted into your own currency (interest starts running immediately). The Visa bill will show date of withdrawal, ATM location number, and conversion rate used. If you're staying longer, open a bank account in baht and get an ATM card with a four-digit secret code (takes about a week to process). Once you have the card, you can deposit as much as you need into the account and access it anywhere in Thailand on ATM networking.

Security

There are lots of video-toting Japanese tourists in Bangkok, so you won't feel out of place flashing an expensive camera, but watch that camera bag—don't leave it unattended. Hotels usually have a security system for valuables—either a safe in the room, or a safety deposit box in the lobby (large enough for money, camera, jewelry). It's common sense not to carry large sums of cash around Bangkok; on crowded buses, watch out for razor artists. If you're traveling up-country, Bangkok hotels can generally provide secure storage for baggage—some have storage lockers.

BANGKOK FAST FACTS

Bangkok Weather

Hot, hot, hot! Bangkok, according to the World Meteorological Organization, is the hottest city on earth. This takes into account year-round average temperatures, and Bangkok is constantly hot and humid. Bangkok is like an open-air sauna: the thermometer hovers around 28° C, and at night, it only drops a few degrees. Fans and air-conditioning are thus of great importance. Some nuances to the heat—there are three seasons: hot, bloody hot, and rainy-hot.

November-February: The ordinary hot season (the Thais call it the "cool" season!) is tolerable because of less humidity: temperatures range 18-32° C (65-90° F). This is the best time to visit.

March-May: The bloody hot season, with temperatures 27-35° C (80-95° F): avoid these months, as extreme heat and pollution are a bad mix in Bangkok.

June-October: The rainy season. During June, July, and August, temperatures range a slightly cooler 24-32° C (75-90° F); there are occasional storms. The average number of rainy days from May to October varies from 14 to 19 a month. In September and October there's possible flooding from swollen rivers—this can severely disrupt traffic, with streets sometimes under a meter of water.

TAT Office

Tourism Authority of Thailand (TAT), tel. 282-1143/7, is located at 4 Rajadamnern Avenue, next to Rajadamnern Boxing Stadium to the northeast of Democracy Monument, and is open weekdays from 0800-1600. Very useful—lots of handouts (pamphlets and brochures on every conceivable subject); they sell full-size posters for B25 (also poster tubes), maps, and color slides. Next door is a branch of TAT called the Tourist Assistance Center, tel. 281-5051 or 282-8129, which deals with emergencies, and complaints about unfair business practices. TAT offices abroad can be found in the Asia-Pacific area (Hong Kong, Kuala Lumpur, Osaka, Tokyo, Singapore, Sydney), in Europe (Frankfurt, London, Paris, and Rome), and in the U.S. (New York, Los Angeles).

Tourist Police

This organization was set up in 1982 to ensure the safety of tourists. Bilingual Tourist Police are attached to TAT offices in Bangkok, Pattaya, Kanchanaburi, Chiang Mai, Hat Yai, and Phuket. As well as the TAT office branch, in Bangkok there is an office of the Tourist Police at the southwest corner of Lumpini Park, at the intersection of Rama IV and Surawong roads. Tourist Police will deal with complaints relating to unfair practices. In an emergency, call the Tourist Police Center, tel. 221-6206/10.

Bookstores

Bangkok has a good selection of English-language bookstores, selling periodicals, general fiction, and specialist reading material on Thailand. In the Silom area, try The Bookseller, 81 Patpong Road; DK Book House, around the corner from Patpong in the basement of the CCT Building at 109 Surawong; and Asia Books on the third floor of Thaniya Plaza on Thaniya Road. In the Siam Square area, there's DK Books on Soi 6, Siam Square, and Bangkok Books at 302 Soi 4, Siam Square. On Sukhumvit there's Asia Books at 221 Sukhumvit (between Sois 17 and 19); there are also several branches of Asia Books in Land-

mark Plaza, near Soi 6, as well as a branch at Peninsula Plaza. Major hotels have their own small bookstores, as do shopping centers.

Measures

The metric system is used. There is a traditional system of weights and measures sometimes used in the markets.

The baht, confusingly enough, is a unit of weight as well as currency—it is equivalent to 15.2 grams, and is used when quoting gold chain weights in Chinatown.

Electricity

220 volts AC/50 cycles throughout Thailand—dual-prong rounded or flat-pin plugs are accepted. Major hotels in Bangkok have 110-volt outlets for electric razors—do not attempt to plug a hairdryer into one of these outlets! There is a complex system of adapters and converters for electrical equipment from North America, unless the device comes with a 220/110 switch. If in doubt whether devices will work or not, have an optional rechargeable battery system (220-volt, two-prong) as backup.

Video

Thailand uses the PAL system, as used in Australia and Europe (with the exception of France, which uses SECAM). This means North American and Japanese tapes (NTSC) will not run on Thai systems, and vice-versa. Some sets in Thailand are equipped for both NTSC and PAL—you can switch from one system to another. Pirated tapes for sale may be available in PAL, NTSC, or SECAM formats.

Photography And Film

Processing for print and slide (E6) films is readily available in Bangkok. The standard is quite high, often with same-day processing. When buying film, purchase from a shop that has air-conditioning, as film can deteriorate rapidly in heat and humidity. Always check the expiration date on the film. When processing, deal with a place that has air-conditioning and a high turnover of chemicals used in processing.

Because Kodachrome cannot be processed in Bangkok (it must be sent to Japan or Australia and cleared through customs—both lengthy processes), little of the stuff is on sale. You can buy Kodachrome 64 ISO and possibly 25 ISO, but rarely Kodachrome 200 ISO. Otherwise, the full range of Ektachrome and Fujichrome films is available, including Fuji Velvia. Film prices are reasonable, but storage conditions may be suspect. There are import restrictions on film, but if you take your film out of boxes and bunch it all together in a plastic bag (so it doesn't look resaleable), customs won't bother you on entry.

For serious photography, you have to be up at the crack of dawn to get the best shots—between 0630 and 0930 there are vibrant colors and excellent shadows. After 1000 the sunlight is so strong that it flattens the subject and the colors lose their brilliance—results are very disappointing, even if you use a polarizing filter. Toward sunset is another possibility for decent photos, but conditions are hazier than at dawn. For temple interiors, a small tripod is useful—there are often low lighting conditions.

Taboo Shots: In most places in and around Bangkok, you can freely photograph subjects—there are few restrictions. In Bangkok, the national museum does not permit interior photography; other museums in and around Bangkok do not permit photos. Anything associated with royalty is highly sensitive. Vimanmek Mansions is both a museum and a former royal residence, so no interior photos are allowed. The Temple of the Emerald Buddha is the innermost royal chapel, so no interior photos are allowed. Movie cameras are not allowed in the Grand Palace—the Thais do not wish footage to end up in the wrong kind of movie.

Most temples will allow you to take photos, with the odd exception. Saffron-robed monks are highly photogenic, but monks may object to having their photographs taken or being pestered by photographers—ask first. The same goes with people in a Chinatown temple. Most bars along Patpong have No Photos signs posted, although patrons do occasionally sneak snapshots.

Business Services

Major hotels have business centers with a wide range of equipment and services—fax, word-processing, printing, secretarial, translation, and interpreting. Hotels are well appointed to handle meetings, seminars, and conferences. For a laptop computer, a surge protector is recommended if running off a power-point. Computer software and equipment can be obtained at Pantip Plaza, 604/3 Petchburi Road, near the Indonesian Embassy. Beware of pirated computer programs—a virus scanning and cleaning disk should be used to screen out potential computer viruses, which include Bangkok's very own Mule virus. CU-Word software will handle Thai and English text on the same program and can be run on IBM-compatibles.

COMMUNICATIONS

Television

There are five color TV channels operating from Bangkok—programs from these are transmitted to all the provinces via relays and substations. Channels 5 and 7 are run by the army; Channels 9 and 11 are state-run; Channel 3 is semiprivate. Some of the programs (such as the news, Western movies, and sports events) are broadcast with English soundtrack on FM radio in Bangkok, but transmission can be erratic. Check *The Nation* or *Bangkok Post* for program details.

English Media

There are three cable-TV channels operated by IBC TV and transmitted by satellite—two operate in English (one for news and sports, the other for movies and entertainment); the third channel has a Thai sound track. Most of the programs are relayed from the U.S., though the news channel has material from a number of international sources. The cable channels are subject to censorship, though sometimes live broadcasts are permitted, such as during the Gulf War.

Thailand has over 200 radio stations, a fair proportion of which are operated by the army. Bangkok has a host of FM and AM stations: several FM stations broadcast only in English. Flip the FM dial to find one (between 95 and 110 MHz), or check newspaper listings. Radio Bangkok (95.5 MHz) and 107 FM broadcast entirely in English. On shortwave you can get VOA, the BBC, Radio Canada, and Radio Australia.

STUDY OPPORTUNITIES

Gemology
Contact the Asian Institute of Gemological Sciences, 484 Rajadapisek Road, tel. 513-2112.

Meditation
Contact the World Fellowship of Buddhists, at 33 Sukhumvit Road (between Sois 1 and 3), tel. 251-1188. The WFB has lots of information about retreats and courses in and around Bangkok and up-country. There is a short meditation class and lecture at the WFB on the first Wednesday of the month at 1800 hours.

Traditional Massage
A 30-hour hands-on course is taught at Wat Po—either done three hours a day for ten days, or two hours a day for 15 days. The cost is B3000.

Thai Language
AUA (American University Alumni Association) at 179 Rajadamri Road, tel. 252-8170, conducts Thai language classes and sells tapes; it also has language labs and a library of Western books. Nisa Thai Language School, 27 S. Sathorn Road (YMCA Building), tel. 286-9323, and Siri-Pattana Language School (YWCA), 13 S. Sathorn Road; tel. 286-1936, both offer courses from beginner to advanced, as well as private tuition. Private tutors advertise in the *Bangkok Post*.

Thai Cooking
Bussaracum Restaurant, 35 Soi Pipat 2, Convent Road; Bangkok, tel. 235-8915, is famous for Royal Thai-style cuisine and is one of the best restaurants in Bangkok. Their ten-day course concentrates on mastering 21 different dishes. UFM Food Center has courses at UFM Baking and Cooking School, 593/41 Soi 33/1, Sukhumvit, tel. 259-0620. Costing an arm and a leg is Oriental Hotel Cooking School, 48 Oriental Ave, tel. 236-0400: there are classes Mon.-Fri. from 0900 to 1200, costing B2500 each, or all five classes for B11,000; one week (15 hours) of instruction concentrates on preparation of ten Thai dishes.

English-language newspapers in Bangkok are the *Bangkok Post* and *The Nation*. The *Bangkok Post* has a wider circulation. Most foreign news publications are available, including the *International Herald Tribune* and *Asian Wall Street Journal*. Although the military governments have made a point of censoring newspapers and magazines, occasionally shutting them down (or banning particular issues of foreign magazines), the Thai press is still amongst the freest in Asia. Speculation or gossip about the royal family is strictly banned.

Post Office
The GPO on New Road has postal, long-distance phone, telegram, and telex services. The postal system is efficient and reliable, with mail reaching Europe or the U.S. in about a week. The GPO is open Mon.-Fri. 0800-2000 and Sat., Sun., and holidays from 0800-1300. The telephone, telegram, and telex services are open 24 hours a day. There is also a philatelic department, and close by the GPO are a number of shops selling Thai stamps and coins for collectors. For Poste Restante (open during regular GPO hours, as above), have correspondents send mail care of Poste Restante, GPO, Charoen Krung Road, Bangkok, and make sure the last name is underlined or written in capitals, or both, as letters can easily be misfiled (due to the importance of first names in Thailand!). You need to show a passport to claim letters. Very convenient is the GPO's packing service (open weekdays 0830-1630; Sat. 0900-1200; closed Sundays and holidays). Parcels are usually permitted up to 10 kgs in weight. From the packing service you can either buy a cardboard box for B5-20 and pack it yourself, or pay B30-50 and have the box packed for you.

Telephone
The IDD code for Thailand is 66. Area codes: Bangkok 2; Chiang Mai 53; Hua Hin 32; Pattaya 38; Phuket 76; Ayuthaya 35; Kanchanaburi 34; Lopburi 36. To get an international call placed in Bangkok, go through hotel reception. You can also dial 106 for an English-speaking operator (it can be hard to get the operator, so keep trying), or place a call through agents along Khao San Road or go to the GPO.

Local calls: Get hotel staff to place the call for you and to set up meetings, whatever. Lines are tricky—sometimes it's hard to get through, and the line may be bad when you do.

Pay phones: Often faulty, or with bad lines. Public phones may use a small one-baht coin, or a small five-baht coin (on some models there are slots for both). If you have a baby five-baht in your pocket, you will come up against a one-baht-only pay phone. If you want to outsmart the pay phones by carrying a supply of small one-baht and small five-baht coins, you will inevitably run into an ancient model phone that will only accept a *large* one-baht coin. One baht will allow you to speak for about three minutes—then the phone will demand another coin or your call will be terminated. The five-baht coins are in theory used for long-distance calling only, but in practice many hotels install them for local calls.

Directories: AT&T issues an annual Yellow Page directory for Bangkok in an English edition—very useful. Major hotels have a copy, as well as a two-volume set of White Pages for Bangkok, also put out by AT&T (which is located on the 15th floor of Amarin Tower on Ploenchit).

Time
Bangkok time is Greenwich Mean Time + 7; Eastern Standard Time + 12, and Pacific Standard Time + 15. When in Bangkok, time in London is -7 hours; Paris -6; New York/Toronto -12; San Francisco/Vancouver -15; Sydney + 3 hours (figures may vary with daylight saving time).

Buddhist Era Calendar: This starts 543 years before the Christian Era, so add 543 to the Western year to get the corresponding B.E. year: thus 1992 A.D. corresponds to 2535 B.E. Both calendars are used in Thailand.

Business Hours: Commercial offices are open Mon.-Fri. 0800-1200 and 1300-1700; government offices: Mon.-Fri. 0830-1200, 1300-1630; banks: Mon.-Fri. 0830-1530. Shops generally keep long hours, open daily 0800-2100; department stores are open 1000-1900.

CUSTOMS AND CONDUCT

CUSTOMS

The Thais are exceedingly polite and helpful people, and they expect similar standards from visitors. Conduct in Thailand is largely a matter of good manners and common sense—much brouhaha is made over things like not pointing your feet at people, but when you think about it, that's not greatly different from going to a job interview and putting your feet up on a desk. Being Buddhists, Thais are remarkably tolerant: as a foreign boor, your lack of sensitivity to local customs and your ignorance of them will be readily overlooked except in two areas—Buddhism and royalty.

Royalty
Thais take their king very seriously—criticism of any Thai king of any dynasty is a serious crime. Lèse-majesté (criticism of the king) is punishable by three to 15 years in jail. The national anthem is played over the airwaves twice a day (at 0800 and 1800 hours) and *all* those within earshot are expected to stand to attention; likewise, the anthem is played in all movie theaters before a show, and the audience stands while the king's portrait is projected onto the screen. It follows that the king's image, which appears on all Thai bills and coins and numerous stamps, must also be treated with great respect. In an argument over restaurant prices, a foreigner scrunched up some Thai bills and stomped on them: a Thai customer sitting nearby promptly punched the foreigner out for tampering with the king's image.

Buddhist Statues
Buddhist temples are sacred places: dress properly when visiting (no shorts, sandals, hot pants,

PLEASE BE ADVISED THAT IMPROPERLY DRESSED VISITORS, SUCH AS THOSE SHOWN ABOVE, WILL NOT BE PERMITTED TO ENTER THE GROUNDS OF THE PALACE

dirty jeans or T-shirts), and remove shoes before entering the main buildings. Treat all Buddha images, ruined or not, with great respect: a Western family was jailed for climbing on top of a Buddha statue and posing there for photos (it's all right to take photos of Buddha statues, but *not* okay to climb on top of one). Do not touch a Thai person's amulets for similar reasons. Buddhists have protested the use of a smiling Buddha image in ads by Qantas Airlines.

Monks
Buddhist monks are forbidden to touch women: a monk cannot even receive a cup of tea directly from a female (the tea would have to be received indirectly by being put down on a table nearby). A female traveler sitting next to a monk on a bus would put the monk in a very awkward position. However, the situation does not generally arise, even on very crowded buses, as monks always sit or stand right at the back of the bus, and women (for safety reasons) generally sit right at the front. The situation does, however, arise quite commonly on the Chao Phraya Express Boat, where monks are huddled at the back of the boat, and passengers have to squeeze past to get off. Menstruating women are not supposed to visit temples in Thailand, and though such taboos apparently do not apply to Westerners, this is mentioned to indicate the Thai attitude toward women in such situations. The temple is a male-dominated precinct (even though nuns sometimes reside in the temples).

Confrontation
One of the major concepts of Buddhism is pursuit of the Middle Way—avoiding extremes. Thais will go out of their way to avoid confrontations—they greatly admire "the cool heart" (*jai yen*) and despise the "hot heart" (*jai ron*). If you lose your temper, they will lose all respect for you: do not raise your voice or display outward signs of anger—smile instead! The Thai smile may replace anger or embarrassment; it is their way of avoiding confrontation. Likewise, direct criticism is not appreciated—it must be indirect. Flattery, on the other hand, will get you everywhere—praise for Thailand and Thai culture will open many doors.

Body Language
The head is high, the feet are low. The head is considered sacred: do not touch a Thai on the head, or in fact anywhere—except when shaking hands. The feet are considered lowly: do not point your feet at a Thai (this means crossing your legs is out; if sitting on the floor, tuck your feet under your body or else kneel). Do not pass food overhead, do not stand over a Thai person, do not step over people seated on the floor to get past them. The Western handshake is

commonly used between Thais and foreigners in official and business circles, but avoid using it with Thai female officials or executives.

CONDUCT

The *Wai*

The Thai form of greeting—the *wai*—avoids physical contact. The *wai*, a prayer-like gesture with a slight bow of the head, is a mark of respect for superiors or elders. Originally this was a method of showing that the person had no weapons by putting both hands forward—that is, the weaker party *waied* the stronger party. This is why the inferior initiates the *wai*, and the superior returns it. Foreigners are not expected to know all the nuances. If you're not sure what to do, do not *wai* at all—just smile and nod. Some situations are very clear. You can always *wai* a monk. Never return a *wai* from a waitress, maid, taxi-driver or from children—or you will make a total fool of yourself! A *wai* to the forehead is reserved for royalty, monks and dignitaries; a *wai* to the nose is for elders; a *wai* to the mouth is for those of higher social standing; and a *wai* to the chest is for those of lower social standing. There are also varying degrees of bowing—a slight nod to a deep bow. You will notice that television newsreaders *wai* the viewers before proceeding with the news—this is because they have no idea who might be watching (If, for example, a head abbot were watching, then a *wai* would be in order).

Socializing

In an informal visit to a Thai home, a small gift for your host is appropriate but not necessary—flowers are ideal, or else a gift-wrapped box of sweets or cookies. It is bad form to open gifts straight away—they are usually opened in private. Remove your shoes before entering a Thai home.

Formal meetings will most likely take place in a restaurant or office. Clothing is important—Thais tend to judge people by the clothes they wear (although shirt and tie are acceptable for even the most formal meeting). Punctuality is less respected than in the West—which may have a lot to do with Bangkok traffic! Do not at-

tempt to split a restaurant bill: the inviter usually pays for the meal. If it is not clear who is to pay, the superior party pays; on the next occasion, the other party will be expected to pay.

The polite form of address in Thailand is to use "Khun" with the first name, which will explain why Westerners are addressed as "Khun Peter" or "Khun Mary" (family names were only

---

THE MEDDLING GOVERNESS

The musical stage-play and the movie, *The King and I*, are banned in Thailand, although the books upon which they are based do not appear to be. The musical and the movie have a peculiar genesis: in the 1860s, Anna Leonowens was a foreign tutor employed by King Mongkut to teach the royal children and those in the harem. After she left Thailand, she wrote two dowdy books based on her six-year stay in the kingdom: *The English Governess at the Siamese Court* (1870), and *The Romance of the Harem* (1872). In both books, she hints at a close relationship with King Mongkut (in fact, it seems he took little notice of her); talks about the tyranny of the king (episodes were rewritten from a French account, based on hearsay, or plagiarized from old books), and claims to have had great influence over the royal children. Far from being the barbarian that Leonowens portrayed, King Mongkut was conversant in ten languages and was an accomplished historian and astronomer.

The Thais were offended by Leonowens' caricature of the king in her books, but further distortions were to follow. In 1943, an American missionary who had been living in Thailand—Margaret Landon—fictionalized Anna Leonowens' adventures and came up with a bestseller called *Anna and The King of Siam*. This was adapted for a 1946 movie starring Rex Harrison and sparked the Rodgers and Hammerstein musical, *The King and I* (1951). The musical was adapted by 20th-Century Fox as a color movie (1956) starring Yul Brynner and Deborah Kerr. Yul Brynner reprised the role in a TV series, "Anna and the King of Siam" (1972), and spent most of his later career playing the role of the king on stage.

introduced this century by King Rama VI). Thais are obsessed with social ranking. To establish rank and status, it is necessary to know a person's family line (royal blood or not), age, job, income, education, and connections. Royal titles are used for those of royal descent: in former times, there were large numbers of children in the royal family, so a system of ranking was devised for later generations. Those of royal lineage received titles in descending order of importance until, after the fifth or sixth generation, heirs reverted to the status of commoners (there are half a dozen ranks of commoners). Almost every Thai has a nickname (Tadpole, Tiny, Froggy, Piggy, Rat, Shrimp) given at birth to ward off evil spirits.

Attempts to learn the language are always appreciated, but be aware that Thai is a tonal language and that grand gaffes can occur when the wrong tones are used—sometimes to the great amusement of Thais, sometimes not. The word for "ambassador" in Thai is close in pronunciation to the word for "bottom": one diplomat in Bangkok used to send people into howling fits of laughter when he talked about his job in Thai.

Meeting People

Bangkokians are very friendly people—they're easy to get along with, approachable, tolerant, and have a great sense of fun and a cheerful disposition. And they love to practice their English. If you meet a student from Chulalongkorn or Thammasat universities, try these subjects: pollution, prostitution, corruption, Bangkok in the year 2000, their hopes and dreams. Monks are quite friendly—you can strike up conversations with them at wats. Quite a few study English, so they're only too pleased to be able to practice. Other ways of meeting Thais and Westerners: through sports (golf, Hash House Harrier runs); in jazz pubs and low-key bars (Thai university students hang out at Soi Sarasin bars). The backpacker info exchange point and meeting-place is Khao San Road.

On the streets of Bangkok you're more likely to run into touts and scam-artists than genuinely friendly Thais. Meeting Thais is better accomplished off the street: on a train, on a long-tailed boat, at the zoo, in a food center.

CAUTIONS

Scams

With monotonous regularity, stories of rip-offs and scams involving irate westerners appear in the Letters to the Editor section of the *Bangkok Post* and *The Nation*. The two biggest scams going involve gem deals and card games.

These things usually start out on the streets, with a well-dressed man walking alongside his victim: "Hot, isn't it," swiftly followed by, "Where are you from? Oh, San Francisco! My sister is studying at Berkeley University, you know. Yes, she's been living there for five years now." Having taken his victim into his confidence, the con-man then proceeds in a roundabout fashion to his uncle's gem store, where fabulous bargains can be had. The victim buys several hundred dollars' worth of stones from "uncle," convinced that the gems are worth many times more than that back in the West. Back in the West, if checked, the stones are discovered to be worthless. Moral of the story: if you know nothing about precious stones, don't venture near a gem store, and certainly not with a tout off the streets.

It seems hard to believe, but travelers who've never played cards for money in their lives somehow end up losing thousands of dollars in rigged card games. This is not a simple ploy—it's a chain of events that are carefully orchestrated and culminate in a card game behind closed doors.

As a corollary to these tricks, you should avoid *all* gem dealers who approach you on the street, *all* card games and card dealers, and anyone with an encyclopedic knowledge of your hometown or claiming to have a relative living on the same street as yourself (con-artists spend hours boning up on big cities like New York, Toronto, London, Sydney . . .) Here's a shortlist of other people to avoid: Boy Scouts in or out of uniform collecting money for a "jamboree"; anybody called Mr. Johnny (or Mr. Jimmy, or Mr. Sammy); "university" students collecting money for charity; friendly turbaned fortune-tellers; anyone who asks, "What are you looking for?"; touts offering sexual adventures, or anyone whose

English is limited to hissing "massage!" into your ear; tall ladies with deep voices; anyone offering you a free tour of the city or a free ride on the canals (they really will take you for a ride!). Even Thais can fall victim to sophisticated hustlers: there have been cases of bogus monks collecting donations for bogus projects.

The best thing to do if approached by touts on the street (and you will be approached) is to ignore them—or say firmly, "Not today, thank you"—or the Thai equivalent, "*Mai ao*" ("don't want any, thanks"). If that doesn't work, tell them you've been in Bangkok for three years. Another tack is not to let them get any questions in: turn the tables and do all the asking. Ask a bogus gem dealer what he does for a living, and he may have trouble answering, or he may get his story mixed up. If he answers that he sells gems, drop him like a hot potato.

Drugs

Penalties in Thailand for possession of drugs are extremely severe—sometimes life sentences, which can only be commuted by a pardon from the king. In 1990, two British teenage girls were caught trying to smuggle heroin out of the country: one got 25 years in jail; the other got 18 years. Foreign embassies can do nothing to help in these cases.

Crime

For a big city, Bangkok is a remarkably safe place. You will feel a lot more relaxed here than you will in larger American cities. Female travelers comment on the fact that they feel quite safe in Bangkok due to secure hotels, readily available transport (frequent taxis), and the large number of Westerners. Locals are willing to help you out if there's any kind of trouble, too. Crime certainly exists in the capital, but foreigners are unlikely to encounter the darker side of Thailand: most serious crimes in Bangkok relate to settling old scores, or to crimes of passion.

Theft is more often linked with frequenters of bars and pick-up joints in Bangkok and Pattaya—usually single foreign males and heavy drinkers. *Katoeys* (transvestites) are particularly dangerous because they're more aggressive—they have been known to spike drinks and take off with valuables. Prostitution is illegal in Thailand but has a de facto status: because of the quasi-legal situation, robbery victims have little recourse for help from the police. Up-country, in more remote places, risks are greater: do not walk alone at night in remote areas or on beach areas.

As in any travel situation, use your common sense in Bangkok and you won't have any problems. Be aware of situations like pickpocketing (in crowded market areas and on buses); do not leave your camera bag unattended; don't flash large sums of cash; put valuables in the hotel safe if going out for the evening; and stay away from touts and scam-artists. If you have any trouble in Bangkok, contact the Tourist Police, tel. 221-6206/10 rather than the regular police. There is also a Tourist Assistance Center, tel. 281-5051 or 282-8129.

HEALTH

HEALTH HAZARDS

Immunizations

Unless arriving from an infected area, no vaccinations are required. However, it's advisable to have standard shots or boosters for tetanus, polio, and typhoid and to carry malaria pills if going up-country. The Thai Red Cross Society on Rama IV Road offers inoculations for typhoid, polio, encephalitis, tetanus, hepatitis B, cholera, and smallpox, as well as treatment for rabies and snakebites.

AIDS

Acquired Immune Deficiency Syndrome (AIDS) is spread by blood-to-blood contact in four main ways: sharing infected intravenous needles; through transfusion of infected blood; through sexual intercourse with an AIDS-infected person; and from infected mother to unborn child. The AIDS virus is also carried in body fluids such as semen. Screening in Bangkok's blood banks is not 100% reliable (the Thai Red Cross screens blood): in the provinces, blood transfusions may be risky. For any kind of inoculation or procedure involving a syringe, insist on a brand new disposable needle. In terms of sexual activity, the risk of acquiring AIDS is minimized (but not eliminated) by use of condoms.

Researchers are hazy on how AIDS spreads: current medical advice is to avoid unsterilized needles; avoid unscreened blood in transfusions; avoid sexual encounters with those who have an unknown or risky sexual history (that includes all prostitutes); avoid any medical procedures that involve improperly sterilized instruments (including tattoos, ear-piercing, acupuncture, electrolysis, and possibly dental work); and avoid sharing razors—and even toothbrushes—since these can carry traces of tainted blood.

There are a lot of question marks about AIDS: at this point it has not been conclusively proven that HIV (Human Immunodeficiency Virus) is the cause of AIDS. According to a recent study, about one-third of HIV-positive cases develop into AIDS within seven years, but there are numerous HIV carriers who have no AIDS symptoms at all, and there are documented cases of people with AIDS who are HIV-negative. From the time HIV is contracted, it can take three months or longer for the virus to appear in testing.

As of early 1991, there were 25,000 recorded HIV-carriers in Thailand—that figure may only represent the tip of the iceberg. A sexual encounter in Thailand with a prostitute or a person not known to be AIDS-free is tantamount to playing Russian roulette.

STDs

Everybody has become so preoccupied with AIDS that they've forgotten what condoms were originally intended for—to prevent pregnancy and the spread of sexually transmitted diseases (STDs) such as gonorrhea, syphilis, chlamydia, and herpes. There are exotic strains of VD in Thailand—some are resistent to penicillin. As a result of greater condom use due to the threat of AIDS, there has been a decrease in cases of venereal disease in Thailand, but the problem certainly exists, as the number of VD clinics in Bangkok will attest to.

Mosquitoes

The bad news is that there are 410 known varieties of mosquito in Thailand, seven of which are malaria carriers (*anopheles* mosquitoes). The good news is that in Bangkok and Pattaya there isn't any malaria—because of the pollution! Anopheles mosquitoes need a clean environment for breeding, and are rather fussy about the water that they lay their eggs in. You'll still get lots of mosquitoes in Bangkok—but not the malarial kind. Further out of Bangkok, malaria is a hazard (cases have been reported at Ko Samet, Ko Chang, and Ko Pangan). Opinions vary as to the effectiveness of taking chloroquine tablets, particularly since mosquitoes can be chloroquine-resistant (and fansidar-resistant); better protection is to ensure that you're not bitten in the first place.

Malaria-carrying mosquitoes bite from dusk to dawn—so at sunset and after it, cover body parts, use a repellent, try and stay indoors in a hotel room with screens on windows and doors, and sleep under a mosquito net. It's unlikely that you will get malaria from one or two mosquito bites; however, frequent biting greatly increases the risk. There were 350,000 registered cases of malaria in Thailand in 1988. The risk of getting malaria is higher during the wet season (July-September), and low during the cool season (Nov-Feb).

Dengue fever, which is carried by the *Aedes aegypti* mosquito, is a low-incidence threat in urban and rural areas. The aedes mosquito is more active during the daytime. Dengue fever is a bit of a mystery—there are several varieties of this fever, and no vaccine available. If a person has symptoms, it's a matter of resting up till the fever passes. Symptoms include fever, headache, severe joint and muscle pains, and a rash.

Sun Exposure And Prickly Heat

Adjusting to the tropics can take up to six weeks. Problems that can occur if you're not acclimatized: heat stroke, sunburn, prickly heat. Take it easy on arrival to allow yourself time to adapt to the new environment—don't indulge in strenuous activity, use a hat, use sunscreen if exposed to the elements, and keep yourself hydrated by drinking lots of fluids.

There is a firm correlation between clothing and health in a tropical setting. Wear loose, light clothing—100% cotton is best because it will breathe and will not shrink. You can get all-cotton clothing made up within 24 hours in Bangkok—just drop into a tailor's for a fitting, or leave a shirt or whatever behind for the tailor to copy. Lighter colors are better because they deflect the heat and are less likely to attract mosquitoes. If you wear tight synthetic clothing (particularly socks and underwear) you may fall victim to prickly heat (an itch and a heat rash) or fungal infections—particularly between the toes and in the groin area. If this occurs, keep those areas clean and dry; switch to very loose cloth-

ing (wear sandals for a few days in the case of the feet; wear boxer-style underwear in the case of groin infection); and cool down with air-conditioning—the problem should go away. Apply talc (baby powder) to the affected areas—this will keep them dry and free of sweat. Prickly heat powder, sold in drugstores in Thailand (a common brand is St. Luke's), has a base of talc with a medicated agent that makes the skin feel cool. Another remedy is to use a soap with an antibacterial agent in it, since fungal infections are caused by certain bacteria. These soaps are usually sold for the treatment of acne, but are equally useful against fungal infections.

Pollution Problems

A normal reaction to Bangkok's pollution is a stinging in the eyes; more severe reactions may be rashes or respiratory problems. Motorcyclists and Bangkok policemen wear gauze masks to cut down on their pollutant intake. If you are reading this book and are not in Bangkok, add the sound of a thousand lawnmowers in unison: Bangkok is *noisy*. Motorcycles, *tuk-tuks*, and other vehicles well exceed acceptable noise levels, and so do longtail boats; discos must be run by deaf disc jockeys—the noise level is painful. If you spend a month or more in Bangkok, you start to go deaf—so protect your hearing by using earplugs. These are not so easy to find in Bangkok: a product called Ear Putty is good—it has a tiny case with two silicone plugs that are reusable and mould to the shape of your ear. The plugs can also be used for swimming and diving.

Water And Ice

Keep to bottled water in Bangkok—there's plenty of it around (Polaris is the most popular brand). Make sure that the seal is intact on plastic bottles. Opinions vary as to the safety of tap water in Bangkok—foreign residents will tell you the tap water is fine for brushing teeth. If in doubt, use bottled water to brush teeth. Beer is always safe to drink. Ice is usually produced under hygienic conditions—the larger hotels use boiled water. However, you will see huge blocks of ice being cut apart with a hacksaw on the sidewalk: the shaved ice at noodle-stands may be suspect.

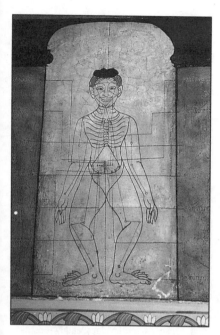

ancient instructional charts for traditional massage and acupuncture

(spread by ticks and mosquitoes—vaccination against it is available in Bangkok). Dangers prevalent in Thailand are snakebite and bites from rabid animals: both can be life-threatening. At the seaside, risks are from jellyfish stings, coral cuts, and from treading on sea-urchins.

HEALTH SERVICES

Medical Facilities
Bangkok has a number of very good hospitals with excellent services available—on a par with those in the West. Many Thai doctors are Western-trained and speak good English; some hospitals have Western doctors on the staff. For medical needs, contact: Bangkok Christian Hospital, 124 Silom Road, tel. 233-6981/9; Bangkok Nursing Home, 9 Convent Road (Silom area), tel. 233-2610/9; Bangkok Adventist Hospital, 430 Phitsanulok Road, tel. 281-1422; or Samitivej Hospital, 133 Soi 49, Sukhumvit Road, tel. 392-0010/9. To find an English-speaking dentist, contact your embassy and ask for a referral.

Personal Health Care
You get pretty dirty in Bangkok—clothing rimmed with dirt, diesel fumes in your lungs, fingernails gritty. Businessmen need two shirts to see the day through. But there are body overhaul places in Bangkok that will make you feel on top of the world again. Service is excellent and cheap. Expert haircutting or shaping? Facial massage? Manicure? Afro-style braiding? Full beauty treatment and Jacuzzi with fresh milk? All of this, and more, can be arranged in Bangkok. The Yellow Pages, under Beauty Salons, is a good place to start—many of the places listed are unisex.

Traditional Massage
Traditional massage places charge around B300 for a two-hour massage—you can get lower rates for a one-hour or 90-minute massage. Most places have small curtained-off areas for massage; you are asked to change into loose pants (provided for men), or loose pants and top (provided for women). Massage can be a sociable affair—you can take a friend or two along and carry on a conversation as you lie on side-by-side pads.

Other Hazards
Contaminated food and water are usually the cause of hepatitis, diarrhea, and worms. Avoid tap water, uncooked vegetables, salads, unpeeled fruit, undercooked meat, raw or undercooked seafood, and unpasteurized dairy products. Hepatitis B can be spread through sexual activity; earth-borne hookworm can be picked up through the skin by walking barefoot. In the case of diarrhea (which may be due just to a change of diet), keep to a plain diet for a one- or two-day period (eat plain rice), and drink fluids such as weak tea or juice to rehydrate yourself. *Nam manau* (ice lemon) is a good rehydrater—a large glass of fresh lemon juice, water, salt and sugar (but perhaps specify no ice-cubes).

In rural areas of Thailand, health hazards increase, particularly during the rainy season when insects are more active. In northern Thailand there's the risk of Japanese Encephalitis

Thai-style massage takes some getting used to—pressure is applied to major blood-flow areas, your muscles and tendons are stretched, and your bones and joints are cracked and worked over.

The massage practitioner uses his or her hands, fist, elbows, feet and other body parts to apply pressure or to stretch muscles. It's a bit like fiery Thai food—makes you want to cry at the time, but afterwards you feel just great! The spinal area is not worked upon. You should indicate any sensitive or sore areas so that these parts will be treated with caution. During the massage, the masseur or masseuse may ask, "Jep?" ("Does this part hurt?") to which you reply, "Jep" ("It hurts—so avoid") or "Mai jep" ("It doesn't hurt—carry on"). For a head massage, a hot towel is often applied. Masseurs and masseuses have a licence obtained from a school such as the one at Wat Po; the best practitioners are said to be the blind ones. You will find numerous Thai massage places in Bangkok (make sure the sign says "Traditional Thai Massage Only"). Some are attached to major hotels.

SPORTS AND RECREATION

To counteract Bangkok's unhealthy environment, health centers have become fashionable among the affluent in the city. Health centers are found in all the major hotels and usually have a gym, and tennis and squash courts. If your hotel doesn't have a swimming pool, find a hotel that does. The YMCA on Sathorn, for example, will allow you to use their pool (open 0700-1900 hours) for B20 a time (including use of locker), upon payment of initial B80 membership. The beach resorts to the south and east of Bangkok have a lot more to offer in the way of water sports—particularly Pattaya and Phuket, where there is diving, yachting, windsurfing, and game fishing. (See "Excursions From Bangkok")

For jogging, Lumpini Park is the place to go. The Hash House Harriers have regular runs for men and women—check the *Bangkok Post* sports pages on Saturdays for details. For kids, there is Siam Waterpark, in the eastern suburb of Minburi—a rambling set of slides, wavepools, waterfalls, with an entry fee of B150 that includes use of all facilities. Siam Waterpark also has amusement rides; near Central Plaza Hotel is Magic Land with a wide range of rides and sideshows. The main spectator sports in Bangkok are Thai boxing (held at two stadiums), and horse-racing (held every Sunday, alternating between the Royal Turf Club and Royal Bangkok Sports Club; betting by the public is permitted).

Golf

There are more than 50 golf courses in Thailand; separate guidebooks to golfing are available in Bangkok, such as *Golfing in the Kingdom,* by David Jern. Golfing is cheap (green fees vary from B250-400 weekdays to B500-1000 weekends and holidays; caddy fees run B150 a day plus tips); equipment is easy to rent; and visitors are welcome. Most courses boast modern clubhouses with restaurants, and pro shops stocking a full range of American and Japanese equipment. Courses are busy on weekends; your best bet is to play on week days, when it's also cheaper. Around Bangkok, there are a number of top-class courses, including the Rose Garden Golf Course (30 km west of Bangkok, tel. 253-0295) and two 18-hole courses at the Royal Thai Army Golf Course in Bang Khen (near the airport, tel. 521-1530).

ACCOMMODATIONS

Bangkok has a great variety of hotels to choose from. Five-star luxury? Medium-priced room with all the comforts? Small, family-run guesthouse? The capital has over 33,000 hotel rooms and more on the way—the city is a permanent construction zone with a skyline that seems to change weekly.

Two important factors influence your choice of a hotel: price and location. If you know what price you want (which basically determines what kind of hotel you'll get), it's really location you have to investigate, because location is everything in Bangkok. Businessmen have been known to change hotels to guarantee getting to an important meeting the next day. Major hotels are concentrated in three areas: the Silom-Surawong business district; the Siam Square commercial district; and in the Sukhumvit area. In addition, there are guesthouses in the Banglamphu area. Two luxury hotels to the north base their entire convention business on the fact that they're ten minutes from the airport: the luxury **Rama Gardens Hotel** (tel. 579-5400, fax 561-1025, 385 rooms) and super-luxury **Hyatt Central Plaza** (tel. 541-1234, fax 541-1087, 607 rooms). Noise is an important consideration when it comes to location: avoid ground-floor rooms or rooms that overlook a busy street, as you will get little sleep.

In the Nov.-Feb. peak season, you might want to fax ahead (662 is the Bangkok code) and reserve a room for the first couple of nights—this will give you ample time to hunt around for the perfect hotel once you're on the spot.

CATEGORIES AND RANGES

Super Luxury
Bangkok has some of the world's finest hotels. Service is what elevates them above the mundane. The Oriental, regarded as one of the world's top hotels, has a ratio of 2.5 staff to each guest. Service is not considered a demeaning job in Thailand, which may explain why hotel guests are pampered beyond belief. Facilities and service in five-star hotels are unbeatable: the Oriental has set high standards, and the other five-star hotels compete with those standards. There seems to be no upper limit on pricing (is that the phone number or the price?) in the super-luxury hotels. Bangkok's hoteliers are masters at providing "the suite life"—sumptuous suites are often uniquely decorated in Thai style. The super-luxury hotels are sights in their own right—if you want an air-conditioned breather, step inside and have a look at the architecture.

Luxury
Major hotels are like mini-states—they have their own conference and convention facilities, 24-hour business and translation centers, communications facilities (fax, telex, and so on), travel services, half a dozen restaurants and bars, swimming pools, health centers, sports facilities, shopping arcades . . . For locations of leading luxury and super-luxury hotels (which also serve as navigational landmarks), see the "Maps and Orientation" section.

Moderate
Moderate-priced hotels offer mid-range tourist class and family accommodations. These do not offer all the trimmings, but are certainly more than comfortable, and are the preferred choice for group tours because of pricing. The Sukhumvit area is popular. Hotel rooms have air-conditioning, hot shower, good plumbing, TV, telephone, small fridge, and sometimes even a safety deposit box in the room. Some hotels have a small swimming pool.

Budget
At the high end, edging up toward B1000, you get all the extras—hot water, fridge, phone, TV, air-con or fan, overseas calling facilities, and so on. At the lower end, around B400 a room, things become more basic. This is a mixed bag—some budget places are super-clean, small and classy; others are large, run-down, and seedy (catering to single men and their escorts). Air-conditioning still reigns in the budget

PRICE RANGES

Price ranges listed here are based on single-room occupancy (the cheapest available at the hotel) per night, and do not include taxes. Most hotels add 10% service charge and 8-11% government tax to the bill: if the bill is B2000 a night, taxes would add another B420. Guesthouses do not charge taxes, and neither do some of the budget hotels; other places may quote a price that includes all taxes. Hotel prices go up constantly—between 1988 to 1991, prices at some of the major hotels *doubled,* cashing in on high occupancy rates. The following is a rough price range only—make upward adjustments to suit. For off-season or longer stays (a month or more) you can negotiate discounts up to 50% for hotels. Group tours also get substantial discounts.

Doubles cost roughly the same as singles—in some hotels the rate is the same; in others, there's a markup of between five and fifteen percent for doubles, so for two people, adjust the rate accordingly. For three people, you can pay a bit more and have an extra bed put in. There's usually no charge for children under 12 staying in the same room as parents. By the way, if you ask for a single room, you'll get a double bed; ask for a double room and you'll get two single beds.

Class	Single Occupancy	Comments
Super Luxury	B3500-6000+/US$140-240+	Most are located in the business/commercial district of Silom-Surawong and in the upscale shopping district of Siam Square-Rajadamri. An older area is around the Oriental Hotel.
Luxury	B2000-3500/US$80-140	Catering to business people, group tours, and well-heeled tourists. Found in same areas as super-luxury hotels, as well as along lower Sukhumvit.
Moderate	B1000-2000/ US$40-80	Mid-range hotels catering to group-tours, tourists, families. Lots of these along the sois off Sukhumvit Road; others found in the Silom-Sathorn area, further back from the business district.
Budget	B400-1000/ US$15-$40	Scattered: some in moderate areas, some in guesthouse areas.
Guesthouses (GH)	under B400/ under US$15	In Banglamphu (Khao San Road), National Library vicinity, Malaysia Hotel area, Hualampong Station area. Catering to young backpackers.

hotels: unless otherwise noted, all the budget hotels listed here have some kind of air-conditioner, even if it is falling off the wall.

Guesthouses

Rock-bottom budget comes in the form of a bed and a fan in the room, and not much else. The air-conditioning runs out here, and so does the plumbing. Guesthouses have shared plumbing, little space, little privacy. These places are small—could be a dozen rooms, or a multi-story place with 60 rooms—what they have in common is low prices. Guesthouses vary quite a lot—some are awful, dark, dank hovels with rooms that resemble prison cells (with warders to match); others are bright, clean, airy places with a pleasant family-run atmosphere. Obviously you'll want the latter—a homey, family-run place that allows you a glimpse into Thai lifestyles. The most important thing in these places, apart from the management, is the res-

taurant area, where backpackers hang out. Since rooms are Spartan and only used for sleeping in, the restaurant area is where you tend to spend a lot of time, and where you meet other travelers.

ALONG THE RIVER

Being near the Chao Phraya River allows you to use the ferries running north and south, but you should bear in mind that the last ferries leave around 1800, so you have to find alternate methods of transport after that. Major hotels operate their own shuttle boats to key destinations from 0800 to 1900 hours. There are at present just a handful of luxury and super-luxury hotels along the river, but half a dozen more are under construction, aiming to challenge the monopoly of the Oriental, Sheraton, and Shangri-La hotels.

Taksin Bridge Vicinity

Menam, 2074 New Road, tel. 289-1148, fax 291-1048, with 727 rooms and 30 suites is a luxury hotel favored by European and Japanese group tours. Located right at the southern end of the express boat line, between Wat Vorachan-yawas and Wat Rajsingkorn landings. Three quarters of the rooms have a river view.

Shangri-La, 89 Soi Wat Suanplu, New Road, tel. 236-7777, fax 236-8579, has 650 rooms and 47 suites that enjoy uninterrupted views of the Chao Phraya. This super-luxury hotel has seven-meter-high glass windows in the Lobby Lounge. The hotel opened in 1986; it is one of the most prestigious in Bangkok, and one of the premier venues for conventions. Located near Sathorn landing.

Oriental, 48 Oriental Ave, tel. 236-0400, fax 236-1939, has 359 rooms and 34 suites. Bangkok's top-rated and oldest hotel—the Authors' Wing dates back to 1887. The Oriental has been voted the world's best hotel for nine consecutive years by New York's *Institutional Investor Magazine*—a ranking backed up by a number of travel magazines.

Royal Orchid Sheraton, 2 Captain Bush Lane, Si Phraya Road, tel. 234-5599, fax 236-8320, has 701 rooms and 74 suites. This super-luxury 28-story hotel has an unbeatable location

Teak bells hang in the lobby of the Oriental Hotel.

GUESTHOUSES

These range B40-80 for dormitory accommodations; B60-160 for singles and B80-200 for doubles. In some of the bigger places, you can get an a/c room with attached bath (up to B350 for a double), at which stage you're looking more at a hotel. A small padlock is useful, as guesthouses may have a bolt on a room door but no locking device. The better guesthouses tend to fill up quite fast. The best way to get into a good guesthouse is to deposit your luggage somewhere and roam budget areas in the late morning, when others will be checking out. Ask to see the room before putting your money down.

Khao San Road

The main budget area, with plenty of cheap guesthouses and travel agents is in and around Khao San Road and in the Banglamphu area toward the Chao Phraya River. It's a ten-minute walk from Pra Arthit landing to Khao San. After you disembark from the ferry (show your ferry ticket at the turnstiles!), head north along Pra Arthit Road, take the first *soi* to the right, and keep going straight ahead till you reach a wall—there's a gateway right here for a shortcut through Wat Chana Songkram, leading to the western end of Khao San Road.

Although there are more than 60 places in the Khao San Road area, the better ones are full by the early afternoon in the peak touring season. Try these: Chart GH, tel. 281-0803; Hello GH, tel. 281-8579;

VIP GH, tel. 282-5090; C.H. GH, tel. 282-2023; Bonny GH, tel. 281-9877; Ice GH, tel. 281-2601; Marco Polo GH, tel. 282-7096. A bit more expensive is Khao San Palace, tel. 282-0578. Khao San Road has lots of services for travelers. If you want to get a haircut, apply for a Vietnamese visa, buy a minibus ticket for Ko Samui, get laundry done, get film developed, and send a fax—all within the space of a few hours—this is the place to do it. Many of the guesthouses do double duty as travel agents or IDD/fax operators.

Some travelers find the Khao San circus not to their liking—too noisy, too busy, too many *farangs,* too much video—and seek refuge in the alleys off Khao San. Leading in from the ferry are two pleasant larger places: Merry V GH, tel. 282-9267; and My House, tel. 282-9263. On Tanao Road, off the eastern end of Khao San, is Privacy GH, tel. 282-7028, and Central GH, tel. 282-0667.

National Library Area

North of Khao San there is a pocket of cheap guesthouses on alleys off Sri Ayuthaya Road, behind the National Library—a ten- to fifteen-minute walk from Tha Thewet landing. Half a dozen small, homey places: Shanti Lodge, tel. 281-2497; Sawatdee GH, tel. 282-5349; Tavee GH, tel. 282-5983; Backpackers Lodge, tel. 282-3231; and Paradise GH, tel. 282-4094—mostly dormitory or shared rooms, but a few private rooms are available.

---

near Si Phraya landing, and next door to River City shopping complex. All rooms have views.

Budget

Swan Hotel, at 31 Custom House Lane, New Road, tel. 233-8444, fax 234-5198, has 72 rooms. A budget-priced anomaly sandwiched in among the giants, further back from the river but still close to the Oriental landing. It has a small pool. Rooms can be grubby, and service is poor. No extras, and air-conditioning is erratic.

Mid-river/Budget

North of River City is **River View GH,** at 768 Soi Wanit 2 (north of River City shopping com-

plex), tel. 235-8501, fax 237-5771, with 30 rooms. It's set back from the river, but some rooms have views. Fan and a/c rooms. The hotel is not conveniently placed for express boats.

A few blocks east of Ratchawong landing is **Chao Phya Riverside GH,** 1128 Songward Road, tel. 222-6344, with 14 rooms—super clean, family-run, safe; guesthouse prices. None of the rooms have views, but there's a pleasant cafe perched right on the banks of the Chao Phraya.

Pra Arthit/Guesthouses

In the Banglamphu area (near Pinklao Bridge) there are several guesthouses right near Pra

GUESTHOUSES, cont.

Hualampong-Chinatown

The Hualampong Station area was once thronged with backpackers, but the trade has folded. Travelers who frequently use Hualampong Station for up-country railway trips find the **TT Guesthouses** useful, as these places are clean and have secure luggage storage. TT #1 GH, tel. 236-3053 (25 rooms) is a ten-minute walk southeast from the station—cross Rama IV Road, walk eastward along Rama IV till you reach Mahanakorn Road, turn down this road and follow signs for the guesthouse. TT #2 GH, with 30 rooms, is found in the same area.

To the west of Hualampong is Chinatown, which has budget accommodations. The area is not recommended—far too noisy, too busy, limited variety of restaurants. The guesthouses tend to be sleazy (short-time places) and are not the cleanest, but there are some better budget-priced hotels, such as **New Empire Hotel** on Yaowarat Road, tel. 234-6990. Another guesthouse zone, at the western edge of Chinatown, is the "Little India" area around Chakrapet and Pahurat roads—lots of Indian-run guesthouses and small restaurants.

Malaysia Hotel Area

There are dozens of guesthouses and budget hotels along Soi Ngam Duphli and Soi Si Bamphen in southeast Bangkok. The **Malaysia Hotel,** at 54 Soi Ngam Duphli, tel. 286-3582, is the budget landmark of the area because of its size and legendary stature. Back in the 1960s the Malaysia was an R&R hotel for American GIs on leave. In the 1970s it became Bangkok's main backpacker destination and was notorious for periodic drug raids on its customers. In the 1980s, the management shifted its attention to wealthier patrons—Saudi Arabians. A ground-floor cabaret featuring Thai women was opened; the Arabs sent the prices up sharply, and the backpackers left. In 1990 three Arab diplomats were killed in Bangkok, which led to a freezing of relations between Saudi Arabia and Thailand: Arabs abruptly moved out of Bangkok. This sent the hotel scrambling for guests, so the prices dropped. Now the Malaysia is a budget hotel catering largely to single men. The area has little to recommend—it is seedy, noisy, full of concrete and traffic fumes. The alleys radiating from the Malaysia Hotel are crammed with guesthouses—the Freddy series is good (Freddy's #2 GH, tel. 286-7826, or Freddy's #3 GH, tel. 287-1665); as is the Lee series (Lee GH, tel. 286-2069); or try L.A. GH, tel. 286-8556.

Arthit landing. Along Pra Arthit Road you'll find **Peachy GH,** tel. 281-6471, with 50 rooms (some more expensive a/c rooms)—it's a larger place with a courtyard restaurant. Nearby is another large place, **Beer GH,** tel. 281-6832, and around the corner is **Apple GH,** tel. 281-6838. In the alleys east of Pra Arthit road are lots of other guesthouses: ten minutes' walk away is Khao San Road. A little way north of Pra Arthit, approached from Wat Samphraya landing, **River GH,** at 18/1 Soi Wat Samphraya, Samsen Road, tel. 280-0876, has 12 rooms.

Krung Thon Bridge Area

Near Sang Hee landing there are two hotels: **Riverside Plaza,** 753 Ratchawithi, tel. 434-0090, fax 435-1642, has 264 rooms. This is a moderate-priced hotel somewhat lacking in atmosphere.

Royal River Hotel, 670/805 Charan Sanitwong Road, tel. 433-0300, fax 433-5880, has 403 rooms, luxury prices, and a relaxed location away from the hubbub. It's popular with group tours; great lunch buffets are served here.

BANGLAMPHU-DEMOCRACY MONUMENT

Luxury: Princess, 269 Larn Luang Road, tel. 281-3088, fax 280-1314, has 170 rooms. The Princess has several top-rated restaurants, and due to its proximity to government buildings, it has become a favorite meeting place for officials and civil servants.

Moderate: Royal, 2 Rajadamnern Klang, tel. 222-9111, fax 224-2083, has 300 rooms. Good location for Bangkok sightseeing, but make sure you get a room away from the road—otherwise it's noisy. The Royal may be run-down, but you can't get a hotel that's closer to the Grand Palace (and some rooms have views of the palace). The Royal is one of the oldest hotels in Bangkok: drop in and have a look—there's a 24-hour coffee shop in the lobby. A less attractive alternative to the Royal is the **Majestic,** at 97 Rajadamnern Klang, tel. 281-5000, fax 280-0965, with 65 rooms.

Guesthouses: See section covering Khao San Road.

NEW ROAD-SILOM-SURAWONG-SATHORN

Super Luxury
Dusit Thani, 946 Rama IV Road, tel. 236-0450, fax 236-6400, has 492 rooms, 33 suites—known as a leading convention and business-person's hotel, with a full range of services including a Reuters wire link-up to world-wide stock exchanges. There's a Press Club located at the top, and rooftop dining in the Tiara Lounge on the 22nd floor. The lineup of dining spots and bars at the Dusit Thani is impressive, with two superb Chinese restaurants, a Japanese restaurant, and an American steak house. **Holiday Inn Crowne Plaza,** 981 Silom, tel. 238-4300, fax 238-5289, has 392 rooms.

Luxury
Tawana Ramada, 80 Surawong Road, tel. 236-0361, fax 236-3738, has 254 rooms, 11 suites. **Montien,** 54 Surawong Road, tel. 234-8060, fax 236-5219, has 483 rooms, 20 suites—modern hotel with spacious rooms. **Mandarin,** 662 Rama IV Road, tel. 233-4980, fax 234-1399, has 343 rooms and caters to groups. **Narai,** 222 Silom Road, tel. 237-0100, fax 236-7161, has 500 rooms; there's a revolving restaurant, La Rotonde, on the top floor.

Moderate
Silom Plaza, 320 Silom Rd. tel. 236-8441, fax 236-7567, has 200 rooms. **New Peninsula,** 295 Surawong, tel. 234-3910, fax 236-5526, has 100 rooms. **New Trocadero,** 343 Surawong, tel. 234-8920, fax 236-5526, has 140 rooms in a vintage building. The Trocadero has seen better days: when the New Road/Surawong area was the *farang* center of things, people like Jim Thompson and James Michener stayed here. Along with the New Fuji, New Peninsula, and Manohra hotels in this area, the Tracadero is somewhat run-down and tattered. **New Fuji,** 299 Surawong, tel. 234-5364, fax 236-5526. **Victory,** 322 Silom, tel. 233-9060, fax 237-1868, has 125 rooms. On the seedy side. **YMCA (Collins House),** 27 South Sathorn Road (set back from the main road), tel. 287-1900, fax 287-1996, has 200 rooms, full-length pool. Great value; despite the name, the YMCA accepts all guests; non-guests can use the pool for a fee.

Budget
Rose, 118 Surawong Road, tel. 233-7695, has 99 rooms. **Bangkok Christian GH,** 123 Saladeng Soi 2, Convent Road, tel. 233-6303, fax 223-5444, has 36 rooms—breakfast included in price. **YWCA,** 13 South Sathorn, tel. 286-1936, has 50 rooms and an excellent restaurant with German-Swiss and Thai dishes. **King's Mansion,** 31 South Sathorn Road, tel. 286-0940, has 120 rooms—staff not very helpful. **Malaysia Hotel,** 54 Soi Ngam Duphli, Rama IV Road, tel. 286-3582, fax 249-3120, has 120 rooms and a pool. There are lots of guesthouses in the area around the Malaysia.

SIAM SQUARE-RAJADAMRI

Super Luxury
Grand Hyatt Erawan, at 494 Rajadamri, tel. 252-9100, re-opened 1991, 450 rooms. **Hilton International,** 2 Wireless Road, tel 253-0123, fax 253-6509, has 350 rooms, 37 suites. Set in an eight-acre landscaped park with tropical foliage, waterfalls, and pleasant walkways. The hotel is a five-story crescent—the wall facing the main entrance is two stories of sheer glass. The pool is the most beautiful in town. **Le Meridien President,** 135/26 Keysorn Road, tel. 253-0444, fax 253-7565, has 400 rooms, 20 suites. This hotel came under new management in 1986 and underwent extensive renovations. The hotel has a continental flavor. **The Regent,**

155 Rajadamri, tel. 251-6127, fax 253-9195, has 407 rooms, 32 suites. This is one of the top-rated hotels in Bangkok. Drop in for afternoon tea in the lobby and take a look at the artwork above—the ceiling is composed of intricately hand-painted silk panels depicting the mythological Thai cosmos. There's also a huge mural commanding the stairway from the lobby. **Siam Intercontinental,** 967 Rama I Road, tel. 253-0355, fax 253-2275, has 347 rooms, 53 suites. The striking design of this hotel successfully blends traditional Thai and modern Western; the hotel is set in 26 acres of landscaped gardens, and has excellent sports facilities. Centrally located within easy reach of Siam Square. **Imperial,** 6 Soi Ruamrudee, Wireless Road, tel. 254-0023, fax 253-3190, has 380 rooms, 20 suites. A sprawling, nondescript hotel which claims to have the largest swimming pool in Bangkok, set in landscaped gardens. **Novotel,** Siam Square, Soi 6, tel. 255-6888, fax 255-1824, has 404 rooms, 25 suites—under French management. Spacious rooms; caters to the businessperson.

Luxury
Asia, 296 Phayathai Road, tel. 215-0808, fax 215-4360, has 568 rooms, 33 suites—a favorite with Japanese group tours and Western businessmen; swimming pools on the 5th and 12th floors with landscaped gardens. **Indra Regent,** 120/126 Rajaprarop Road, tel. 252-1111, fax 253-3849, has 391 rooms, 48 suites. **Baiyoke,** 130 Rajaprarop, tel. 253-0362, fax 254-5553, offers 240 rooms; the Sky Lounge on the 43rd floor has great views.

Budget
Reno, 40 Soi Kasemsan 1, Rama I Road, tel. 215-0026, has 70 rooms. **Florida,** 43 Phayathai Road, tel. 247-0990, has 107 rooms. The Florida was an R&R hotel for GIs on leave in the Vietnam War era—decor hasn't changed much since then.

SUKHUMVIT SOIS 1-21

Super Luxury
Landmark, 138 Sukhumvit (between Sois 4 and 6), tel. 254-0404, fax 253-4259, has 360 rooms and 55 suites plus aerial-view dining at the Hibiscus Room on the 31st floor. The hotel opened in 1988 and is angled for businesspeople, with a 24-hour business center. **Mansion Kempinski,** 75/23 Soi 11, tel. 253-2655, fax 253-2329, has 120 rooms. The hotel opened in 1991, and is under German management.

Luxury
The Boulevard, 17 Soi 7, tel. 255-2940, fax 255-2950; has 129 rooms. A businessperson's hotel. **The Ambassador,** 171 Sukhumvit between Sois 11 and 13, tel. 254-0444, fax 253-4123, has 932 rooms; good for families. Worth a visit to see the exotic birds and animals caged along the entranceway; inside the hotel is a huge aviary that can be viewed from the second-floor coffee-shop. There are 20-odd restaurants and nightclubs in The Ambassador: the hotel entices even backpackers to its food center, with low-priced stalls. **The Somerset,** 5 Soi 15, tel. 254-8500, fax 254-8534, has 76 rooms.

Moderate
Grace, 12 Soi 3, tel. 253-0651, fax 253-0680, has 542 rooms. Due to their proximity to Nana Plaza, the Grace, Rajah, and Nana hotels were notorious as hangouts for single men. Now the clientele has shifted to group tours. **Rajah,** 18 Soi 4, tel. 255-0040, fax 255-7610, has 450 rooms. **Nana,** 4 Soi 4, tel. 252-0121, fax 255-1769, has 334 rooms. **Manhattan,** 13 Soi 15, tel. 255-0166, fax 255-3481, has 186 rooms.

Budget
Golden Gate, 22/3 Soi 2, tel. 252-8126, fax 253-9494, has 50 rooms. **White Inn,** 41 Soi 4, tel. 252-7090, features Tudor-style lodgings; small and cozy. **Vital House,** 39 Soi 8, tel. 253-3410, fax 253-5125, with 50 rooms is super-clean, very secure, and has a small pool. **Mermaid's Rest,** 6/1 Soi 8, tel. 253-5123, fax 253-2401, has 26 rooms in a converted mansion—Scandinavian-run, very clean, great value. **Comfort Inn,** 153/11 Soi 11, tel. 251-9250, fax 254-3562, has 28 rooms. **Bangkok Inn,** 155/12-13 Soi 11, tel. 254-4834. **Federal,** 27 Soi 11, tel. 253-0175, fax 253-5332, has 93 rooms. **Miami,** 2 Soi 13, tel. 253-5611, fax 253-1266, has 123 rooms. **Honey,** 31 Soi 19, tel. 253-0646, fax 254-4716, has 75

rooms—caters to single men, due to its location near the nightlife of Soi Cowboy. **Quality Inn,** 8/7 Soi 19, tel. 254-4783, fax 255-7340, has 35 rooms.

SUKHUMVIT SOIS 21 AND UP

Luxury/Moderate
Windsor, 10 Soi 20, tel. 258-0160, fax 258-1491, has 235 rooms. A former R&R hotel used by GIs in the Vietnam War era, this hotel has been upgraded and is favored by tour groups. **Jade Pavilion,** 30 Soi 22, tel. 259-4675, fax

258-2328, has 225 rooms. **Ariston,** 19 Soi 24, tel. 259-0960, fax 259-0970, has 160 rooms. **Impala,** 9 Soi 24, tel. 258-8612, fax 259-2896, has 200 rooms. **Tara,** 18/1 Soi 26, tel. 259-2900, fax 259-2896, has 200 rooms, 14 suites.

Moderate/Budget
Crown, 503 Soi 29, tel. 258-0318, has 63 rooms. **Rex,** 762/1 Sukhumvit (opposite Soi 49), tel. 259-0106, fax 258-6635, has 131 rooms. The Rex is too far out of town; if you make frequent trips to the east coast, however, the Rex is located near the Eastern Bus Terminal.

DINING OUT

If you want a country of great libraries and grand operas, Thailand is hardly the place. But if you want to be able to sit under palm trees with a Mekhong-and-soda or a beer, with a table groaning under the fruits and curries and noodles and soups and sweets . . . well, then, Thailand is paradise on earth.

—prominent Thai author and statesman Kukrit Pramoj, quoted from an interview

THAI FOOD

You could spend several years in Bangkok, eating well three times a day, and never visiting the same place twice. There are over 30,000 registered restaurants in the metropolitan area, and that doesn't begin to take in the number of streetside foodstalls. To cover Bangkok's restaurants in detail really requires a separate guide—recommended for the gourmet is *Bangkok Restaurant Guide* (Asia Books), with listings in English and Thai (the last edition was dated 1988, which means the prices are out, but the maps are invaluable—it's easy to find restaurants with the Thai script). Meanwhile, the listing of restaurants given here should keep you busy for a month or so!

The recommendations here emphasize Thai and Asian food—and there is a smattering of restaurants which are mainly for Thais (hence inexpensive, and no compromise for the Western palate). Thai food, the saying goes, is no

good unless it makes you want to cry—or at least makes the sweat run down your forehead so you'll "cry" that way. The most common Asian cuisines in Bangkok are Chinese and Indian. Chinese restaurants are found throughout Bangkok, and many restaurants have mixed Chinese and Thai food on the menu. Bangkok has excellent Indian restaurants, with good vegetarian and non-vegetarian selections.

Dining Experiences
Food Centers: To get started with Thai and Asian food, try visiting a food center. These are self-serve centers with a variety of stalls—you buy coupons at one booth, go around to the various stalls and get what you want, then get a refund for unused coupons at another booth. The stalls offer an incredible selection at very low prices—every regional kind of Thai food, and most Asian cuisines. Three big food centers are at the Ambassador Hotel (Bangkok's original food center), Mahboonkrong Shopping Complex near Siam Square, and at Central Plaza in the Lad Prao area (en route to the airport).

Foodstalls: Streetside foodstalls serve very cheap food, but that doesn't mean you get a drop in quality—quite the contrary. At foodstalls you can get whole dried squid or barbecued chicken, or even crunchy fried grasshoppers, all cooked up before your eyes on charcoal braziers. The vast number of streetstalls in Bangkok is partly explained by the fact that in some areas residents live in one room, with water but no cooking facilities (and no cooking allowed). Streetstalls may not open till night in some zones because of traffic regulations. Hygiene is of some concern—but if you stick to well-cooked food, no problem (avoid the ice).

Seafood Supermarkets: Though Thai food is cheap, seafood is pricey. There are several "seafood supermarkets" around Bangkok—you go shopping with a trolley, pick out the food you want and hand it over, specifying the cooking method. The food is charged by weight, with an extra price for cooking. Exorbitant bills of over B800 per person are common.

Royal Thai Cuisine: In terms of presentation, Thai food is ranked alongside French and Japanese for its finesse. The most visually appealing of all Thai styles is Royal Thai, a cuisine once prepared only by palace chefs—whose methods were closely guarded secrets. The style uses tiny portions, exquisitely presented, with "sculpted" vegetables and fruit. Royal Thai food can be experienced at **Bussaracum Restaurant.**

Restaurants with Classical Dance: A number of tourist-type restaurants stage classical and folk dancing at dinner. These range from tourist rip-off set menus to quite reasonable food: in any case, the reason you go is for the classical dance. For details, see "Bangkok by Night" entries.

Dinner Cruises: Restaurants and hotels along the Chao Phraya River offer dinner and cruise combinations at night—refer to the "Along the River" restaurant listing that follows.

Etiquette

Specify how hot you want your food when ordering. *Mai phet* means "not hot"; *phet nitnoy* is "a little hot." Salt is replaced by *nam pla* (fish sauce) on the table. *Mai sai nam kheng* means "no ice." Thais use a fork and spoon for eating—the spoon is the main implement, and may be used in place of a knife to saw up food. Thais are not particular about how you eat or in what order you eat dishes. If you wish to eat with your hands, so be it (some dishes, such as sticky rice or chicken wrapped in pandan leaves, leave no alternative). Rice is the basis of a Thai meal. A full Thai dinner will include steamed rice, soup, a steamed dish, a fried dish, a spicy salad, and dessert and fruit. As with Chinese food, it is best to share dishes to have a greater range. All the dishes are served at the same time (except the dessert and fruit), and you spoon whatever you want onto your steamed rice. If you put the fork and spoon separately on your plate, this is a semiotic signal to the waiter that you are not finished; if you put the fork and spoon neatly together, the waiter will clear the dishes off the table.

cauldrons of spicy food in a morning market

SINGHA

LAGER   BEER

เบียร์เหมสุทธิ์   ชำระภาษีแล้ว   3 5 5 ซ.ม.³

BOON RAWD BREWERY CO.,LTD.
BANGKOK

On The Menu

The range of Thai food is quite astonishing, and the items presented here are only the barest essentials. Thai cuisine has absorbed many influences: what makes it distinctly Thai is the spicing and sauces—utilizing lemongrass, coriander, ginger, garlic, tamarind, coconut milk, basil, and peanuts, to name a few condiments. And, of course, chilies.

Drinks: Drinks immediately spring to mind because of chilies! Actually, while most drinks do not counter the effect of chilies, lime juice is something of an antidote. A good Thai drink is *nam manau* (fresh lime juice with salt, sugar, and ice cubes) which will rehydrate your system into the bargain. Fresh juices go well with Thai food—you can drink coconut juice direct from the shell. In the alcohol line, Thai beer is good—common brands are Singha and Kloster. Beer is served ice-cold, or else with ice. Mekong whiskey, mixed with lime and soda, is the local firewater meant to complement Thai food.

Rice: Keep a good supply of steamed rice on hand in a side dish just in case you come across a "rat-shit pepper"—one of those tiny volcanic yellow ones. Rice is either steamed, fried, or sticky. A second staple food is noodles.

Soup: Thailand's culinary masterpiece is *tom yam*, a sour soup that is made with various kinds of meat or fish. The most famous is *tom yam gung*, or lemon prawn soup; there's also *tom yam gai*—the same broth with chicken. Floating in the soup are spices which are not eaten—lemongrass, citrus leaves, garlic, lime juice, and chilies. Or try *tom kah gai*—chicken cooked in coconut milk.

Main Dishes: These are based on chicken *(gai)*, beef *(neua)*, pork *(muu)*, duck *(ped)*, or seafood. Most curry dishes utilize coconut milk. Try *kaeng phet* (hot curry), *kaeng wan* (green chili paste curry), *kaeng gai* (red chili paste curry), *kaeng matsaman* (a milder curry) or *kaeng kari* (yellow or Indian curry). Other main dishes are based on the same meats—which could be barbecued, steamed, deep-fried, or sautéed with combinations of vegetables. There are tasty separate plates of vegetables—such as broccoli with garlic sauce, or peppered eggplant.

Seafood: Dining on Thai food in Bangkok is very low-priced, but seafood can be expensive. In some restaurants, the price quoted on the menu is *by weight*, so inquire about prices per serving to avoid unpleasant surprises. A great range of seafood dishes (both saltwater and fresh) is available. Some suggestions are curried crab, fried sea bass seasoned with lemon or green chili sauce, mussels steamed in a pot, freshwater lobster baked in a clay pot with herbs, or fried squid with hot sauce.

Salads: These usually consist of meat or seafood mixed with fresh vegetables and a spicy dressing. Try *yam pla muk* (squid salad), *yam het* (mushroom salad), *yam mamuang* (green mango salad), or *yam neua* (beef salad).

Desserts: You'll be pleased to know that no hot spices are used in desserts, although Thais are prone to sprinkling chili powder on their fruit (especially sour green mangoes). Thai desserts have an amazing variety of tastes and textures, with the major flavor being coconut. This is a whole new language of food, and you're best advised to go to a food center to help identify the

KAREN WHITE

jackfruit

(clockwise from top left) 1. jammed up on Sathorn Road; 2. traffic policeman with face-mask to counter pollution; 3. motorcycle-taxi operators, waiting on street corner; 4. *tuk-tuks* buzzing down a sidestreet; 5. strange things you might find in Bangkok traffic

(clockwise from top) 1. Grand Palace area: buildings in this zone are not supposed to exceed the height of the palace buildings; 2. in the Silom business district: makeshift homes on vacant lot (at left) amid highrise banks and condominiums; 3. a condominium tower springing up next to much older form of housing—a barge on the Chao Phraya; 4. urban sprawl of Bangkok; 5. Robot Building, Sathorn Road

(top) fruit-seller setting up stand in Thonburi; (bottom left) vendor fanning dried squid on portable charcoal brazier; (bottom right) seafood on a streetside barbecue

(clockwise from top left) 1. lotus buds; 2. chilis; 3. rambutans; 4. garlands of flowers

desserts. Thais prefer their desserts to have a fragrance, so jasmine and other aromatic flowers are soaked in water and this is used to make a syrup. Try lotus seed in coconut cream, taro and pumpkin in coconut milk and syrup, sugar palm nut (toddy palm) in syrup, or stuffed chestnut in coconut cream. Thais love the small cakes made from mung beans, yams, glutinous rice, coconut, and agar sugar, usually flavored with fresh fruit and sweetened with coconut cream and palm sugar.

Fruit: One of the great delights of Thailand is its fruit. You have to be a budding botanist to keep track of the many species available in this tropical wonderland. Sliced fruit is readily available from street vendors at very low prices, but restaurants do not usually serve fruit salad or fruit shakes—this is a Western habit (the major hotels catering to Westerners serve fruit salad, and you'll find fruit salad dishes at the eateries along Khao San Road). Bananas, oranges, coconut, pineapple, papaya, and guava are available year-round. The more exotic types of fruit—mango, durian, langsat, tamarind, jackfruit, mangosteen, pomelo, rose apple, custard apple, sapodilla, rambutan—are seasonal. You can get jackfruit, rambutan, durian, or coconut ice cream. Durian is definitely an acquired taste—this fruit, which is prickly, green, and the size of a football, has a thick yellow pulp that is a cross between custard and a potent old cheese. Fruit aficionados love the March to June season when you can get *khao neeo mamuang*—mangoes with sticky rice and coconut milk.

KAREN WHITE

mangosteen

RESTAURANTS BY AREA

The better restaurants in Bangkok are buried down sidestreets to escape the traffic—so they're often hard to locate. Using the maps provided, you should have no trouble finding the ones listed here. There is a great variation in atmosphere from cafeteria types to palatial converted mansions. In the evening, and on weekends, some of the more popular smaller restaurants may require reservations. Although a restaurant may be high-priced at night, lunch could be much more reasonable—and without the crowds. Most of the restaurants have Thai and English menus.

Pricing

The following price ranges are per head and do not include tax, service charge, or drinks. Taxes range from zero to 7.5%-12% government tax and 10% service charge on top of that (which makes a total of 22% tax in some cases). One place charged an 8% "entertainment tax" because music was provided by a guitarist! A small-size Singha beer can run anywhere from B30 to B80; any kind of wine or imported liquor will be very expensive—wine being about B80 a glass. It's quite all right to check your bill before paying—this can be complicated by the fact that bills are often written up only in Thai. In noodle places or lower-priced places, no tip is expected. Tipping is not necessary if you've already paid a service tax, but it is polite to leave five or ten baht on the silver plate. Keep in mind that "expensive" in this price scheme means expensive by Bangkok standards—the minimum wage in Bangkok being B100 a day:

◊◊◊◊◊—very expensive/over B650/US$26
◊◊◊◊—expensive/B450/US$18-26
◊◊◊—above average/B300-450/ US$12-18
◊◊—reasonable/B150-300/ US$6-12
◊—inexpensive/B50-150/US$2-6

DINING ALONG THE RIVER

Along the Chao Phraya there's alfresco, dining with pleasant breezes—away from the diesel fumes. These places are very easy to get to for lunch, but the last ferries on the Chao Phraya leave their terminuses at 1800 hours, so plan to get home by some other means if dropping in for dinner.

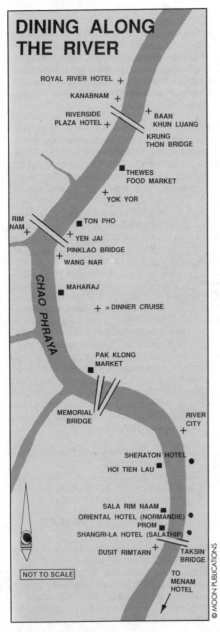

DINING ALONG THE RIVER

ROYAL RIVER HOTEL

KANABNAM

RIVERSIDE PLAZA HOTEL

BAAN KHUN LUANG

KRUNG THON BRIDGE

THEWES FOOD MARKET

YOK YOR

RIM NAM

TON PHO

YEN JAI

PINKLAO BRIDGE

WANG NAR

CHAO PHRAYA

MAHARAJ

+ = DINNER CRUISE

PAK KLONG MARKET

MEMORIAL BRIDGE

RIVER CITY

SHERATON HOTEL

HOI TIEN LAU

SALA RIM NAAM

ORIENTAL HOTEL (NORMANDIE)

PROM

SHANGRI-LA HOTEL (SALATHIP)

DUSIT RIMTARN

TAKSIN BRIDGE

TO MENAM HOTEL

NOT TO SCALE

© MOON PUBLICATIONS

Dinner Cruises

At night, hotel terraces are lit up with strings of lights, and you can take a ricebarge or boat tour along the river. Boats attached to major hotels are expensive—around B600 including meal, and may require reservations. Those attached to restaurants on the river are decidedly cheaper. Their boats are usually smaller and don't have a kitchen on board—you eat at the restaurant, or food from the restaurant is served to you on the boat. For this reason, you must be at the restaurant an hour before departure so that you can order and have the cooked food served to you. You pay for the food as ordered, plus an extra fee for the boat, usually around B50. To ensure a place, drop by during the day, make a booking (or have a Thai speaker phone in a booking for you), and return that evening. The schedules may change from the ones given here, which is another reason for inquiring in advance. Boats can also be chartered from these places by groups. If you have money to burn, hey, what the heck! Charter the Oriental Queen for dinner and invite a hundred guests. *Note:* Restaurants in the following listing which offer dinner cruises are in ***bold italics***.

Taksin Bridge Area

Menam Hotel (buffet ◊◊), tel. 289-1148, right near the southern terminus of the Chao Phraya express boat. The Menam has a buffet breakfast for B180 (ground floor) and a more expensive buffet lunch. The hotel is set back slightly from the river.

Dusit Rimtarn (Thai/seafood ◊◊◊), tel. 437-9671, in Suppakarn Shopping Center. Upstairs serves traditional cuisine; downstairs serves seafood, with an air-conditioned section and a riverfront terrace. A classical dance show is performed in the evening. Free shuttle-boats run to Suppakarn Condominium from the Oriental landing. ***Suppakarn Floating Restaurant,*** tel. 437-9603, offers a trip up the river, departing 1915 and returning 2200 hours, daily except Mondays, and costing B250-500.

Shangri-La Hotel, tel. 236-7777. One of the better restaurants here is Salathip Pavilion (Thai ◊◊◊) with traditional and Royal Thai dishes served on a patio next to the river (dinner only). You have a choice of dining indoors—with lavish

Thai architectural surroundings—or outdoors under the stars.

Prom (Thai ◊) is a small open-air place on the Thonburi side. Take the boat from the pier at the foot of the Shangri-La Hotel.

Oriental Hotel, tel. 236-0400, at the Oriental landing. A rooftop restaurant, The Normandie (French ◊◊◊◊◊), is designed to resemble an Orient Express dining car—it has panoramic views of the Chao Phraya and top-rated French food, with top prices; jacket and tie required for men. Lord Jim's (seafood ◊◊◊◊◊) features local and imported seafood served in a setting evocative of a 19th-century steamer, overlooking the Chao Phraya; has a buffet lunch and full à la carte dinner. Ciao (Italian ◊◊◊◊◊), has a romantic setting and offers superb pasta and pizza. There is also a nightly Western-style barbecue at the Riverside Terrace; across the river is Rim Naam Terrace, serving Thai cuisine (buffet lunch also served). The Sala Rim Naam (Thai ◊◊◊◊◊) has a dinner/classical dance show.

Sheraton/River City

Sheraton, tel. 234-5599, at Si Phraya landing. Although it is billed as the Sheraton's best restaurant, Captain Bush Grill (Continental ◊◊◊◊◊), on the first floor, has no windows or view, and the food is conventional. The Sheraton also stages a nightly riverside buffet (Thai/Western ◊◊◊◊) with a classical dance show. On the other side of the river in River House Condominium complex is Hoi Tien Lau, an expensive Chinese restaurant operated by the Sheraton (a shuttle boat is provided to cross the river).

River City: There are several restaurants in this shopping complex, but only two with river views. Approach River City from the Si Phraya landing. **Savoey Seafood** (seafood ◊◊◊◊) on the ground floor terrace, tel. 234-9365, gives you a choice of dining in a/c comfort, or outdoors on the terrace. **The Beer Garden**, on the 5th floor open-air rooftop (Thai/Western food ◊), is one of Bangkok's bargains—barbecued food, great views, reasonable prices, open evenings only, from 1730 to 2330.

Boats from River City: These two cost around B550-650 a person, including cruise and dinner: ***Chao Phya Charter Co.***, tel. 433-5453, operates a deluxe ricebarge, the ***Wan-***

fah, with kitchen on board; bookings right at the pier. Departs from River City daily at 1900 hours for a two-hour cruise to the Krung Thon bridge area and back. Traditional music played on board. The barge can be chartered—it holds up to 120 guests. The ***Loy Nava Company,*** tel. 437-4932, operates two cruises, departing 1800 and 2000 hours, to Krung Thon Bridge—two hours' duration.

Mid-river

Pak Klong Talad: Wholesale food markets with some vendors and foodstalls; get off at Tha Rajini or Tha Saphan Phut.

Maharaj Restaurant (Thai ◊◊), right at Maharaj landing, tel. 221-9073, is the restaurant with the bright red interior. Mediocre food, but a nice setting. Also superb **foodstalls** just north, in tiny places hanging over the river, near Tha Prachan landing—frequented by students.

Pinklao Bridge Area

Rim Nam (Thai/Chinese ◊◊◊) just south of Pra Pinklao bridge on the Thonburi side (get off at Pra Pinklao landing), tel. 424-1112, has a great setting with an open-air terrace as well as an a/c dining room. The *Rim Nam's* large cruiser parked next to the restaurant departs daily at 1900 and 2030 for a B40 extra charge.

Wang Nar (Chinese/Thai ◊◊) on the south side of Pra Pinklao bridge near Pra Arthit landing, tel. 224-8552, open 1100 to 2300. Large venue, large servings, good value. More expensive seafood and Chinese exotic dishes are available. *Wang Nar* has a boat for cruises on the Chao Phraya.

Yen Jai (Thai/seafood ◊◊) just south of Pra Arthit landing, tel. 281-6843, open 1100-2000 daily except Sunday. For an extra charge, *Yen Jai* offers a boat-cruise on the Chao Phraya—you eat your food at the restaurant before departure.

Ton Pho (Thai ◊◊), just north of Pra Arthit landing, tel. 280-0452, is open 1100 to 2000.

North Of Pinklao Bridge

Yok Yor (mixed ◊◊) right at Visutkasat landing, tel. 281-1829, open 1100-2300 daily, has an ambitious menu—seafood, Thai, Chinese, and some Japanese and Korean. *Yok Yor* has a

EXPERIMENTING WITH THAI FOOD
by Jeffrey Alford

You can eat extremely well in Thailand without knowing a word of Thai, and without knowing much about the cuisine. Thais have a very good sense of food—a gift which influences boiling an ear of sweet corn as much as preparing a complicated curry. You can order Thai fried rice in a different restaurant or from a different street vendor every day for a month, and it will almost always taste very good.

But chances are you'll want to taste more, and to explore. One place to begin is a reliable Thai cookbook: *Thai Cooking* by Kurt Kahrs is excellent. Read through the recipes and see what sounds good, then go out in search of particular dishes. Or look at the section on ingredients, and then head to the market to taste and identify all that's unfamiliar.

While seasoning a curry, a salad, or a stir-fry, Thai cooks work to achieve a balance between hot, salty, sour, and sweet. When Thais go abroad—whether it's to a university in the cold of Wyoming or to the oil fields of the Middle East—and have little access to familiar ingredients, their cooking is still distinctively Thai, always trying to achieve this balance.

"Hot" means chili *(prik* in Thai); "salty" means fish sauce *(nam pla)* or ordinary salt; "sour" means lime juice or tamarind; and "sweet" is simply sugar, or palm sugar. When you order a plate of *som tam* (green papaya salad) in the market, the person preparing it will offer you a spoonful of the salad just before serving, asking for a final decision about what last-minute adjustments should be made. Many of the condiments set out on a restaurant table are there for the same purpose.

Many of my favorite foods in Thailand fall into a category called *gap glum,* or "drinking foods." Like *tapas* in Spain, *gap glum* are eaten when people get together for a glass of Mekong whiskey, beer, or freshly squeezed orange juice. These dishes stand easily on their own, and they are anything but bashful or bland. *Gap glum* are an important part of Thai food, just as getting together with family and friends for food and drink is an important part of Thai life.

A balance of tastes is essential to the success of most *gap glum. Yam neua,* a popular *gap glum* served all over Thailand, combines grilled strips of beef with fresh coriander, fresh mint, shallots, lime juice, fish sauce, chilies, and a little sugar. Balance is the make-or-break of *yam neua.* Many other *yams,* or "salads," are also in this category. Even if you don't see one offered on a menu, ask for *yam pla muk* (squid salad), *yam het* (mushroom salad), or *yam wun sen* (cellophane noodle salad). *Yams* are usually delicious! To go along with *yams,* order a small plate of sticky rice *(khao neeo),* and then juice or a beer, of course.

Turning Up The Heat

If you are not accustomed to hot food—or even if you are—chilies in Thailand can catch you by surprise. Thai children generally don't get started with really hot food until they are well into their teens, and some Thais never develop a taste for chilies. Consequently, there are many dishes which aren't hot. But most Thais like chilies, and food is generally hotter in the home than it is on the street or in a restaurant. When I first lived in Thailand, my friends would take me on Sundays to visit their relatives. I was, I thought, very accustomed to eating hot foods, but often my lips would be burning so intensely that I would wonder if I actually had a minor burn. I'd then look around at the other people eating, and no one would appear in the least bit uncomfortable.

In Thailand I've had consistently hotter food than I've had anywhere else in the world (with the possible exception of Padang food in Sumatra). The heat source is the tiny yellow chili that the Thais call *prik kee noo.* It comes in red, green, yellow, and orange, and it's about an inch long. It's a very good-tasting chili, but beware of eating an entire *prik kee noo* in one bite. Try *nam pla prik,* the little sauce that is served with fried rice *(khao pad).* With tiny slices of *prik kee noo* floating in fish sauce, it's a great introduction to how good Thai chilies and chili sauces can be. When ordering food, you can try asking for a less hot version by saying *phet nitnoy* (a little hot) or *mai phet* (not hot). If you find yourself with a curry which your first bite tells you is HOT, try not to touch your lips to your food when eating. Notice how most Thais eat hot food: their lips seldom close, as if they were tasting a very hot soup. Mouthfuls of rice will also reduce the heat.

At restaurants where there are a lot of tourists, the food is generally good though not very hot. But the trick to experimenting with Thai food is, of course, not to eat where you see a lot of tourists. Tourist-type food is limited in range, whereas Thai food isn't.

Regional Cuisines

Bangkok, or central Thai food, is only one of several different regional Thai cuisines. The cuisines of the north, northeast, and south are all distinctive and equally delicious. I am very fond of northeastern food—or *ahan essan*. Street food favorites *gai yang* (grilled chicken) and *som tam* (green papaya salad) come from the northeast, as do many of the foods traditionally served with sticky rice *(khao neeo)*. *Essan* food is similar to Lao food: the tastes are more direct, many foods are grilled. *Ahan essan* has become quite popular in Bangkok in the last few years, but the problem for restaurateurs has been how to capitalize on what has been for so long considered poor people's food.

The food of the north, like *essan* food, is generally eaten with sticky rice. Beef and pork are the main meats, and fish is uncommon, as is coconut milk. There is a long tradition of sausage-making in the north, and of homemade cracklings and preserved garlic, and so on. This may sound a little like northern European food, but it's not—the taste is distinctly Thai. Most "jungle curries" are also northern in origin. Where northern food is available, ask for two sauces: one is green, *nam prik num;* the other is red, *nam prik ong*. A simple but delicious meal can be had with these two sauces, a plate of fresh garden vegetables, and a basket of sticky rice.

Southern food—the opposite end of the spectrum from northern food—uses a great deal of coconut milk, and meals tend to revolve around fish and seafood. There is a strong Malay and/or Muslim influence in southern food, as is shown in the use of ground, dried spices. Early in the morning at a market, or even for lunchtime, ask around for a *kanom jeen* stand—easily recognized as it looks like a Thai version of a North American salad bar. You will be served a bowl of *kanom jeen* noodles mixed together with a delicious tamarind-based sauce. From there the rest is up to you: select a few fresh herbs, a slice of tiny eggplant, a little more cucumber . . .

Sampling The Foodstalls

One of the best ways to eat in Bangkok is simply to explore the markets. Twenty years ago this was not the case, as people cooked primarily at home, and markets were for purchasing raw ingredients. But fast food, Thai-style, is now a way of life in Thailand, and a wonderful one at that. Not all markets sell prepared dishes, but ask around and someone will direct you to a market that does. Certain markets specialize in lunchtime preparations, and others in suppertime foods. A bag of this or that (in clear plastic, and tied ingeniously with a rubber band) will seldom cost more than five or ten baht. You can buy a bag of fresh salad vegetables, and another of sticky rice or fragrant Thai rice. Invite a friend, find a nice shady place to sit, and enjoy an excellent Thai meal.

Eating in the market definitely offers the greatest choice and variety of foods—it is, after all, where an increasing number of Thais eat all the time. But then there are also streetside restaurants, and street vendors, and all those wonderful specialized concoctions which sell for one or two baht, and which no one in their right mind would ever bother to prepare at home, even if they knew how. There has at times been talk of restricting Bangkok's street vendors to designated places, and of stricter licensing, a little like the Singapore model. Public outcry, however, has always drowned out those feeble voices.

You will not necessarily find better Thai food by walking into an expensive restaurant. The atmosphere will be different, but the food probably will be. When people prepare something on the street or in the market, they can perfect a single dish in a way that is difficult to duplicate at home or in a restaurant. It is not at all uncommon to see a Mercedes with blacked-out windows drive up to a little night-hawker stand, and for someone dressed to the nines to step out and wait in line for a plastic bag full of curry or *guay teeo* (noodles).

Some last advice before you embark: try everything at least once, and always order small portions. And always leave a little room for what you'll discover around the next corner . . .

nightly boat trip on the river to Rama IX bridge. You must be at the restaurant at 1900 hours to eat, and the boat leaves at 2000 for a two-hour cruise (B50 charge for the boat plus food charge as ordered).

Thewes Food Market: Stroll a short distance from Tha Thewet landing and you'll come to a large food market, where you can purchase fruit or sample some foodstalls.

Krung Thon Bridge Area

Riverside Plaza Hotel, tel. 434-0090, has departures daily to Rama IX bridge, Sun.-Thurs. 2000 to 2245, and Fri.-Sat. 2030 to 2245; costs B50 plus dinner as ordered.

Kanabnam Restaurant (Thai/seafood ◊◊) right at the Sang Hee landing (at Krung Thon bridge), tel. 433-6611, has great Thai food in a pleasant outdoor setting. Because this place caters mainly to Thais, there is a lot of fire-power in the dishes—watch out for flamethrowers like the sour-hot beef salad. Open daily 1100-2330. Several boats belonging to *Kanabnam* are moored nearby—one being a ricebarge. Food is served to you on board before departure; there's no kitchen on the boat. Two departures—1900 and 2000 hours—for the three-hour return trip to Rama IX bridge; there's a B50 boat charge.

Baan Khun Luang (Thai ◊◊) on the east side of Krung Thon bridge (no cross-river boat—take a bus across the bridge, or a *tuk-tuk),* tel. 243-3235. This place can seat up to 1,000 diners; group tours are dropped here by the bus-load, and consequently the quality of the food is not the best. The lunch buffet, however, is a bargain—B90 a person for a huge selection. *Baan Khun Luang's* boats can be chartered by a group; their regular cruise from the restaurant to Rama IX bridge, from 2000 to 2230, costs B50 in addition to food.

Royal River Hotel (Buffet ◊◊), tel. 433-0300, has a ground-floor Chinese/Western buffet (indoors, but close to the river) from 1100 to 1400 hours for B180, and a dinner buffet on the riverside terrace for B300. The *Royal River* has a large cruiser of the same name, which does a B300 buffet-cruise on the Chao Phraya, Saturdays only, 1900-2200.

DEMOCRACY MONUMENT-KHAO SAN ROAD

There are dozens of eateries lining Khao San Road, all serving cheap, basic food—particularly good for Western-style breakfasts and fruit

NEW ROAD-SILOM-SURAWONG RESTAURANTS

NOT TO SCALE

© MOON PUBLICATIONS

shakes. Toward the police station, just down an alley, is a branch of the **Royal India** serving very cheap and tasty Indian cuisine. The New World Department Store, three blocks north of Khao San, has a food center with a variety of cheap food. Around the corner from Khao San, at the Democracy Monument, are some good Thai restaurants catering to public servants who work in the area. **Vichit** on the northeast side of the Democracy Monument serves Thai and Western food—it has low prices, but desserts in this traffic-exposed area are liable to get covered with diesel. Ditto for **Sorndaeng** restaurant, at the southeast side of the monument. If you want something a touch classier, try the places down by Pra Arthit pier (Wang Nar, Ton Pho and Yen Jai restaurants) described in "Dining Along the River."

NEW ROAD-SILOM-SURAWONG

Himali Cha Cha (Indian ◊◊), 1229/11 New Road (actually set in an unmarked sidestreet 40 meters south of Surawong Road), tel. 235-1569, features Northern Indian cuisine, Muglai Muslim, and vegetarian; full range of tandooris, curries, and *kormas*. Reservations recommended for dinner.

Muslim Rendezvous (Indian ◊), 1221 New Road (opposite and north of Soi 38), tel. 233-1010, has plain greasy-spoon decor but good Indian and Thai food at very low prices.

Café India (Indian ◊), 460/8 Surawong Road (opposite the Trocadero Hotel), tel. 234-1720, open 1100 to 2300. There is actually a string of Muslim restaurants from the subcontinent in this location, but Café India has a better atmosphere and service. Offers tandoori chicken, and a good range of vegetarian and non-vegetarian food.

Yoi (northern Thai ◊) lists 322 Silom is their address, but actually this place is down an alley off Silom, about 100 meters on the right, signposted in Thai only, tel. 233-9070. Northern-style Thai food (My God—get me a cold drink, quick!) is the specialty here, with bargain-priced appetizers served in a cafeteria atmosphere.

Coca (Chinese ◊◊), 8 Soi Tan Tawan (the first *soi* west of Patpong 1), tel. 236-9323. Palatial Chinese decor,banquet tables and some smaller tables to the sides. As long as you stay away from the more exotic offerings (sharkfin soup), prices are reasonable.

Dee's (Thai ◊), down Soi 6 off Silom; an open-air Thai hangout with good seafood and plastic tableware. There are hardly any open-air restaurants in the Silom-Surawong area because thousands of swallows make their homes in the eaves of banks and other high-rises around the area, showering the place with a steady rain of bird-goop. Dee's is tucked into a corner immune from direct hits.

Le Cam-Ly (Vietnamese ◊◊◊), Patpong Building 2F, just off Surawong Road, above the 7-Eleven store, tel. 234-0290, open 1130 to 1430 and 1800 to 2200. You wouldn't expect to find such elegance in this neck of the woods, but here it is, complete with a swank decor of bamboo and ceramic jars—and a large tree in the middle (try and work out if it's real or not!). Excellent service.

Trattoria da Roberto (Italian ◊◊◊), Plaza Arcade on Patpong 2, close to Surawong, tel. 233-6851. Excellent food, but pricey. "Roberto" is actually of Chinese descent, and he owns nearby Bobby's Arms (a British pub-restaurant). Perhaps Brasserie de Robert is next?

Thai Room (Mixed ◊), 30/37 Patpong 2, tel. 233-7920. Mixed menu—Thai, Western, even some Mexican dishes. The menu and the greasy spoon decor are explained by the fact that this was a hangout for American GIs during the Vietnam War era. The food is hearty, and the price is right.

Silver Palace (Imperial Chinese ◊◊◊◊◊), 5 Soi Pipat 1 (a short way from Silom Road, and next door to Bangkok Bank), tel. 235-5118, open 1100-1400 (dim sum lunch is served) and 1800-2200. Reputed to be the best Chinese restaurant in Bangkok, and certainly one of the most expensive. Banquets are best—a party of ten people is ideal, with entire banquets costing from B3700-11,000. Culinary exotica includes bird's nest, snow frog, turtle with Chinese herbs, and sharkfin soup.

Bussaracum (Royal Thai ◊◊◊◊), 35 Soi Pipat 2, tel. 235-5160, open 1100-1400 and 1700-2230. Here the emphasis is on presentation—dishes are so beautifully laid out that it seems a crime to eat them. The Bussaracum serves

*streetside foodstall
selling fruit*

Royal Thai food—small portions exquisitely presented with brass cutlery, blue-and-white china crockery, and fired clay pots. Curry spicing has been toned down to suit the tourist palate. Presentation is remarkable: shrimps are presented to look like birds; mushrooms are cut in the shape of turtles; carrots are carved into roses. Fruit and vegetable carving goes back to the days of the royal court when chefs and assistants had ample time for such delicate pursuits. The Bussaracum is quiet at lunch-time, but busy in the evening, when classical music is provided in the background. There's a branch of the restaurant around the corner in the Trinity Complex at 425 Soi Pipat 2; another branch operates in the Dusit Thani Hotel.

Alliance Française Café (Western ◊) Inside the French Cultural Center at 29 South Sathorn Road, open 0700 to 1900 daily. Good for breakfast, light lunch, or afternoon snacks. Limited menu, but a pleasant place to catch up on postcards or have a quiet chat.

Western: There are many Western restaurants in the Silom-Surawong area including Bobby's Arms in the Carpark Building on Patpong 2, serving British food; Angus Steakhouse on Soi Thaniya; El Gordo on Silom 8 (the *soi* opposite Bangkok Bank), serving Mexican food; and Sarah Jane's on Convent Road, offering Italian cuisine. With Western food, expect Western prices.

LUMPINI PARK-SIAM SQUARE

Somboon Seafood (Seafood ◊◊), 22 Soi Chula 60 (near intersection of Rama IV and Phayathai roads), tel. 251-5653, open 1100-2400. This place looks a bit run down, but has excellent fresh seafood, and the best crab curry in Bangkok. Don't be put off by the ground-floor salon that overflows onto the street with customers—Somboon has floor after floor of seating and eating.

Samyan Foodstalls: Close to Somboon Seafood in the Samyan area (Soi Chula 42) are the best seafood streetstalls in Bangkok. East down Rama IV Road, past Lumpini Park, is a cluster of foodstalls outside Lumpini Boxing Stadium.

Pop (Thai ◊), at the north end of Lumpini Park, tel. 252-4015. Open-air dining, 0630 to 2200; good range of ice-creams, sundaes, and northern Thai dishes.

Guan Lee (Chinese/seafood ◊◊), on the corner of Soi Lang Suan and Soi Sarasin, tel. 251-8366. Soi Lang Suan and Soi Sarasin are restaurant and nightlife areas, with many restaurants and clubs. If you head east on Soi Sarasin, there is a string of jazz bars where "drinking food" is served—motorized stalls sidle up to customers sitting at sidewalk tables drinking Mekong whiskey.

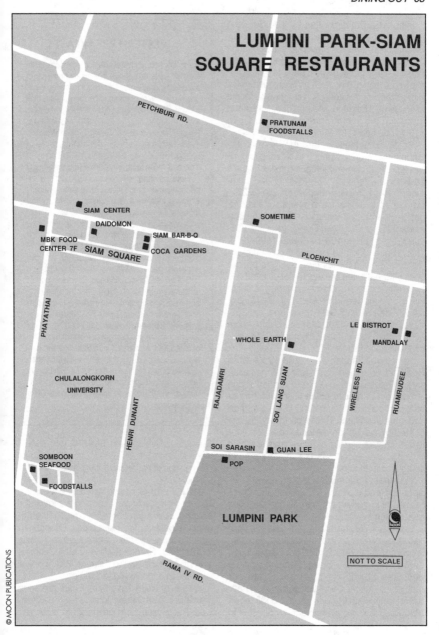

LUMPINI PARK-SIAM SQUARE RESTAURANTS

PETCHBURI RD.

■ PRATUNAM FOODSTALLS

■ SIAM CENTER

DAIDOMON

■ SOMETIME

MBK FOOD CENTER 7F

SIAM BAR-B-Q

COCA GARDENS

SIAM SQUARE

PLOENCHIT

PHAYATHAI

LE BISTROT ■

MANDALAY

WHOLE EARTH ■

CHULALONGKORN UNIVERSITY

HENRI DUNANT

RAJADAMRI

SOI LANG SUAN

WIRELESS RD.

RUAMRUDEE

SOI SARASIN

■ GUAN LEE

SOMBOON SEAFOOD

■ POP

■ FOODSTALLS

LUMPINI PARK

NOT TO SCALE

RAMA IV RD.

© MOON PUBLICATIONS

Whole Earth (vegetarian ◊), 93/3 Soi Lang Suan, tel. 252-5574, vegetarian and non-vegetarian food in pleasant atmosphere. Large range of curries and salads. Excellent tofu replaces meat in many of the dishes; there are imaginative vegetarian dishes such as fried mushrooms with cashew nuts, vegetarian curry with coconut milk. Some Thai food and seafood, and worth trying are the yogurt-and-fruit shakes. Open 1130-1400 and 1730-2400.

Soi Ruamrudee Restaurants: This road has a number of stylish restaurants catering to businesspeople and to the embassy crowd. There's **Le Bistrot** (French ◊◊◊◊◊) at 20/17-19 Ruamrudee Village, Soi Ruamrudee, tel. 251-2523—overpriced, overblown, and overrated food. Opposite Ruamrudee Village is **Mandalay** (Burmese ◊◊◊), at 23/17 Soi Ruamrudee, tel. 255-2893, open daily 1100-1400 and 1800-2230. This is Bangkok's (and Thailand's) only Burmese restaurant—with dishes that look Thai but are quite different in the spicing. Order coconut rice to go with a selection of dishes. Nearby is Bangkok's only Indonesian restaurant, **Bali** (Indonesian ◊◊◊) at 15/3 Soi Ruamrudee, tel. 250-0711, open 1100-2200 Mon.-Sat. and 1700-2200 Sun. It has outstanding curries and saté, and excellent rijsttafel.

Sometime (Italian ◊◊◊), 133/19 Keysorn Road, tel. 253-7604, has seafood done Italian style (Thai style, actually) and a good range of coffees, in a cozy place filled with bric-a-brac, antiques, old lamps and fittings, and art nouveau woodwork. Prices on the menu are quoted by weight for seafood, so watch your wallet. There's a group of restaurants and bars in same area—Moon Shadow (at 145 Keysorn) being similar in idea.

Pratunam Foodstalls: On both sides of Rajaprarop Road (near the Indra Hotel and Pratunam clothing market) are lots of foodstalls, open well into the evening.

Sukiyaki Restaurants: In these cheap places, cooking is done at the table, Asian style. **Daidomon** (◊) 266/13 Soi 3, Siam Square, open 1100-2300, caters to college students and the lunchtime crowd; cheap chicken, prawn, or sashimi set lunch. **Coca Gardens** (◊), corner of Soi 7 and Henri Dunant, tel. 251-3538, open 1030-2230 features a menu entirely devoted to

WESTERN BREAKFAST

Bangkok has some of the top-rated Western food in Asia, but prices are steep because of imported ingredients—although "imported beef" on your menu may mean imported from the next province. Much cheaper are the fast-food chains that are found all over Bangkok—McDonald's, Pizza Hut, and so on. Few of these Western restaurants have been listed here because of space limitations—with such a great array of Thai and Asian food, why bother with the others?

Hotel catering, which is usually superb, is expensive, and comes minus local atmosphere—which is half the thrill of dining out. Many foreigners, however, are reluctant to experiment with breakfast foods. If you have a severe craving for muesli, cereal, toast and jam, or bacon and eggs, try a hotel breakfast buffet—prices plummet for breakfast and lunch and you can generally get a buffet for B150-300 per person before taxes. You can find good breakfast buffets at the Menam Hotel, Dusit Thani (basement), and The Ambassador—to name a few. Bourbon Street, on Sukhumvit Soi 22, features a lumberjack breakfast. Khao San Road has lots of eateries where you can get a Western breakfast or fruit salad, or both. Saigon Bakery at the corner of Convent and Silom sells excellent fresh croissants and pastries; there is a Danish Bakery behind Villa Supermarket on Soi 33/1, Sukhumvit; and there are small bakeries in the Siam Square area.

Chinese sukiyaki. **Siam Bar-B-Q** (◊◊) 414/16 Henri Dunant, tel. 255-2835, open 1100-2300, has a range of barbecue, Japanese dishes, Thai sukiyaki.

MBK Food Center: (Mixed ◊) On the 7th floor of Mahboonkrong shopping complex and Tokyu Department Store, this place is enormous, stretching for half a block. Despite the size, it's always packed, which says something for the food. Great selection of stalls, serving everything from Thai to Asian to Western—all very cheap. Open 1000 to 2100 daily.

Western: Neil's Tavern, on Soi Ruamrudee (near the U.S. embassy) serves steaks and seafood. The restaurants in the major hotels such as the Regent, Hilton, Siam Intercontinental, and Le Meridien President have good Western food.

SUKHUMVIT SOIS 1-21

B&H (Vietnamese ◊◊), 70/1 Soi 1, tel. 254-3390, open 1130-1430 and 1730-2300. Tucked right down the end of the *soi*—elegant decor; dishes can be pricey. You can find better Vietnamese food in Bangkok than in Saigon because chefs in Bangkok can get fresher, higher-quality in-

gredients—better pork, for example.

La Grenouille (French ◊◊◊◊), 220/4 Soi 1, tel. 252-0311. A small, intimate French-managed restaurant—there is an upstairs section.

Akbar's (mixed Indian and middle-eastern ◊◊), 1/4 Soi 3, tel. 253-3479, serves dishes from north and south India, as well as Pakistani and Arabic food.

Moghul Room (Indian ◊◊), 1/16 Soi 11, tel. 253-6989. There is actually a string of Indian, Pakistani, and Arab restaurants along here—some serving excellent vegetarian dishes. The

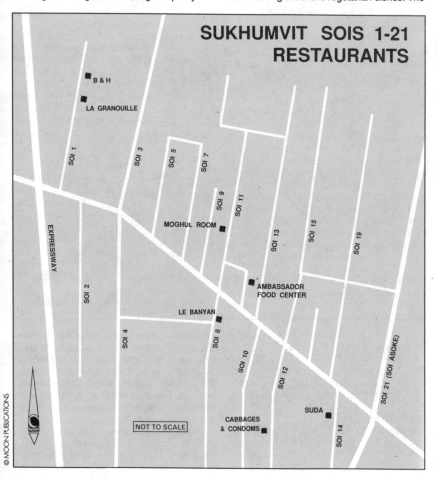

SUKHUMVIT SOIS 1-21 RESTAURANTS

■ B & H

■ LA GRANOUILLE

SOI 1
SOI 3
SOI 5
SOI 7
SOI 9
SOI 11
SOI 13
SOI 15
SOI 19

EXPRESSWAY

MOGHUL ROOM ■

SOI 2

■ AMBASSADOR FOOD CENTER

LE BANYAN ■

SOI 4
SOI 8
SOI 10
SOI 12
SOI 21 (SOI ASOKE)

SUDA ■

SOI 14

NOT TO SCALE

CABBAGES & CONDOMS ■

© MOON PUBLICATIONS

SUKHUMVIT SOIS 21 UP RESTAURANTS

LE DALAT

SOI 21 (SOI ASOKE)

SOI 23

L'OPERA

SOI 33

SEAFOOD RESTAURANT

BAITARL

PAN PAN

FUENG FAH

SOI 39

LAICRAM

SOI 18

SOI 20

SUKHUMVIT

SOI 22

SOI 49

SOI 55

DJIT POCHANA

LEMONGRASS

SOI 24

FOODSTALLS

SOI 38

NOT TO SCALE

© MOON PUBLICATIONS

Moghul Room stands out because of its tasteful decor and wide choice of dishes.

Le Banyan (French ◊◊◊◊), 59 Soi 8, tel. 253-5556, has a charming Parisian ambience—located in a restored mansion, and serving adventurous food with French flair. A gourmet's delight. Open lunch 1200-1400 Mon.-Fri., and dinner 1900-2200 Mon.-Sat.

Ambassador Food Center (mixed/Asian food ◊), on Sukhumvit between Sois 11 and 13, open 1000 to 2300. The walkway leading to the

Ambassador Hotel has caged flamingos, cockatiels, barking deer, toucans from the Amazon, macaws . . . and Bangkok's original food center. An amazing range of food at very low prices—Halal Muslim, Hainan, Vietnamese, Korean, southern Thai, northern Thai, and other self-serve foodstalls. A great place to experiment with Thai and Asian food.

Cabbages & Condoms (Thai ◊◊), about 200 meters down Soi 12 off Sukhumvit, tel. 251-5552, open 1100-2200. You'll find great food at reasonable prices in a relaxed atmosphere. You can eat in the Vasectomy Room or the Condom Room. On sale in the foyer are condom key-chains and safe-sex T-shirts: this place is a fund-raising vehicle for the PDA (next door) which is responsible for birth-control programs and an anti-AIDS campaign.

Suda (Thai/Chinese ◊), on Soi 14 just off Sukhumvit, tel. 252-2597. Cheap, basic Thai and Chinese food, with some sauces that will give you dragon-breath—order lots of steamed rice in this place! No compromise for the Western palate, but still popular with Westerners—which goes to show that Thai food does not have to be toned down to appeal. Try the *yams* (spicy salads), and fried cashews with chicken and curry paste.

Western: There are a number of (expensive) steak houses, beer gardens, pubs, and Western restaurants catering to foreigners living in the Sukhumvit area. These include Jools on Soi Nana Tai, Steak and Lobster on Soi 11, Prime Beef on Soi 13 (behind Ambassador Hotel), and Haus München on Soi 15.

SUKHUMVIT SOIS 21 AND UP

The nocturnal landmark for the intersection of Asoke and Sukhumvit is the giant red neon lobster that graces the **Seafood Restaurant.** That's about all you'd want to say about this seafood supermarket restaurant—fun, but very expensive fun (bills of B800 and up per person are common).

Le Dalat (Vietnamese ◊◊), 47/1 Soi 23, Sukhumvit Road, tel. 258-4192, open 1130 to 1430 and 1800 to 2200. The restaurant is in a converted mansion—two floors in the main building and an outdoor section in the garden (where you may get eaten—by mosquitoes). Can be crowded on weekends—reservations recommended.

Djit Pochana (Thai ◊◊), 62 Soi 20, tel. 258-1597, open 1030-2230. Popular with group tours, so the spices are often toned down to suit. Features a low-priced lunch buffet.

Soi 33 Restaurants: You can't miss down this *soi*—there's a string of good restaurants. **Fueng Fah** (Thai ◊) about 100 meters on the right, at 8/1 Soi 33, tel. 246-2050, just past White Rabbit Restaurant, has good Thai food and seafood in an unpretentious environment, with low prices. Opposite the Fueng Fah is **Baitarl** (Thai ◊◊), at 3 Soi 33, tel. 258-5711, one of the best Thai restaurants in this area. Just north of this is **Pan Pan** (Italian ◊◊◊), tel. 258-9304, with pizza and homemade ice-cream.

Lemongrass (Thai ◊◊◊), 5/1 Soi 24, tel. 258-8637, reservations recommended. In a pleasant converted mansion with decor featuring antiques. Nouvelle Thai cuisine—tasty but small portions; the specialty of the house is fiery southern Thai food. The restaurant is popular with ex-pats, and service can be slow. Open 1100-1400 and 1800-2300 daily.

L'Opera (Italian ◊◊), 55 Soi 39, tel. 258-5605. Open daily 1130-1400 and 1800-2230. Food varies in quality—from delicious pasta to mediocre pizza.

Laicram (Thai ◊◊◊), at 11/1 Soi 49, tel. 392-5864. Hard to find, but worth the trouble, this restaurant features some unusual items such as prawn-tail curry and homemade coconut ice-cream. This gourmet restaurant has been so successful that it has opened two other branches—at 120/12 Soi 23, tel. 258-2337; and at Thaniya Plaza, Silom District, tel. 231-2117. Open daily 1100-2000.

Soi 38 Foodstalls: On Soi 38, just off Sukhumvit, there are excellent foodstalls, especially good for noodles and Thai-style desserts. If you make it alive across Sukhumvit, on the opposite side around Soi 53 is another foodstall area.

Western: There are many European and American-style restaurants in the Sukhumvit area. Among them are: Bei Otto, a German pub-restaurant on Soi 20 opposite the Windsor Hotel; Bourbon Street, a Cajun-Creole pub-restaurant on Soi 22; Angus Steak House on Soi 33 (near Villa Supermarket); The Two Vikings, a Danish restaurant on Soi 35; and The Cedar, serving Lebanese-Greek food, on Soi 49.

SHOPPING

TIPS

Comparing Prices

Shop around for the item you want, and examine goods carefully. Although an item may look the same in different shops, there is great variation in materials and quality of workmanship—which will make a big difference to pricing. Department stores generally have fixed prices, which will indicate the rough value of an item.

Touts

Touts get a 10-40% commission on the purchase price of an item. Thus a taxi-driver may take you only to the gem dealer where he can get a commission—the quality of the goods is not a consideration. Stay away from any kind of tout or shop agent.

Bargaining

After you have researched the pricing for the item you want, you're in a position to bargain effectively. You can generally bargain 10-40% off the asking price, but do this in a pleasant manner. Thais will lose respect for you if you use a loud voice or lose your temper—maintain your sense of humor, and your manners. Department stores have fixed prices, but may offer a discount on expensive items like jewelry or furniture. Try and get any packing included in the price (and for larger items, some of the freight and insurance costs). Prices plummet if you're buying in larger quantities or wholesale direct from factory outlets—but make sure they are real factory outlets.

Payment And Paperwork

For more expensive items, get a full receipt (with proper store address on it, date, full description of goods, price, and so on). For jewelry and antiques, get a certificate of authenticity (this certificate is not a guarantee of quality—it merely states that it's a genuine stone or antique). Once purchased, most items cannot be exchanged or returned, but it may be possible to get a 90-day guarantee with option of full refund for more expensive items.

Payment by credit card provides some basic insurance, since the credit card company can assist in recovering your money and returning the goods in the event of misrepresented goods. The bottom line is that businesses accepting these cards must maintain a certain standard of honesty and integrity. When paying by credit card always specify on the slip whether the amount is in U.S. dollars or in baht (write US$200 or Baht200, for example). Some places will try to charge you up to six percent extra to cover the cost of credit card transactions—this is illegal, but many shops in Asia still do it. When you're bargaining, clarify whether extras will be added. Always keep your credit card within sight when a transaction is being completed—extra imprints can be run off out of sight.

Some exports are not allowed (Buddha images, antique bodhisattva images, some antiques and art objects): if in doubt, make the sale of the item contingent on the shop obtaining an export certificate from Bangkok's Fine Arts Department.

Packing And Shipping

Most shops can arrange for packing and shipping, including the completion of documents such as insurance, customs, and other permits. Try and have packing done right at the store where you purchase an item, and take items with you immediately if possible (to avoid switching of items). Good insurance is essential, and covers you in the event of non-shipment by the shop concerned. For larger items or bulk shipment, several Bangkok companies specialize—try Hong Kong Transpack, tel. 259-0088; and JVK International, tel. 375-2921. For small shipments (weight limit of 10 kg for a parcel), the GPO has a packing section—either they pack it for you, or you purchase the materials from them (box, tape, and so on) and do it yourself for a lower fee.

Complaints

Complaints are handled by TAT, tel. 282-1143/7, or by a branch called Tourist Assistance Center, tel. 281-5051. The Tourist Police, tel. 221-6206/10, can help—if they return with the buyer, the best that can be hoped for is a partial refund (maximum 60-80%, with the remainder claimed by the shop as "expenses"—which may include a commission already paid to a tout). If you paid by credit card, contact the company and inform them of the problem. Another agency that can help is the Consumer Protection Committee, tel. 281-0580. Major fraud is handled by the Police Economic Crimes Division, tel. 234-5808.

Resources

There are a number of specialist guidebooks for shopping, which you can buy in Bangkok. Some of these are: *A Guide to Buying Antiques, Arts & Crafts in Thailand,* by Robin Brown; *A Buyer's Guide to Thai Gems and Jewellery,* by John Hoskin; and *Factory Outlet Shopping,* by Pat Nervo.

WHAT TO BUY

Traditional Crafts

A stunning array of home decor items and furniture is produced by Thailand's artisans, and by factory operations using traditional techniques. Thai craft labor is inexpensive, and the standard is usually excellent—most crafts require painstaking attention to detail. In addition to traditional designs, Thai artisans can produce outstanding copies of Western designs, or custom designs to order. Some of the more popular home decor items are described here.

Wickerware: Thailand's abundant vegetation (reeds, vines, rattan, bamboo, coconut palm) is turned into a profusion of attractive items—baskets, lamps, trays, fans, hats, purses. Rattan and wicker furniture is widely available; try the shops between Sois 43 and 63 on Sukhumvit.

Bronze, Brass, and Pewter: Used for a variety of housewares—vases, cups, plates, and candlesticks. A popular purchase is bronze cutlery—though buyers should be aware that bronze or brass pieces require a silicon coating to prevent them from tarnishing; this does not work fully, however, with pieces that come into contact with liquids. Nickel-plated bronzeware will tarnish less.

Nielloware: This intricate craft of applying etched designs on silver or gold receptacles is thought to be of Portuguese origin—it is mainly used to produce trays, boxes, lighters, vases, or jewelry.

Lacquerware: Of Chinese origin, this painstaking art requires the application of a design during the process of coating an object with seven layers of lacquer. There are two types:

hand-painting umbrellas in northern Thailand

TAT

black and gold, and a distinctive red lacquer-ware—both are used on trays, plates, boxes, bowls, and ornaments. Some lacquerware is inlaid with mother-of-pearl.

Ceramics: Fine ceramics were first produced for export in Sukothai over 700 years ago. Most designs are of Chinese origin; there is a large variety of goods—dinnerware, vases, lamp bases, figurines, water jars, planters. Three popular types are blue-and-white porcelain; Bencharong (made from porcelain decorated with multicolored enamels); and celadon (usually a jade-green color).

Curios: There is really no end to shopping in Bangkok! You can purchase theatre art objects such as papier-mâché *khon* masks, buffalo-hide shadow puppet figures, or dolls in elaborate classical dress. *Kalagas* are bulging tapestries, Burmese in origin, which depict kings and mythical animals—these wall hangings are mass-produced in Thailand, and thus reasonably priced. Villages in Thailand's northern hills supply hill tribe embroidery (used on jackets, cushion covers, and bags) and silver jewelry (bracelets, rings, necklaces and heavy headdresses). Other attractive purchases are hand-painted umbrellas from Chiang Mai, items inlaid with mother-of-pearl or having shells as decoration, delicately handmade artificial flowers, and stylish wood-carvings.

khon *mask*

Fabrics And Clothing

Thai Silk and Cotton: Thai silk has a coarse texture and is heavier than Chinese silk. A test for pure silk is to burn a scrap of the material. Pure silk forms droplets, synthetics vaporize. Because of bright colors and traditional designs, Thai silk is more suited to home decor items than clothing—it is used for pillowcovers, bedspreads, drapery, upholstery, and placemats. Thai cotton comes in many different weights and patterns—100% cotton is great for the tropics and you can have items tailor-made. Dressmakers and tailors buy their fabric from **Pahurat Cloth Market** and nearby **Sampeng Bazaar** in Chinatown—these have a wide variety of local

and imported fabric. Another large market is **Pratunam;** in addition, there are shops specializing in silk and cotton, and department stores usually sell fabric.

Ready-made Clothing: Quantity-wise, there is lots of ready-made, cheap clothing in Bangkok. Quality-wise, the selection is poor, so check for loose stitching (buttonholes, hem, collar) and for fabric and color quality. Zippers will be the first thing to go—check the quality. Designs and colors are mostly for Thais and may look unusual when you get the clothing home. Large sizes are hard to find. Cheap clothing may not be the bargain you think it is—the clothing tends to fall apart after a few washes.

Tailor-made Clothing: Take your time selecting a tailor. Scrutinize the sample racks, and watch out for shoddy workmanship. Tailors are specialized: some do men's suits, others specialize in women's clothing—the skills are not the same.

Clear communication with the tailor is essential. Misunderstandings can arise over material quality, over fittings (get everything written down clearly, have fittings done several times), and over timing (allow extra time for delays). Tailors are not always familiar with Western fashion—try and take along a garment to copy, or at least a photo of what you want. Thai tailors (especially those for women) seem unfamiliar with loose-fitting garments for Westerners and tend to make tight-fitting jackets and so on. Once made, these are difficult to alter—and the last thing you want to wear in a hot, sticky place like Bangkok.

Many places around Bangkok advertise unbelievable deals—things like two suits and three shirts for US$100, ready within 24 hours. You get what you pay for in a case like this—don't expect good quality for that amount of money or that time frame. While an item like a blouse can be made in 24 hours from a single fitting session, a suit might take three or four days to have made up, and might require two or three fittings.

Leatherwork: Working with leather is a new art in Thailand, and craftsmanship and styling are not impressive. The quality of Thai leather it-self is not the greatest—fake leathers are some-times used (fake leather belts are sold in tourist markets, but shops usually have genuine leather). Items for sale include leather shoes, handbags, purses, briefcases, and belts. Items like belts and leather shoes can be custom-made.

Gems And Jewelry

Bangkok is a leading world center for cutting and setting of colored gemstones, with jewelry exports a major foreign-exchange earner. Stones mined in Thailand include rubies, sap-phires, zircons, garnets, and turquoise; there are pearl farms in the south. Because Thailand has largely exhausted its domestic supply of gems, the emphasis has shifted to importing gems and colored stones for cutting and set-ting—rubies and jade, for example, are import-ed from Burma. Thai artisans working with gold and silver are especially skillful. Under con-struction at Surawong and Mahasek Roads is what promises to be the largest gem-dealing center in the world: the 29-story Bangkok Gems and Jewelry Tower.

Buying gems and jewelry is a matter of ex-pertise. If you are not an expert, forget about bargain gem purchases. Canny Bangkok deal-ers know the worth of the goods on the interna-tional market—the best you can hope for is good value for money (which means that *genuine* gems are still much cheaper than in the West). Do not buy gems for the purpose of resale or in-vestment—this will almost certainly backfire.

A high proportion of synthetic stones are now found in Thai jewelry. Even natural gems are heat-treated to enhance their coloring and clar-ity. This process is not deemed fraudulent as it duplicates what could have happened naturally, but this interpretation has been stretched to in-clude the heating of worthless stones from Sri Lanka and their transformation into "sapphires." Instead of Burmese jade, some customers are sold soapstone or green plastic; garnets or spinels are sometimes substituted for rubies. Thai civil law says that the cost of jewelry de-pends on negotiations between buyer and trad-er: it does not require merchants to identify and itemize the products they sell. Unfortunately, a

minority of gem-dealers in Bangkok have ex-ploited this loophole and made fraud their busi-ness. Dishonest shops will only be required to supply a partial refund in the event of rip-off allegations: they pocket the rest and carry on with their business unhindered. Fraudulent sale of gems and jewelry is the major source of com-plaints to Bangkok's TAT office.

To protect yourself, choose a shop carefully, examine goods thoroughly, get a full receipt, ask for a certificate of authenticity, and try and get a guarantee of a full refund within 90 days of purchase. Before making a major purchase, phone TAT to find out if any complaints have been filed against the shop you're dealing with. This "blacklist" is only verbal—no printed list is available. Even shops that are under investiga-tion continue to remain on TAT's printed lists of recommended shops. There is no central or-ganization for jewelry appraisal in Thailand. Un-mounted gems can be certified for a B500 fee at the Asian Institute of Gemological Sciences, 484 Rajadapisek Road, tel. 513-2112, but the in-stitute will not assess pricing.

Caveat Emptor: Even a buyer diligently tak-ing every precaution can get burned. In 1991, an American travel magazine printed a letter from a Californian who had traveled with his wife to Bangkok to buy a sapphire for her wedding ring. The couple comparison-shopped for three days, looked only at establishments listed in the TAT brochure (which supposedly guaranteed quali-ty at competitive prices), and when ready for a purchase, were going to pay by credit card and request a certificate of authenticity from the dealer. As a back-up, they contacted American Express in Bangkok and asked if they could cancel the deal (to be billed on an American Express card) if the stone's U.S. appraisal value differed from the guarantee certificate. They then asked the gem-dealer, Betty Thai Silk and Jewelers Co. Ltd., whether a sale contingent on appraisal in the U.S. and subject to cancel-lation would be acceptable—to which the deal-er replied "yes." The couple paid US$5,515 for a sapphire; when they got it back to the States, it was appraised at US$1,540. Betty Thai Silk and Jewelers refused to acknowledge the fraud or honor the guarantee; American Express could not retrieve the money from the company, but the couple managed to get the difference back from American Express. Moral of the story: be very, very careful when buying gems.

Antiques And Art Objects

The same advice goes for antiques—the dealers know the worth of the goods, so there are very few bargains to be had. Real antiques are expensive and exceedingly rare, and, catch-22, you may not be allowed to take them out of the country. The main trading center for antiques and reproductions in Bangkok is **River City** (next to the Sheraton), with 70-odd dealers located on the 3rd and 4th floors, and shops crammed full of wood, bronze, terra-cotta and stone statuary, and artifacts. Antique pieces may derive from Thailand, China, Laos, Cambodia, Vietnam, or Burma. There is an auction on the first Saturday of every month on the 4th floor of River City—auction items can be previewed up to two weeks beforehand. On the third floor of River City is the Thai Antique Dealers Association, which issues authentication certificates, but will not value an item.

With antiques, even the experts can flounder. A Thai-Chinese sculptor called Yas does such good copies of Khmer pieces that a consultant to the National Museum had trouble distinguishing them from 11th century originals. Yas uses sandstone blocks from northeast Thailand—similar to the stone found at Angkor temples. He breaks the head from a sculpted body (as happened to many of the old sculptures), heats the stone with a hairdryer, and then buries it in the earth for a fortnight to age it. He even puts his signature (discreetly) on his better works! He passes the "antique" sculpture on to a dealer, who employs a Cambodian refugee to spin a yarn about looting from a crumbling Cambodian temple, and the tourist pays several thousand dollars for an "ancient" sculpture.

Reproductions: In the 1980s, the market was flooded with clever fakes, and dealers realized that they were actually in the business of selling reproductions rather than antiques. There are so many fine reproductions in Bangkok that it makes more sense to shop for those (at lower prices) than for "antiques" of dubious vintage. Reproductions are good buys—well-crafted, and great home decorations. Among

the offerings are rosewood furniture, Burmese tapestries, and Chinese and Thai porcelain. Local Thai painters produce excellent work—some do modern themes, others specialize in reproductions of classic murals. Local framing is of high quality, inexpensive, and easily custom-ordered. Buyers purchasing large wood-carvings should be aware that such pieces (particularly those made of newer wood) can crack when introduced into temperate climates.

Export Regulations: There are strict controls over exporting antiques and art objects. All items need an export certificate from the Fine Arts Department of the National Museum, tel. 224-1370, and certain antiques are not allowed out of the country at all. Usually the dealer will arrange the paperwork for a piece being purchased—this process can take up to two weeks. The documentation requires two postcard-sized photographs of the item, and submission of passport and photocopies of passport pages, plus a fee. Fake antiques do not actually need export permits, but airport customs can't tell if they're real or not, so you have to get permits anyway.

Buddha Images: The Fine Arts Department forbids the export of all Buddha images, except for religious or study purposes. Also forbidden is the export of bodhisattva images or fragments (heads or hands). Tiny images, such as Buddhist amulets or very small Buddha statues, may be taken out; mythical figures and animals such as those from the *Ramayana* can be exported. Thais are simply concerned about where the statues will be used: when visiting Europe they have been horrified to discover large Buddha statues used as decorations—one in a hotel hallway leading to a washroom; another in a market, where items of underwear for sale were draped around a Buddha.

Pirated Goods

Pirated cassettes and videos, and copies of designer clothing and watches are on sale cheaply everywhere in Bangkok. Piracy knows no limits in Thailand—well, almost no limits. The pop song "One Night in Bangkok" is supposedly banned in Thailand—but none of the bars on Patpong take any notice of that—they play it regularly (a pirated version, of course). The only

River City, one of the many shopping malls in Bangkok

material that appears to be taboo for pirates is Thai originals. Apparently what they fear here is not the long arm of the law, but "instant justice" meted out in revenge by the original party—which is to say someone may get shot. This will explain why a Western music tape costs B25, but a Thai tape may cost B70.

Threats by the U:S. Government and by European manufacturers have done nothing to stem the massive contravention of copyright and patents by Thai pirates. This includes not just designer clothing, cassettes and video-tapes—it extends to books, comics, computer disks, photographs, trademarks, patents—you name it. It's possible that copies may be seized by customs in your own country because of trademark violation, but it's unlikely customs would stop a single copy coming through. They would, however, balk at 15 "Rolex" watches—some fast talking in order here!

Apart from having the brand name prominently displayed on the item, what the buyer of pirate-ware has to look for is quality. Not all copies are the same quality. There are four grades of fake Lacoste T-shirts, for example. Audio cassettes are not the same—those recorded from compact discs are more expensive. If you want that fake Rolex or Cartier watch to last, test it out after purchase: those made in Taiwan are supposed to have better Seiko innards than the ones made in Hong Kong.

Those contemplating pirate software purchases, take note: Bangkok is rife with computer viruses, some of which are rather nasty.

Fakes have generated some amusing stories—there's one about a Pattaya bargirl who took a Swiss man's genuine Rolex to a few pawnshops—where the item was rejected as a worthless fake. On the reverse side of the equation, a British shopper in Bangkok was startled to find a pair of very low-priced shoes with a label marked Made in England. On the reverse side of this label was the warning: Beware of Frakes.

WHERE TO SHOP

Bangkok is a shopper's paradise: you can shop around the clock, shop till you drop. You can even shop when you're stuck in the traffic—kids come along selling flower garlands and news-papers. There are sidewalk stalls everywhere—so many, in fact, that they're obstructions for pedestrians. Bangkok is famous for its street markets (most of these are introduced in the touring itineraries in this book). Even if you're not interested in buying anything, go along to observe the lively commerce.

Certain shopping streets have clusters of shops selling the same kind of goods—the principle being that shoppers are more likely to go to an area where they can be sure of a purchase.

An example of this is Yaowarat Road in China-town with its string of goldsmiths. Offering air-conditioned comfort but lackluster atmosphere and higher prices are numerous shopping arcades (shopping plazas, shopping complexes) and department stores around Bangkok. A department store may serve to anchor a shopping complex, so the two become one. The two largest department store chains are Robinson's Department Store and Central Department Store—each with five stores in Bangkok. Sogo, Thai Daimaru, and Tokyu Department Stores are Japanese-run. There are many shops attached to major hotels in Bangkok. These places are expensive but tend to be reliable, as their reputation (and that of the hotel) is at stake.

For shopping map locations, see map of Bangkok in the "Maps and Orientation" section. The abbreviation "DS" in the following descriptions stands for "Department Store."

Northern Bangkok

Markets: Chatuchak Weekend Market—on Paholyothin Road, near the Northern Bus Terminal—is the biggest indoor/outdoor market in Bangkok. It is held from 0800 to 1800 on Saturdays and Sundays. You can easily spend several hours getting lost in here. The market has every kind of merchandise—fabric and ready-made clothing, household goods, furniture, foodstuffs, traditional crafts (wickerwork, baskets, bronze tableware, hill tribe items, ceramics, Burmese and Chiang Mai crafts . . .), plants, animals, birds. The best guide to this maze, if you need one, is *Nancy Chandler's Market Map*, which has a detail map for Chatuchak. Good luck!

Arcades/Department Stores: A little further north along Paholyothin Road is Central Plaza—the largest arcade in Bangkok. It's along the route to the airport; Hyatt Central Plaza Hotel is next door.

Banglamphu Area

Markets: At Banglamphu Market on Prasumane and Chakrapong Roads the focus is on retail and wholesale ready-made garments. Khao San Road has many stalls selling crafts, clothing, audio cassettes, second-hand books—carries on into the evening. Opposite Wat Saket is an amulet and Buddha market.

Arcades/Department Stores: New World DS is at 228 Chakrapong.

Chinatown

Markets: Pahurat Cloth Bazaar (cloth, sarongs, saris, Indian jewelry) on Pahurat Road; east of Pahurat is a narrow alleyway called Sampeng Bazaar, selling fabrics, household goods, and office supplies.

Shops: On Yaowarat Road, there are many shops selling jewelry, also gold chains and bracelets (18-karat to 22-karat), purchased by weight with an extra charge for workmanship. Other shops sell Chinese ceramics and herbal medicines.

Arcades/Department Stores: Central DS on Pahurat Road; Cathay DS at 263 Yaowarat; Merry Kings DS at 902 Mahachai.

New Road-Silom-Surawong

Markets: Patpong Night Bazaar, which spills over onto Silom and Surawong, runs from 1900 onward (crafts, Burmese tapestries, clothing, pirated goods).

Shops: The Silom-Surawong-New Road area is the main business district of Bangkok. Running the full length of Silom and Surawong are silk, jewelry, clothing, art and antique shops, craft shops, and tailors. Some of Bangkok's more renowned Thai silk and cotton stores are located in this area: Jim Thompson Thai Silk at 9 Surawong Road; Anita Thai Silk at 294 Silom, and Design Thai at 304 Silom. New Road—from the River City area down to Shangri-La Hotel—has antique shops and boutiques. River City Shopping Complex specializes in antiques and art objects.

Arcades/Department Stores: Oriental Plaza (near Oriental Hotel—antiques, clothing, crafts—50 boutiques on three levels); River City Shopping Complex (near Sheraton—antiques, jewelry, crafts, clothing); Charn Issara Tower (located on Rama IV Road between Silom and Surawong, exclusive jewelry and clothing stores); Robinson's DS (Rama IV and Silom) and Central DS (306 Silom).

Siam Square

Shops: Lots of boutiques, restaurants, and small shops (jewelry, handicrafts, books, audio cassettes, clothing) crammed into the alleys of Siam Square.

Arcades/Department Stores: Opposite Siam Square is Siam Center Building, with several floors of fashion boutiques. Around the corner on Phayathai Road is Mahboonkrong Shopping Complex, with seven floors of emporiums—it merges with Tokyu DS. Both places are popular with young Thais.

Ploenchit-Rajadamri-Pratunam

Markets: Pratunam clothing market, on Raja-praprop Road near the Indra Hotel, has a huge selection of materials and cheap ready-made clothing, with over 300 garment wholesalers, retailers, and exporters.

Shops: From the Rajadamri-Ploenchit intersection, spreading eastward to Sukhumvit, there are lots of stalls and shops (crafts, clothing, tailors, home decor items). Rajadamri, from Ploenchit to Pratunam, is lined with shops and stalls. Bangkok Dolls, 85 Soi Rajatapan, Rajaprarop Road (east of expressway), manufactures dolls and has a doll museum—there's a branch at Peninsula Plaza.

Arcades/Department Stores: The Ploenchit-Rajadamri-Pratunam area is the largest indoor shopping district in Bangkok, with a dozen department stores and arcades found around the Rajadamri-Ploenchit intersection. Just east of the intersection is Amarin Plaza, anchored by Sogo DS; one block south is Peninsula Plaza, anchored by Galleries Lafayette DS; just west is Zen DS in the World Trade Center; to the north are side-by-side shopping centers: The Mall and Rajadamri Arcade, anchored by Daimaru DS. The first two floors of The Mall are dominated by Naraipan, a state-run handicraft emporium with a large selection. Eastward along Ploenchit at Chitlom Road is a giant branch of Central DS.

Sukhumvit Area

Shops: The Ploenchit shopping district continues along lower Sukhumvit, from Sois 1-15, with tailors, craft shops, streetstalls, and so on. Specialty stores in the Sukhumvit area include Celadon House, on Soi 21 (Asoke, north of Sukhumvit)—with an excellent showroom of Celadon pottery; and Corner 43, at the corner of Soi 43 and Sukhumvit, which sells stylish wicker furniture.

Arcades/Department Stores: Landmark Plaza, on the ground floor of the Landmark Hotel between Sois four and six, has excellent bookstores, as well as Asian Mystique, a silk shop. Robinson's DS is on Sukhumvit between Sois 17 and 19.

KAREN WHITE

durian

TRANSPORTATION

ARRIVING IN BANGKOK

Arrival By Land
By Rail: There is a regular train service from Singapore to Bangkok. The full trip takes two days, with train changes in Kuala Lumpur and Butterworth (the stop for Penang). There is no third class on the route, so the train is expensive if a/c, sleeper, and express charges are added in. The train is suited to those who enjoy the romance of train travel and prefer to savour the sights along the way; it's best to plan a few stops to break up the journey.

By Road: There are three road-crossings on the Thai-Malaysian border (at Padang Besar, Betong, and Tak Bai). Most travelers cross by private bus, which runs from Penang (Malaysia) directly across the border up to Hat Yai, then stops at a beach resort like Phuket or Ko Samui before continuing up to Bangkok.

Arrival By Air
Bangkok, Hong Kong, and Singapore are the transport hubs of Asia—served by all major carriers, with frequent connections and cheap onward ticketing. Over 45 carriers fly into Bangkok, with frequent direct and discount flights from Europe, North America, and Australia. However, it is advisable to book well in advance (three months or more, especially for discount fares) as airline bookings can be heavy in the peak tourist months (Nov.-Feb.). The national carrier, Thai Airways International, is highly regarded by travelers.

Customs On Entry
You can bring any amount of foreign money into Thailand, but amounts above US$10,000 in assets have to be declared upon entry. Importation of Thai currency is limited to B2000 per person, or B4000 per family. Duty-free allowances are 200 cigarettes or 250 grams of tobacco, and one litre of wine or spirits. These duty-free items would be greatly appreciated as gifts by Thais. Foreign-brand cigarettes are not allowed to be sold in Thailand, though streethawkers sell them everywhere; foreign-brand liquors and wines are expensive.

Don't be put off by the customs form requiring you to itemize all your stuff in preparation for tax tariffs. Anything that's for your personal use is nontaxable, so don't put it down. Customs is only interested in expensive "gifts" that you may be bringing in. Good quality electronic items are

Sao Ching Cha area

TOURIST TRAFFIC

There were 5.29 million foreign arrivals recorded in Thailand in 1990. Heading the arrivals list were Malaysians, followed by Japanese, Taiwanese, Hongkongers, Singaporeans, Americans, Germans, Australians, British, and French. The most popular tourist destination is Bangkok (with over 35,000 hotel rooms available), followed by Pattaya Beach (over 21,000 rooms) and Phuket (over 14,000 rooms). There were 3.9 million foreign arrivals recorded for Bangkok's Don Muang Airport; the remaining 1.39 million visitors were mainly cross-border arrivals (largely Malaysians on weekend or longer visits), arrivals at other airports in Thailand, and the odd arrival by cargo ship (at Klong Toey) or cruise ship (at Pattaya). To ease the airplane traffic jam at Bangkok's airport, authorities are encouraging direct flights into other parts of Thailand. There are flights from Singapore, Hong Kong, and Kuala Lumpur direct to Hat Yai, Phuket, and Pattaya; a few overseas charter flights also fly to these destinations as well as to Chiang Mai; Bangkok Airways has a flight from Chiang Mai to Pagan in upper Burma.

expensive in Thailand, so if you have something like a laptop computer, customs may want you to guarantee that you'll be taking out the same item when you leave the country. Officially, you're only supposed to bring in one still camera (plus five rolls of film) or one movie camera (plus three rolls of movie film), but unofficially, nobody really gives a hoot.

Logistics

Flights into Bangkok can arrive at two in the morning. It is rather unnerving to arrive in a big city—any big city—at this hour but, armed with the right information, you should do fine. The International Passenger Terminal at Bangkok's **Don Muang Airport** has extensive facilities—a bank (with good exchange rates), hotel booking office, transport counter, duty-free shops, post office, several dining areas, and a TAT counter (tourist information, brochures). There's a Left Luggage Room which charges B20 per item

per day, with maximum storage up to three months. If arriving at two in the morning, go to the hotel booking counter at the airport to reserve a room—this ensures that the hotel will be open when you arrive. Right opposite the international terminal is the Airport Hotel, with rooms in the B2000 range.

Transfers Into Bangkok

The international airport is 20 km to the north of the city; the domestic airport is just south of the international terminal. A ride into Bangkok, depending on the time of day, will take 45 minutes (taxi) to 1 1/2 hours (bus).

Transport Service Counter: The ground floor of the International Passenger Terminal has a Limousine Service counter offering "limousines" for B300 to downtown hotels. These look and act like regular taxis; the only difference is that they sign you in and out. Two, three, or even four passengers can split the fare. You can also get a seat on a minibus for B120 pp (with direct hotel drops), or a shuttle-bus for B60 to the Asia Hotel (located north of Siam Square). There's a direct bus to Pattaya for B200 pp, leaving several times a day.

Taxi: There is a public taxi stand south of the arrival hall. A ride into town is B180. Make sure your taxi has yellow plates and a rooftop taxi sign. Cheaper taxis (B120-180 depending on destination) can be flagged down on the highway in front of the airport. Make sure you negotiate rates before getting into the vehicle; it is not customary to tip taxi-drivers.

Train: You can take a hike over the highway adjacent to the airport via a footbridge, and head south 100 meters to Don Muang Station. From here to Bangkok's Hualampong Station it takes 45 minutes, and there are no traffic delays. Trains usually operate from 0600 to 2200 (earlier or later departures are possible); cost is B5 diesel train, B25 rapid train, and B35 express.

Local Bus: Passengers can walk to the bus stop on Vibhavadi Rangsit Highway. Maximum fare on air-con buses is B15. To get to the Banglamphu area (Khao San Road) take a 59 bus or 3 air-con bus to Democracy Monument. The 4 air-con bus runs past the Erawan Hotel (Pratunam area) and then down Silom (within striking distance of the Malaysia Hotel). The 13 air-con bus goes down to the Erawan Hotel, then swings eastward all the way along Sukhumvit to the Eastern Bus Terminal.

INTERNATIONAL DEPARTURE

Airline Ticketing
For a complete current listing of airline addresses, refer to the Yellow Pages for Bangkok (there are two entries—Air Travel Ticket Agencies, and Airline Companies).

Unusual Connections
Kunming (China) on CAAC (also known as China Southern Airlines) once a week (you can get a visa for China in Bangkok without too much trouble); Ho Chin Minh City (Saigon) on Air France, Thai International, or Hang Khong Vietnam; Hanoi direct on Hang Khong Vietnam; Phnom Penh on Air Cambodia (very expensive); Vientiane direct on Lao Aviation or Thai International. Inquiries for Hang Khong Vietnam and Lao Aviation go through Thai International, tel. 233-3810.

Ticket Agents
Some Bangkok travel agents do not have a good reputation. Put your money down only when you have a confirmed ticket in hand, have checked all the details and restrictions on that ticket, and have checked the airline's reservation list. There are a number of discount travel agencies on Khao San Road and around the Malaysia Hotel. The Khao San Road agents operate lots of private buses and minibuses running toward Malaysia, or on to Penang.

Red Tape
Get to the airport well ahead of time as security checks are elaborate. Take into account that you can get stuck in traffic on the way to the airport, unless it's before 0630. Departure tax for international flights is B200 (for Thai nationals and permanent residents, it's B1000). Anyone who has a work permit or assessable income in Thailand is required to have a tax clearance certificate from the Revenue Department: failure to produce this document will mean not being allowed to leave.

AIRLINES

Aeroflot tel. 233-6965/7

Air France tel. 233-9477

Air India tel. 256-9614/8

Air Lanka tel. 236-9292/3

Alitalia tel. 233-4000/3

Bangkok Airways tel. 253-4014/6

Bangladesh Biman tel. 235-7643

British Airways tel. 236-0038

CAAC (China Southern Airlines) tel. 235-6510

Canadian Airlines tel. 255-5862/6

Cathay Pacific tel. 233-6105/9

China Airlines tel. 253-5733

Egyptair tel. 233-7601/3

Finnair tel. 251-5012

Garuda tel. 233-0981/2

Japan Airlines tel. 233-2440

KLM tel. 235-5155/9

Korean Air tel. 234-9283/9

Lufthansa tel. 255-0370/1

Malaysian Airlines tel. 236-5871/5

Northwest Orient tel. 253-4822

PIA tel. 234-2961/5

Philippine Airlines tel. 233-2350/2

Qantas tel. 236-0102

Royal Brunei tel. 234-0007

Royal Jordanian tel. 236-0030

Royal Nepal tel. 233-3921/4

SAS tel. 253-8333

Singapore Airlines tel. 236-0440

Swissair tel. 233-2935/8

Thai Airways tel. 233-3810 international, and 280-0070 domestic

Tradewinds tel. 255-2884/7

United tel. 253-0558

INDOCHINA OPENS UP

For the first time in over 30 years, Indochina is accessible to group tours and individual travelers. Bangkok is the gateway to Indochina—with regular flights to Saigon, Hanoi, Vientiane, and Phnom Penh. There are also less frequent flights between these cities—Vientiane to Phnom Penh, and Hanoi to Vientiane, for example. Travel in Indochina can be a frustrating experience for those on their own, mostly because of bureaucratic obstacles. This makes a trip to Vietnam not what you'd call a vacation—it's better described as an adventure. It has poor facilities, poor transport, and poor communications; even so, authorities and locals are prone to overcharging foreigners.

Money

While in Bangkok, stock up on U.S. cash. Take lots of small bills ($1, $5, $10, $20) as cash dollars are the unofficial hard currency in Indochina—and make the wheels turn quickly. Off the track in Indochina there may be problems with traveler's checks—you can cash them easily in Saigon or Hanoi, but may have trouble elsewhere. Therefore carry some larger U.S. bills (some travelers carry everything in cash for Indochina). Credit-card companies (nor any other companies) from the U.S. cannot do business in Vietnam, under the Trading with the Enemy Act. Though U.S. Express travel checks can be cashed, it is preferable to have traveler's checks of UK origin, such as Thomas Cook or Barclay's Bank checks. At the moment, American Embassy officials in Bangkok say that no more than US$100 worth of Vietnamese merchandise for personal use and put in accompanying baggage may be taken back to the U.S.

Visas

The initial visa is expensive—US$100 and up in Bangkok. The visa must be obtained through a travel agent—you cannot apply directly to the Vietnamese or Lao embassies in Bangkok for a visa, except if you're going on business. The cheapest visas come from the agents along Khao San Road. Other agents are sprinkled around the city, and some have better connections than others, so deals vary. More expensive, but well connected, is MK Ways on Wireless Road. Shop around—some agents will provide a cheap package of visas and air tickets.

Allow about five working days in Bangkok for a visa to either Vietnam or Laos. Both visas are valid for about two weeks from date of entry (the Vietnamese visa starts running from the date of issue, but will take into account your expected entry date). Visas are renewable once in Vietnam or Laos. Cambodian visas cannot be issued in Bangkok—a telex will be sent to Cambodia via the travel agent, and you will get the visa stamped into your passport on arrival (allow five days in Bangkok for the paperwork). However, you can pick up a cheap Cambodian visa in person in Vientiane, Hanoi, or Saigon.

Unless you're in a tearing hurry, it's only necessary to pay through the nose for the visa of the first Indochinese destination. Once in Indochina, you can get the next visa much cheaper. In Hanoi you can get a Laotian transit visa valid for five to seven days for US$15 cash, usually within a day. Coming from Laos, you can pick up a Vietnamese visa in Vientiane for US$15 cash, valid for two weeks. In Saigon you can get a Cambodian visa for US$15 (including a Vietnamese reentry permit), but it will take about five to seven working days to come through.

Itineraries

Your Vietnamese visa is automatically valid for Saigon (Ho Chi Minh) and Hanoi—travelers usually start out in Saigon because it's easier to get onward travel permits there than it is in Hanoi. There are no restrictions on your movements in either Saigon or Hanoi: you can stay at the hotel you prefer—some guesthouses are as cheap as US$7 a night. The most popular routing for Indochina is: Bangkok-Saigon-Hanoi-Vientiane-Bangkok. Allow at least two weeks for this route; a month would be more reasonable. Some details: Bangkok to Saigon flights are US$150; an optional Saigon to Phnom Penh return sidetrip costs US$90 return flight; Saigon to Hanoi overland by train (foreign price) is US$45/seat or US$120/sleeper; you can also do the trip by rented minibus with a small group, stopping at towns like Hue and Dalat along the way if you have permission; Hanoi to Vientiane flights cost US$130; from Vientiane you can cross the Mekong by boat to Nong Khai, and go overland back to Bangkok very cheaply. In Vietnam, beware of confusing travel regulations and permits: travelers have been fined US$100 cash by provincial police for purported violations of travel rules.

continued on next page

INDOCHINA OPENS UP, cont.

Laos, just across the Mekong, has a lot in common with Thailand—similar cultural background, similar customs, similar language (you can speak Thai in Vientiane, and use Thai baht). Laos is Thailand without the bustle—a sleepy backwater.

The trickiest destination in Indochina is Cambodia. Flights directly into Phnom Penh from Bangkok are ridiculously expensive. However, from Vientiane you can fly one-way into Phnom Penh for US$130, and from Saigon you can fly to Phnom Penh (US$45 one-way, or US$90 round-trip). Once in Phnom Penh a reentry visa for Vietnam is easy to arrange. Travelers use this sidetrip to extend their time in Vietnam.

Angkor Wat

Angkor Wat is the prized destination of Indochina—indeed, of Southeast Asia—and the Cambodians know it. Anything to do with Angkor is very expensive. Most agents try to talk you into a one-day pack-age tour from Phnom Penh for US$250 (flights, guide, transport, entry-fees), but you spend only a short time at Angkor. Extended time is US$50 a day extra. Travelers have gotten to Angkor on their own, through bribery: you can fly into Siam Reap for US$90 and pay officials US$100 under the table so they will leave you alone and let you wander around for a few days. Be wary though—Angkor is close to guerrilla activity, and the area around Angkor is mined, so don't stray from the ruins. Exiting Cambodia, it's possible to go from Phnom Penh overland to Saigon. The local bus is a few dollars, but it's infrequent and packed—it's more likely that you'd get together with other travelers and rent a minibus for about US$40 a head. The road trip from Phnom Penh to Saigon takes about six hours straight through—but you may be dropped at the border and have to wait for onward transport. There has been talk of starting up a direct flight from Bangkok to Angkor Wat.

Export of Buddha or bodhisattva images or fragments is forbidden. Exporting antiques, reproductions, or art objects requires proper documentation—see section on antiques under "Shopping." Visitors are allowed to take only a small amount of Thai currency out of the country—currency can be converted to U.S. cash at the airport banking facilities.

GETTING AROUND BANGKOK

The fastest and most pleasant way of getting around Bangkok is along the Chao Phraya River—gets you away from the pollution, though not necessarily the noise. For information on getting out of Bangkok to destinations like Ayuthaya, refer to the "Excursions from Bangkok" chapter.

WATER TRANSPORT

Bangkok's commuter craft include express boats and cross-river ferries on the Chao Phraya, and longtailed boats that operate up and down major *klongs*. These vessels may or may not leave from the same landings. Sometimes landings are adjacent to each other—one landing for express boats, the second for longtailed boats.

Chao Phraya Express Boats
The Chao Phraya Express Boats *(rua duan)* run from Wat Rajsingkorn (downstream from Menam Hotel) in the south to Nonthaburi in the north. For landings from the southern terminus to the Krung Thon Bridge, see the map accompanying the "Along the River" tour. Different vessels hold 40, 60, or 90 seated, and upwards of 50 standing. Boats run about every 20 minutes; there are 38 stops along the 18-km route on the Chao Phraya. The riverboats do not automatically stop at each landing—they may only make a stop if there is a demand, so to make sure the boat will stop where you want, tell the ticket-collector, or push a buzzer at the back of the boat to inform the "pilot." Fare is B3 to B8, depending on distance. Hang on to your ticket as it may be requested at the other end, and inspectors may board the boats. Passengers should be aware that none of the express boats or longtails have any safety equipment, and that they are frequently overloaded during peak hours.

Red Flag/Green Flag Express Boats: Although every ferry says "Express Boat," the fastest are the red-flag express boats, which run intermittently during peak hours. Red flag expresses have a triangular red flag flying at the stern, stop at only half the landings along the

route, and cost one baht extra for the ride. There are also a few green flag expresses that run a little north of Nonthaburi to Pak Kred. The red-flag express service operates from 0630 to 0830 and from 1600 to 1800 except on Sundays. If a red flag express happens to pass your stop, just get off and wait for a regular express boat which stops at that landing.

Cross-river Ferries
These ferries *(rua kham fak)* operate from piers adjacent to most express boat landings; rides cost one baht. These are connectors or "bridges" serving the Thonburi side, since the Chao Phraya express boats don't stop much on that side. In addition to the cross-river boats near Chao Phraya landings, there are other junctions up and down the river that cope with busy points. One of these is Tha Prachan near Thammasat University. Tha Prachan is not a Chao Phraya express boat stop; it has three cross-river trips that head in different directions—one to Prannok, another to Siriraj Hospital, and a third direct to Pra Pinklao landing. Two other landings that only have cross-river boats: River City landing, and the landing at the foot of the Shangri-La Hotel.

Longtail Boats
Longtails *(rua hang yao)* are shallow-bottom boats with enormous engines at the rear designed to negotiate the narrow *klongs*. They're called longtails because of the long propeller that extends off the engine (they could also be called "long-nosed boats"). Longtails seat about 30 to 40 passengers; wider versions can seat up to 70. Fixed routes cost B3-15, according to distance. To get the longtail to stop at an upcoming pier, raise a high-school hand, and pay after you alight. See "The Left Bank" tour for a map of routes and more details.

Longtail piers are adjacent to Chao Phraya Express Boat piers. All the commuter longtails operate to left bank destinations except for one: a service along Klong Saensaep from Wat Saket to Bang Kapi (northeast, near Ramkamheng

University). It takes 50 minutes to cover the entire route, and charge is B5-15 depending on distance. There are 34 stops along the way, mostly near bridges that cross the canal. For stops on the initial part of the route, see map accompanying "Siam Mystery Tour."

Small Craft Rentals

Longtails can be rented from the same piers as commuter longtails for B100-300 an hour: the lower rate comes from having a smaller group, going out for a longer period (say three hours), and bargaining very hard. Keep repeating the negotiated price, and write it down on paper to confirm it—boatmen have been known to "misunderstand" and later demand higher rates. Never go out in a longtail alone.

Better than a longtail is a motor launch *(rua yon)* holding up to ten passengers. It chugs along at a canal-viewing speed, and doesn't throw up a lot of spray.

Hotel Boats

The major hotels have motor launches, longtails on tap, craft resembling the Chao Phraya Express Boats (but fitted with reclining seats), and converted ricebarges for touring the Chao Phraya and the canals. For longer tours, such as trips to Ayuthaya, there are large air-con cruisers such as the *Oriental Queen* and the *River Sun*. The Shangri-La Hotel has a spectacular red barge with golden *nagas* mounted up front, as on the royal boats.

Hotels have their own shuttle-boats for hotel guests only, but there are a few free services. From the Oriental landing, there's a free shuttle to Suppakarn Condominium complex. The River City pier is used as a launching site for many tour groups. Regular shuttles are operated to River City pier by the Oriental (every 15 minutes), Shangri-La (hourly), the Menam (hourly) and the Royal River Hotel (every two hours), usually from around 0800 to 1900 hours.

LAND TRANSPORT

As in most countries in Asia (except China), traffic moves on the left in Thailand. All passenger vehicles in Bangkok have yellow plates, except for hotel-compound taxis and passenger motorcycles (both have white plates). Registered taxis have a taxi sign mounted up front (lit up at night) and yellow plates. Do not accept rides from other vehicles as they may not carry proper insurance, and may pose a security problem.

Buses

Bangkok Mass Transit Authority operates a comprehensive bus network with rock-bottom fares. In most places you only have to wait 10 or 15 minutes for a bus, though certain routes have been known to have 25-minute waits. Buses are jammed in peak hours, and pickpockets have been known to operate under such conditions (to avoid them, keep to the front of the bus). Thai women complain of being handled by men under crowded conditions, which has resulted in the idea of having special buses just for women. It's hard to decipher routings from a regular bus map—get a bus-guide booklet. Buses have one advantage over the rest of the traffic: they have their own lane running the wrong way down a one-way street during peak hours!

Air-conditioned buses are blue, have more comfortable seats, and charge B5-15, depending on distance. Regular buses are blue-and-white (B2) or red-and-white (B3)—the only difference is that the red-and-white versions have automatic doors and are supposed to be newer. There are usually fans on board. Certain "express" buses charge up to B6. Running along the same routes as the a/c and regular buses are green minibuses, which charge B2 a ride. These are operated by small businesses which belong to a bus association, and are supposed to pick up passenger overflow from the regular bus system, particularly during rush hours. Buses generally run 0500 to 2300 hours; there are some routes with all-night service.

Taxis And *Tuk-tuks*

Hotel Taxis: These have white licence plates and a rooftop taxi sign. They charge up to double the cost of street taxis, and there are usually fixed rates, which are posted in the hotel lobby. The drivers usually speak some English. The taxis can also be rented by the hour or by the day.

Street Taxis: These have yellow plates, as do most passenger vehicles in Bangkok, plus a rooftop taxi sign, and can be flagged down on the street.

None of the taxis in Bangkok have meters, so everything (except for hotel taxis) must be negotiated. Never get into the cab until you have agreed on a price—the method of negotiation is to hold up the appropriate number of fingers, with prices proceeding in multiples of ten baht. Taxi fares are from B50-100; for really long rides, such as crossing town from one end to the other, the fare could go up to B120; a trip to the airport costs B150-180 including a B10 expressway toll. Taxi drivers will size you up from what you're wearing, how good your Thai is, how gullible you look—and what your destination is. For example, if your destination was the Oriental Hotel, the first fare quoted would be a ridiculous B200; if you said the Oriental ferry pier, that price would drop considerably. Taxi drivers are always short of change or slow to give it, so if you are using taxis frequently, carry lots of change (B20 and B50 bills are useful). It's not necessary to tip a taxi-driver, and there are no extra charges for driving at night. You should, however, make upward adjustments in the fare if your taxi has been caught in traffic for a long time.

For longer rides, street taxis are preferable to tuk-tuks because you get insulation from noise and diesel fumes, tinted glass, and a degree of comfort and privacy. And air-conditioning! If you have a number of stops you want to make, you might consider hiring a taxi or tuk-tuk by the hour—it will be cheaper and more convenient. A lot of taxi and tuk-tuk drivers act as agents for shops and massage parlors—they get a cut if they deliver a customer. If offered any of these, decline firmly but politely.

Tuk-tuks: Cheaper than the taxis are tuk-tuks. A tuk-tuk is a cross between a motorcycle, a bumper car, and a lawnmower—and the drivers are schizoid about it too (sometimes they careen around a corner on two wheels instead of three). These chariots have elaborate chromework decorations with dragons and metal roses, icons to appease the gods of the traffic, and an array of popping lights that seem to have little function except to add to the fairground bumper car effects.

Negotiating strategy for tuk-tuks is similar to that for taxis. Tuk-tuk drivers can be difficult to negotiate with—they will invariably mumble something about "one way" and point at a watch: sometimes you can get a regular taxi for 20 baht more. If you can't agree on a price with a tuk-tuk driver, put in your final bid, and start walking off slowly in the direction of the traffic flow—the driver may move alongside and indicate he has accepted your price, in which case you jump in. Fares range from B30-80; you might have to pay more for a peak-hour ride. An average ride is B50. These chariots are not recommended for longer rides if you value your lungs and your eardrums (and your posterior: tuk-tuks have next-to-no suspension). Some rumors about tuk-tuk drivers: because of long shifts, drivers have been known to take drugs to stay awake; and there seems to be a correlation between the fare paid and the speed of the tuk-tuk (that is, the lower the fare, the higher the speed to make up the time).

Most of the time, tuk-tuk and taxi drivers will practically run you over trying to get your business. However, it is extremely difficult to find a taxi or tuk-tuk around 1530 or 1600, when most of them are heading back to a central depot as their shift ends. Very few taxi or tuk-tuk drivers own their vehicles, and they're fined if they're late getting back. This will explain why they will refuse to take you for any price if you're not headed in the direction of the taxi depot.

Language Problems: Taxi and tuk-tuk drivers on the streets speak limited English. Try to have your destination written out in Thai script—perhaps get a hotel clerk to write up a series of destinations in Thai for you on business-size cards. To get back to your hotel, make sure you have a hotel card with Thai script on it. Bilingual maps are useful when dealing with taxi-drivers—you can point to the Thai characters. Be imaginative—you'll draw a blank if you tell a taxi-driver you want the "TAT office"—but if you hold up your fists, mime kick-boxing and say "Rajadamnern," a driver will know exactly where you want to go—to Rajadamnern Boxing Stadium, which is right next door to the TAT office. Most of the tuk-tuk and taxi-drivers are boxing fans! If you have trouble explaining your destination, pick a wat nearby, or a large hotel, or

DRIVING IN BANGKOK
by Geoff Flack

For the hardy—or the foolhardy—there are many car-rental outlets in Bangkok. Driving in Bangkok is not recommended for relaxation; however, for out-of-town day-trips or overnight journeys, driving is pleasant enough (for more details, refer to "Excursions from Bangkok"). The following notes on driving in Bangkok may be used indirectly by pedestrians and vehicle passengers: draw your own conclusions, and make allowances for Bangkok Rules.

Vehicle Rentals
There are car and motorcycle rental agencies all over Bangkok—you will find a number of them in the Sukhumvit area and others listed in tourist brochures and in the Yellow Pages (a dozen pages of ads under Automobiles—Renting & Leasing). Avoid the smaller places that have only one or two cars—if there's a mechanical problem, they may not be able to replace your car.

An international driver's licence is required; you must also show your passport (a xerox copy of the initial pages will be taken, but *do not* surrender the passport) and a credit card (a blank imprint is taken). Most rental cars have standard transmission only. Make sure you get a car with seat belts and air-conditioning, and tinted windows if possible. The insurance form is usually in Thai only, with an accident deductible of B2000 (payable in advance, in cash; it will be refunded if you are not in an accident). Make sure you get a contact number from the rental agency in case of an accident, as someone may have to come out to a police station if you are negotiating damages. You are only given one key, and often the agency doesn't keep back-up keys, so if renting for a longer period, make extra sets of keys! The gas tank will be practically empty when you get the car—find out where the nearest gas station is, and drive there immediately. There are big savings on rented cars for longer periods (say a month), but it's best to test the car out for a few days to see if you can handle the traffic before deciding on a long-term rental. You can also get off-season rate reductions.

Problems
There are two major problems: driving, and knowing where you're going. It's very difficult to perform both functions at the same time. This is true of any major city, but in Bangkok the situation is compounded because there are so many one-way streets, overpasses, ramps, freeway exits and entrances, and because you have to keep changing lanes (you may have to charge across five lanes of traffic to make a turn). If you're doing the driving yourself, you either worry about driving and miss your turn-off, or you worry about making your turn and you smash into somebody. So you really need a navigator.

Certain quarters of Bangkok are labyrinths—the back-*soi* "shortcuts" are best left to experienced maze-masters. In fact, avoid backstreets altogether—they can result in dead ends. Chinatown should be avoided at all costs—the area is crowded with shoppers and small trucks making deliveries. There are scores of one-way streets, and canals in the area make navigation difficult because you have to find a bridge to cross a canal. Thonburi is a zoo—it's riddled with canals and it's very easy to get lost there. If you get well and truly lost, pay a taxi driver to lead you out.

A big problem for North Americans is driving on the left—in a panic situation you may use right-hand reflexes instead of left-hand ones. The driving "rules" are different, too. You are actually expected to perform U-turns at certain places to get past concrete median strips. Traffic does not necessarily keep to lanes, either—*tuk-tuks* and motorcycles do not occupy entire lanes, giving larger vehicles their only chance to push in (*tuk-tuk* drivers expect you to squeeze in). Motorists fight for every meter in the peak hour. The motorist's greatest fear is running out of gas while stuck in Bangkok traffic, but nobody turns off their engine in a rush-hour traffic jam in case there is a minuscule gain to be made. That means cars can sit there idling for forty minutes or more, and after a while you start to get giddy from the fumes.

When you finally reach your destination, there's usually no parking. In certain areas, Bangkok residents cannot find parking near their own homes—and they know every backstreet and alley. Sometimes they have to park up to a kilometer away and walk. The richer folk have off-street parking spots within housing compounds. There are such things as paid parking lots, but they're few and far between.

You will also encounter attendants in uniform who direct you to regulated parking outdoors (such as in the Siam Square area), and who expect a B10 or B20 fee. In other areas there are unofficial "attendants" who also expect a fee—to make sure your car doesn't have its windshield wipers ripped off, or scratches down the paintwork when you return. It's best to pay the small fee for this "protection."

You rarely see a tow-truck on the streets of Bangkok, but if a car is towed, it will probably be taken to the closest police station. Regulations change frequently—confusing parking regulations may lead to a tow-away. On Asoke Road (Soi 21 off Sukhumvit), for example, parking regulations stipulated that you could park on one side of the road on alternate days—but nobody could figure out which side on which day.

Special Hazards

There appear to be few restrictions on drinking and driving, although officially the two are not mixed. Drag-racing takes place on drunken weekend evenings along Sukhumvit Road—Mercedes versus Mercedes, *tuk-tuk* versus *tuk-tuk,* or motorcycle versus motorcycle. The speed limit in Bangkok is supposedly 60 km/hr, but nobody pays much notice, and traffic policemen urge cars along expressways at much higher speeds. Seat-belts are usually only found in the front seat and most macho Thais don't wear them. During the rainy season, visibility can be very poor, and during heavy flooding the road and a nearby canal (or ditch) cannot be easily differentiated. Unless you want to end up in a canal, it's better to park the car and wait till the rain eases off.

Hopefully you won't have an accident, but if you do, it's very important to choose whom you have an accident with. It's much better to have an accident with a cheaper second-hand car than it is to crash into a Mercedes driven by a police general. Avoid accidents with army personnel above the rank of colonel. Most Thai drivers do not carry insurance: minor traffic accidents are settled on the spot between drivers; other accidents are settled at the nearest police station. Taxi and *tuk-tuk* drivers are prone to taking off from the scene of an accident, and hit-and-run accidents are on the rise. I once saw a truck-driver come out of a sidestreet onto Sukhumvit and smash into a motorcyclist, flipping him through the air. The truck screeched to a halt, then turned around to take off. Dragging a limp leg, the motorcyclist leapt onto the back of the truck as it disappeared down a *soi.*

Other than at an accident, you will rarely encounter police in Bangkok. If you have been at fault, and are pulled over, you may be allowed to pay an on-the-spot "fine" of B100-200 and depart.

Motorcycles are one surefire method of beating the traffic.

the nearest large intersection. This will get you into the general area and you can direct the driver from there.

Other Transport

Taxi-bikes: For those with nerves of steel and good life insurance, riding pillion on a motorcycle is the way to go. There are flying squads of riders on many street corners—easily identified by their bright jackets or waistcoats with a number on it. No helmet is provided for you, and it is dubious whether any insurance is involved (this motorcycle service has yet to be recognized by the law in Bangkok—the operators have white plates, not commercial yellow ones). Helmets are not mandatory in Bangkok.

The number of motorcycle operators has mushroomed over the last few years because Bangkokians have become fed up with traffic jams. You can cross the entire city in peak hour in an amazing 25 minutes on a motorbike, darting through holes in the traffic, weaving through a maze of fenders, grills, rear-view mirrors, and other chromework (watch your kneecaps). There are estimated to be over 20,000 taxi-bikes in the city. Fares are cheap—B10 for short rides; B20-40 for longer trips—about 30-40% lower than taxi fares. If there are two passengers, no problem—all three of you get on the bike. No research on the casualty rates, but motorcycle accidents are commonplace in Bangkok. Put it this way: if you stay in Bangkok for a few months, you are bound to witness half a dozen motorcycle accidents. This has got to be one of the few places in the world where motorcyclists have head-on collisions. Cycle operators wanting to pass a line of cars sometimes pull out abruptly to the center of the road—and can hit oncoming motorcyclists. In one case, this occurred at the crest of a hill, with riders approaching from opposite directions.

Songtaos: These are pick-up trucks with two long seats; they're privately operated, and charge about the same as buses. You can flag one down or get off anywhere along a fixed route. Banned from the busiest areas, they are now found only in peripheral Bangkok. You can also rent the entire pick-up and use it as a kind of taxi in locations on the outskirts of Bangkok.

Trishaws: Some suburban areas in Bangkok still have trishaws (bicycle-driven cabs), and outside Bangkok you will see many. Fares start around B10.

Getting Around On Foot

Most will scoff at the idea of walking in Bangkok, but there are areas where strolling is pleasant enough—some are described in detail in the "Exploring Bangkok" section. Paving on the sidewalks is often uneven, or worse—watch out for missing chunks. Sidewalks can narrow to a foot or so in places; elsewhere, sidewalk vendors may reduce it to that margin or force you to walk on the road. You may hit Bangkok during the dreaded Hole-digging Season: this is when government workers dig great numbers of holes, excavate roads and sidewalks, and then leave everything as is, returning several months later to fill in the holes.

A major problem for pedestrians is crossing busy streets. "Busy" may mean 10 lanes of fast-

odd things in the traffic: the family sedan

(top) line of barges loaded with teak logs, north of Nonthaburi; (middle) tugboat towing a rice-barge on the Chao Phraya; (bottom) Chao Phraya Express

(clockwise from top left) 1. taking the geese for a spin; 2. Wat Paknam presides over canal housing on Klong Bangkok Yai; 3. longtail terminal on Klong Saensaep, below the Golden Mount; 4. longtail commuter boat blasting along a canal; 5. your trusty tillerman at the helm

(top) the fantastic domain of Wat Pra Keo, in the grounds of the Grand Palace; (bottom) a demon Yaksha statue guards the entrance to a glittering cloister at Wat Pra Keo

(top) Phra Ram and Phra Luxaman encounter the half-bodied demon Kumpon; (bottom) partly restored murals from W
Pra Keo courtyard, showing characters from the Ramayana: a Goddess, (left) and the monkey god Hanuman (right)

moving traffic—pedestrians have been struck and killed negotiating streets like this. It can take up to 20 minutes to cross a major street. I have only seen one set of traffic lights specifically for pedestrians—on New Road, just down from the GPO. The lights hold off the cars for less than a minute while pedestrians scurry across. The best method for crossing a street is to find an overhead footbridge. If there isn't one, form a pedestrian-power group by linking up with others, and forge over a crosswalk (normally these are ignored by drivers). Keep eyes in the back of your head—what appears to be a one-way street may allow buses to travel in the opposite direction, apparently to nail unwary foreigners, as the notices about two-way buses usually appear in Thai. And just when you think you're safe—on the sidewalk—along comes a motorcyclist at full throttle, trying to bypass blocked-up traffic.

To add insult to injury, pedestrians are regarded as a nuisance by traffic policemen, whose sole aim in life is to keep the traffic mov-

BEATING THE TRAFFIC

Bangkok residents still joke about an attempted coup d'état in the 1980s that failed because the perpetrators got caught in morning traffic—the tanks stopped at a red light. Being in Bangkok traffic at 1700 hours is a bit like being in the middle of a war-zone anyway (did the other drivers even notice the tanks?). Up to 50 motorcyclists roar off when the lights change at an intersection, scores of tuk-tuks make a deafening racket, and dozens of buses belch out diesel fumes. Because of the traffic, you'll find it takes a long time to get anything done in Bangkok. Given that the traffic is chaotic, unpleasant and unreliable, you have to plan your day around it. Peak hours run 0630 to 0930 and roughly 1530 to 1930 (later on Fridays). In some parts of the city, "rush hour" seems to last most of the day. Do any longer-distance traveling before 0630, between 0930 and 1500, or after 2030—otherwise you might spend a long time stuck in the traffic. Bangkok's bars do quite lucrative "happy hour" business between 1600 and 1900 with patrons wanting to avoid rush hour.

Taxi-drivers have special ways of dealing with the traffic—so don't be surprised if a driver appears to be going in the opposite direction from your destination. If you want to go from Chinatown to South Sathorn Road, for example, the driver would most likely cut across Pra Pokklau Bridge over the Chao Phraya into Thonburi, head south, and go back over the Taksin Bridge onto Sathorn Road, thus cutting a wide arc around traffic bottlenecks.

Whatever you do, avoid Rama IV Road during peak hour. It has some of the world's longest traffic lights—they've been variously timed at taking eight to twelve minutes or longer to change (operated manually by a traffic policeman). The Silom Road-Rama IV Road intersection is especially bad: if you're in a taxi, it's better to get out and walk to the other side of the intersection, and get another cab.

During the dreaded peak hours, there are only three sure-fire ways of beating the traffic. The first is to use the Chao Phraya express boats between 0600 and 1800—the river has no jams, though express boats can be crowded. The second (deadly) option is to use a motorcycle, or ride on the back of a motorcycle-taxi. The third option is to walk: what appears on the map to be around the corner may actually be a long way in a taxi because of one-way streets. At a five km/hr pace, you're almost up to the average traffic crawl of eight km/hr, and in some areas you can actually move faster on foot for short distances (assuming that breathing in the diesel fumes doesn't incapacitate you). It can take up to four hours to cover 10 km in gridlocked Bangkok traffic.

If you can't beat the traffic, you may as well amuse yourself while sitting it out. Bangkok car commuters, knowing they will be caught, come prepared: some even have a TV mounted on the dashboard tuned into a Thai boxing match while crawling along; others eat, or read the paper. Businessmen do their reports while sitting in traffic—and you could no doubt carry on a meeting as well.

Sundays are great—light traffic and no rush hours, but attractions may be closed, and so are most business areas. Sunday is a big shopping and entertainment day for Thais. They crowd the malls or markets that are open (such as Chatuchak Weekend Market to the north of the city), throng the theaters, and also visit parks—or boxing stadiums or horse races. There can be jams on Sundays coming back into Bangkok from places like Pattaya or Ko Samet due to weekend vacationers returning.

ing—doesn't matter where to, just *moving*. On occasion, there have been crackdowns, with fines levied on "jaywalkers"—a jaywalker being, by definition, anyone who attempts to cross a Bangkok street. This is not as radical as a new solution being attempted in Indonesia: the police there make jaywalkers do push-ups on the spot as punishment.

William Warren, well-known author and long-time Bangkok resident, describes some special pedestrian hazards in an article titled "I Crossed Ploenchit *Alone*": "Only in Bangkok . . . have I ever seen someone run over by a kitchen—that is, by one of those sizeable noodle shops on

wheels, complete with the entire cooking apparatus." In Bangkok, these noodle shops are often motorized, with motorcycle-type controls at the back. Warren goes on to describe some seasonal dangers, such as the hazard of open manholes concealed by flood waters during the rainy season. Crossing Silom or Surawong roads during certain months after dark is especially hazardous as the pedestrian has to face not only the traffic but also the random droppings of swallows nesting in the buildings above and lining the overhead wires. Once, he writes, there was a short-circuit during a downpour—and hapless pedestrians were pelted with dead swallows.

MAPS AND ORIENTATION

MAPS

A large city like Bangkok really requires a book of section maps, but there isn't one available at present. That being the case, you may end up carrying a bunch of different maps. The *sois* (sidestreets) hardly show up on the maps available, and yet it is the *soi* detail that you often need in locating a restaurant or a sight. Those carelessly placed location dots on maps you buy in Bangkok can be way off. A number of section maps of Bangkok giving fine detail are included in the "Exploring Bangkok" section of this book. Two larger maps are also included— Along the River (Chao Phraya landmarks and landings), and The Left Bank (canals of Thonburi). Check the maplist at the front.

Bus Maps

These can be useful for getting your bearings, even if you don't use the buses. The best map costs B35, has a green and red cover, and about six different titles on the front—*Bangkok, Bus Map & River Taxi, No. 1 Best Seller, Latest Edition Tour & Guide Map . . .* This map has English with matching Thai script interspersed throughout—very useful for pointing at destinations. The map says "Latest Edition" but doesn't reveal the year, so you have no way of telling if it's an older map or not. You need a magnifier to pick out some of the places on the bus map, and you will have a lot of trouble finding out the exact route of a bus from the mass of information given. Makes a great sunshade, however, if you forgot to bring a hat. If you want to solve the

DECODING MAP FEATURES

amphoe	district	khao	mountain	singha	lion
ao	bay	klong	canal	soi	sidestreet
ban	village, house	ko	island	suan	garden
bang	place on the water	menam	river	talad	market
-buri	suffix for town	muang	town	tha rua	boat landing
chang	elephant	nakhon	town, city	thanon	street
chiang	town	nam	water	tham	cave, grotto
chedi	pagoda	pak nam	river mouth	tong	gold
hat	beach	phom	fort	wang	palace
hin	stone	saphan	bridge	wat	temple

Bangkok street sign

"head-and-tail-end" problem for buses, get a pocket-sized booklet called the *Bus Guide* for B35, which has routing diagrams.

Other Maps

Nancy Chandler's Market Map is hand-drawn and annotated—lots of detail, very useful for markets. The edition date is given on the front of the map. For the canals, the best navigation aid available is *Canals of Thonburi*, one of a series of four cultural maps (a package costing B80) put out by the Association of Siamese Architects in 1981. It shows all the *wats* on the canals in Thai and English script.

Spellings

There is no standard system of rendering Thai into English, so English spellings vary wildly from map to map. Petchburi Road can be spelled Phetburi, Petburi or Phetchaburi. Si Ayutthaya is the same as Sri Ayudhya. Some of the place names and street names given in this book may not match your bus-map locations, but they'll be phonetically close. Street signs are usually given in Thai and English. Pronunciation is something else again: a Thai person may not recognize your version. "Th" is generally pronounced "t" (as in "Thailand"), so that Thanon, Thonburi, Sathorn and Nonthaburi are pronounced Tanon, Tonburi, Satorn, and Nontaburi.

Addresses

The main arteries of Bangkok are used to help determine the location of an address. A cross-street is useful to know because these roads can be lengthy. The address *8/1 Soi 33, Sukhumvit Road* means you would first look for sidestreet *(soi)* 33 running off the main road (Sukhumvit Road), then look for the number 8, which might be a group of buildings in an enclosed compound. After gaining entry to the compound, you would look for building 1, the first of the row. Usually the *sois* are even-numbered on one side of the road, and odd-numbered on the other. This does not mean, however, that they will roughly match. For example, on Sukhumvit, Soi 38 is opposite Soi 55.

Landmarks

To get your bearings, familiarize yourself with the major landmarks. These are the high-rise hotels (Baiyoke Tower, Shangri-La Hotel, Dusit Thani . . .), department stores, prominent features like the Democracy Monument and the Grand Palace, and prominent *wats*—the Golden Mount and Wat Arun, for instance. Major *wats* are important—many of the Chao Phraya landing-stages are for *wats;* streets leading to *wats* are often named after them (so Soi Wat Rakang Khositaram is the sidestreet leading to Wat Rakang); and taxi-drivers know where all the *wats* are (even if they don't know the locations of

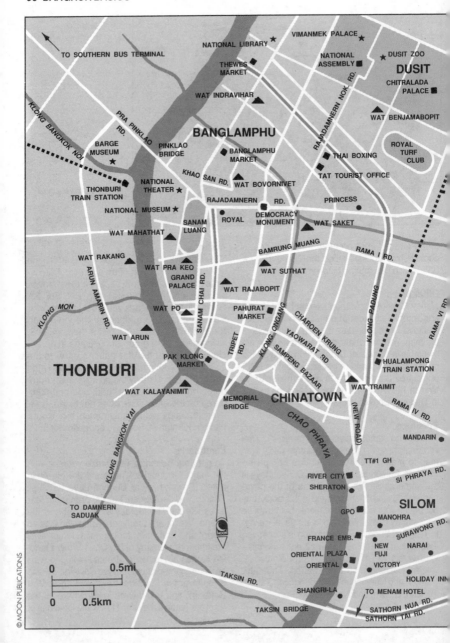

TO SOUTHERN BUS TERMINAL

NATIONAL LIBRARY

VIMANMEK PALACE

THEWES MARKET

NATIONAL ASSEMBLY

DUSIT ZOO

DUSIT

CHITRALADA PALACE

WAT INDRAVIHAR

KLONG BANGKOK NOI

PRA PINKLAO RD.

BARGE MUSEUM

PINKLAO BRIDGE

BANGLAMPHU

WAT BENJAMABOPIT

ROYAL TURF CLUB

BANGLAMPHU MARKET

THAI BOXING

RAJADAMNERN NOK RD.

THONBURI TRAIN STATION

NATIONAL THEATER

KHAO SAN RD.

WAT BOVORNIVET

TAT TOURIST OFFICE

NATIONAL MUSEUM

RAJADAMNERN RD.

PRINCESS

SANAM LUANG

ROYAL

DEMOCRACY MONUMENT

WAT SAKET

WAT MAHATHAT

BAMRUNG MUANG

RAMA I RD.

WAT RAKANG

WAT PRA KEO GRAND PALACE

WAT SUTHAT

ARUN AMARIN RD.

SANAM CHAI RD.

WAT RAJABOPIT

KLONG MON

WAT PO

PAHURAT MARKET

CHAROEN KRUNG

KLONG PADUNG

RAMA VI RD.

WAT ARUN

TRIPET RD.

KLONG ONGANG

YAOWARAT RD.

SAMPENG BAZAAR

HUALAMPONG TRAIN STATION

THONBURI

PAK KLONG MARKET

WAT TRAIMIT

RAMA IV RD.

KLONG BANGKOK YAI

WAT KALAYANIMIT

MEMORIAL BRIDGE

CHINATOWN

(NEW ROAD)

CHAO PHRAYA

MANDARIN

TT#1 GH

TO DAMNERN SADUAK

RIVER CITY

SHERATON

SI PHRAYA RD.

GPO

SILOM

MANOHRA

SURAWONG RD.

FRANCE EMB.

NEW FUJI

NARAI

ORIENTAL PLAZA

ORIENTAL

VICTORY

0   0.5mi

HOLIDAY INN

0   0.5km

TAKSIN RD.

SHANGRI-LA

TO MENAM HOTEL

SATHORN NUA RD.

TAKSIN BRIDGE

SATHORN TAI RD.

© MOON PUBLICATIONS

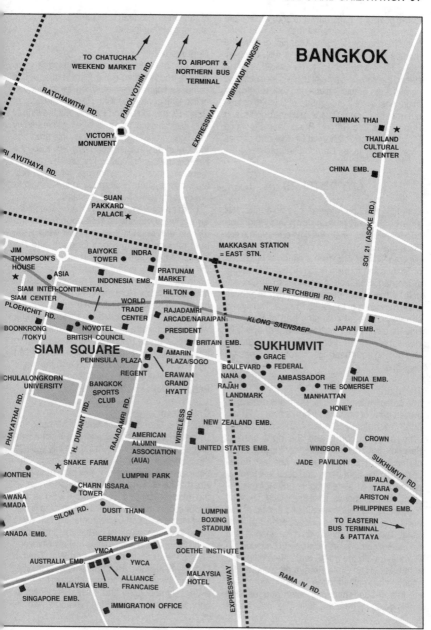

BANGKOK

TO CHATUCHAK
WEEKEND MARKET

TO AIRPORT &
NORTHERN BUS
TERMINAL

RATCHAWITHI RD.

PAHOLYOTHIN RD.

VIBHAVADI RANGSIT

EXPRESSWAY

TUMNAK THAI

THAILAND
CULTURAL
CENTER

VICTORY
MONUMENT

CHINA EMB.

RI AYUTHAYA RD.

SUAN
PAKKARD
PALACE ★

SOI 21 (ASOKE RD.)

MAKKASAN STATION
= EAST STN.

JIM
THOMPSON'S
HOUSE
★   ● ASIA

BAIYOKE
TOWER ●

INDRA ●

PRATUNAM
MARKET

INDONESIA EMB. ■

NEW PETCHBURI RD.

SIAM INTER-CONTINENTAL
SIAM CENTER

HILTON ●

PLOENCHIT RD.

WORLD
TRADE
CENTER

RAJADAMRI
ARCADE/NARAIPAN

KLONG SAENSAEP

JAPAN EMB. ■

BOONKRONG
/TOKYU

NOVOTEL ●
BRITISH COUNCIL

PRESIDENT ■

BRITAIN EMB. ■

SUKHUMVIT

SIAM SQUARE

PENINSULA PLAZA ●

AMARIN
PLAZA/SOGO

● GRACE

CHULALONGKORN
UNIVERSITY

REGENT ●

ERAWAN
GRAND
HYATT

BOULEVARD ● FEDERAL

NANA ●

AMBASSADOR

INDIA EMB. ■

BANGKOK
SPORTS
CLUB

RAJAH ●

LANDMARK

● THE SOMERSET

MANHATTAN

PHAYATHAI RD.

H. DUNANT RD.

RAJADAMRI RD.

WIRELESS RD.

● HONEY

AMERICAN
ALUMNI
ASSOCIATION
(AUA)

NEW ZEALAND EMB. ■

CROWN

CHULALONGKORN
UNIVERSITY

★ SNAKE FARM

UNITED STATES EMB. ■

WINDSOR ●

JADE PAVILION ●

SUKHUMVIT RD.

MONTIEN

LUMPINI PARK

IMPALA ●
TARA ●
ARISTON ●

AWANA
AMADA

CHARN ISSARA
TOWER ●

PHILIPPINES EMB. ■

SILOM RD.

DUSIT THANI ■

LUMPINI
BOXING
STADIUM

TO EASTERN
BUS TERMINAL
& PATTAYA →

ANADA EMB.

GERMANY EMB. ■

YMCA ■

GOETHE INSTITUTE ■

AUSTRALIA EMB. ■

YWCA ■

ALLIANCE
FRANCAISE

MALAYSIA
HOTEL ●

RAMA IV RD.

EXPRESSWAY

MALAYSIA EMB. ■

SINGAPORE EMB. ■

IMMIGRATION OFFICE ■

all the hotels). A hundred years ago, when there were only a few roads, all locating was done from the position of *wats* or canals, or from the houses of nobles. Navigation is now done by major streets, which in some cases have replaced the canals. Some of these streets change names three or four times along their length: the major east-west thoroughfare of Bangkok starts out from the Grand Palace as Bamrung Muang Road, turns into Rama I Road, then Ploenchit Road, and then Sukhumvit Road—and carries on all the way to the Cambodian border!

CITY DISTRICTS

Bangkok, like Los Angeles, has no center. It is an urban sprawl broken down into neighborhoods—villages within the city, each with a distinct character. This, in fact, is how the city evolved—it was originally a series of hundreds of villages and farming communities that started to overlap. Bangkok is younger than Los Angeles—the oldest sections of town are those lining the banks of the Chao Phraya. The river is certainly the most charming part of Bangkok, with its own hotels, restaurants, transport, its own set of rhythms. For the purposes of touring and getting your bearings, here are a few area divisions.

Thonburi

The collective term used for the many districts on the left bank of the Chao Phraya river is "Thonburi." Technically, the left bank of the Chao Phraya is Thonburi, and the right bank is Bangkok, but Thonburi falls under the jurisdiction of Bangkok. Thonburi is poorer and less developed than the right bank, and sees few foreigners because it has few sights and (for the moment) no major hotels. Until the 1930s, Thonburi had almost no roads—an idyllic district of fruit trees and market gardens accessed only by canal. The roads arrived with a vengeance, and the market gardens are now only to be found further west. With the prime real estate along the right bank of the Chao Phraya all snapped up, attention has shifted to the Thonburi side: there are lots of condominiums, town houses, and hotels going up near the river. The main tourist attraction of Thonburi is its canals, with market gardens further inland.

Rattanakosin

The original royal city of Bangkok was once walled, and is called Rattanakosin Island. It is composed of two sectors. When it was founded in the 18th century by King Rama I, the core of Bangkok was the **Grand Palace** and the strip of land enclosing that (the artificial island created by the digging of Klong Lot). Today, this area has the key sights in Bangkok (Wat Pra Keo, the National Museum, Wat Po) as well as government ministries and Thammasat University. Rattanakosin is a term that refers to the Bangkok-era dynasty as well as to the island.

Under King Rama I, the royal area doubled—an eastward expansion was bounded by the digging of Klong Ongang, and city walls were built encompassing Klong Ongang and the banks of the Chao Phraya. This outer half of the old royal city is today quite diverse. At the north end is **Banglamphu,** a residential district near Democracy Monument with cheap guesthouses on Khao San Road; in the middle is the **Sao Ching Cha** neighborhood ("Giant Swing"), which is a mixture of government offices and residential areas (city hall is located here); to the south end is a mixed Chinese and Indian residential and warehouse area with the major bazaars of **Pak Klong Talad** (food market) and **Pahurat Cloth Market.**

Chinatown

When the Grand Palace was to be built, the Chinese community occupying the area was requested to move just outside the city walls to the Sampeng area. Bangkok has many Chinese areas, but historically, this part, from New Road (Charoen Krung) to the Chao Phraya, is the oldest Chinese community, and is the strongest in Chinese influence. The area is riddled with alleys and backstreets; on Yaowarat Road there are jewelers, herbalists, and shops with Chinese foodstuffs. Sights include Chinese-style bazaars and temples, and Wat Traimit (Temple of the Gold Buddha). There are budget hotels in this area, but no major hotels; the area is densely populated and noisy. Chinatown is bounded on the east by Klong Phadung, which was dug during King Rama IV's reign as a new city boundary line. It was his intention to fortify this line with a series of forts, but few were actually built.

Dusit Area

Around 1900, King Rama V had a European-style retreat built to the northeast, with palaces and wide boulevards. A number of Thai nobles followed suit, so that this northern district contains some elegant architectural features, teak mansions, and classic gardens. Dusit Zoo and the Marble Temple are located here, too. King Rama IX lives in the Dusit area today, in Chitralada Palace, and the area has the National Assembly Building and a number of government offices. Rajadamnern Avenue is the boulevard leading to this quiet administrative district.

Farang Quarter

In the mid-19th century, Europeans established diplomatic links with Siam, and opened trading. The area from River City shopping complex down to the Shangri-La Hotel, on the banks of the Chao Phraya, is the area where foreign embassies, warehouses, banks, and trading establishments were located. Today the area is still a "farang quarter" with four of Bangkok's classiest hotels (including the famed Oriental Hotel) located between New Road and the river, and lots of shops catering to well-heeled tourists. It is known locally as the Bangrak area.

Silom-Surawong District

Silom and Surawong roads form the main business district of Bangkok—a transformation that has only taken place in the last few decades.

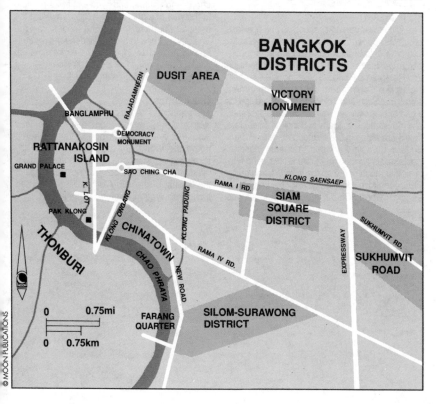

© MOON PUBLICATIONS

Originally, this sector, bounded by New Road, Surawong, Sathorn, and Rama IV Roads, was an eastward extension of the "farang quarter," with consulates, churches, and European residences. Silom and Rama IV roads used to have canals running alongside them (Sathorn Road still has a murky canal running down the middle of it). Today major banks and company headquarters are located in the Silom-Surawong district, and the parallel streets are lined with multi-story buildings. The area is Bangkok's leading gem-trading center, and has many airline offices, major hotels, a host of ritzy shops and restaurants, and the infamous nightlife of Patpong. Embassies are strung along Silom Road and Sathorn Road; to the southeast of Sathorn is a European and Thai residential area, and a guesthouse zone around the Malaysia Hotel.

Siam Square

This is a newer upmarket shopping and business area, with department stores, shopping plazas, and hotels. Lots of department stores are concentrated along Rama I, Ploenchit, Rajadamri and Rajaprarop Roads. These include the chain stores like Central, and Japanese department stores like Sogo and Tokyu. Siam Square itself is a grid of *sois* with boutiques, shops, restaurants, and movie-theaters. Many of Bangkok's first-class hotels are found in the district bounded by Siam Square, Lumpini Park and Pratunam Markets. Restaurants abound, but there is little in the way of sights: much of the space here is taken up by Chulalongkorn University and by the Royal Bangkok Sports Club. Embassies and airlines are centered around Wireless Road (Witthayu) to the east. North of Siam Square is **Victory Monument,** a nightlife, hotel, and restaurant area catering mainly to Thais.

Sukhumvit Road

After WW II there was rapid expansion in Bangkok, with many new zones and neighborhoods formed. The expansion took place along certain roads rather than around a particular site. Sukhumvit, once little more than a country lane, was caught up in a construction boom in the 1960s, when it was a favored R&R center for American troops. Today, the *sois* leading off Sukhumvit have a number of foreign embassies, and Sukhumvit is a residential area for foreigners and affluent Thais. It's a moderate-priced tourist neighborhood, full of hotels, restaurants, shops, nightclubs, and bars—but has nothing in the way of sights and is a long way from the river. Sukhumvit Road is the longest road in Thailand—it has to be subdivided for direction-finding. Sois 1 to 21 (from the expressway to Asoke Road) is the first logical division; the next is Sois 21 to 55 (Soi Thonglor).

Outer Zones

The peripheral zones of Bangkok comprise the slum and port area of Klong Toey, and polluted industrial areas (Din Daeng to the northeast being the worst). In the suburbs there are sprawling satellite housing developments clustered around huge shopping complexes—one of the largest of these is Central Plaza, located along Paholyothin, the road to the airport.

EXPLORING BANGKOK

Bangkok offers a huge selection of sights. There are over 400 temples in this city, so you have to be selective in your sight-seeing. You can catalogue, cross-reference, and index the sights but this doesn't make a whole lot of sense. Better than a long list of "ingredients" is a prepared itinerary, which blends items into a more palatable form. To extend the metaphor: your author-and-chef has prepared a selection of different dishes—different slices of Bangkok—it's up to you to choose.

A cogent reason for setting up itineraries is that Bangkok's soul is to be found in its small corners—the fascinating little shrines or back-alley markets. With these small corners you can cut Bangkok down to size: such places, however, are quite tricky to find, and if your time is short, the logistics are daunting—an itinerary will give you clear directions.

Logistically speaking, you're much better off spending an entire morning exploring one area. If you can put together transport, sights, shopping, and restaurants within a manageable radius, you're on the right track. The early riser

will catch Bangkok at its best: saffron-robed monks walking around with alms-bowls; *tai-chi,* jogging, and aerobics in the parks; food markets in full swing—and it's relatively cool. By the early afternoon, after a hard day's touring, the heat rises (you get sticky and sweaty), and the traffic turns nasty (the *tuk-tuk* drivers raise their hackles and their prices). You have basically two choices: get back to your hotel and relax, or relax where you happen to be, and sit out the rush hour and the heat. And remember that one of the major sights of Bangkok is the inside of a good restaurant!

Countless tour agencies can organize your day for you if you want—the Bangkok Yellow Pages lists ten pages of "Travel Bureaus." Using an agency is convenient but may be expensive and unsatisfying—ultimately, agencies deprive you of the thrill of getting lost, or getting into trouble—and you miss out on the adventure. Agencies control the schedule, limit the amount of time you spend at a particular place, and will herd you through over-touristed areas. They can be useful, however, for exploring the *klongs* (join a small group at a landing on the midsection of the Chao Phraya and rent a boat); and if going out of Bangkok (30 km to 100 km or more), agencies can package four or five sights, which may save time and money (for more details, see "Excursions from Bangkok").

There is a double-tier pricing system for attractions in and around Bangkok: a small fee for Thais, and a whopping mark-up for foreigners. This is not a problem for most temples, which charge a nominal B5 to B20 entry fee, but it can make a big difference at a place like the Samphran Elephant and Crocodile Farm, which charges foreigners B190 to get in, and considerably less for locals. The Grand Palace is B100 entry for *farangs*, but free for Thais.

The itineraries in this chapter delve into nine selected areas of Bangkok. Feel free to adapt, change, add, subtract, do a tour in reverse, or go off at a tangent. You will most likely end up straying from where these itineraries are designed to take you—in which case, all the better. It's what you find along the way, and the people you bump into, that make Bangkok memorable. These itineraries just provide a way in—you have to improvise the rest. Explore!

ON THE MENU

The number in brackets following an entry corresponds to one of the nine tours described in this chapter. Thus (5) corresponds to detailed itinerary number five, The Left Bank. Those places marked with an asterisk * are not included in the detailed itineraries.

Essential Viewing
Chao Phraya River—18 km on the river to Nonthaburi (1)
The Grand Palace and the Royal Chapel, Wat Pra Keo (2)

Canal Trips
The Left Bank—mini-trips on Thonburi canals by small boat, viewing snippets of waterborne life (5)

Major Thai Temples
Wat Arun—Temple of the Dawn; viewpoint over Bangkok (1)
Wat Po—Reclining Buddha; Traditional Medicine College (1)
Wat Suthat—fine interior murals; Giant Swing (6)
Wat Benjamabopit—the Marble Temple; European touches (8)
Wat Rajabopit—unique temple artwork and circular design (6)
Wat Traimit—housing the world's largest gold Buddha (4)
Wat Saket—The Golden Mount; viewpoint over Bangkok (7)
*Wat Indravihar—houses large Standing Buddha

*Wat Bovornnivet—important center of learning
Wat Mahathat—Buddhist university and meditation center (6)
Wat Paknam—known for its powerful amulets (5)

Other Temples And Shrines
Erawan Shrine—Brahman shrine (7)
Lak Muang—City Pillar, founding shrine (6)
Pho Sua—Chinese Confucian temple (6)
Sanjao Dtai Hong Kong—Chinese Mahayana temple (4)
Leng Noi Yi—Chinese Buddhist temple (4)

Museums
National Museum—largest of its kind in Southeast Asia (6)
Royal Barges Museum—royal ceremonial vessels (5)
Coin Museum at Grand Palace—coins, royal decorations (2)
*Royal Thai Air Force Museum—located near airport—fine collection of antique aircraft. Check with TAT for details.
*Thai Human Imagery Museum—30 km west of Bangkok—lifelike fiberglass figures of Chakri dynasty kings
*Medical Museums—in Siriraj Hospital; of specialist interest

Teak Mansion Museums With Gardens
Vimanmek Mansion Museum—former royal residence; antiques (8)

Suan Pakkard Palace—traditional housing; Ban Chiang ceramics (8)

Jim Thompson's Thai House—traditional housing; antiques (7)

Kamthieng House—ethnology museum at Siam Society (8)

Galleries, Theatre, Cultural Events

*National Art Gallery

*National Theatre

*Thailand Cultural Center

*Thai boxing stadiums

For more details, see "Bangkok by Night"

Markets, Shopping

Pak Klong Talad—wholesale food and flowers (3)

Pahurat Cloth market—little India (3)

Chinatown—cloth, materials, food (4)

River City—antiques (9)

Wat Rajanada, Wat Mahathat—amulets, antiques (7/6)

*Tha Thewet—plant and food market at Thewet landing

*Chatuchak Weekend Market—large general market opposite Northern Bus Station on Saturdays and Sundays; plant section open weekdays.

For more details on markets, refer to the Shopping section under "Bangkok Basics." For details on floating markets, see Damnern Saduak section under "Excursions from Bangkok."

Natural Sights

Snake Farm at Thai Red Cross Society (9)

Dusit Zoological Gardens (8)

*Rama IX Royal Park—200-acre park and botanical gardens off Sukhumvit Soi 103 to the southeast of Bangkok

*Safari World—300-acre African and Asian wildlife park in Minburi, a suburb to the northeast of Bangkok—drive through yourself, or the park will provide coaches; not far off is Siam Waterpark, with pools, giant slides, and an amusement park

*Crocodile/Elephant farms—see Samut Prakarn and Samphran entries under "Excursions from Bangkok."

There are many orchid and butterfly farms around Bangkok, including one at the Rose Garden Resort.

DETAILED ITINERARIES

Tour 1: **Along the River**—by boat on the Chao Phraya (p. 98)

Tour 2: **Heart of Bangkok**—the Grand Palace & Wat Po (p. 104)

Tour 3: **The Grand Bazaar**—large food, cloth & general markets (p. 113)

Tour 4: **Dragon Path**—Chinatown temples & shopping on foot (p. 116)

Tour 5: **The Left Bank**—adventuring on the *klongs* of Thonburi (p. 120)

Tour 6: **Walking Buddha**—aspects of Buddhism in Rattanakosin (p. 130)

Tour 7: **Siam Mystery Tour**—mysterious places (p. 137)

Tour 8: **Teak Mansions, Classic Gardens**—Dusit area antiques (p. 142)

Tour 9: **Tales from the Farang Quarter**—Oriental Hotel area (p. 146)

BOB RACE

lotus

ALONG THE RIVER

There it was, spread largely on both banks, the Oriental capital which had yet suffered no white conqueror; an expanse of brown houses of bamboo, of mats, of leaves, of a vegetable-matter style of architecture, sprung out of the brown soil on the banks of the muddy river . . . Here and there in the distance, above the crowded mob of low, brown roof ridges, towered great piles of masonry, king's palace, temples, gorgeous and dilapidated, crumbling under the vertical sunlight, tremendous, overpowering, almost palpable, which seemed to enter one's breast with the breath of one's nostrils and soak into one's limbs through every pore of the skin . . .

— Joseph Conrad's first impressions of Bangkok, from the novel, *The Shadow Line*

The skyline has radically altered since Joseph Conrad's arrival in 1888, but there is no finer introduction to Bangkok than a cruise along the Chao Phraya River. In Conrad's day the Chao Phraya was the only "highway" to Bangkok—the sole access was by sailing ship or steamer. Conrad's sense of awe and wonder at the opulent palaces and temples is a feeling you can easily capture with a trip at dawn or dusk, when the lighting is more dramatic.

You never seem to tire of the perspective from the Chao Phraya—a number of trips are recommended to take it all in. You can run the full length of the river on the Chao Phraya Express Boat; get off at random and explore areas along the banks, or structure your trip with planned stops. A one-way fare for the entire 18-km route along the Chao Phraya is only seven baht, about 25 cents: this is Bangkok's greatest touring bargain. Other riverboats can be easily hired or used by a group—ricebarges are the best craft because they are stable and move along the river at a slow pace. Longtailed boats were designed for the canals—they don't perform too well on the sometimes choppy waters of the Chao Phraya. River City advertises a private boat for the run to Nonthaburi (one way) at B500, an exponential difference from the seven-baht fare on the Chao Phraya Express Boat.

The following description starts at the southern terminus for the express boat and goes north. The full ride from terminus to terminus takes about 75 minutes in a regular express boat (all stops—which is the better option for river-viewing—avoid crowded peak-hour boats

longtail on the Chao Phraya

which only make selected stops). Ride all the way from the south to the north, spend some time in Nonthaburi, and then work your way slowly back, making stops along the way. This way you can easily spend a day along the river. If you want to make sure you get a good seat, board the boat at the southern terminus of Wat Rajsingkorn (which is off Charoen Krung Soi 74, past the Menam Hotel). To avoid spray and engine noise, take the foremost seat you can. If you can't get a seat (boarding further up the river), the next best place to be is standing up at the back on deck.

There are a number of restaurants, cafes, and noodle stands at (or near) landings with excellent dining. For more details on these, consult the restaurant listing under "Dining Along the River"—this also has suggestions for evening dinner cruises.

South Terminal To Memorial Bridge

Starting at Wat Rajsingkorn, the boat passes an area of docks and warehouses—similar to what it was in the Bangkok of a century ago. Further toward Taksin Bridge are fishery plants on the right bank, and lumberyards on the left. Suppakarn condominium and shopping complex looms up near Taksin Bridge. Condominium-building started in the 1980s and is the wave of the future—these structures are sprouting along both banks, as are new hotels and shopping centers. After Bangkok spent fifty years spreading eastwards—divorcing the river—it has turned back again to the Chao Phraya as the "in" center. Herein lies a controversy as the Chao Phraya is dying—and the new growth along its banks is hastening its demise.

After Taksin Bridge, on the right bank, the white shapes of the major riverside hotels come into view. The first is the Shangri-La Hotel, at present the largest on the river, with a new shopping and office complex being built next door. In the wink of an eye, you'll see Assumption Convent (with Assumption Cathedral behind it), the East Asiatic Company building, the Oriental Hotel, the French Embassy, the former Customs House, the Royal Orchid Sheraton, and River City shopping complex (for further description of this area, see "Tales from the Farang Quarter").

Housing takes a distinct nosedive after River City—corrugated tin shanties, and more warehousing near the Ratchawong area, which is in Chinatown. After that you pass under three bridges spanning the Chao Phraya—two of them being Phra Pokklau Bridge, and the older one being Memorial Bridge. Memorial Bridge was the first bridge to span the Chao Phraya, and was opened by King Rama VII in 1932, on the 150th anniversary of the Chakri dynasty. Two months later, a bloodless coup ended absolute monarchy.

Memorial Bridge To Pinklao Bridge

This is the "royal mile" of old Bangkok—with an extraordinary density of wats, and a waterfront view of the Grand Palace. This is the busiest section of the Chao Phraya: you'll see barges loaded with sand or crates of soft drink, naval launches, cross-river boats, longtailed boats, hotel shuttle-boats—and maybe even a police-boat or a speedboat. On the right bank, Pak Klong market—the largest in Bangkok, with lots of longtails loaded to the brim with produce. On the left bank, in a row, are the chedis of Wat Prayoon (the "turtle wat," known for its turtle pond), the spire of Santa Cruz Church, and the tall prayer hall of Wat Kalayanimit.

On the left bank appears Wat Arun, the Chao Phraya's most distinctive landmark; then Wat Po and the Grand Palace on the right bank. Chao Phraya means "River of Kings" and this is the true regal section. Between Tha Tien and Tha Chang there is a royal landing, used only by royal craft. Those other than royal used to approach the Grand Palace from Tha Tien or Tha Chang. The area opposite the Grand Palace is connected with the navy—it has naval headquarters with a library. The navy operates its own cross-river ferries.

Around Tha Maharaj there are usually some monks boarding or disembarking—they travel from other monasteries to Wat Mahathat (close to Maharaj landing) for special lectures or studies. Wat Mahathat functions as a Buddhist college—one of the best in Bangkok. The monks travel free on the ferries, and even have their own exits and entrances at the piers; because they travel free, they always stand at the back of the boat.

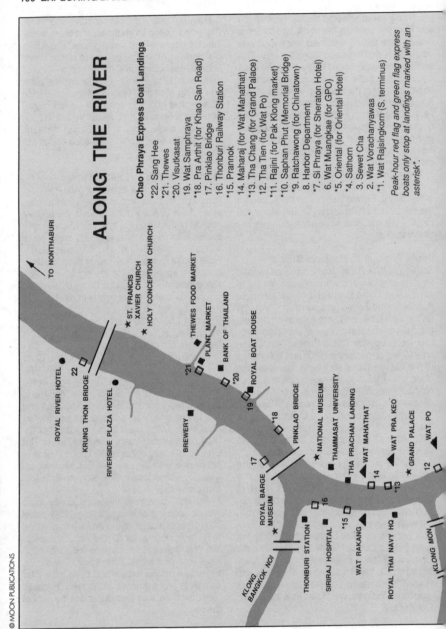

ALONG THE RIVER

TO NONTHABURI

★ ST. FRANCIS XAVIER CHURCH
★ HOLY CONCEPTION CHURCH

ROYAL RIVER HOTEL
KRUNG THON BRIDGE
RIVERSIDE PLAZA HOTEL

BREWERY
THEWES FOOD MARKET
PLANT MARKET
BANK OF THAILAND
ROYAL BOAT HOUSE

PINKLAO BRIDGE
★ NATIONAL MUSEUM
■ THAMMASAT UNIVERSITY
THA PRACHAN LANDING
▲ WAT MAHATHAT
▲ WAT PRA KEO
▲ GRAND PALACE
WAT PO

ROYAL BARGE MUSEUM
THONBURI STATION
SIRIRAJ HOSPITAL
▲ WAT RAKANG
ROYAL THAI NAVY HQ

KLONG BANGKOK NOI

KLONG MON

© MOON PUBLICATIONS

Chao Phraya Express Boat Landings

*22. Sang Hee
*21. Thewes
*20. Visutkasat
19. Wat Samphraya
*18. Pra Arthit (for Khao San Road)
17. Pinklao Bridge
16. Thonburi Railway Station
*15. Prannok
14. Maharaj (for Wat Mahathat)
*13. Tha Chang (for Grand Palace)
12. Tha Tien (for Wat Po)
*11. Rajini (for Pak Klong market)
*10. Saphan Phut (Memorial Bridge)
*9. Ratchawong (for Chinatown)
8. Harbor Department
*7. Si Phraya (for Sheraton Hotel)
6. Wat Muangkae (for GPO)
*5. Oriental (for Oriental Hotel)
4. Sathorn
3. Sewet Cha
2. Wat Vorachanyawas
*1. Wat Rajsingkorn (S. terminus)

Peak-hour red flag and green flag express boats only stop at landings marked with an asterisk.

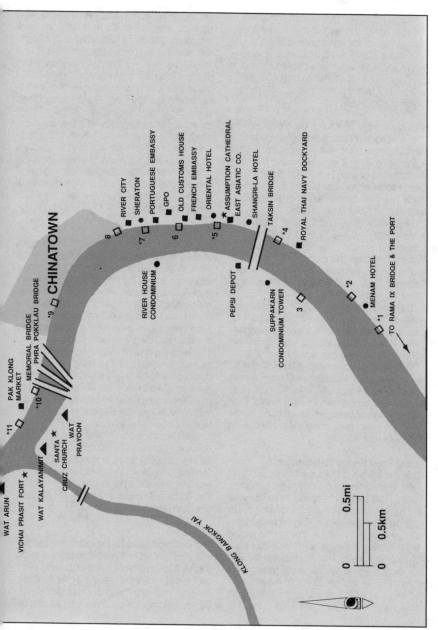

Farther north is Thammasat University on the right bank, founded 1934; on the left bank is Siriraj Hospital, the first modern hospital to open in Thailand (1888). Siriraj has a number of small museums, open weekdays (find an attendant); they're really of specialist interest (Congdon's Anatomical Museum has some preserved embryos of Siamese twins).

Pinklao Bridge To Krung Thon Bridge
The area north of Pinklao Bridge gives way to an exclusive residential area—condominium-building is going on at a rapid rate here. Near Wat Samphraya landing is a Royal Boat House, where some of the royal barges are kept in dry dock: the main barges are kept at the Barge Museum on Klong Bangkok Noi.

Right near Visutkasat landing, you'll see a huge mustard-colored Bank of Thailand office, formerly a palace. Between Visutkasat and Thewes landings there is a Tudor-style red-roofed building, half hidden by trees. The present Queen of Thailand, H.M. Queen Sirikit, grew up in this mansion.

Thewes (pronounced "Tay-WAIT") has a plant market strung along a street leading from the pier, with wholesale plants and gardening supplies. There is a fascinating food market just north and parallel to that, across a canal.

Two landmarks near Krung Thon Bridge are the spires of Holy Conception Church, and St. Francis Xavier Church. There are lots of sand-barges and house-barges near Krung Thon Bridge. Another variety is the charcoal-barge: these supply cooking charcoal to houses via vendor-boats.

Krung Thon Bridge To Nonthaburi
Near the bridge is the towering Royal River Hotel, and condominiums (with more going up). North of that the river becomes more industrial and rural in character—with factories, houses hugging the waterline, swaying coconut palms, wats, and the odd mosque. You get the feeling you're leaving Bangkok, which is in fact what you're doing. The express boat speeds through this section—there are not many passengers embarking. As you get closer to the riverside housing, you'll see kids and adults jumping off vantage points for a swim or a wash in the dirty

old Chao Phraya. You also see people throwing garbage straight into the river, although there are campaigns on TV to counter such thoughtlessness. Tossing garbage into the Chao Phraya is nothing new—in the 19th century when cholera plagues broke out, King Mongkut passed a decree that no dead animals were to be thrown into the river. But in former times, dead dogs notwithstanding, "garbage" here meant organic wrappings of banana leaves, which were not a problem. The only time a long-tail operator will take any notice of the garbage problem is when a piece of plastic fouls the boat's propeller (the offending item is removed and then tossed back into the Chao Phraya). Another naval menace is water hyacinth, which drifts in large clumps.

In Nonthaburi
Half an hour in Nonthaburi, the northern terminus of the express boats, is enough to take in the markets there, or you can linger a few hours and visit a *wat* on the left bank and go to a restaurant near the pier. When you arrive, if you walk straight from the pier due east (past the clock tower) there is a natural history museum just a few minutes away, on the right-hand side of the street. It's a small museum with stuffed Thai sealife and wildlife. Another five minutes or so down the same street will bring you to a huge covered market with fish, vegetables, and fruit. Nonthaburi, on the outskirts of Bangkok proper, has a wider (and cheaper) selection of unusual fruit. Retrace your steps—there's a floating restaurant just south of the pier.

If you have some more time, try a trip to Wat Chalerm Phrakiet on the opposite bank. There's an alternate way back to Bangkok via Klong Om and Klong Bangkok Noi—it takes about 1 1/2 hours without stops (for details on this, and on Wat Chalerm Phrakiet, see the end of the tour, "The Left Bank").

After Dark
The last express boats leave at 1800 (so the last trips are not completed till around 1900 hours). If you catch one of the last boats, you'll get the magic rays of the sun low over the Chao Phraya. Then activity on the river dies down, but you can still carry on. If you want a romantic

Rama IX Bridge

night on the water, board a vessel for a dinner cruise. Boats will cruise past the Royal Palace (spectacular illumination in the early evening), Wat Arun (fully lit), the strings of lights around hotel terraces, and weave in among huge hulls—heavy shipping—near Rama IX Bridge. For more details, refer to "Dining Along The River" in the "Dining Out" section.

The Port

Bangkok is one of the world's great ports, so it is worthwhile getting to see the southern section of the Chao Phraya—as far as the Gulf of Thailand. This is the historic passage to the capital—the port is home to container vessels, oil tankers, freighters, fishing vessels, navy ships, and other heavy shipping. The skyline is framed by cranes that loom up like giant praying mantises; dominating one section of the river is Rama IX Bridge, qualifying for the largest cable-stayed single-span bridge in the world.

The port is out of range of the regular ferry, so you would have to hire a vessel. A small launch *(rua yon)* or a longtail boat will require about two hours to go down past Rama IX Bridge, and another two hours to return, making it a four-hour trip. You might consider hiring a vessel down to Samut Prakarn (Pak Nam), getting off, and returning by road. The hovercraft also passes through the port on its way to Pattaya or Hua Hin, taking one hour for the section from Bangkok to the Gulf of Thailand.

HEART OF BANGKOK

It makes you laugh with delight to think that anything so fantastic could exist on this somber earth. They are gorgeous; they glitter with gold and whitewash, yet are not garish; against that vivid sky, in that dazzling sunlight, they hold their own, defying the brilliancy of nature and supplementing it with the ingenuity and playful boldness of man.

—Somerset Maugham, describing Bangkok's temples in *The Gentleman in the Parlour* (1930)

Wat Pra Keo—Grand Palace— Wat Po—Wat Arun

Timing: The Grand Palace (which encloses Wat Pra Keo) is open daily 0830 to 1200 and 1300 to 1630, with last tickets sold at 1530 hours. The B100 entry fee includes a small booklet on the palace, a ticket to the Coin Museum, and one to Vimanmek Mansions (valid for a month). The palace is a royal area, so there is a strict dress code in effect—no shorts or sandals (enterprising vendors sell or rent long pants and sarongs near the gates). Also questionable are T-shirts, halter tops, and dirty jeans. Wat Po and Wat Arun are open daily 0800 to 1700, as are most temples in Bangkok.

The heart of Bangkok is the extraordinary grouping of palaces and *wats* near the banks of the Chao Phraya. This is the spiritual and historical center of the city, and there is such a rich profusion of architecture and statuary that you can't absorb it all in one visit.

The best way to approach the Grand Palace and temple complex is the royal way—by boat along the Chao Phraya to Tha Chang landing (there is a special landing further south, called Tha Rajavoradit, which is reserved for royal boats. You can see a riverside pavilion there). If

you arrive around 0800, hang around the landing at Tha Chang to observe the unloading of express boats, cross-river boats, and dozens of longtailed boats in what amounts to a waterborne rush hour. Walk east after getting off the boat: there's only one way of getting into the palace complex—through the north gate (see map).

Close to the ticket booth is the two-story **Coin Museum,** housing a collection of Thai coins, a display of medals and decorations awarded by the king, and a display of royal regalia. It takes a while to inspect the museum and most find it a distraction from the real fare—probably better to see the museum on your way out of the palace, or see it another day.

WAT PRA KEO

For pure fantasy, few places can surpass the royal chapel of Wat Pra Keo. The bizarre group of structures and statues is the stuff of legends—the perfect setting for tales about the gods. Many mythical figures from the *Ramakien* and other legends, in fact, are found at Wat Pra Keo in statuary or in frescoes. Wat Pra Keo lies within the grounds of the Grand Palace: the *wat* is the most sacred of all Thai temples. The first structures on this site were put up in the 1780s; they have been renovated or replaced over the past two hundred years.

The first thing to strike the eye is the gigantic *yaksha* statues that guard the entrance to the chapel. These six-meter-high demons from Thai mythology hold giant clubs and guard all the entrance gates—each *yak* has a name, and a different color.

North of the entrance is a group of buildings fronted by a glittering pagoda, **Pra Si Ratana Chedi,** containing Buddhist relics. Construction began in 1855, and a mosaic coating was added during the reign of King Rama V. The **Mondop** (Library), next door, contains the *Tripitaka* (Buddhist holy texts). The building is closed to the public, but the exterior alone is dazzling—when you stand at the base and look upward, you get a perspective of soaring grandeur. North of the library is a small stone **model of Angkor Wat,** the 12th-century Khmer citadel. The model was built in the reign of King Rama V, when Thailand held sway over Cambodia. On the model you can identify the Khmer *prangs* that influenced Thai temple architecture. On the terrace around the east side of the Royal Pantheon, you will see a fabulous collection of statues—mythical half-animal, half-human hybrids. Among them are golden *kinnarees,* which are half-bird, half-woman figures from a mythical forest in Buddhist cosmology, located in the Himalayas. Male versions are called *kinnara.* Also in this area are two gilt *chedis,* with base sections supported by mosaic-covered demons and simian figures that seem to grimace under the weight.

Wat Pra Keo and the Grand Palace serve as the best introduction you can get to Thai royal and religious architecture, since so many different structures are grouped in the same area (see "Mythology and the Arts" in the main Introduction). The **Royal Pantheon** (Prasat Pra Thepidon) is a religious *prasat* or ceremonial hall—a cruciform shape with a Khmer-style *prang* rising out of its rooftop. The original building was constructed 1855; however, in 1903 a fire broke out, and the structure was rebuilt. Inside are life-sized gold statues of eight Chakri kings—the building is open to the public only one day a year, on Chakri Day (April 6).

Temple Of The Emerald Buddha

The most revered Buddha image in Thailand is housed in the Temple of the Emerald Buddha. Emerald refers to the color of the statue—the Buddha is reputedly carved from a block of jadeite, or possibly jasper. The *bot* was constructed especially to house this tiny image. The Buddha is only 75 centimeters in height, and is thought to have miraculous powers. It was discovered in Chiang Rai in 1434 when lightning struck a *chedi,* revealing a stucco image; a few years later the stucco cracked and revealed a green image that emanated a supernatural glow. The Buddha is seated in a meditation posture, common to Sri Lankan art, which may give clues as to its origin. The statue was eventually taken to Chiang Mai; in the 16th century it was removed to Laos; in 1778 it was captured by a Thai general, later crowned Rama I. He brought it back in triumph to Bangkok, where the talisman has remained since—bestowing good fortune on the kingdom.

The Emerald Buddha sits in the highest place in the temple, perched on an altar; taking up the rest of the vertical space around it is a conglomeration of lesser Buddha statues and decorations. There are rich murals on the surrounding walls, based on Buddhist themes: on the wall above the entrance is a magnificent fresco showing Victory over Mara—the point of Buddha's enlightenment when he overcomes temptation, and the earth-goddess Torani

Rama and Luxamen encounter the half-bodied demon Kumpon. (From the Ramakien murals at Wat Pra Keo.)

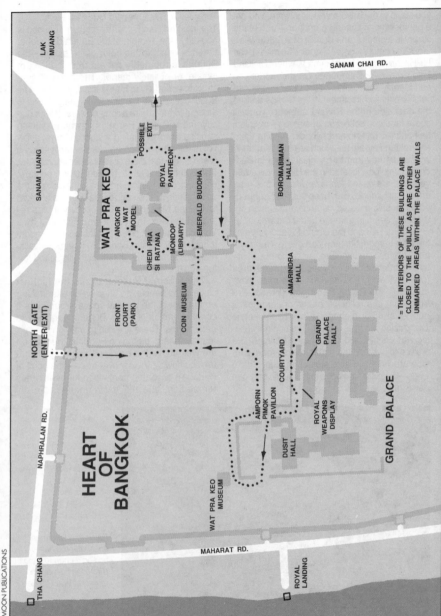

HEART OF BANGKOK

WAT PRA KEO

GRAND PALACE

LAK MUANG

SANAM CHAI RD.

SANAM LUANG

NAPHRALAN RD.

MAHARAT RD.

THA CHANG

ROYAL LANDING

POSSIBLE EXIT

ROYAL PANTHEON

ANGKOR WAT MODEL

CHEDI PRA SI RATANA

MONDOP (LIBRARY)*

EMERALD BUDDHA

BOROMABIMAN HALL*

AMARINDRA HALL

FRONT COURT (PARK)

COIN MUSEUM

NORTH GATE (ENTER/EXIT)

AMPORN PIMOK PAVILION

COURTYARD

GRAND PALACE HALL*

ROYAL WEAPONS DISPLAY

DUSIT HALL

WAT PRA KEO MUSEUM

* = THE INTERIORS OF THESE BUILDINGS ARE CLOSED TO THE PUBLIC, AS ARE OTHER UNMARKED AREAS WITHIN THE PALACE WALLS

© MOON PUBLICATIONS

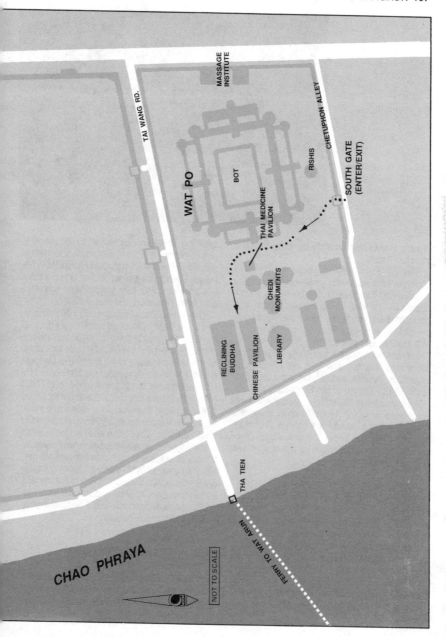

*detail from
Wat Pra Keo's
Ramakien murals*

drowns Mara's demon army by wringing water from her hair.

The Emerald Buddha goes through three changes of dress every year—summer, rainy season, and cool season. The ceremony is conducted by the king or his representative, and holy water is sprinkled on those waiting outside the hall. Though Wat Pra Keo may be overrun with tourists, it is an important place of worship. There are no monks attached to the *wat*, but many supplicants come to make offerings of lotus buds, incense, and candles in the courtyard opposite the Temple of the Emerald Buddha.

After you leave the temple, examine the exterior base, which, in Ayuthaya-style, is curved. Along the base section are strings of bronze *garudas* (mythical birds) clasping *nagas* (serpents); the three doorways to the chapel are guarded by pairs of bronze lions.

Ramakien Murals

Don't be in any hurry to leave Wat Pra Keo—it's the highlight of the entire palace area. Once you leave the enclosure, no returns are allowed on your ticket, so before you move on to the Grand Palace, take another sweep around the *wat* to inspect the Ramakien Murals. The murals run clockwise for the entire length of the walls (starting from the north side, opposite the gate facing the Angkor Wat model) and tell the story of lovers Rama and Sita, the kidnapping of Sita by the

evil King Tosakan, her rescue by the monkey-god Hanuman and his simian army, and the final slaying of Tosakan—with many subplots in between. Even if you are not familiar with the story, this ancient comic strip yields many fine snippets from Thai court and village life.

The murals date from the reign of Rama III, and have been retouched numerous times—a constant renovation project. Major restorations of Wat Pra Keo and the Grand Palace took place for the 1882 centenary of the founding of Bangkok (under King Rama V) and for the 1982 bicentennial celebrations. In 1982, with a budget of US$8 million, Thailand's Fine Arts Department mobilized 2,000 painters, carpenters and masons to retile, regild, and restore the art and architecture of the royal complex. They were assisted by modern technology—a computer camera was used by a team of artisans to duplicate intricate old mosaics on parts of Wat Pra Keo. Opening the bicentennial celebrations at the Grand Palace was an outdoor performance under a full moon by 2,525 classical dancers—2525 being the year on the Buddhist Era calendar.

THE GRAND PALACE

The Grand Palace, bounded by crenelated walls and forts, was the residence of successive kings from 1782 till 1946, with many architectural additions and deletions made during that period, and since that period. The palace covers 60 acres, and was modeled on the one destroyed by the Burmese in Ayuthaya. Apart from the king's residence, in previous centuries the palace contained a great variety of public offices (the main court, the mint), royal chapels (including Wat Pra Keo), the royal library and theatre, the king's harem, a large contingent of soldiers, an armory, and stables for war elephants and horses.

A few government offices, such as the Ministry of Finance, are still located within the palace walls, but most of the buildings are unused—the present king lives in the Chitralada Palace in the Dusit area to the northeast. The ceremonial and audience halls in the Grand Palace are occasionally used for royal occasions or state receptions for VIPs.

As you come out of Wat Pra Keo, on your left is **Boromabiman Hall,** a bland mustard-colored edifice of French design. It was the residence of King Rama VI and later crown princes,

and is sometimes used to lodge visiting heads of state. Both the Hall and nearby Sivalaya Gardens are off-limits to tourists. You are allowed into **Amarindra Hall,** which in early Bangkok served as a justice court; later it became a coronation and audience hall. Outside are red poles to which the elephants of visiting dignitaries were tethered.

Lying between Amarindra Hall and the Grand Palace Hall is a doorway that was used by only one man—the king. It led to the **Inner Palace**—the royal harem—which was guarded by a force of women with Amazonian prowess in combat. This was a self-contained city run by women. At its peak, under Rama V, the harem had up to 3,000 residents, including queens and consorts (from present or previous reigns), royal children, daughters from aristocratic families seeking a court education, and scores of female attendants. The first kings of the Chakri dynasty kept large harems: Rama I had 43 children; Rama II, 73 children; Rama III, 51 children . . . . The practice of polygamy was abandoned by Rama VI and Rama VII, but the harem door still stays firmly shut, with no access to the dilapidated queens' residences beyond.

Grand Palace Hall

The Grand Palace Hall ("Chakri Maha Prasat") was completed by 1882 (to mark 100 years of the Chakri dynasty) by King Rama V, who employed British architects for this stunning centerpiece. During construction, it was decided that the building looked too European, so Thai-style spires were added to cap off the Italian Renaissance design of the base. The Thais refer to it as a *farang* wearing a *chada* (the headdress worn by classical Thai dancers). The Grand Palace Hall was used as the residence of King Rama V; a section of it is now used for receiving foreign envoys and for state dinners. The interiors are European in style—the walls are decorated with large portraits of Chakri kings, and bygone diplomatic receptions.

Shortly after completion of the hall, King Rama V had a brief audience with Carl Bock, a Norwegian naturalist whose journeys in Thailand were supported by the king. Carl Bock describes the meeting in his book *Temples and Elephants* (1884):

H.M. King Chulalongkorn

The room itself was a long chamber, containing many fine oil paintings, and an array of splendid ornaments . . . Adjoining this was the drawing-room, a stately and spacious saloon, furnished entirely in the European style in the most luxurious manner. As we entered I saw, at the opposite end of the room, his Majesty Chulalonkorn, King of Siam and Lao—a very handsome man, of about thirty years of age, slim of figure and very erect, with a very fair complexion for a Siamese, and beautiful dark, beaming eyes—who, as we stopped to make the customary triple bow, advanced to meet us . . . The abolition of the old etiquette, which required all who entered the august presence of the sovereign to prostrate themselves before him, was one of the first acts of the king on his accession in 1868 . . .

The Grand Palace Hall interiors are inaccessible, but there's a small room at ground level with a **Royal Weapons Display.** Part of the Grand Palace once served as an armory—firearms and other weapons were manufactured and stockpiled at the palace.

West of this is a tiny Thai-style structure, **Amporn Pimok Pavilion** ("Amporn Pimok Prasat"), where the king would transfer from his palanquin and disrobe before entering Dusit Throne Hall. This structure is considered a classic, and was reproduced by King Rama V in a famous pavilion at the summer retreat of Bang Pa-In.

Dusit Hall

Dusit Maha Prasat was completely burned down in 1789 after being struck by lightning. The teak throne, inlaid with mother-of-pearl, was said to have been carried out by King Rama I himself. The hall was immediately rebuilt, and is a fine example of Thai architecture from the Rattanakosin period. Especially fine is the steep roof, which has *garudas* mounted high up in the gables. Dusit Hall was once used for royal audiences, and later as the final resting place of kings before cremation.

If you continue west from Dusit Hall, there's a small cafe—a good place to park yourself after all that exhausting architecture and culture. If you still feel up to it, you can go and look at Wat Pra Keo Museum on your way out, and also the Coin Museum (near the ticket booth). Though it's tempting to try and exit by the west gate, you will most likely have to leave the palace by the north gate. From there you can walk down to Wat Po, or take a *tuk-tuk*.

yaksha (demon)

KAREN WHITE

WAT PO

This monastic complex once functioned as a Buddhist open university—Thailand's first—and was particularly strong on medicinal instruction. The first structures built here date back to the

16th century, with later embellishments and additions by Kings Rama I and Rama III. There are some 250 monks presently attached to the *wat*—their living quarters are just south of the main temple complex. The *wat* is a cluster of places of worship, study, and meditation; there's an elementary school toward the west wall, and a school of traditional massage toward the east wall.

The main attraction at the temple is the massive Reclining Buddha in the northwest corner. As you approach this area from the south gate, you pass four large **Chedi monuments,** built by King Rama I (green *chedi*); Rama III (white *chedi*, yellow *chedi*); and Rama IV (blue). Right near the northernmost *chedi* is a small pavilion with a huge drum—called **Thai Medicine Pavilion.** If you take a closer look at the interior, you'll see diagrams of the human body etched into stone—these are instructional charts for traditional massage and acupuncture; other tablets bear script with recipes for herbal remedies. These disciplines are taught at the *wat,* and patients come for treatment.

Next to that is a gateway guarded by four huge stone figures with beards and top hats. These **top hat statues** were brought as ballast on boats from China in the early 19th century. Barges set out from Thailand with full loads of rice, dropped their loads in China, and then needed some sort of weight for the return trip—so the Chinese obliged with stone statues or bundles of tiles. The statues at Wat Po with top hats and big noses, though dressed in Chinese garb, represent European demons. One story has it that King Rama I ordered these sets from China—he specified European-type images so he could show the Thais what a European looked like. If this is true, the Chinese certainly supplied some comical caricatures of Europeans.

Reclining Buddha

Housed in a building barely bigger than itself in the northwest corner of Wat Po is the colossal Reclining Buddha. This statue is made of brick, covered with cement, and coated with gold leaf. It is 46 meters long and 15 meters high and was constructed in the reign of Rama III, in 1824. A Reclining Buddha is a dying Buddha—the last position before passing into nirvana. The soles

of the feet are inlaid with intricate mother-of-pearl designs depicting the 108 auspicious signs of Buddha, derived from Pali scriptures. At the other end, during restoration in the 1980s, it was discovered that the mighty head was about to fall, because the entire weight was resting on a single strut inside the hand—the strut was reinforced. You'll find the Reclining Buddha a real challenge to photograph. It's dark in the hall (you need a tripod), and you can't back off from the statue to get it all into the frame (super wide-angle needed).

In the same compound as the Reclining Buddha is the small **Chinese Pavilion,** containing a shrine and a sacred well. Behind that is a large Bodhi tree, said to be an offshoot of the same Bodhi tree that Buddha meditated under. Just south is the **Library,** housing old manuscripts on medicine, astrology, and other subjects. The eastern courtyard of the temple is entirely taken up by the huge **Bot,** which is usually closed—at least to visitors.

Wat Po is one of the most relaxing *wats* in Bangkok—a good place to hang about, have a drink, unwind. Around the place are fortune-tellers, who will read your palm and butter you up about your rosy future—for the right fee. To really unwind, try a massage at the **Massage Institute** at the east wall—for B140 for an hour, or B80 for a half-hour session, strong fingers will work your weary bones over—*really* work them over. These are students doing their practicums; you can take courses here, too.

Stone statues in the grounds of Wat Po were originally designed to help students diagnose medical ailments. On your way out of the *wat,* take a closer look at a collection of statues known as *rishis* (hermits) near the south gate. Other statues around the monastery were donated by thankful patients. Patients at Wat Po Traditional Medicine School (herbal medicine) are treated in the late afternoon.

WAT ARUN

With batteries recharged, you should now be ready for the final jaunt of the day—to Wat Arun, Temple of the Dawn. Head through the street-side markets to the Tha Tien landing and take a cross-river ferry to Wat Arun. Here, you clamber up steep sections of the 82-meter *prang* for a fabulous view of Bangkok across the Chao Phraya.

Wat Arun is the Eiffel Tower of Bangkok. The landmark is found on countless bits of tourist literature and advertising, used on numerous postcards, used as a logo by TAT, and featured on the 10-baht coin. It is the tallest *prang* in the kingdom—the height of a 20-story building. If you examine the *prang* carefully, as Carl Bock did with astonishment in 1881, you'll find ". . . The general part of the structure is of brick; the tracery is composed of bits of broken plates, glass, cups and saucers, in fact all kinds of broken pottery and crockery. . . ." In fact, decorated with millions of pieces of Chinese porcelain. Around the base of the *prang* are some fine stone Chinese warriors—once ballast on riceboats trading with China, and now priceless antiques; guarding the temple precincts are pairs of giant *yakshas*.

Wat Arun already existed when King Taksin set up the new capital of Krungthep; Taksin built his palace right next door, thus making it his royal *wat*. King Rama I began reconstruction work on the central *prang*, elevating its height, but the work was not completed until the time of King Rama III. The phallic-shaped structure derives from Brahmanic worship in Cambodia, and symbolizes the paradise of Mt. Meru, center of the universe in Hindu-Buddhist cosmology. The base has groups of demons who appear to be supporting the structure (or possibly dancing around it); on the uppermost levels are four niches with statues of the Hindu god Indra riding a three-headed elephant—and right at the top is a Hindu thunderbolt.

This temple is named after Aruna, the Indian god of the dawn, but in terms of photography, the *wat* is far better toward sunset. At this time, the sun slants into the right bank if viewed from the top of the *wat*. If you want to get the classic postcard shot of Wat Arun itself, cross to the right bank, walk south to the turnoff for Wat Po entrance, but then go west toward the riverbank. There you can wait for the reddish sun (a color that comes from the polluted haze) to slip down behind Wat Arun, giving it a dramatic silhouette.

THE GRAND BAZAAR

The grand bazaar of the city was Sam Peng, the Chinese quarter, where almost every house was a shop and the houses were jammed into a square kilometre of land fronting the river.... Here an immense trade was carried on; shoppers thronged the narrow, crooked alleyways all day, revellers thronged the gambling houses, opium dens and brothels all night. Still, the floating market carried on. Scores of boats, each loaded to the gunwales under great piles of merchandise, massed together before sun-up, traded with that intensity common to markets and dispersed before the sun had climbed uncomfortably high.

—Larry Sternstein, describing turn-of-the-century Bangkok, in *Portrait of Bangkok*

Tha Rajini—Pak Klong Talad— Pahurat Cloth Bazaar—Sikh Temple— Little India—Sampeng Bazaar— Tha Ratchawong

Timing: Pak Klong markets are open 24 hours a day; Sampeng Bazaar is busy in the daytime from 0930 hours till the afternoon.

This tour starts at **Tha Rajini,** which is a short distance from **Pak Klong Talad,** Bangkok's main wholesale food and flower market. Produce comes in by pickup truck or minibus (fresh flowers are unloaded at night because they're cut in the afternoon)—or by longtail boat from the orchards and market gardens down the *klongs.* You will sometimes see a "vegetable boat"—a longtail loaded to the brim with wicker baskets of fruit, or chilies, or possibly roses—speeding down the Chao Phraya for Pak Klong. This is where restaurateurs and sidewalk vendors come to buy in bulk, so the place is bustling.

If you want to find out where those special Thai smells come from, follow your nose through the market to the spice section (shops toward the Tha Rajini side), where you'll find lemongrass, ginger, chilies, and garlic in bulk. More appealing to the eye are the stalls along Chakrapet Road, piled high with fruit in eye-catching patterns—spiky green jackfruit, or smooth-skinned reddish mangoes. Some more exotic specimens to identify (depending on season): rambutans, mangosteens, and pomelos.

Across the street is the cut flower section: a blaze of color with a fantastic array of roses, jasmine, orchids, gardenias, cape marigolds, amaranths, and lotus buds. You can see women threading garlands of flowers—the smaller ones *(puang malai)* are made of jasmine and gardenias, with an orchid tassel or rose-petal decorations. These originated in the 13th-century kingdom of Sukothai. They are used as offerings—placed on Buddha images or on spirit houses, and sometimes hung from windows and doors, or suspended like chandeliers from the ceiling.

Aside from offerings and merit-making occasions, flower garlands or bouquets are used on auspicious occasions such as birthdays, weddings, and festivals. You can pick up one of these fantastic works of art for a song—place it at one of the shrines along the way, or save it for your hotel room. The larger flower arrangements or bouquets have flowers embedded in, or sewn over, a mound of damp clay or sand—usually in a pyramidal design resembling a lotus bud. Thailand is the world's largest exporter of orchids:

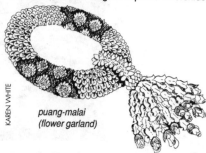

KAREN WHITE

*puang-malai
(flower garland)*

they are air-freighted to the West—at Pak Klong you can get orchids and bunches of roses at ridiculously low prices.

Heading eastward along Chakrapet, you'll see a statue of Bangkok's founder, King Rama I. The seated statue was created by Corrado Feroci, an Italian who founded Silpakorn University of Fine Arts in 1943. This statue is a shrine as well as a memorial—the belief that Thai monarchs possess divine powers was absorbed from Cambodia in the 14th century.

Turn northward up Triphet Road, and walk up to the next big avenue, Pahurat Road. Turn right along Pahurat, and you move into a very Indian presence, with **Pahurat Cloth Bazaar,** where cotton is sold by the meter—one of the best places in Thailand to buy cotton for saris and sarongs. You can get ready-made saris, batiks, and sarongs—as well as elaborate Thai sarongs used for special occasions. The market sells other clothing fabrics, bedding and curtain supplies, Indian costume jewelry, and wedding accessories.

Little India

Take note of your bearings here—there's an overhead footbridge that leads directly to Sampeng Bazaar. But stay on the west side of the road for the moment, for a short excursion to Amritsar. The Indians in the Pahurat area are mainly Sikhs. They do not mix with the Thais, rarely intermarry, and the Indians run their own schools to preserve their customs. They keep a low profile, and generally go about their business (cloth trade, factories, jewelry, condominium sales). One of the few concessions they make to living in Bangkok is to speak Thai.

If you want to get an idea of how the Sikh community preserves its customs, walk 100 meters down Chakrapet Street and follow the nearest turban into a tiny alley—which leads to a white-and-gold edifice called Siri Guru Singh Sabha. You step into one of Bangkok's strangest temples—not a Thai face to be seen. The **Sikh Temple** has six floors of marble and carpets—a vertical version of Amritsar's Golden Temple (the Amritsar temple is shown in a fresco over the elevators on the ground floor). The plan of the temple is: ground floor—offices and clinic; second floor—kitchens serving food; third floor—for meetings; fourth floor—main temple; fifth and sixth floors—elementary school. The temple is very active from early morning till about 0930. You're welcome to visit the temple on the fourth floor—where the focus is a golden structure housing Sikh holy books. Just make sure you leave your shoes on the ground floor, and wear a head-covering before entering the temple section (there are pieces of cloth available for this purpose at the fourth floor).

There's a market area around the temple—Indian teashops, restaurants, sweetshops, videorentals, emporiums, and cheap guesthouses. At 392 Chakrapet is Royal India Restaurant—drop in for snacks or sweets, *masala dosas* or a

vendor at Pak Klong Talad

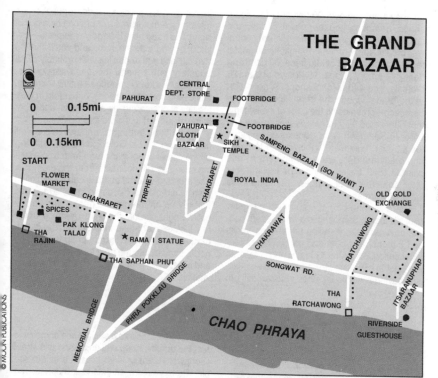

mango *lassi*. After poking around Little India, go back to the overhead footbridge, which leads to Sampeng Bazaar.

Sampeng Bazaar

Though the western end of Sampeng Bazaar is dominated by Sikhs, you soon move into a Chinese area. "Chinese" is misleading as the community is well integrated into Thai society: second-, third-, or fourth-generation Chinese think of themselves as Thais—they've never been to China, and may not even read Chinese (though they can speak it). There has been so much intermarriage and mixing of customs in Bangkok that it's almost impossible to distinguish the two groups today. Nevertheless, the Sampeng Bazaar area has a long association with the Chinese community. When King Rama I decided to relocate his capital to Bangkok, a

sizeable Chinese community living on the present site of the Grand Palace had to move. They shifted to the Sampeng area (just outside the city walls), with junks and houseboats moored abreast on the river nearby.

In 1882, King Rama V ordered a register of the population for postal and planning purposes—and for assessment for head tax, which was levied on the Chinese. According to the postal register, there were 169,300 residents in Greater Bangkok, of which roughly one-fifth were non-Thai—most of them Chinese. The inner city area of Bangkok showed a higher percentage of Chinese—although the Chinese were distributed throughout the city, their presence was strongest in the Sampeng area.

Most Chinese in Bangkok at the time were employed in marketing, manufacturing, and commerce, but some other statistics cropped up: they managed over 90 percent of all liquor shops, gambling houses, pawn shops, and opium dens. The only vice they did not control was prostitution. For Inner Bangkok, the postal register showed 245 opium dens, 69 gambling dens, 11 lottery shops, 154 pawn shops, 26 brothels, and 440 alcohol shops. A good part of the "trade" was in the green-light district of Sampeng—green being the color of the lanterns that illuminated the brothels. Naturally, law and order in Sampeng were nonexistent—gangs fought over "business" rights for the territory, and grisly murders were committed. At one point, in 1889, the army had to be brought in to quell an outbreak of gang-land feuding—this led to 800 arrests.

There is none of that opium-and-gangster stuff left today: Sampeng is a an innocent canvas-covered bazaar selling underwear, socks and buttons, and pots and pans. The bazaar (now called Soi Wanit 1) is about as close as you'll get to a walking street in Bangkok—which isn't saying a whole lot since you can still get jostled, or run over by a handcart-pusher (or a matron on a motorcycle), or brained by a bolt of cloth! The trade here is largely wholesale—ask about buying a dozen items and you'll find the little old lady you're dealing with probably owns a factory with several thousand employees. The west end of Sampeng is mainly clothing, fabric, and household goods, but tucked in here are tiny shops selling jewelry, batiks, and other items of interest to the visitor.

A long stroll through Sampeng Bazaar will bring you to the old **Gold Exchange Building** (at the corner of Soi Mangkorn), with a gold-selling business still operating from the premises. The mustard-colored building can be identified from its red *garuda* ("birdman") statue mounted halfway up on the outside (make sure you've got the right *garuda:* there's an identical one a few blocks east). Itsaranuphap Bazaar is one block east of this: at Itsaranuphap you can go north, straight into the next tour, or head south and call it a day, finishing at **Tha Ratchawong** landing.

DRAGON PATH

Bangkok's Chinatown, unlike similar districts in Western cities, is more of an historical manifestation and less of a cultural or ethnic one.
—John Hoskin, *Bangkok*

Tha Ratchawong—Itsaranuphap Bazaar—Yaowarat Road—Leng Noi Yi—Sanjao Dtai Hong Kong—Wat Traimit

Starting point: You can start this tour from Ratchawong landing—or just carry on from the previous tour at Itsaranuphap Bazaar.

Tha Ratchawong is where barges and ships used to unload their wares for market—if you go up a block and turn right, you will see goods being shifted from trucks to warehouses. You'll see tattoo-covered porters hard at work, and you may also see a company inspector who will thrust a steel tube into a sack of rice or maize to test the quality. Keep walking along this street (Songwat Road) until you reach a small temple, where you turn left onto Itsaranuphap. The old temple is definitely Chinese in style—oddly enough (given its history), Chinatown doesn't have much Chinese architecture. Apart from the temples, there is only a smattering of Chinese-style two-story shuttered storefronts.

In a city where probably half the population is of Chinese origin, you can hardly talk about "Chinatown"—the Chinese influence pervades Bangkok. Historically speaking, though, you can talk about the Chinese settlement around Sampeng and Ratchawong. The Ratchawong "Chinatown" area has lost a lot of its character over the last few decades, but you can still find narrow lanes and back-alleys where the Chinese pulse is strong.

Itsaranuphap Bazaar

One of these is Itsaranuphap Bazaar, a walking street that cuts right across Chinatown to the north. The business at this end is mostly wholesale, but retail markets pop up farther in, with a bewildering range of foodstuffs and merchandise stacked to the ceiling. Chinatown takes a lot of "decoding": at first, you may not recognize a single kind of foodstuff—after food has been dried, salted, candied, or pickled, it's hard to identify. Try this for a shopping list: dried fish maw; fish balls; candied pomelo skin; lotus seed; dried sharkfin. The sharkfin is horrendously expensive and is used (sparingly) in soups. Dried fish maw (made from fish-stomach or innards) is also used in soups—on sale in Chinatown, it is light brown in color and resembles thick, curly wafers. Speaking of fish—off to the side is a 200-year-old market called Talad Kao where you can slip and slide around like an eel on the hosed-down floor. It only operates in the morning.

Yaowarat Road
North of this, you reach Yaowarat Road, which is one of Chinatown's main arteries—at this intersection it's at its busiest. Take careful note of the semiotics of this junction as you will return to the same spot, but on the opposite side of the street. On Yaowarat you get a strong whiff of China—a smell of dried fish, cabbage, and herbal medicines—and all the signs are in Chinese characters. Do a quick circuit west along Yaowarat to check out the tea stores, the drugstores stocked with dried herbs and powdered horns (the former for cleansing the system; the latter used as aphrodisiacs), lottery-ticket sellers, and jewelers. You'll see theaters showing kung fu movies, mainly from Hong Kong—these choreographies of violence dominate the theaters and TV, and have killed off Chinese opera in Bangkok.

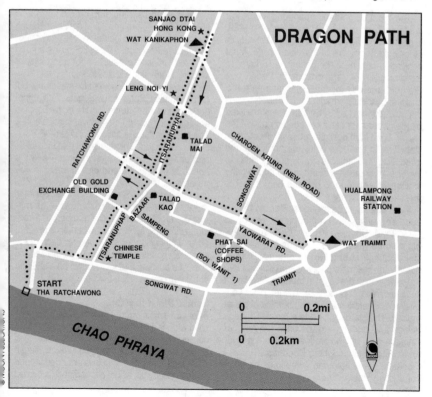

joss-stick holder at Chinatown temple

The most common shops along Yaowarat are those of goldsmiths, who do a roaring trade in gold chains. If you want to buy gold chains or other gold items, this is the place to go. Most necklaces sold here are based on 18-karat to 22-karat gold (24-karat is too soft). People buy the gold and pay for the workmanship (on a chain or bracelet); when it's sold back they sell the gold alone. The buy and sell rates are fixed by the government and are posted outside the shops. Apart from gold, the predominant color on Yaowarat is red—the color of happiness and good luck. Red lanterns signify good luck; blue lanterns may mean a death in the house (why foreigners continue to buy the blue lanterns mystifies the Chinese).

If you go back to Itsaranuphap Bazaar, there's another market section that brings you up to New Road (Charoen Krung): here, make another sortie westward—this time to visit Leng Noi Yi temple. **Leng Noi Yi** means "Dragon Lotus"—on the main doorway you will see two dragons, which are royal symbols, enclosing a lotus, a symbol of Buddhism. The temple is very busy with incense-burning and burning of paper money. The statuary here is a mix of Chinese deities and Buddha—at the back are rows of Chinese-style fat and prosperous-looking Buddhas, and a few laughing Buddhas. Chinese monks at the temple can sometimes be seen conducting funeral rites.

Go back to Itsaranuphap on the north side of New Road—here you'll find a section selling fruit, and pink temple cakes with fillings of vegetable or sticky rice. The cakes are stamped with red Chinese characters for good luck or long life. North of this is a section that deals in incense and paper goods—not for stationery, but for the afterlife. Paper houses, cars, TVs, refrigerators, and other items for use in the next life are sold, then burned on the evening of a burial. The paper artform is called *klong tek*.

It is an ancient Chinese belief that evil spirits and energies travel in straight lines—and if a house is right at the end of a street, it is vulnerable. A mirror can deflect evil spirits. You can see small *feng shui* mirrors (called *pat kwa*) in many places around Chinatown—the mirrors are eight-sided (a lucky number) and contain a yin-yang symbol at the center, surrounded by *I Ching* ideograms—one for each of the compass points. Just glance up at the second floor of a building that looks down an alley, and you'll see one of these mirrors.

Sanjao Dtai Hong Kong

After you exit Itsaranuphap at the north end, the road widens. Walk past the *wat* on your left, and continue up past stalls selling paper goods. Here, on the edge of Chinatown, you'll reach Sanjao Dtai Hong Kong. The temple is arranged around an outer courtyard, where paper money is burned in a dragon-embossed urn—sending it, via the smoke, to departed relatives to ease their afterworld lives. Most often, the money is in the form of a receipt, given after a donation to the temple (the receipt ensures no corruption). Wealthier worshippers can purchase birds for release, or even eels or turtles. The interior of the temple is thick with incense smoke. The main Buddha image is at the back of the temple, and is called Po Tek Sien Tung, a protector or helping Buddha—symbolizing help and rescue of people. This is also the name of the foundation behind the temple that does extensive charity work.

Besides money, donations are made in the form of sacks of rice, which are later distributed to the needy. Sanjao Dtai Hong Kong is a Mahayana Buddhist temple, which may explain its helping-hand orientation: on one wall in the courtyard are pictures showing temple workers on the scene of a disaster—a major accident, flood, fire, or a building collapse. There is a large foundation backing up the temple—they stockpile food for the needy, run their own modern hospital, ambulances and rescue vehicles, and employ their own uniformed workers. At the back of the temple you will see some of the temple's rescue vehicles. These are usually first on the scene of a disaster; Thai provincial governments have nothing to match them.

Retrace your path back down Itsaranuphap to Yaowarat, and turn left. Although Yaowarat is heavily Chinese, you'll notice that Chinese restaurants are curiously absent. The reason is that the value of property in Chinatown is extremely high, and restaurants require a large space—they do not turn over enough income to sustain high rentals, whereas gold-trading shops do. Thus, Chinese restaurants are scattered throughout Bangkok, and you'll find a lot with mixed Chinese and Thai menus. In Chinatown you'll find lots of streetside vendors—meals on wheels. As for teahouses, those are rare, too, but a string of teahouses (the kind where debating goes on) survives along Phat Sai Road, just south of Yaowarat.

Wat Traimit

It's a little hike to get to the last destination of this tour—follow Yaowarat east till it meets New Road at a crazy roundabout. There you proceed to a sidestreet called Thanon Traimit and find Wat Traimit, which houses, in a rather ordinary building, the largest gold Buddha image in the world—three meters high, and weighing in at over five ton. The gold is reckoned to be 18 karat, or about 80% pure: there are lots of Chinese who come to pay their respects to this Buddha for good luck! The serene Sukothai-style seated Buddha was discovered by accident in 1953. It was originally covered in stucco—when being moved by crane, the statue slipped and the stucco cracked to reveal its secret. The gold Buddha was probably cast in the Sukothai period, and covered with plaster in the 18th century to prevent capture by the Burmese attacking Ayuthaya. There is a glass case showing pieces of the stucco casing; there are also some smaller Buddha statues to which devotees apply gold leaf. The temple is open daily from 0830 to 1700 hours.

THE LEFT BANK

All this tract is occupied by Gardens and Orchards of Cocoanuts, Durians, Pomeloes, Oranges, Betel, Ceri etc. being densely inhabited and well watered by innumerable canals generally of small size.

—description of Thonburi from
Dr. Bradley's map of Bangkok (1870)

Timing: Boat trips described here are best done in the early morning when it's cooler and there are more frequent departures.

Adventuring on the *klongs* of Thonburi involves hired boats, hotel boats, or commuter longtailed boats. These trips hark back to the Bangkok of 150 years ago, when there were no roads, and all transport was done by rivercraft on the canals. A series of trips is described here—enough to keep you busy for several days. Navigation on the *klongs* is done by *wats*—the canals have confusing names; with *wats* you can pinpoint locations. The best available map showing the *wats* along the canals is called *Canals of Thonburi*, which comes in a package of four cultural maps (costing B80) produced by the Association of Siamese Architects. Although it was printed in 1981, the *wats* are certainly still in place; names of *wats* are printed in both Thai and English, which is very useful for getting around.

There is one murky *klong* trip on the Bangkok side (right bank)—50 minutes one way from Wat Saket out northeast to Bang Kapi (for a short description and map, see "Siam Mystery Tour").

The *klongs* bring river life up close—in some places the *klongs* are so tight, and the bridges so low, that even the longtails have trouble negotiating them. You sail past housing that varies from majestic teak structures to modern concrete—or else an ancient building that is crumbling into the canal. Outside the dwellings you can see spirit-houses—small shrines mounted on poles, with offerings of flowers, incense, or food. There's a lively water-borne commerce—boats delivering food, delivering mail, dropping passengers, or floating vendors plying their wares.

In many places you can see boys leaping off bridges or landings into the canals, and adults lathering themselves with soap. Crocodiles used to lurk in the waters, but there are none left now—in fact very little can live in the *klongs* now. In case you wonder about the water: the locals have developed an immunity to whatever lurks in the depths. A foreigner who went to live with a Thai family on a *klong* was talked into a swim one day: he turned white as a sheet and was sick for two days. Even the fish can't survive: dead catfish have been spotted floating in some canals. Thais will throw all their garbage and human waste into the canals, but will still drink from it and swim in it.

BOAT RENTALS AND ORGANIZED TOURS

Boat Rentals

If your time is short and your legs are long, you'll probably want to band together with some other travelers and rent a longtail or a launch by the hour (generally costing B250-300 per hour for the boat, but some have bargained it down to B150 an hour or less, with the boat taken for three hours). Longtails are easy to get from busier right-bank piers in the zone from Pinklao Bridge to Taksin Bridge. Those at the northern end of things (Tha Maharaj, Tha Chang, Tha Tien, Rajini, Saphan Phut piers) are better for bargaining—the ones to the south (Oriental Pier, pier at Shangri-la Hotel) are more expensive due to dealings with the well-heeled hotel folk in that vicinity.

Longtail rentals have ample leg-space, padded seats (unlike the hard-bottomed commuter longtails), and you can tell the tillerman to stop or slow down if you see something of interest and want to investigate. The small motor

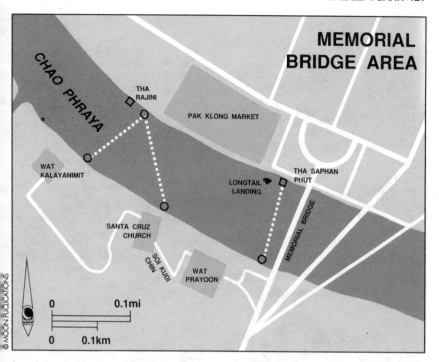

launch *(rua yon)* is actually preferable to a long-tailed boat for exploring. It looks like a tugboat, seats up to 10 passengers, who face each other (rather than being in rows); this also allows for better all-round viewing. Compared to a long-tailed boat, the motor launch is quieter, slower, and you ride higher off the water, thus avoiding spray.

One-hour Trip
Klong Mon—Klong Chak Phra—
Klong Bangkok Noi—Royal Barge Museum
On this ride you get to see a mix of architectural styles—from Western churches to century-old temples to old mosques—crowding both banks of the river.

The **Royal Barge Museum,** housed in a building resembling an aircraft hangar, holds the most spectacular of the royal barges in dry dock. The huge barge in the middle, with the prow fashioned in the head of a mythical bird, is

called *Suphannahongse* ("Golden Swan"), and belongs to the king. It weighs 15 tons, is 45 meters long, and requires 54 oarsmen to propel it. The other barges have prows sculpted in the shapes of mythical figures—*yaksha, hanuman, garuda, nagas.*

The barges used to move in procession down the river once a year, but they have been dry-docked since 1967 as an austerity measure. In 1981, 51 of the royal barges were renovated at a cost of US$3.5 million and brought out for the 1982 bicentennial celebration. King Bhumibol stepped out of his yellow Rolls Royce and boarded the *Suphannahongse,* propelled by 54 rowers dressed in crimson uniforms: the barge glided down the Chao Phraya like a giant mythological bird. As gold-encrusted conch shells and silver trumpets sounded a fanfare, several hundred thousand Thais gathered along the riverbank, straining to get a glimpse of the king and his entourage. The cruise went off without a hitch:

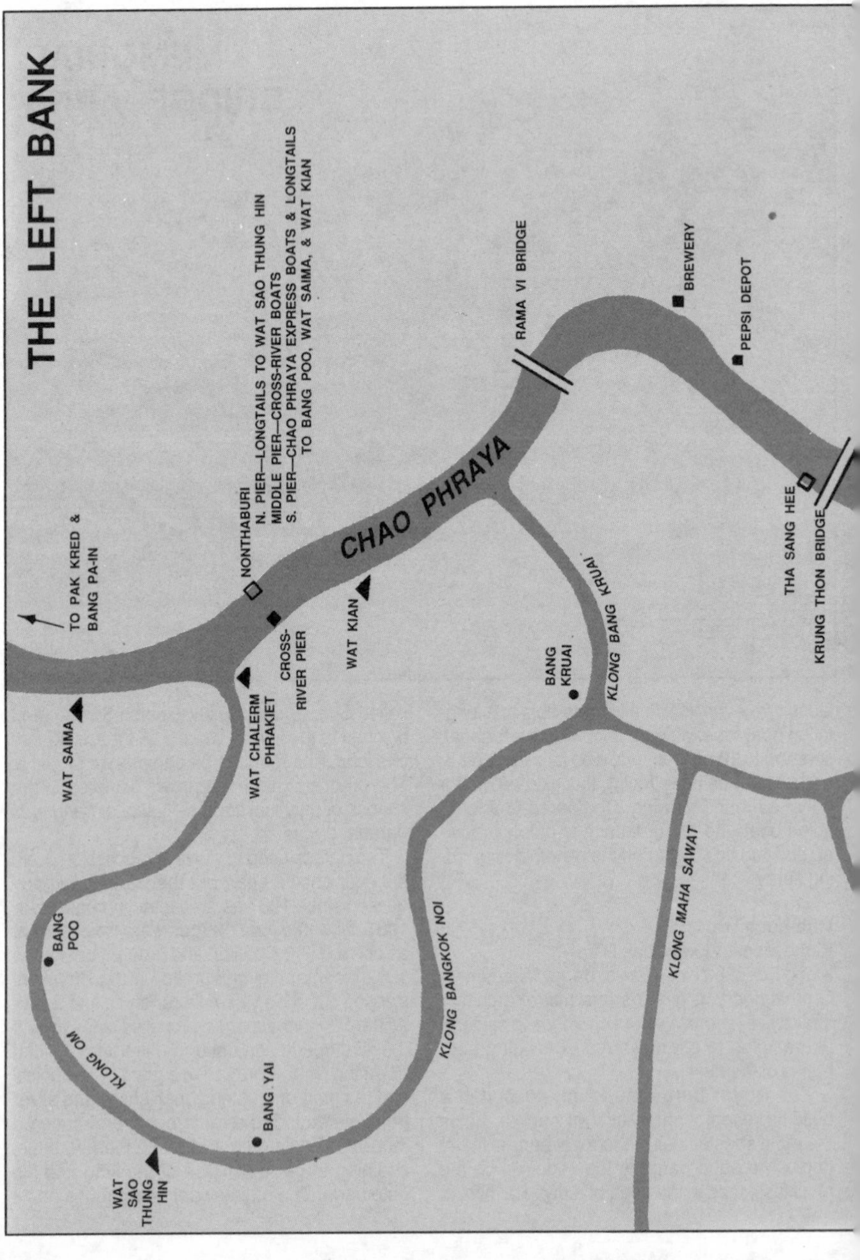

THE LEFT BANK

© MOON PUBLICATION

TO PAK KRED &
BANG PA-IN

CHAO PHRAYA

NONTHABURI
N. PIER—LONGTAILS TO WAT SAO THUNG HIN
MIDDLE PIER—CROSS-RIVER BOATS
S. PIER—CHAO PHRAYA EXPRESS BOATS & LONGTAILS
TO BANG POO, WAT SAIMA, & WAT KIAN

WAT SAIMA

WAT CHALERM
PHRAKIET

CROSS-
RIVER PIER

WAT KIAN

RAMA VI BRIDGE

BREWERY

PEPSI DEPOT

THA SANG HEE

KRUNG THON BRIDGE

BANG
KRUAI

KLONG BANG KRUAI

BANG POO

KLONG OM

BANG YAI

KLONG BANGKOK NOI

KLONG MAHA SAWAT

WAT SAO
THUNG
HIN

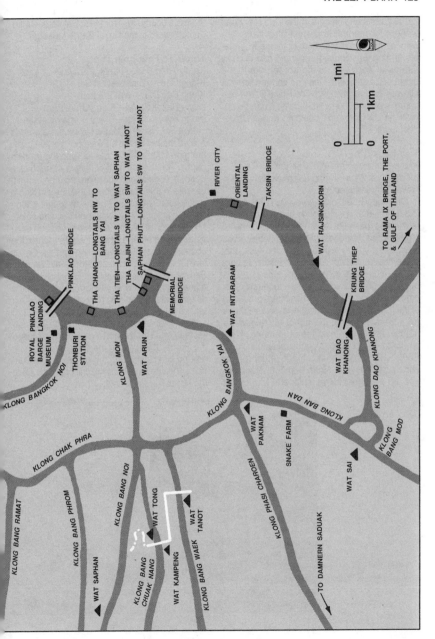

2,000 cadets and officers of the Thai Navy had worked for months to perfect their oarsmanship, as the royal barges are notoriously unstable. In previous times, the barges had to carry strings of coconuts as life-preservers in the event of an accident, since no commoner was allowed to touch the king. The Royal Barge Museum is open 0830 to 1630 daily; it can be approached by land also—see entry under "Cross-river Sorties."

Two-hour Trip

Klong Bangkok Yai—Wat Paknam—
Klong Chak Phra—Klong Bangkok Noi—
Royal Barge Museum

On Klong Bangkok Yai you can't miss **Wat Paknam**—the russet roofing of the monastery dominates the entire area. Wat Paknam has no big Buddhas, and most of the monastery looks new, but if you're looking for good luck, this place has buckets of it. The monastery is very active—some 400 monks in residence—and is popular with Thai worshippers because of its amulets. These small clay images are produced at the monastery, and their special power comes from the blessing of the abbot of Paknam, a highly esteemed meditation master. New amulets cost about B100; unusual amulets cost B6000-9000; and amulets made under former abbots can cost more than B30,000. The amulets are a magnet for worshippers, who crowd the main courtyard. From Wat Paknam, continue northward to the Royal Barge Museum.

Three- To Four-hour Trip

Krung Thep Bridge (Chao Phraya)—
Klong Dao Khanong—Wat Sai—
Klong Ban Dan—Wat Paknam—
Klong Bangkok Yai—Klong Chak Phra—
Klong Bangkok Noi—Royal Barge Museum

Wat Sai Floating Market takes place around a fixed market on the banks: occasionally a few matrons take to the water to keep the tourists happy. The floating market here is as dead as a dodo. At "peak-hour" there are so many tourist vessels in this narrow *klong* that they create a traffic jam. There are hordes of tourist shops selling over-priced artifacts, clothing, and so on. The irony of all this is that there is no such thing as a floating market where tourists gather: the observers destroy any genuine trading. Out of town is one that is more authentic—at Damnern Saduak (see "Excursions from Bangkok"). Since a floating market is anything more than half a dozen boats trading, you may stray across other places on the *klongs* which qualify.

An interesting alternative to the floating market is to head for the port—cruise down toward the Rama IX Bridge on the Chao Phraya, turn around and cut through the canals to Wat Paknam. Then do a clockwise circuit of the canals to the Royal Barge Museum.

vegetable boat on its way to market

spirit house on a klong

Organized Boat Trips

Numerous hotels and operators from the Chao Phraya piers have scheduled canal tours, priced from B100 to B150 (and up) for three hours. They use a variety of vessels, from longtails and small motor-launches to larger express boat-type vessels. You don't need a tour to get to places like Wat Arun—that's easy to do by yourself; you might want to eliminate that from the schedule, and spend more time elsewhere (just wave the boatman on—tell him you don't want to stop there). A few of the tours:

Longtail and Ricebarge Cruise: From River City—1500 to 1700 hours, starts with longtailed boat trip running along Klong Mon and Klong Bangkok Yai—about 45 minutes; then transfers to a ricebarge that cruises up and down the Chao Phraya for another 45 minutes (fruit and drinks thrown in), costing B300 a person.

Floating Markets and Snake Farm: From Tha Chang, daily at 0730 to Wat Sai Floating Market and Wat Sai Snake Farm, with return trip catching Wat Arun and the Royal Barge Museum if there's time. Other trips run from the same place during the day, and cost B150 a person. A number of other operators at Chao Phraya landings advertise similar deals, particularly at the Oriental pier. Both destinations—the floating markets and the snake farm—are tourist traps. However, what you see along the way on the canals still makes the trip worthwhile. Wat Sai Snake Farm charges B100 entry, and features a show where daredevil handlers slap the snakes around, swing them over the heads of the terrified audience, get them to pop balloons, and—the *pièce de résistance*—handler bites snake! There is a menagerie of other animals here—birds, tigers, monkeys, crocodiles, and a few elephants who obligingly pose for photos.

CROSS-RIVER SORTIES

There are two kinds of public boat transport linking Thonburi to the right bank of the Chao Phraya: the most common of these is the cross-river boats; delving deeper into the canals are the longtailed boats. You can mount forays into Thonburi using combinations of Chao Phraya Express Boats, cross-river boats, and buses, or you can use longtailed boats and buses. There are quite a few cross-river boats serving Thonburi because the Chao Phraya Express Boats mostly serve the right bank. The left bank *wats* are not nearly as spectacular as those on the right bank, but they have their own derelict charm—and they're not often visited by tourists. Here are some mini-trips using cross-river boats:

seven-headed naga
graces the prow of a ˙
royal barge

Wat Prayoon—Santa Cruz—Wat Kalayanimit

Start at Saphan Phut landing and take a cross-river boat for one baht (or walk across Memorial Bridge) to Wat Prayoon. This *wat* is known for a memorial rockery, with a pond that is chock-full of turtles. The turtles have been released into the pond by merit-seekers; feeding the turtles with fruit is also a form of gaining merit. If you keep walking through the monastery to the back, there's an exit gate that you can take—turn left, and follow an alley to Soi Kudi Chin, then turn right. This brings you to Santa Cruz Church, which wouldn't look out of place in Florence. Actually, the church is Portuguese—after Ayuthaya fell, a small band of Portuguese settled in this area, creating Santa Cruz Village, which was a foreign enclave for a considerable period. The church was rebuilt in 1834 and 1913. On Good Friday, a Passion Play is held at the church.

From Santa Cruz, you can take a cross-river boat back to Rajini landing, or you can carry on to Wat Kalayanimit and take a cross-river boat from there. To get to Wat Kalayanimit on foot from Santa Cruz, take a rather roundabout route through a maze of housing—wait for someone to come off the cross-river boat at Santa Cruz and follow them out to the roadway, then keep asking for the *wat*—you'll get there eventually. Like Wat Prayoon, Wat Kalayanimit was constructed in the reign of Rama III. While Wat Prayoon is an active monastery, Wat Kalayanimit is something of a derelict shrine—the lofty main hall has a large seated Buddha, with Chinese-style temple decorations. In the rambling grounds of the *wat* is a massive bronze bell.

Wat Rakang

You can take a cross-river boat from Tha Chang landing to get to this small *wat,* dating from the Ayuthaya period. In the western compound of the *wat* is the library, housed in an 18th-century traditional building on stilts, with beautiful carved doors, shutters, and murals illustrating scenes from the *Ramakien.* The murals were the work of priest-painter Pra Acharn Nak—one of the rare early artists whose name is known today. The house was the residence of King Rama I before he came to the throne.

Royal Barge Museum

As previously mentioned, the Royal Barge Museum is a stopping point on a tour by longtail boat. However, you can get there by a few other methods. You can get on a commuter longtail at Tha Chang landing (the longtail is headed for Klong Bangkok Noi, all the way to Bang Yai)—the operator will most likely want a ransom of B10 to drop you off at the Royal Barge Museum (make sure the operator knows where you want to get off by showing a map with Thai characters).

From the Royal Barge Museum there is a concrete walkway leading to the north: it branches into two paths—the one going northwest is a five-minute walk to Arun Amarin Road; the other going northeast is a 15-minute walk that zigzags through fascinating back-alley housing and ends up at Pra Pinklao (express boat) landing. Here you can have a drink at the Rim Nam Restaurant, overlooking the Chao Phraya. It follows that you can visit the Royal Barge Museum by starting from Pra Pinklao landing (if arriving by express boat, walk south under the bridge, and then follow signposts). There is also a cross-river ferry from Pra Pinklao landing to Tha Prachan (Thammasat University).

COMMUTER LONGTAILS

Commuter longtails can be cramped and crowded, but they put you in closer touch with the locals—you get to see how the boats drop passengers literally right at the front door. Sometimes the entire longtail is full of schoolkids in uniform; or it could have women headed for Bangkok markets with various unwieldy loads; at other times of the day, the front section could be filled with monks in bright saffron robes.

There are several strategies for touring in the commuter boats: the most important is to remember that they are commuters, and they will be crowded in peak times. Time yourself accordingly. You can cruise to the end of the line, and just stay in the boat and come back to the Chao Phraya pier. Or you can get off, walk off, and connect with a bus going back through Thonburi. In some cases, you can connect with another longtail boat (see suggestions at end of this section).

Starting from the southern end of things, here are the commuter longtails:

From Saphan Phut Landing: Longtails operate to Klong Bang Waek, passing Wat Paknam and terminating a short way past Wat Tanot. A one-way trip takes about 30 minutes. Boats run every 15 minutes from 0300 to 2200—the reason for these long hours being that Saphan Phut sits at the edge of Pak Klong Market. Price is B5 one-way for a run, but *farangs* are often charged more—maybe B10 or B15.

The longtail landing is just north of the Chao Phraya Express Boat landing.

From Rajini Landing: Rajini, the next landing north, also has longtails to Klong Bang Waek. Boats run every 20 minutes from 0600 to 2100, go past Wat Paknam, and terminate just past Wat Tanot; costs B5 one way.

From Tha Tien Landing: Longtails run along Klong Mon (due west), and then up Klong Bang Noi, terminating to the west of Wat Saphan. The ride takes 30 minutes and the canal tapers to a very narrow section past orchid nurseries and market gardens supplying Bangkok—a great trip! Cost is B5 one way; B10-15 for *farangs*. Frequency varies from every 15 minutes to once an hour, depending on the time of day. The schedule looks something like this: a boat at 0630, 0730, 0900, then on the hour till 1600, then variable frequency (every 20 to 30 minutes) until 1930, then 2030, 2100, and 2200 (this schedule is liable to change).

From Tha Chang Landing: There are two longtails running. The first is not of much use—it runs to Klong Mon and on to Klong Chuak Nang, terminating around Wat Kampeng, but the journey only takes place in the afternoon, from 1600 to 2100 hours (every half hour; cost is B10). This is a one-way trip only—the incoming trips (Wat Kampeng to Tha Chang) only take place in the morning from 0700 to 0900.

The second longtail departure, however, is a great river trip to the north, to the town of Bang Yai on Klong Bangkok Noi. Boats leave every 30 minutes from 0830 to 2300, and the fare is B7, local price. The journey takes around 50 minutes one way. From Bang Yai, you can carry on to Nonthaburi.

LONGTAIL COMBINATION TOURS

Southern *Klongs*

Tha Tien—Klong Mon—Klong Bang Noi—
On foot to Wat Tanot—Return to Saphan Phut via Klong Bang Waek and Klong Bangkok Yai—Possible stops at Wat Paknam and Wat Intararam

Allow a minimum of three hours for this journey—longer if you plan on stopping. The walk from Klong Bang Noi to Wat Tanot is about half an hour.

The Tha Tien boat only has hourly departures in the morning in the direction of Klong Mon because the commuters are all headed the other direction. Try and get an earlier boat, say at 0730, because it's cooler then and busier on the river—you'll see people coming the other way in boats, headed to work or to school or to market. Hardly anybody is headed west at this time, so you'll virtually have a private boat for B10. Establish the price early on (check before boarding), because the helmsman may try to charge more than the regular fare. When the boat leaves Klong Mon and enters Klong Bang Noi, the canal tapers to several boat-widths, and you glide into an area filled with the scent of jasmine, the sound of birds, and full of market gardens—orchid farms, coconut groves, bamboo thickets. A trip to the end of the line will take 30 minutes.

A bit of logistics here: if you consult the map, the trip down Klong Bang Noi is further than the trip down Klong Bang Waek, so in order to link up, you'd have to get out halfway along Klong Bang Noi. In order to see the entire *klong* and still have the shortcut, what you can do is ride the boat to the end of the line, wait for the boatman to turn it around, and then ride it back to the point for the crossing to Klong Bang Waek. The boatman may wait at the terminus (which is in the middle of nowhere) for half an hour, but that's okay—gives you more time to take the place in, and appreciate some silence. (Remember silence?) If you want, you can get off at a small canal-side shop about five minutes before the terminus, and wait there for the boat to return.

On the way back, ask for Wat Tong, and mention the fact that you're going to Klong Bang Waek. The turnoff for this overland section is about 15 minutes on the way back to Bangkok. You actually get off at someone's house (mind the dogs!) but this quickly gives onto a concrete walkway that will lead out in the direction of Wat Tong.

You will have to keep asking for directions, because there is no way of describing where that concrete walkway goes. After passing Wat Tong, ask for directions to Wat Tanot. About 10 minutes later, you'll reach a dirt road, and then a real paved road, complete with *tuk-tuks* and motorcycles—walk along this till you see a bridge,

keep walking, turn right shortly after the bridge, and the path leads to Wat Tanot. Here, cross to the south side of the canal, and you're almost at the terminus of the longtails on Klong Bang Waek. There are departures every 15 or 20 minutes headed to Pak Klong market on the right bank of the Chao Phraya.

Along the way are several interesting *wats* where you can make stopovers. Wat Paknam is about ten minutes from Wat Tanot—get off at a landing just near a Caltex sign. For a description of Wat Paknam, see longtail rental tour previously described. Five minutes further on by boat is Wat Intararam, which is one of the oldest in Bangkok. There are two *chedis,* containing the relics of King Taksin (reigned 1767-1782) and his queen, and several shrines with statues of King Taksin. There is a tall *viharn* with beautiful doors—the interior walls are decorated in what looks like wallpaper, but is actually painstakingly handpainted. From here, it's a ten-minute longtail ride back to Saphan Phut landing.

Northern *Klongs*

Tha Chang—Klong Bangkok Noi—
Bang Yai—Wat Sao Thung Hin—Klong Om—
Nonthaburi—Back along the Chao Phraya

Travel time alone is about 2½ hours, so allow at least four hours for the circuit—more if you wish to explore at stopping points.

You can catch a commuter longtail going to Klong Bangkok Noi from the pier next to the express boat landing at Tha Chang. Regular departures from 0830 onwards, every 30 minutes, or when the boat is full, whichever happens first; tickets are B7. About 25 minutes out, you reach the town of **Bang Kruai** where there's a temple in the shape of the principal royal barge, *Suphannahongse*—the "Golden Swan" in Thai mythology. It takes about 50 minutes to get to the town of Bang Yai from Tha Chang (see map). From here you have two options: take a land route to Nonthaburi (by bus), or carry on along the *klongs* to Nonthaburi.

Land Route From Bang Yai To Nonthaburi

If you walk about 100 meters away from the landing you arrived at, there are buses that head east to the riverbank opposite Nonthaburi, where you can catch a cross-river boat. If you go this route and have sufficient time, make a sidetrip to **Wat Chalerm Phrakiet** on the left bank of the Chao Phraya, facing Nonthaburi. You can traipse along the shore through plantations to get there. If you don't want a long hike, you can ride pillion on a motorcycle to the *wat,* which will only take a few minutes. Wat Chalerm Phrakiet is a classic *wat* built by King Rama III; the gables of the *bot* are decorated in multicolored ceramic tile. The monastery has touches of Chinese architecture, such as a rockery with an odd collection of stone animals. The setting and the architecture are inspiring, and the monks are quite approachable—the *guttis* here (monks' quarters) are on stilts, with classroom activity taking place in the open lower area. To get to Nonthaburi from the *wat,* there is a longtail landing right at the waterside near the *wat*—flag down a vessel. Or you can make your way back to the cross-river pier opposite Nonthaburi.

Klong Route From Bang Yai To Nonthaburi

The more adventurous option for getting from Bang Yai to Nonthaburi is to carry on along the *klongs* using two small craft. From Bang Yai,

hop in a tiny river-taxi for B20 (for the entire taxi) for the trip to Wat Sao Thung Hin, which is a few minutes upstream (it is possible to hire a river-taxi all the way into Nonthaburi, but that will cost a lot more than the regular commuter boats). You might have to wait at Wat Sao Thung Hin for up to 45 minutes for the next craft, the daily rocket (a ten-man longtail), which will zip you up Klong Om and around the corner, past Wat Chalerm Phrakiet (you can get off here if you want and pick up another longtail later), and on to Nonthaburi. This trip costs B10 a person, and takes 20 minutes. Klong Om is rather pleasant—much cleaner than the canals to the south, and with some newer teak stilt housing, jungle areas, and durian plantations. At Nonthaburi, you can visit the markets (a few hundred meters due east of the boat landing), have lunch at a floating restaurant south of the boat landing, and then return to Bangkok on the Chao Phraya Express Boat.

If doing this trip in the reverse direction (that is, Express Boat to Nonthaburi first), the landing for boats to Klong Om (Wat Sao Thung Hin) is the northernmost one. Nonthaburi has numerous longtail departures, but most of them are short hauls to places like Wat Saima or Wat Kian.

WALKING BUDDHA

Thinking about my yearnings and wantings, I recalled vividly the day at Wat Sraket when my teacher had pointed out that monks don't paint, write great novels, compose music, or create movie extravaganzas because these are forms of cravings or wantings. It was difficult for me to understand that writing a book was a craving, particularly when being creative was a coveted trait in Western society.

—Jane Hamilton-Merritt,
A Meditator's Diary

**Wat Suthat—Giant Swing—
Bamrung Muang—Sanjao Pho Sua—
Lak Muang shrine—Sanam Luang—
National Museum—Wat Mahathat—
Amulet market**

Timing: The National Museum is closed Mondays, Tuesdays, and holidays—but there's plenty on this tour without the museum. Actual walking time is just over an hour, but it will take a complete day to cover the ground and absorb the sights. If taking a taxi or *tuk-tuk* to the starting point, just say *Sao Ching Cha* (the Giant Swing), and everything will be understood.

Buddhist temple decoration in Thailand is exclusively done by lay people as a method of gaining merit. This contrasts with other branches of Buddhism—in Tibetan Buddhism, for instance, monks are actively involved in the creation of artwork for merit. In Thailand, large Buddhas are cast in bronze in a foundry, bought by a group of lay people, and presented to a temple as a special gift—or else they are commissioned by the monastery. Two questions that come to mind when entering a Thai temple: why, if Buddha is not a god, are there so many Buddha images in the temples? And why are there so few monks to be seen?

Wat Suthat

The area around the palace has a great number of *wats* which were built under royal sponsorship. Wat Suthat is one of the earliest of these projects, started under King Rama I—like Wat Po, Wat Suthat has a lot of Chinese touches in the architecture and statuary. The *wat* has an especially tall prayer hall, housing a 14th-century bronze Buddha, transported on barges all the way from Sukothai. Wat Suthat is a bit off the tourist track—no spectacular drawing card, but the *viharn* has a collection of gilded Buddha images, and the interior walls have lively murals showing scenes from the *Jataka* (former lives of Buddha). These date from the reign of Rama III and are reckoned to be among the finest in Thailand. King Rama II is believed to have personally carved the massive teak doors at the back of the *viharn*. A courtyard to the rear has some odd stone statues—European sailors and soldiers with bemused expressions on their faces. The statues are Chinese in origin—most likely donated to the temple by 19th-century merchants (involved in ricebarge trading) who didn't have space for them.

Wat Suthat occupies a huge block; farther to the south are the *guttis* (monks' quarters). Most monasteries have a separate compound for the monks—this is where they spend most of their time, in study and meditation. The monks are usually assigned four to a room in these simple residences. You can walk around the *guttis* if you want—perhaps even find a monk to show you around. Bangkok's temples are open to visitors from 0800 to 1700, but the monks are not around the temples much during that time—they usually gather before sunrise, or after sunset. From 0600 to 0700 monks go out with alms-bowls for food. At Wat Suthat, they will be around a morning food market in an alley to the west of the *wat*. Just before noon they may gather for the last meal of the day—sometimes special "treats" are brought in by worshippers. No food is eaten after 1200—only drinks are allowed. In the afternoon, the monks study or

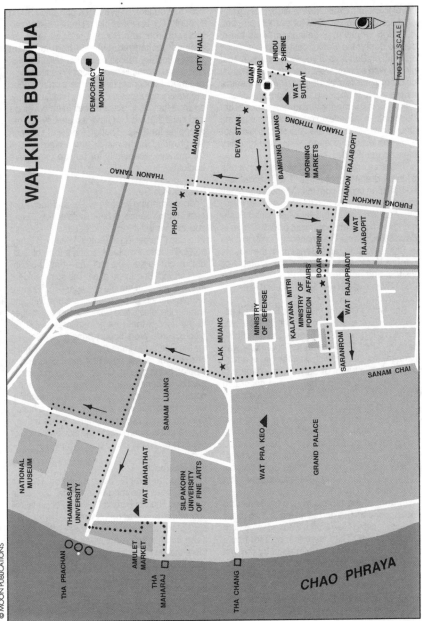

WALKING BUDDHA

NOT TO SCALE

DEMOCRACY MONUMENT

CITY HALL

GIANT SWING

HINDU SHRINE

WAT SUTHAT

MAHANOP

DEVA STAN

THANON TANAO

BAMRUNG MUANG

THANON TITHONG

MORNING MARKETS

THANON RAJABOPIT

PHO SUA

FURONG NAKHON

BOAR SHRINE

WAT RAJABOPIT

WAT RAJAPRADIT

KALAYANA MITRI
MINISTRY OF FOREIGN AFFAIRS

MINISTRY OF DEFENSE

LAK MUANG

SARANROM

SANAM CHAI

SANAM LUANG

WAT PRA KEO

GRAND PALACE

NATIONAL MUSEUM

THAMMASAT UNIVERSITY

WAT MAHATHAT

SILPAKORN UNIVERSITY OF FINE ARTS

THA PRACHAN

AMULET MARKET

THA MAHARAJ

THA CHANG

CHAO PHRAYA

© MOON PUBLICATIONS

travel to other monasteries to study; they gather at around 1900 or 2000 for evening prayers. Although monks may deliver sermons to lay people during the week, most temple services are held on Sundays. If you wonder about Thai monks who smoke, wear designer sunglasses, or carry a stereo blaring rock music: some monks are only on board for a short period, as a retreat or as a merit-gaining procedure. Thai Buddhism is very flexible—some sects permit smoking, while others are very strict and do not allow the monks to even wear sandals (they must go barefoot).

The area around the front of Wat Suthat has a strong Brahman presence. The Thais inherited Brahman beliefs from the Cambodians. Many royal and state ceremonies are Brahman in origin, and are conducted by white-robed Brahman priests. To the northwest of Wat Suthat is **Deva Stan**, a small Brahman temple with statues of Shiva, Vishnu, and Ganesh; to the east is **Sanjao Kack**, a Hindu shrine with a statue of Vishnu; and right in front of Wat Suthat is the Giant Swing, which was formerly used in an annual Brahman ceremony.

Sao Ching Cha, or the Giant Swing, an assembly of colossal teak pillars painted red, was moved to its present location at the turn of the century. Until 1935 (when the ceremony was banned) the Giant Swing was the site of a two-day festival in honor of Shiva, with a parade of war elephants, military bands, and decorated trucks. During the festival a daredevil stunt was performed by young Brahman priests. Teams of four priests would get on a swing (hung from the crosspiece of the teak structure): as the swing gained momentum, one of the men would attempt to snatch, with his mouth, a purse of money mounted on a 15-meter bamboo pole to the west of the swing. Over-zealous swinging could lead to a free-fall from the swing.

In front of the temple you're on **Bamrung Muang**, one of Thailand's first roads. Two roads (the other being New Road) were adapted from elephant trails. They were first built for horse and carriage, and were later used by the first cars in Thailand, belonging to the king and the royal family. Bamrung Muang at the turn of the century was a walking street, with the odd rickshaw or pony cart using it—hard to imagine

now as you look at five lanes of traffic roaring through. The business of the street—selling religious objects and Buddha images—has remained unchanged. On sale here are giant brass Buddhas, massive candles, bells, monks' clothing, and temple decorations. You may even see monks shopping here. In the stricter orders, monks are not allowed to directly handle money, so what they do is place money in an envelope and hand that over, or have temple boys do the shopping for them. Though food and lodgings are provided for the monks, there is still a need for money—especially for buying expensive books.

Sanjao Pho Sua

Follow Bamrung Muang west, and turn right onto Thanon Tanao. A ten-minute walk will bring you to a very different kind of temple—Sanjao Pho Sua ("Father Tiger Temple"). Many of Bangkok's Chinese temples practice a form of Buddhism, but some—like this one—have no connection with Buddhism at all. The spirit resident in this Confucian temple is a tiger—in the inner temple there is a row of small statues, with the tiger on the far left, and Confucius several statues to the right of that (the golden image with the black beard). Worshippers bring paper clothing for the Confucian image, and they bring chunks of raw pork for the tiger (the meat is later distributed to the needy). Other offerings include gigantic red candles and incense sticks. People come to Pho Sua for guidance—the divination, as at Thai temples, is done by shaking a bunch of sticks till one pops out. That stick has a number—and it is taken over to the side and a slip of paper is given out (in Thai or Chinese).

Wat Rajabopit

Leaving the temple, head south on Thanon Tanao, cross Bamrung Muang, and the street turns into Thanon Furang Nakhon. Follow this till you come to a *wat* on a corner. Ah yes, you say, just another *wat* on a corner—after you've been in Bangkok for a week, and you know there's a *wat* on just about every corner, you start to get jaded. But this one is *different!* Wat Rajabopit is, quite simply, unique. This delightful *wat* was built in 1870 and reflects King Chulalongkorn's early preoccupation with Western

tile-work detail from Wat Rajabopit

art and architecture. The entrance doors have soldiers in European uniform carved on them; the interior of the *bot* looks like a Gothic cathedral, with chandeliers, arches, and high ceiling. But the most startling feature of the *wat* is the use of a Western architectural form not found in any other Thai temple—the rounded form. The soaring central *chedi* has four pavilions attached with rotund galleries; this assembly is enclosed by a circular cloister. The artwork at Wat Rajabopit is superb—the doors and windows are finely detailed. The delicate yellow tilework is not made of broken pieces as at Wat Arun, but of specially ordered tiles.

Wat Rajapradit

If you continue west of Wat Rajabopit, you'll come to a small bridge over a canal—on the other side is a gilded boar mounted on a lump of stone. This weird shrine was erected to commemorate the birth year (Year of the Pig) of King Rama V's consort, Queen Saowapha. A short walk brings you to Wat Rajapradit. Wat Rajapradit is not on the regular tourist traffic routes, which is a blessing if you're looking for some peace and quiet. The main building is covered in grey marble and flanked by two Khmer-style *prangs*. Check out the stone lions around the compound—as with other Chinese stone lions that grace Bangkok's temple courtyards, these have free-rolling balls ingeniously lodged in their mouths. Poke a few fingers in and roll the ball around for good luck. If you examine some of the statuary carefully, you'll notice that on at least one statue the body doesn't match the head—the head was hacked off by looters, and the monastery replaced it with a concrete one. That's why important statuary is under lock and key in the National Museum.

Continue west, turn right on Sanam Chai, and you'll pass the Ministry of Foreign Affairs building. This is French colonial in style: not built by the French, but copied from the French—the Thais saw a lot of French architecture in Indochina. Farther up is the Ministry of Defense, with a collection of old cannons parked on the front lawn.

Lak Muang

North of this is Lak Muang, one of the city's busiest shrines. The shrine houses the founding pillar of the city—a *lingam*-shape in honor of the god Shiva. Supplicants put strips of gold leaf on this pillar; a second pillar represents Thonburi, which now falls under Bangkok's jurisdiction. Distances throughout Thailand are measured from here. Just about every form of Thai wish-fulfillment and worship is indulged in at this shrine—offering lotus-buds, burning incense, releasing birds, applying gold leaf to wooden elephant guardians, shaking "lucky sticks" to read fortunes . . . but of special interest to visitors are the performances of *likay* dance-drama. These take place in a small theater at the shrine, and are paid for by grateful worshippers—those who have had their wishes granted. *Likay* is a kind of village-fair entertainment—classical dance mixed with bawdy slapstick.

From Lak Muang, continue north a bit, and then cross **Sanam Luang**, the "Field of Kings," a vast open area sometimes used for ceremonies or festivals, but more often used for local sports. In March and April, when it's windier, the whole area is taken up by kite-flyers. Kite combat is a serious adult sport, with company-sponsored teams—one team flies a huge "male" kite that attempts to snag a lighter (but faster) "female" kite and drag it across a dividing line. *Takraw* tournaments also take place at Sanam Luang in March and April—one version is net *takraw*, which is very much like volleyball played with the feet, using a hollow rattan ball.

National Museum

At the northwest end of Sanam Luang is the National Museum—a treasure-trove of material on Thai history, archaeology, art, and culture. It houses a stunning collection of Hindu and Buddhist statuary. To do the place justice really requires a whole day, or several half-day visits. The museum is closed Mondays, Tuesdays, and holidays, otherwise open 0900 to 1600, with last tickets sold at 1530. A pamphlet with a map is supplied when you purchase a ticket, so you can easily find your way round; you can also buy a detailed guidebook to the museum. The best time to visit is mid-week, when there are escorted tours. The tours given by volunteers in English on Wednesday at 0930 (Thai Buddhism) and on Thursday at 0930 (Thai art and culture) are highly recommended.

Meanwhile, with an entry fee of B20, it won't hurt to drop in for an hour or so and see some of the Buddha images. These are housed in the S-section (two floors of Asian art and Thai) and the N-section (two floors of Thai Buddha images, including one room devoted to Bangkok period). Here you see the great diversity of styles and materials—Buddhas made of marble, limestone, wood, or stone; Buddhas in Dvaravati, Khmer, Sukothai, or Ayuthayan styles; Buddhas large and small; Buddhas in a great variety of poses: preaching posture, gesture of Dispelling Fear, Victory over Mara posture. And what exactly did Buddha look like? Unknown—but to make him readily recognizable, Buddhist authorities invented 32 special features as a guideline for sculptors and artisans—a cranial bump, hooked nose, arched eyebrows, long earlobes, and so on. And the Buddha is shown in stock positions with hand gestures (called *mudras*—

see Buddhism in the Introduction for details) that correspond to important events in his lifetime.

You've probably seen a Seated Buddha, a Reclining Buddha, and a Standing Buddha—but have you seen a Walking Buddha? In the N8 section of the museum is a famous **Walking Buddha**—a delicate bronze statue with asexual features, done in Sukothai style. The weight of the statue rests on its right foot, and its left hand is extended with palm out in the gesture of Dispelling Fear (said to have originated when Buddha raised his hand to subdue a rampaging elephant). Made in the 15th century, this small statue gives a real impression of a body in motion, which was a complete breakaway from traditional artforms at the time. The Walking Buddha posture is rarely seen in Indian art—and then only in relief. The Sukothai period saw the development of a fully in-the-round Walking Buddha—the first images of this type date from the 14th century. The significance of Walking Buddhas is enigmatic—some scholars think that it is connected to Buddha leaving sacred footprints; another scholar claims the Sukothai Walking Buddhas were the talismans of forest-dwelling monks, who had to make lengthy daily walks to collect food from lay people in the towns.

The long arms seen in this statue are one of the special features of Buddha, as are the flat feet with projecting heels; on top of the head is the Thai flame, symbolizing the Buddha's radiant energy—this is a Sukothai invention. Nothing is known about the sculptor of this piece—nor, indeed about *any* of the artisans whose pieces grace the museum's collection. This kind of art springs from an anonymous well.

There is a style of meditation called "walking meditation." In some disciplines, seated meditation (in the lotus position) concentrates on breathing—and so walking meditation focuses on the act of walking. In this style, monks slowly pace up and down a five-meter space—sometimes for 20 minutes, sometimes for up to an hour, with heads slightly bowed, arms clasped loosely together at the front or back, and eyes lowered to a spot two meters in front of the forward step. Concentration on movements is focused like this: *I am raising my left foot, I am*

*Buddha statues
in the courtyard of
Wat Rajabopit, awaiting
relocation after
renovations*

*moving it forward, I am putting it down. I am
raising my right foot, I am moving it forward, I am
putting it down. I am stopping. I am turning. I
am moving forward again. I am raising my left
foot, I am moving it forward.* And so on.

As mentioned, the National Museum is worth
a half-day on its own, preferably on a volun-
teer-escorted tour. If you have more time, or if
you return for another visit, be sure to see **Buddhaisawan Chapel,** which was once part of a
palace. Under the early Chakri dynasty kings,
there were two sovereigns in Thailand: the National Museum sits on what was formerly the
palace of the second king, covering an area
(called Wang Na) that included Thammasat University, the National Museum, and the National
Theater. This area was bounded by a wall and
comprised housing, workshops, warehouses,
and military barracks. The last of the second
sovereigns was Pra Pinklao (the nearby bridge
on the Chao Phraya is named after him). He
was also given the name George Washington,
after the American president; on his death in
1885, the office of second sovereign was abol-
ished by King Rama V.

The interior walls of Buddhaisawan Chapel
have some of the oldest murals in Bangkok.
One set of murals depicts scenes from the life of
Buddha (some are dark and in bad condition—
you need a flashlight). Here is where the angels of Bangkok (the "thep" in *Krung Thep,* City
of Angels) are to be found—there are five rows
of them on the walls, kneeling in respect to the
Buddha image. The chapel was built in 1787 to
house a Buddha statue, **Pra Buddha Sihing,**
which is made of bronze, plated with gold—and
considered second in importance only to the
Emerald Buddha. This seated Buddha image
is believed to date from the 15th century—legends trace its origin to Sri Lanka.

All The Buddhas Of Bangkok

A statistical problem to ponder: just how many
Buddhas are there in Bangkok? To begin this
calculation, figure that most residences in
Bangkok have a Buddhist shrine, or a collection of Buddhas in a special Buddha Room; hotels, shops, and offices have their own shrines;
each *wat* has hundreds of images—statues,
frescoes, and so on; and most Thais carry a
small Buddha image as an amulet. Why so
many Buddhas?

Buddha declined to have images of himself
made during his lifetime—he preached non-
attachment to material objects. It was not until
hundreds of years after his death that statues,
murals, and icons started to appear. This was
because, at a simple level of Buddhism, people
demanded a physical presence for worship—
something they could focus on. Later on, creating artwork for the temples was considered meritorious—and no temple would refuse to accept

a Buddha statue (leading to a surfeit of statues in some temples). Buddha statues also became regarded as talismans—for the home, for the monastery, or even for the entire country (as with the Emerald Buddha). The power of a Buddha statue or amulet is said to come from its consecration: if it was blessed by a high-ranking abbot, it may have special powers.

It's not enough to simply own one of these Buddhas—special care must be taken of the image. The statue and the area around it must be kept clean; the image must be presented with garlands of flowers and other tributes; the statue must occupy a high place; and, above all, the owner must have faith in the statue's powers.

In the temples, Buddha images can be used for instruction—a wall mural depicting the life of Buddha is much more than a decoration. At a higher level, Buddha sculptures are used as meditation aids: by focusing on Buddha's serene face, the meditator can initiate a contemplative state.

One of the best-known meditation centers in Bangkok is **Wat Mahathat,** not far from the National Museum. Wat Mahathat offers free lec-tures on Buddhism and Vipassana meditation on the first and third Saturday of each month at 1600 at Vicayun Hall. The *wat* houses Mahachulalongkorn Buddhist University, one of the two highest seats of Buddhist learning in Thailand. For the casual visitor, there's not much to see in this rather austere place—but nearby is a thriving **amulet market.** It runs along the sidewalk north of the monastery, with dealers selling Buddha statues, amulets, wooden penises for virility, photos of Chakri kings, medallions struck with figures of revered abbots or kings—there are so many types that you need a catalogue to figure it all out (the dealers sell those, too, as well as magazines on identifying amulets). If you follow this road to the end, you'll find an entrance to a large covered market. At the north end there are some excellent cheap sit-down food areas near the river; further in, there is a large amulet market. Make your way through this, and you'll eventually surface right near the express boat landing at **Tha Maharaj.** At the landing there's a good restaurant with bright-red decor—also called Maharaj—where you can sit overlooking the Chao Phraya.

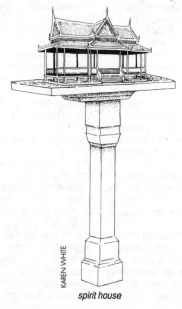

KAREN WHITE

spirit house

SIAM MYSTERY TOUR

The Thais cannot help regretting that Buddhism offers no guidance in such important everyday matters as forecasting the results of the next state lottery, putting through a successful business deal or increasing a woman's fertility, and that it provides no special rituals for weddings, coronations or similar rites.
—John Blofield, *Bangkok*

Wat Saket—the Golden Mount—bird market—Wat Rajanada amulet market—The Iron Wat—Klong Saensaep by longtailed boat—Sanjao Mae Tuptim—Erawan Shrine—Siam Square—Jim Thompson's Thai House

Timing: Jim Thompson's house is closed Sundays.

Before you set out, a few mystery trivia questions to ponder:

What happened to all the canals on the east bank of Bangkok? Why do buyers purchase small wooden phalluses at Wat Rajanada? What is the most common offering at the shrine of Mae Tuptim? What did a Queen Victoria statue represent to the Thais? What form of worship is said to please the Hindu god Brahma? Why does the Sogo Building have Ionic columns? And what happened to millionaire Jim Thompson?

The starting point for this trip is **Wat Saket,** which is open from 0700 or even earlier. There's not a whole lot to see at Wat Saket itself (the Convocation Hall, lined with gold Buddha statues, is worth a visit); what you go there for is the view from the top of the **Golden Mount.** This is the imposing structure that looks like a medieval fortress—or a battle cruiser. Ascend the stairs to the very top and you'll come out on an open-air terrace with bird's-eye views of Bangkok's urban sprawl. In early Bangkok this was the highest viewpoint in the city—sitting on a man-made hill. The original Golden Mount, ordered by King Rama III, collapsed during construction—King Rama IV rebuilt it.

From here you can see where you'll be going next: a murky canal below, and a fort with ramparts which holds the bird market. The octagonal fort is one of two left from the original 14 watchtowers, once part of the city wall girdling Rattanakosin Island. Wat Saket lay just outside this wall. Commoners could not be cremated within the city walls, so during 19th-century cholera plagues in Bangkok, the bodies of paupers were brought to Wat Saket for disposal—they were either cremated or left for the vultures.

Walk down from the Golden Mount to a bridge, and stroll around to the small **bird market** inside the fort by the canal. The birds are singing doves, some worth a fortune—as in China, the birds are entered in singing competitions, with big prizes. This enclosure has a few "antique" stalls, but there's a bigger collection of Buddhas and amulets in the grounds of the *wat* on the opposite side of the road.

The dim stalls at **Wat Rajanada** have a collection of fake antiques, brand-new kitsch, and maybe even some real pieces. Wat Rajanada is famed for its amulets—which will protect against disasters as varied as plane crashes and sterility. Also on sale are small wooden phalluses (which Thai males wear on a string around the waist to ensure virility; they are also placed on altars to induce fertility). In the background is **Lohaprasat,** known as The Iron Wat. This steel castle is based on a Sri Lankan temple and was built about 155 years ago. The model was destroyed, leaving Lohaprasat the only temple of its kind in the world. You can walk around the temple, but no entry is allowed—the way is blocked by entrance-gates with wrought-iron Buddhas.

Klong Saensaep

If you backtrack a little to the canal you passed, you will see a landing for longtailed boats. Get on a commuter longtail and ask for Tha Saphan Wit-

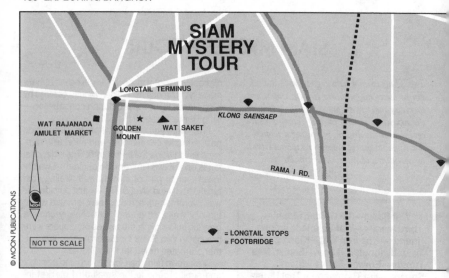

SIAM MYSTERY TOUR

LONGTAIL TERMINUS

KLONG SAENSAEP

WAT RAJANADA
AMULET MARKET

GOLDEN
MOUNT

WAT SAKET

RAMA I RD.

= LONGTAIL STOPS
= FOOTBRIDGE

© MOON PUBLICATIONS

NOT TO SCALE

tayu ("Wittayu Bridge Landing"); the trip takes 18 minutes. When you board the boat, you'll find out why this *klong*—Klong Saensaep—is the very last on Bangkok's east bank to still be used by longtails—the other ones died, or were filled in to make roads in the 1960s (Silom Road was once a canal). So here is the boat to Hades, home of the dead, on the River Styx—and Charon, your trusty boatman, will propel you through the black muck for a mere seven baht. Riders hide behind newspapers or hold tissues over mouth and nose to avoid black spray from the canal. (My apologies for subjecting you to such a smelly experience, but it does save a lot of time— next time, bring a shower cap and a face mask). At one time Klong Saensaep must have been a very pretty canal, with leafy trees overhanging it—looks almost Parisian in parts. Amazing the way office workers in high heels, chic skirts, and immaculate hairdos step on and off the longtail landings without a single wobble.

On your left, if you peer closely, you'll see a kick-boxing academy with a ring right next to the river. And you have to wonder: has any losing boxer gone right over the ropes and into the canal? Or does that increase motivation—you fight well, or else you end up polluted from head to toe. This section of the river is fronted by shanties—this is back-alley Bangkok up close. Rubbish is strewn under the houses; the canal is filled with all kinds of pollutants. The most poverty-stricken are those who make use of a bridge for a roof over their heads, with makeshift straw matting for a shelter. There are even a few places built smack under a railway bridge. The longtail you're on goes all the way out to Bang Kapi (another 45 minutes further) to the northeast of Bangkok, where you actually get to see green water and bougainvillaea and coconut palms—but for the purposes of this tour, get off at the Hilton.

The approach to the stop you want—Saphan Wittayu—is signaled by a large "3" on top of a building to the north—(TV Channel 3 offices). Make sure you wave your hand to stop the boat at Saphan Wittayu—it's not a common passenger stop. (The guests at the Hilton certainly don't arrive this way!) It's a short walk from the boat landing to the grounds of the Hilton.

You couldn't find a greater contrast than that between the opulent glass-and-steel palace of the Hilton and the murky, garbage-strewn *klong* and run-down housing a few hundred meters away—but that's Bangkok for you. Walk through the lush grounds (through a parking lot) to the far corner of the Hilton facing the canal.

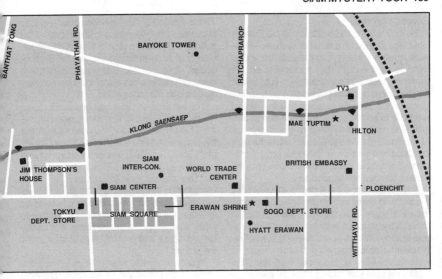

Sanjao Mae Tuptim

Overlooking the canal is Sanjao Mae Tuptim, one of the strangest shrines in Bangkok. It has a small spirit-house, with the usual offerings of lotuses, incense, and food, but there is another kind of offering—wooden phalluses. Hundreds of these carved and painted phalluses, ranging from small to gigantic, surround the small shrine. The origin of the shrine, or how this custom of leaving phalluses came to pass, is unknown, but it is thought that the phalluses symbolize the Hindu god Shiva. Thailand's cult of phallus worship is said to have originated in Cambodia in the 13th century. The female spirit (called Mae Tuptim) is believed to reside in a tree at the site, and promotes prosperity in general, so both men and women come to pay homage— hoping for success in the lottery, or for the successful birth of a child. You can make your way from here back inside the Hilton—perhaps stopping for a drink in the Garden Restaurant, which overlooks the lushest hotel grounds in Bangkok. In the absence of a botanical gardens in Bangkok's city zone, the grounds of the Hilton are Mecca for the plant lover.

After you exit the Hilton, it's about a 20-minute walk to the next destination—Erawan Shrine.

You can shorten the not-so-interesting walk by taking a *tuk-tuk,* but the traffic runs one-way against you on Wireless Road, so you'll have to walk up to Ploenchit. Along the way, you pass the large walled compound of the British Embassy. There are over a dozen Gurkhas on duty at the embassy—you may glimpse a Gurkha officer with khaki outfit, black beret, and *kukri* (a razor-sharp machete) sheathed on his belt. On Ploenchit Road, through the former front gates, you can peek at a statue of Queen Victoria, sitting in the garden. At the base of the statue, it reads: Victoria, Queen of Great Britain & Ireland, Empress of India, Erected in loving memory by her subjects in Siam, 1903. The statue was moved back from the gates of the embassy in 1907 because it attracted too much attention for worship as a fertility symbol—not so strange when you consider that the Thais worship their own kings as gods. A Thai ambassador despatched to the court of the great queen reported, in great admiration, that she appeared in her aspect and bearing "a beautiful and majestic white elephant."

From this point, cross a footbridge and take a bus or *tuk-tuk* to Erawan Shrine—look for Greek columns a short way down on the left.

Erawan Shrine

In the 1950s the construction of the old Erawan Hotel was dogged by a series of mishaps—there were mysterious delays and accidents; a ship bringing marble from Italy was lost at sea. A Brahman priest was consulted, who put forward the theory that because some trees had been cut down on the site, the resident tree spirits had no place to call home—hence the run of bad luck. The priest recommended the construction of a shrine to Brahma to accommodate the spirits. Once this was done, the hotel project proceeded at a rapid pace, and the shrine became famous as a source of good luck.

Brahma appears at the shrine as a four-headed multiarmed deity set on an altar. "Erawan" means three-headed elephant: the elephant is Brahma's mythical mount, which explains why one of the offerings at the shrine is a wooden elephant statue. There's a steady stream of worshippers offering joss sticks, food, and lotus buds to Brahma, or gilding elephant statues—making requests for health, wealth, and success in various endeavors. Those who have had wishes granted will often pay for brightly costumed dance performers to do a few rounds of the Brahma statue—this is one of the few places in Bangkok where you can see classical dance movements up close. Brahma is said to be pleased by the female form, and women who've had wishes granted are rumored to have danced topless (or naked) in front of the shrine.

These extremely rare performances naturally take place when there is nobody around—after midnight. You will notice that anybody in the vicinity of Erawan Shrine will *wai* the Brahma statue—this includes bus passengers going past, and, rather more alarming, drivers as they hurtle along Ploenchit Road.

The old Erawan Hotel was eventually pulled down, and a massive new structure erected— the Grand Hyatt Erawan. You won't fail to notice the crazy architecture at Erawan Sogo Department Store, Amarin Tower, and the Grand Hyatt Erawan—Greek Ionic pillars juxtaposed with the Thai classic style of Erawan Hotel. It's a combination that is described by the architects as Greco-Thai, and described by others as an eyesore. It's all part of marketing strategy—to make an ordinary department store look classical and classy, and put McDonald's really "under the arches."

You may wonder what relation shrines like those at the Hilton and Erawan hotels have to Buddhism. The answer is: very little. Both shrines derive from Brahmanism, with a dose of animism. Buddhism, Brahmanism, and animism are independent fields fulfilling separate needs, but the three can complement and reinforce each other, and the Thais see no conflict between them. Buddha focused on the central issue of man's suffering, its causes, and its removal. This left many other questions in the more mundane world unanswered—how to deal

A classical dancer takes a break at Erawan shrine.

with the erratic forces of nature, the material world, well-being, and survival. The gods of the spirit world were never specifically denied by Buddha—Brahmanism and animism fulfill the popular need for images that have a magical power to grant wishes.

After visiting Erawan Shrine, take an air-conditioned breather at **Siam Center.** A bus or a *tuk-tuk* is recommended for the trip to Siam Center down Ploenchit (which turns into Rama I Road); otherwise it's a 15-minute walk. This area is a magnet for Thai teenagers and university students, drawn by the ritzy boutiques, coffee-shops, and by the numerous movie theaters. Siam Center is the large green block on your right—there are a number of pleasant cafes within—try **UCC** on the ground floor, or **Tramps** on the 4th floor. Siam Center boutiques may capture your attention, and there are some great tailors there, too (try the 2nd floor).

Jim Thompson's Thai House

Ten minutes of walking from Siam Center will bring you to Jim Thompson's Thai House. It's on Soi Kasemsan 2, and is clearly signposted—the house is right at the end of the *soi*. Open 0900 to 1700 daily except Sundays, the house is a cool place to be during the afternoon heat. Entry to the grounds is free; if you want to see the interior of the house, you pay a B100 entry fee (B40 for students), which includes a tour with a volunteer guide.

Jim Thompson was such a legendary figure in Thailand that a letter addressed to him, care of Bangkok, would find its way to this house. The American entrepreneur arrived in Bangkok after WW II, and single-handedly set about reviving the Thai silk industry. In March 1967, at the age of 61, Thompson disappeared while on a stroll in the Cameron Highlands, a jungle area in Central Malaysia. Theories about the disappearance range from CIA involvement to communist insurgent activity; from being eaten by tigers to being kidnapped by love-starved aboriginal women. The fact that Thompson's elder sister was murdered in America the same

BOB RACE

Thai classical dancers

year lent weight to the intrigue-and-plot theories, but neither case has been solved. Thompson's will was not found till two years later: it was folded into the blueprints for the Thai House. Thompson's nephew, Henry Thompson III, was the sole beneficiary of the estate. He established a foundation to maintain the house and its art collection, and to open it to the public, with proceeds going to various charities and to research projects for Thai arts.

The Thai House is more or less preserved as Thompson had lived in it—except that his animals are not around anymore (he had several dogs and a cockatoo). In 1958, Thompson (a practicing architect before coming to Bangkok) decided to buy a group of existing traditional (19th century) teak residences—these can be readily disassembled and moved. One house came from a silk-weaving village that he dealt with; other buildings came from as far afield as Ayuthaya. The group of six buildings was completed by 1959. Thompson adapted classical concepts to a contemporary lifestyle—an innovation that sparked a great renewal of interest in Thai-style housing.

On permanent display inside is Thompson's collection of Asian artifacts, including Cambodian stone figures, wooden Burmese statues, and a superb collection of Bencharong porcelain pieces. He scaled down his collecting of Thai artifacts because some Thai pieces he had bought were questioned by Thai authorities: Thompson promptly took the pieces under investigation to the National Museum and left them there.

Thompson used to approach the residence by boat along the *klong*—in fact, the road entrance is the back door. There is a landing for a longtailed boat on the opposite side of Klong Saensaep, not far off from the house, but you can't reach it directly—you have to walk down to Rama I Road, walk back down the next *soi* to the west, and cross a bridge to get to that landing (which is a fair walk). You can then ride back to Wat Saket. Otherwise, walk out of Soi Kasemsan and sit out the rush-hour in a restaurant or bar in the Siam Square area.

TEAK MANSIONS, CLASSIC GARDENS

The classic northern house, rectangular in shape, is raised a considerable distance off the ground on sturdy round posts, oriented north and south to expose it to the prevailing winds. Wood is used throughout, and the walls, doors, windows and gable ends are made as separate units, an early form of prefabrication that was being practiced in Thailand centuries before its advantages were recognized by Western architects.

—William Warren, *Thai Style*

Teak was once the most abundant building material in northern Thailand, and the wood favored for construction of better houses, both in north and central Thailand. Today, "teak" is synonymous with "antique," as the wood has been almost logged out in Thailand. The places described in this tour are old teak mansions, now museums, which preserve an older, more regal lifestyle. The pleasant gardens in the grounds are good for quiet reflection or conversation.

This tour starts with Vimanmek Mansions, which can be reached from **Tha Sang Hee** landing on the Chao Phraya. If you approach along the Chao Phraya from the south, keep an eye out for some regal mansions near Visutkasat landing—these were built during the reign of King Rama V. At Tha Sang Hee, walk off the boat and head west for about a hundred meters to a bus stop. Catch an 18 or 28 bus headed east, and tell the conductor you want Vimanmek Mansions. It's a short ride—about five minutes—and you get off right opposite the gates for the mansions.

Vimanmek Mansions

Vimanmek Mansions ("Celestial Palace") is the world's largest golden teakwood structure. The three-story palace was built for King Rama V in 1900 and only used for several years before he moved to the nearby Dusit Palace. Vimanmek was renovated for the 1982 Bicentennial. It does not look Thai in style—it more resembles a Victorian manor, with high-ceilinged rooms,

---

**Tha Sang Hee—
Vimanmek Mansions—
Dusit Zoological Gardens—
Marble Temple—Suan Pakkard
Palace—Baiyoke Tower—
Kamthieng House (Siam Society)—
Tumnak Thai Restaurant**

Timing: Vimanmek Mansions is open daily from 0930 to 1600 with last tickets sold at 1500. Because it's a royal area, there's a strict dress code in effect—no shorts or sandals. Suan Pakkard Palace is closed Sundays, otherwise open 0900 to 1600 hours. Kamthieng House is closed Sundays and Mondays, otherwise open 0900 to 1200 and 1300 to 1700. There is a fair bit of ground to cover in this tour: assuming that between 30 minutes and 80 minutes is spent at each site, you will end up with a very full day.

Alternate routing suggestions: You can do the route in reverse, starting at Kamthieng House on Asoke—and then catching bus 38 to Pratunam. End point would be Tha Sang Hee landing, which has a nearby restaurant (also ricebarge dinner cruise, starting 1830).

Alternate starting point: The Marble Temple. An unusual aspect of this temple is that in the morning, from 0600 to 0700, the monks line up outside the temple in a parking area with their alms-bowls, and wait for locals to come and offer donations. This differs from the other *wats* in Bangkok, where the monks wander around on foot and collect the food. If you want to go to the Marble Temple at the crack of dawn (taxi suggested), you can visit the temple after the alms-giving, and then continue on to Vimanmek, and resume the tour from there.

anterooms, halls, terraces, and verandahs (although no nails were used in its construction as is the Thai style—wooden pegs were used). You get to see about a third of the 81 rooms at Vimanmek—the most interesting of which are the king's quarters. The rooms display artifacts, royal regalia, and period furniture. Other curiosities include Thailand's first shower-head, the first electric light, and elephant-foot umbrella stands. Vimanmek is open 0930 to 1600 (last tickets sold 1500; admission B50, or use ticket stub from Grand Palace). You can't get into the main building by yourself—there's a 45-minute guided tour, which is included in the ticket price. After that, though, you're free to walk around the beautiful grounds.

The Dusit area has a very European look to it—which was intentional on the part of King Rama V, who had visited Europe in the 1890s and wanted an area of Parisian boulevards and parks. His Champs-Élysées was Rajadamnern Avenue; also in this area is the European-style National Assembly Building, and an equestrian statue of King Rama V. The Royal Plaza near the statue is used for ceremonies such as the trooping of the colors in December. From Vimanmek, you can stroll down the northern end of Rajadamnern Avenue, and cut through Dusit Zoo toward the next destination, the Marble Temple. It's a pleasant 20-minute walk. Surprising for such a place, Dusit Zoo has well-kept tropical flora throughout the grounds, so it would be more accurate to describe it as **Dusit Zoological Gardens.** In fact, these were at one time King Rama V's botanical gardens. Here you can see Thais in a relaxed environment—feeding bananas to the hippos, or pedaling boats around the lake.

The famed white elephants of Thailand—a dozen of them—are lodged across the way, in the grounds of Chitralada Palace, where King Rama IX today resides: naturally, the palace grounds are off limits. White elephants are actually grey elephants with albino markings: they have a whiteness between skin folds, and a lack of pigment in the eyes. These rare elephants have always been an auspicious symbol of royalty, since the days of old Siam when elephants were commonly used as "tanks" in pitched bat-

tles. The finding of a white elephant was a rare event and wars were fought between the Thais and Burmese over possession of these creatures.

If you exit Dusit Zoo at an eastern gate opposite Chitralada Palace and continue south, you'll reach the Marble Temple.

The Marble Temple
Last of the royal-sponsored *wats,* **Wat Benjamabopit** was built at the turn of the century when Rama V moved to the Dusit area. The structure is faced with white Carrara marble; the orange roof tiles are Chinese. Flanking the entrance to the *bot* are large Khmer-style lions (considered guardians of Buddhist teaching); inside the main hall is a bronze replica of a highly revered Buddha image, the original of which is up-country at Phitsanulok. Throwing light on the interior are magnificent stained-glass windows with Thai artwork—the windows were made in Florence. Prince Naris, the king's half-brother, was responsible for this impossible yet pleasing assembly of Thai, Italian, and Chinese styles. To the rear is a large courtyard with galleries containing 50 Buddha images of different styles and periods—some copies of famous statues, some from other countries, and all intended to be educational.

When you leave the Marble Temple, cross the street and walk west, and you'll find a bus stop where you can catch a 72 bus. This will take you past Chitralada Palace, and a ten-minute ride will land you right opposite the next stop, Suan Pakkard Palace (ask the conductor for the exact stop). There's an overhead footbridge to cross the street.

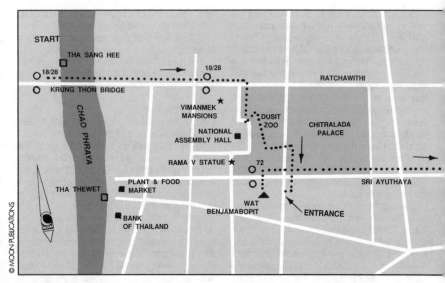

Suan Pakkard Palace

Traditional Thai teakwood houses were still to be found in Bangkok of the 1950s and up-country, but are rarely found now—victims of "progress" and westernization. Today they are collectors' items, with wealthy buyers offering villagers large sums of money for ancestral homes. Once bought, they are easily disassembled and shipped to a new location—the Thais thought of pre-fabricated housing long before Europeans. Traditional Thai housing was well-adapted to the Thai climate, with breezy, open living quarters. The houses were usually raised off the ground to protect them from flooding, and to keep them above livestock.

Suan Pakkard Palace is the former home of Prince Chumbot and Princess Chumbot—both of royal lineage. They were leading art collectors; Princess Chumbot was an avid gardener. In 1952 they had a traditional-style pavilion built to display their collection. Suan Pakkard ("Cabbage Patch") is now a museum comprising five traditional Thai houses and a pleasant landscaped garden. Centerpiece is the Lacquer Pavilion, which is constructed from two Ayuthaya-vintage pavilions—it is decorated with magnificent gold-leaf and lacquer murals de-

picting the life of Buddha. There's a priceless display of Asian art and antiques, particularly strong on Ban Chiang artifacts and ceramics. Suan Pakkard sells antiques too, but beware of fakes. Open Mon.-Sat. 0900 to 1600, admission B80.

Retrace your steps to the bus-stop, and catch the same 72 bus. Ride the bus for exactly three stops, and alight on Rajaprarop Road, opposite Indra Theater and shopping complex. You can cross a footbridge that leads to Pratunam clothing market and **Baiyoke Tower,** where you can see what's been done to Bangkok over the last 40 years—ride to the 43rd floor to the Sky Lounge, which has extensive views over Bangkok. Pratunam is the best clothing market in Bangkok—for wholesale, tailored, or ready-made.

Siam Society

To get to the next stop—the Siam Society—go back to the same bus-stop opposite the Indra Theater and catch a 38 bus. Ride eastwards for about 10 to 15 minutes (non peak-hour ride)—look for a Shell station on your right, as the Siam Society is hard to spot. The Siam Society is at 131 Asoke Road.

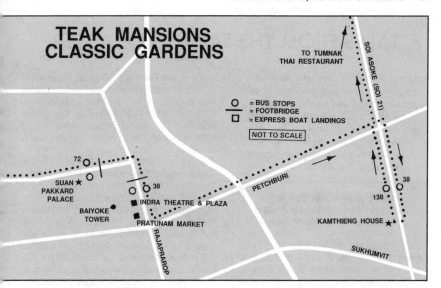

The century-old teakwood mansion here—called **Kamthieng House**—was donated to the Siam Society, and moved section by section from Chiang Mai. It has been fitted out as a northern Thai farmer's house—with a well, granary, kitchen, and so on, and has displays of farming, fishing, household items, and hilltribe costumes. Admission is B20. The Siam Society runs a library, organizes events, and publishes scholarly material on Thailand. The library located here charges B300 per visit for nonmembers.

You might like to take some time out—browse around Sukhumvit until about 1830 hours or so. For dinner, try something bizarre: go to **Tumnak Thai,** billed as the world's largest restaurant. At full capacity, it can seat 3,000 patrons and is popular with group tours. Orders to the kitchen are computer-coordinated, and dishes are delivered to a mid-station area by waiters gliding along on roller-skates. A large array of Thai dishes is served in an open-air setting of Thai-style pavilions—the food is passable, but nothing special. Assuming light traffic, a bus ride to get there from the Siam Society should take 10-15 minutes—take a 138 bus headed north on Asoke Road to Tumnak Thai, at 131 Rajadapisek Highway. Look for the restaurant sign on the left—it's near a large blue building (Robinson's Department Store). There are classical dancing shows from 2030 to 2130 nightly at Tumnak Thai.

TALES FROM THE FARANG QUARTER

Our guests were of every type, from newly arriving diplomats to fortune-hunters, adventurers, spies and crooks. As everyone claimed to be a VIP with a heroic war record, was well-groomed and fairly well-behaved, it was impossible to assess them accurately.
  —Germaine Krull, describing guests arriving at the Oriental Hotel in 1947

**Snake Farm—Robot Building—
Bangrak—Farang Quarter around
Oriental Hotel—River City**

Timing: From Monday to Friday, the Snake Farm has two daily shows—at 1030 and 1400; on weekends and holidays, there is only a morning show at 1030. Some shops at River City are closed Sundays.

To start, some breakfast suggestions in the area close to the Snake Farm. The Dusit Thani Hotel offers a huge breakfast buffet for B260 a person, plus taxes. This is in the street-level section (don't go up the ramp)—sumptuous food for hearty appetites (fruit, juices, croissants, muffins, muesli, eggs, bacon . . .). At the opposite end of the spectrum—that is, cheap and Thai—try Pop, which is in Lumpini Park at the north side. It is open-air and has a great range of ice cream, sundaes, some Western food, a lot of Thai food, and is open from 0630 onwards. From here, it's a 15-minute stroll through Lumpini Park to the Snake Farm. You can enter the Snake Farm from Rama IV Road or from Henri Dunant Road. (Dunant, by the way, was the 19th-century Swiss founder of the Red Cross Society.)

Be at the Snake Farm by 1015, in time for the 1030 slide presentation (walk right to the back of the compound), followed by the snake handling show at 1100. There is another slide show at 1400, with snake show at 1430. Admission is B70.

The **Snake Farm** is the only establishment of its kind in Asia, and what you see and learn here is unique. The farm was established in 1923 with foreign resident funding, through the initiative of Dr. Leopold Robert, the first director of the Science Division of the Thai Red Cross Society.

There are some 160 varieties of snakes in Thailand—46 of them poisonous (roughly half of those being sea snakes). The purpose of this establishment is primarily educational—informing people how to identify snakes, and how to deal with deadly bites. There are sleeping vipers and cobras on display in glassed-in cases, and there is a small museum at the back with stuffed and pickled specimens, and other exhibits. The Snake Farm is a research institute: the antivenom serum produced here is sent to hospitals around Thailand.

Different bites require different antivenin—the doctor can usually tell which snake it was from the puncture marks on the skin. The most powerful poison is delivered by the Siamese Cobra—a bite will kill a human within the hour. The venom milked from a single Siamese cobra is enough to kill a thousand rabbits! There is an excellent half-hour slide presentation on the institute and its work, in English, starting at 1030. After the slide show, there is a demonstration of snake handling, including venom milking of one variety of snake. Unlike the "cobra cowboys" you'll see at other snake farms around Thailand, these handlers do not harass the snakes

by beating them. Star attraction of the snake show is the king cobra, the largest of all poisonous snakes—some four meters in length.

From the Snake Farm, walk across Surawong Road to **Jim Thompson Thai Silk Shop.** This is not a plug for the shop, but a stop of interest (prices here are higher than at other silk retailers because of the Thompson name, but you can find out the range and quality of Thailand's silk products in this shop). The shop—and the company—are the legacy of a man who was instrumental in reviving the Thai silk industry. At the end of WW II, 40-year-old Thompson, an American officer, found himself in Bangkok, staying at the Oriental Hotel, looking for a change of career. He at first considered renovating the Oriental Hotel, but he clashed with Germaine Krull over plans for this. Krull, a former French war correspondent, had stayed on in Bangkok looking for a change of pace, too—she went on to manage the Oriental Hotel for the next twenty years.

Thompson, meanwhile, turned his attention to Thai silk, and managed to establish a market for it through contacts in New York. He set up the Thai Silk Company in 1948. At this stage, silk production was a cottage industry in Thailand: Thompson introduced color-fast dyes and new looms, and the venture became successful beyond his wildest expectations. For his efforts, he was awarded the prestigious Order of the White Elephant by the king in 1961. Since Thompson's mysterious disappearance in 1967, the international company has continued to thrive under American directorship, with most of the executives being Thai. Of all silk exported from Thailand, Jim Thompson Thai Silk accounts for about a third.

Robot Building

It's quite a distance from here to the next destination, which is the Oriental Hotel area. You can take a *tuk-tuk* to the Bangrak vicinity; along the way, take a look at some of Bangkok's more bizarre architecture. At 33 Surawong Road, near Jim Thompson's, there's the Wall Street Tower; on Thaniya Road there's Thaniya Plaza Building. Both have Greco-Roman features on the exterior—a mix of architectural styles that has raised a few eyebrows. Halfway down Sathorn Road is a building that does more than raise eyebrows—it blinks back at you! The Robot Building (Bank of Asia head office) is the brainchild of Dr. Sumet Jumsai, a peripheral member of the royal family, philosopher, mountain climber, historian, newspaper columnist, television host, painter—and architect.

The Robot Building was completed in 1986 at a cost of US$10 million. It attempts to introduce a human element—and some humor—into architecture. The big round eyes at the top look across Bangkok like the wide eyes of a child. As Dr Jumsai says: "The building makes people smile, and that's what a building should do. It should make people happy." And happy people open bank accounts—so business has been brisk, to the delight of the Bank of Asia managers.

The Robot Building has a head with steel louvre eyelids, two "legs," Caterpillar-type "wheels" at the base—but no arms. Stuck on the outside are the world's biggest nuts and bolts (3.8 meters in diameter), but the Robot Building is more than a gimmick—each part is functional. The two antennae at the top, for example, do double duty as communication aerials and lightning rods. You can only visit the ground floor—there are some robotic sculptures in the foyer. Dr. Jumsai was also architect for the headquarters of the Nation newspaper group—which was constructed in the shape of a stylized journalist hunched over a computer terminal, writing a story. It's along the Bangna-Trad Hwy., on the way to Pattaya—motorists passing by are undecided whether it's innovative or ugly.

Oriental Hotel Area

From the Robot Building, take a bus or *tuk-tuk* and ask for the Bangrak area, at the southern end of New Road. There's a lot of reconstruction going on in this area (Shangri-La Hotel shopping and office complex) and Bangrak market is a casualty—but one interesting section remains along New Road (Charoen Krung) between Sois 46 and 44, with a sidewalk flower and fruit market. From here you can walk up to the Oriental.

The area around the Oriental Hotel is the old farang quarter of Bangkok—maps a century old show European consulates and trading companies located along this stretch of the river.

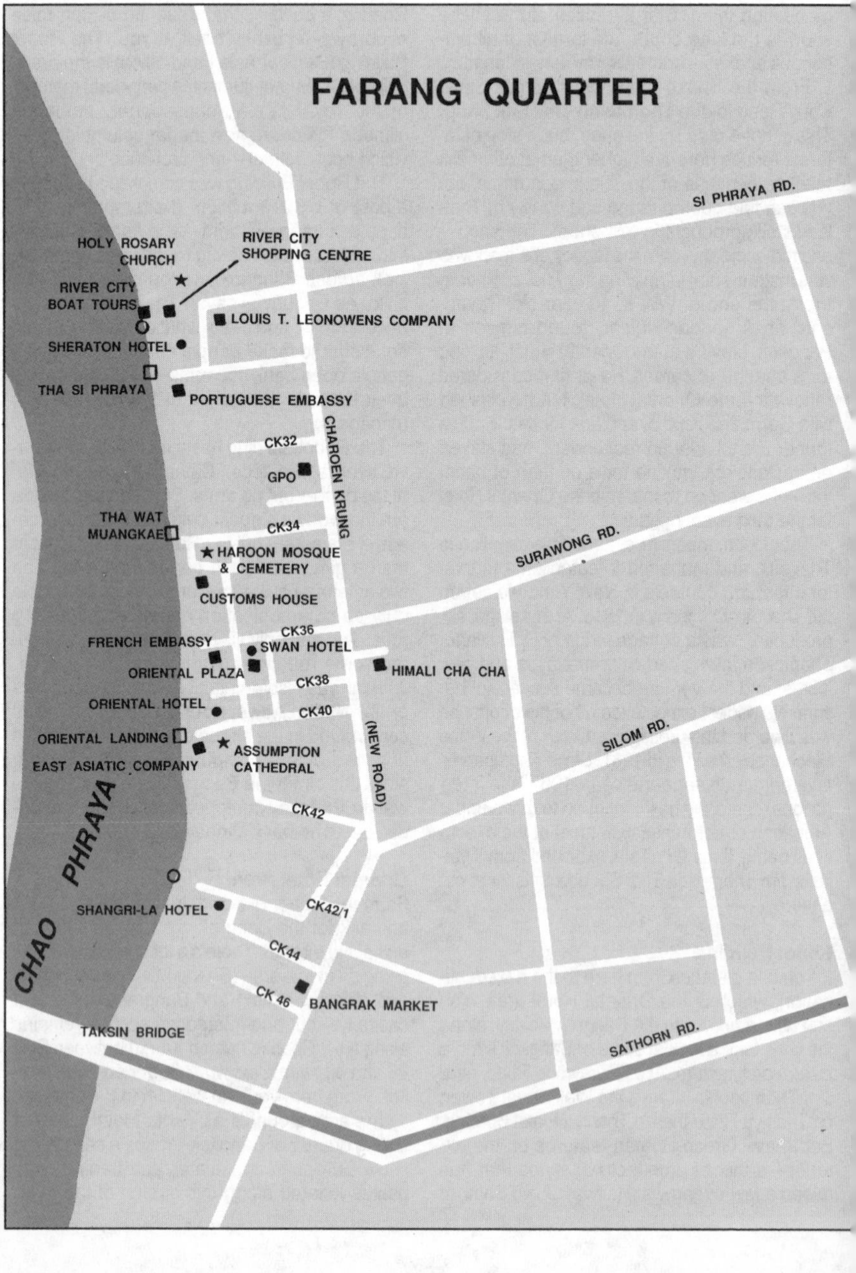

FARANG QUARTER

SI PHRAYA RD.

HOLY ROSARY
CHURCH

RIVER CITY
SHOPPING CENTRE

RIVER CITY
BOAT TOURS

SHERATON HOTEL

LOUIS T. LEONOWENS COMPANY

THA SI PHRAYA

PORTUGUESE EMBASSY

CHAROEN KRUNG

CK32

GPO

THA WAT
MUANGKAE

CK34

SURAWONG RD.

HAROON MOSQUE
& CEMETERY

CUSTOMS HOUSE

CK36

FRENCH EMBASSY

SWAN HOTEL

ORIENTAL PLAZA

HIMALI CHA CHA

CK38

ORIENTAL HOTEL

CK40

ORIENTAL LANDING

EAST ASIATIC COMPANY

ASSUMPTION
CATHEDRAL

(NEW ROAD)

SILOM RD.

CK42

CHAO PHRAYA

SHANGRI-LA HOTEL

CK42/1

CK44

CK 46

BANGRAK MARKET

TAKSIN BRIDGE

SATHORN RD.

© MOON PUBLICATIONS

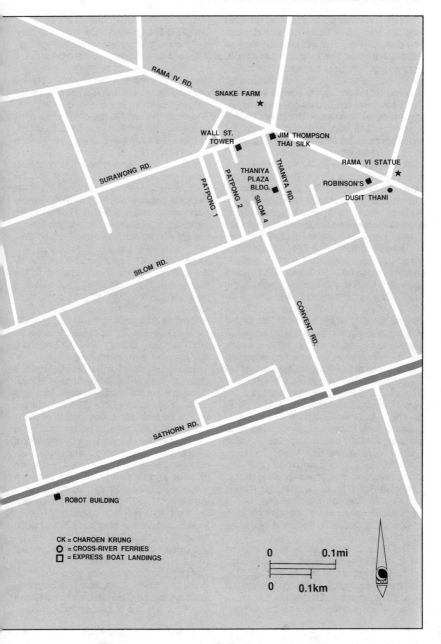

The community was clustered around the south end of a road—New Road—which foreigners had persuaded King Rama IV to build, paving an old elephant trail. The area was riddled with bars and guesthouses frequented by foreign sailors, but the only large hotel was the Oriental. The French and Portuguese embassies are still in the same location, and the area remains foreign-dominated, although the heavy trading these days has more to do with tourism, and many shops in this area cater to tourist shoppers, particularly antique-hunters.

If you walk down Soi 42 you'll come to a group of Western buildings. There's **Assumption Cathedral,** built in 1910 to replace another cathedral constructed some 90 years previously. This Catholic church has a lofty, vaulted ceiling with a rococo interior and a marble altar from France; next door is a school run by the church.

At the waterfront is the **East Asiatic Company** building, constructed in 1901, and run today as Denmark's most successful trading enterprise. Founder of the company was Captain H.N. Andersen, a merchant seaman who arrived in Bangkok in his twenties, seeking his fortune. In 1883, at the age of 31, he loaded the hold of a ship with teakwood, and sailed all the way to Europe. Teakwood was a rare commodity in Europe at the time, and Andersen sold the load at a 100% profit. He then set sail for Bangkok with a full load of coal. In Bangkok he started up a trading company next to the Oriental Hotel (which he owned from 1884 to 1893). In 1897, Andersen bought a three-masted schooner to ply a direct trade with Europe, transporting goods and passengers, and the same year he launched the East Asiatic Company, backed up by Danish shareholders. The company extended operations to Hong Kong, Shanghai, Kuala Lumpur, and Singapore in the early 1900s. Andersen eventually returned to his native Denmark, where he held the position of Consul General for Thailand, and lived to the ripe old age of 85.

The **Oriental Hotel** can be traced back as far as 1876, when two Danish sea captains put up the first structure on this site. In 1886, H.N. Andersen tore down the existing structure and hired an Italian architect to design a new luxury hotel—which survives today as the Authors'

Residence—the oldest hotel still in business in Bangkok. The Oriental Hotel itself is snooty, and the doormen may not let you in, especially if there is some special event in progress. If you're wearing shorts or sandals (or carry a daypack, or forgot to brush your hair), you will probably be refused entry. If you do gain the hallowed sanctum of the inner quarters, visit The Verandah (where you can have a drink overlooking the river) and the Authors' Lounge.

There are three wings at the Oriental—the River Wing (a highrise completed in 1976); the Garden Wing (1958); and the tiny Authors' Residence (two-story structure built in 1887). In the Authors' Residence, high tea is served in the **Authors' Lounge** from 1500 to 1800, with live piano music usually provided. The four suites above the lounge are all named after famous authors who stayed in the hotel—Joseph Conrad, Somerset Maugham, Noel Coward, and James Michener. There are books written by the authors and other memorabilia in the suites—which cost a cool B12,000-14,500 a night each. In the River Wing are suites dedicated to other illustrious guests—Barbara Cartland (with 500 romance novels on the shelves?), Kukrit Pramoj, Jim Thompson (suite decorated with Thai silks), Graham Greene, Gore Vidal, and John Le Carré among them.

Around the corner from the Oriental Hotel is a group of "colonial" style buildings—**Oriental Plaza** (antique and handicraft shops housed in 1908-vintage building); the **French Embassy** (built in the mid-19th century; peer through the gates) at the old **Customs House** (built in the 1880s, now used as a residence by members of a fire brigade situated along the riverbank. Continue past back-alley residences to **Haroon Mosque and Cemetery.** You don't see too much of Bangkok's Moslem community, but there are over 150 mosques in Bangkok—serving a sizeable religious community (mostly Malays, who are well integrated). Almost all the mosques are Sunni Moslem, as is this one.

To get out of this maze of back-alleys, you exit on Soi 34, heading back to New Road (Charoen Krung). A little digression here—back down New Road, on a *soi* 40 meters down from Surawong Road is a small Indian restaurant called **Himali Cha Cha.** It is one of the best Indian restau-

(top) locals presenting food to monks at the Marble Temple as a way of earning merit; (bottom left) view of the Golden Mount from Wat Saket; (bottom right) novice monk

(top) ornate door at Wat Rajabopit; (bottom left) Chinese warrior guard, on a chapel doorway at Wat Po; (bottom right) mural at Wat Rajabopit

(clockwise from top) 1. releasing a cage of birds to earn merit and bring good luck; 2. burning paper money at Sanjao Dtai Hong Kong; 3. lighting candles at Pho Sua Temple, Chinatown; 4. deafened by fireworks at lion dance for a special occasion outside Pho Sua Temple

(clockwise from top left) 1. amulet salesman: he recommends that you wear a dozen to ensure full protection; 2. browsing through amulets, believed to have supernatural powers, Wat Mahathat area; 3. applying gold leaf to a small Buddha statue; 4. the mysterious shrine of Sanjao Mae Tuptim; 5. magical tattoos are believed to protect the body from bullets and knives

THE LEGENDARY LOUIS

Meanwhile, back at the GPO—and the horrendous traffic on New Road: the first street north of the GPO is Soi 30, which is also known as Captain Bush Lane, named after a 19th-century master navigator, Captain John Bush, who at one time tutored King Rama V. Captain Bush was harbormaster of Bangkok from 1864 to 1904, and if he were to return today, he would have a bit of trouble recognizing this part, as the 28-story Royal Orchid Sheraton occupies the site of his residence. Down the end of Captain Bush Lane is the **Portuguese Embassy**, hidden behind high walls and better viewed from the river. This is the oldest diplomatic residence in Bangkok, built in the early 19th century. There are a few other Western-style buildings in this area. To the north of River City is the Portuguese-founded **Holy Rosary Church**. The original church was built in the 18th century; the present version was constructed 1987. Bangkok has more than 125 Catholic and Protestant churches.

On Si Phraya Road, past the Sheraton Hotel, you will see a sign for **Louis T. Leonowens Company,** a multinational trading company dealing in tools and machinery. The building is bland, but the story behind the company is extraordinary. The present building was put up in 1968 on the site of the original company founded by Louis Leonowens. Louis was the son of Anna Leonowens, who left Siam in 1867 for Europe and North America, where she launched a lucrative career of writing distorted memoirs about the Court of Siam (these memoirs much later formed the basis for another book, and eventually for the movie, *The King And I*). The memoirs offended the Thais, but they bore no grudge against her son. In 1882, at the age of 30, Louis returned to Siam, appointed a cavalry officer by King Rama V (whom Louis had grown up with).

Louis sought fame and fortune—and the hand of comely Fanny Knox, daughter of the British Consul and his Siamese wife. Also in pursuit of Fanny was the Regent of Siam, who wished her to marry a relative to forge a link between his house and the mighty British Empire. Fanny rejected Louis' advances, and in 1884, he ended up marrying her sister, Caroline, with whom he later had two children. The headstrong Fanny rejected the Regent too: she secretly married a Thai nobleman called Preecha. The Regent, furious, had Preecha arrested on trumped-up charges and thrown into jail. This caused a diplomatic crisis: the British despatched a gunboat to Bangkok. Preecha was spared the axe because of pressure from the British, and on compassionate grounds, as Fanny was pregnant.

Meanwhile, Louis had resigned from the king's service, and started working for the Borneo Company in the north—where he befriended the Prince of Chiang Mai, was granted leases for extracting teak, and accumulated a considerable number of native wives. Louis was apparently a flamboyant character with a flair for practical jokes, and a weakness for Siamese women and alcohol.

In 1892, a series of tragic events occurred. Shortly after Fanny Knox gave birth to a son, Preecha was executed. Less than a year later, Caroline (Louis' wife and Fanny's sister) died of pneumonia. Depressed, Louis took his children to England—they were later sent to Canada and placed in the care of Anna Leonowens. Louis returned to Bangkok in 1893, bought the Oriental Hotel from Captain Andersen, and began private teak trading with Burma; in 1895 he started up his own logging business. Louis proposed to Fanny for a third time, but again she rejected him. In 1899, Louis married the twenty-year-old daughter of a Bangkok businessman—the same year he sold his interests in the Oriental Hotel, and in 1905, he sold controlling interests of his business as well. The company by now dealt in spirits, cement, typewriters, and engineering products as well as teak. Louis Leonowens died in 1919; when his wife died in 1936, she left most of the Leonowens estate to Siamese charities, as requested by Louis. Fanny Knox Preecha moved to a rented house in an alley off New Road, not far from the Leonowens Company. She spent the latter part of her life devoted to the cause of democracy in Thailand; she died in 1925.

Though it changed hands, Louis' company continued trading under the same name—one of the best-known European names in Thailand. Most Thais call it "Borisat Louis," or simply "Louis." In 1986, it was taken over by the Getz Corporation from America. There is no longer any teak trading, but the company logo remains the Giant Swing, for which the company donated teak timber for 1920 renovations in memory of Louis Leonowens.

rants in Bangkok, and there's a story behind its creation as complex as a Moghul curry. Back in the mid-'70s as the Vietnam War and related flare-ups came to an end, a number of Westerners gravitated to Bangkok—among them mercenaries, spies, disaffected veterans, and freelance war reporters. Two who drifted into town were Cha Cha and John Everingham. Cha Cha means "uncle" and is the nickname of an Indian cook, K.L. Sircar, who worked for various Indian ambassadors abroad. This led to a posting in Vientiane, Laos; Cha Cha eventually quit the diplomatic "service" and set up his own restaurant near the Vientiane markets. A steady customer was John Everingham.

In 1976, John Everingham, an Australian photographer, was the last Western journalist left in Vientiane after the communist takeover of Laos. His presence was tolerated because he presented material sympathetic to the communist cause—but at the same time, he was secretly filing stories with Western news media sources. Everingham had a few other complications—he was having a dangerous affair with a Laotian woman called Keo. He was in the habit of meeting his Laotian paramour in a discreet section of Cha Cha's restaurant. Everingham was eventually followed, arraigned on charges of spying, and thrown in prison for a couple of weeks. His slide library, the result of ten years' work in Indochina, was destroyed by the authorities. He was then thrown out of the country, but later swam back across the Mekong with scuba equipment to spirit Keo away.

In the interim, Cha Cha and his Thai wife had left Laos. Cha Cha and Everingham had joked that if they met again they would open a new restaurant. By chance they bumped into each other on the streets of Bangkok, and in 1980 the restaurant became a reality—the Himali Cha Cha—created and financed by Everingham,

and entirely run by Cha Cha. Everingham's daring rescue of Keo was the subject of a movie made in 1982. He is based in Bangkok, and runs ArtAsia Press, which operates from an office behind the Shangri-La on Soi 44—publishing magazines, postcards, calendars and books. On the stands around Bangkok you will see many of Everingham's postcards.

River City

On to the final destination for this tour. River City is basically a group-tour dropoff point for boats, and shops cater to those staying at the large hotels like the Oriental and the Sheraton, so prices can be steep. But it is the antique-buying center of Bangkok with a plethora of shops on the third and fourth floors. A good percentage of the offerings are reproductions—nobody is sure what percentage. On the ground and second floors, River City has custom tailors, shoemakers, gems and jewelry, handicrafts, and a wide range of other goods.

And now, the moment we've all been waiting for—an ice-cold Singha beer, or a fresh juice. There are a few places in the River City complex where that can be arranged, along with supporting seafood. But the perfect place doesn't open till 1730 hours. So try and fill in a bit of time by shopping or otherwise—this place is worth the wait. It's very hard to find a place near the river in Bangkok that's reasonably priced and has a view, but River City has one. It's the Beer Garden on the rooftop—this place is open-air, naturally cooled, and high enough that you can enjoy great views of river traffic without being bothered by pollution or noise. And the food is great, too. Open daily 1730 to 2330; take the elevator to the 5th floor. You can just have a drink if you want, or take after the local Thais and try a barbecue set menu, which is cooked at the table.

BANGKOK BY NIGHT
SOME *SANUK*

WHAT'S ON

Bangkok is the cultural center of Thailand, and offers movies, theater, classical dance and drama, puppet performances, orchestra, live music, or concerts by visiting international artists. You can check the entertainment listings in *The Nation* or the *Bangkok Post,* particularly on the weekends when lengthier rundowns are given. TAT puts out a bimonthly brochure listing cultural activities and exhibitions (exhibitions of modern works are often staged at the **National Art Gallery**, open 0900 to 1600, closed Mondays and Tuesdays). The city has two orchestras—the Bangkok Philharmonic and the Bangkok Symphony. Watch for special events—offerings range from visiting orchestras to Madonna-impersonating Thai singers. Speaking of impersonations, an entertaining transvestite revue takes place nightly in a large theater on Suk-humvit—see entry for Calypso Cabaret, toward the end of this chapter.

Some theatrical and musical performances take place in major hotels. Embassy-related venues include the Alliance Française Auditorium (29 South Sathorn Road); the Goethe Institute (18 Soi Attakarnprasit, off South Sathorn Road near the Malaysia Hotel); the British Council (428 Soi 2, Siam Square, behind Lido Cinema); and the AUA Auditorium (American University Alumni, 179 Rajadamri Road). These places screen foreign films. Imported films are subject to stiff taxes in Thailand—a measure designed to encourage the local film industry. Very few foreign movies are shown in Bangkok theaters (usually blockbusters or second-rate movies), but with the advent of video and large-screen TVs, foreign films are shown in many bars and cafes. Locals thrive on a steady diet of Thai and Chinese movies. Thai movies are not the kind of thing to recommend: they're based on standard (usually romantic) story lines, with lots of violence—all in Thai, though some have English subtitles.

Traditional Performing Arts

Longer dance-drama pieces are periodically performed at the **National Theater** (adjacent to the National Museum near Sanam Luang). There are usually special exhibitions every second Friday, Saturday, and Sunday each month, and on the last Friday and Saturday of each month—these could be daytime performances. Seats are B300-500 and performances are lengthy—three hours or more. Since they're all in Thai, you will miss the story line, which can reduce you to watching the movements and costumery. If you arrive toward the end of a performance you may be allowed a peek at the stage. Another venue is **Thailand Cultural Center**, on Rajadapisek Road (the northern continuation of Asoke Road), which also occasionally stages *hun krabok* puppet theater or classical music performances. Both the National Theater and Thailand Cultural Center are used by visiting ballet and theatrical companies. For details on what's coming up, get a current program from TAT.

Restaurants With Classical Dance

The easiest way to see Thai dance styles is to go to dinner-dance places which put on packaged shows for tourists. Music is provided by the small, traditional *pipat* ensemble: these shows are generally a mixture of classical dance (excerpts from *khon, lakhon,* and *likay),* folk dances from northern Thailand (fingernail dance, candle dance—usually performed as a gesture of greeting or good luck), and martial art forms such as *krabi krabong* swordfighting. *Krabi krabong* is a martial art using poles, swords, or knives, and originally used by warriors to hone their combat techniques.

BOB RACE

Thai dancer

Pricing is usually around B300-500 for the set dinner and dance; shows start around 2030 and last an hour or so. Most venues have traditional Thai housing with polished teakwood floors. Don't expect great Thai food from these places—most provide set menus that cater to the Western palate. At **Chao Phraya Paradise Hotel** in Thonburi, the "Thai" food is precooked, served lukewarm in set dishes, and portions are anemic, devoid of spices, some even totally unpalatable.

An amusing venue is **Tumnak Thai**, on the Rajadapisek Highway northeast of Bangkok, out near Thailand Cultural Center. You can order your own food there in an open-air setting. The place is so big (seats 3,000) that there are simultaneous classical dance shows on several stages, from 2030 to 2130 hours daily. A cut above the rest, and pricier, are **Baan Thai Restaurant** and **Piman Thai Restaurant**, both out at the far eastern end of Sukhumvit. The Oriental's **Sala Rim Naam** stages nightly shows of *khon* dance-drama—the food and dance show tab runs B600 a head.

Dinner Cruises

For ricebarge and boat cruises along the Chao Phraya River after dark, refer to Dining Along the River in the restaurant listing under "Bangkok Basics."

Thai Boxing

Matches are held daily at two alternating venues: at **Rajadamnern Stadium** (next to TAT office, Mon., Wed., Thurs. at 1800, and Sun. at 1700), and **Lumpini Stadium** (Rama IV Road, east of Lumpini Park, on Tues., Fri., and Sat. at 1820). Seats vary from B150 to B1000 each. The best bouts are said to take place on Tuesdays (Lumpini) and Thursdays (Rajadamnern). Bouts are shown on television on Sundays.

Hotel Venues

All the hotels have at least one bar, cocktail lounge, or pub; some have several, and many have their own disco or lounge with aerial views or river views. Live music, ranging from classical to piano bar to rock, is sometimes provided. Hotel venues are expensive by Bangkok standards: for the discos, cover is B200-400 and

classical dancers

folk dancing from the north

up; drinks run around B150 each. These places cater mainly to a sedate, older crowd of foreigners.

Pub-restaurants

These are hybrids—some are quiet and have darts, attempting to duplicate an English pub; others stress the food; others beef up the music. Relaxed atmosphere—these oases serve as happy-hour shelter for refugees from the traffic, or as watering holes for ex-pats who drop in for a pint after work. Some pub-restaurants are semi-hostess in nature, with a remarkable line-up of pretty waitresses.

Jazz Pubs, Blues Bars

The stress here is on live music and drinking: live music gets going around 2130; you can order food in these places too. One of the largest venues for jazz is a place called **Saxophone**, at the southeast side of Victory Monument—takes

a bit of effort to get to, but well worth the trip (open till 0230).

Beer Bars

In contrast to the hotel prices, there are thousands of beer bars around Bangkok where you can park yourself over a 40-baht beer. Khao San Road is full of them. It may sound strange to say "beer bar," but you have to somehow distinguish them from the many other kinds of bars. Watering holes proliferate around nightlife areas, usually in an open-air setting, as a counterpoint to the heavier going of the go-go bars. You'll feel right at home sitting on the sidewalk at a beer bar and watching TV, or watching the world go by.

Discos

Discotheques and videotheques are good places to cap off the evening. Most start around 2300, get going round midnight, and close at 0300 or later. They usually charge a cover of

THAI BOXING

Muay Thai (Thai boxing) is a national sport—a martial art with a 400-year history. Boxers go through many years of rigorous training. In Thai boxing, contestants are allowed to use almost any part of their body to strike, except the head (no biting or butting allowed). In addition to using regular boxing gloves, the boxers use bare or taped feet to strike at an opponent. The punches and kicks are meant merely to soften up the opponent, however: the deadliest strikes come from knees or elbows. When a boxer hisses "sok sok," it means he intends to use his elbows to punish his opponent; a hard knee-blow can result in instant collapse of the opponent. Shoving and pushing are allowed, but wrestling is not. Points are awarded for any blow to the opponent's body: all parts of the body can be struck, even the groin (which is protected, of course). Because Thai boxing is exhausting, bouts are short: usually five rounds of three minutes each, with a two-minute interval between rounds.

Music is important to the matches, and is usually provided by a Thai oboe, two drums, and cymbal sets. Before a bout, the boxers perform a ritual dance to music—honoring their trainer as well as the guardian spirit of Thai boxing. Boxers wear a sacred headband and armband (which contains an amulet) for this part of the proceedings: the ritual dance lasts about five minutes and also acts as a warm-up and stretch for the contestants. The ritual dance is actually a series of stylized fighting movements, and is difficult to master—bets are often placed on the boxer's performance.

When the boxers come out of their corners and start to pummel each other, the ringside musicians build up to fever pitch, rising and falling along with events in the ring. In the crowd, feverish betting and shouting—all very noisy and exciting.

Thai boxing

B100-200, which includes a few drinks; the discos attached to major hotels usually charge B200-400. On the outskirts of Bangkok are two wild mega-discos, vying for the honor of largest in the world: **Nasa Spacedrome** (at 999 Ramkamheng Road, toward Ramkamheng University, eastern Bangkok; stages spacecraft laser show), and the Palace (on Vibhavadi Rangsit Highway out toward the airport; has a "bucking bronco" to amuse the Thai young set). Over in Thonburi on Arun Amarin is another mega-disco called the Paradise. Noise levels in most of the discos and go-go bars are very high: the disc jockeys must be hard of hearing.

ON THE SLEAZY SIDE

Much of Bangkok's nightlife is angled for single men. What stuns first-time visitors to Bangkok is the openness and sheer scale of the sex trade in the capital. Sex is big business, and police and politicians with an economic interest in the proceedings turn a blind eye. Prostitution has been part of Thai life for centuries, and even the smallest Thai town has one or two brothels. In the late 1950s, at the same time as opium was banned, prostitution was outlawed by the government in response to international pressure. While opium use was wiped out (replaced by heroin), prostitution continued to flourish in massage parlors and bars, especially in the 1960s and '70s when Bangkok was an R&R destination for U.S. troops. Today, with an estimated 80,000 to 300,000 prostitutes in Bangkok, there is a plethora of subtle fronts for prostitution: the really open activity, however, is confined to a handful of red-light zones.

It is estimated that up to a third of tourist arrivals in Thailand are "sex tourists." In 1988, a British-made film, *Foreign Bodies,* was shown on European television: the film-makers interviewed a German pederast and two Thai children he allegedly hired, and followed a bargirl back to her northeastern village. Although there was a public furor over the film in Bangkok, little was done to change the situation: Thailand has not yet signed the Convention on the Rights of the Child. Jumbo-loads of men from European countries like Germany and Denmark continue to arrive in Thailand on openly advertised sex junkets; the Japanese advertise similar junkets. Worldwide publicity about AIDS in Thailand has had some impact: there has been a decline in the sex trade in Bangkok since 1989, with a number of massage-parlors going out of business.

Whatever you think about the trade, in one way or another you're going to have to deal with it if you stay in cheaper accommodations, or if you stay near one of the red-light areas (likewise for visiting Pattaya or Phuket). You're going to have to deal with Westerners who reveal sexual habits they don't normally reveal, and who act very differently when on holidays.

Cabarets And Hostess Bars

Cocktail lounges and cabarets mainly cater to Thais. Usually these places have lots of pictures of the crooners in glittering costume posted outside. Inside, after singing, the girls will sit with customers. A variety of hostess bar is the "no hands" dining places, where groups of men are hand-fed and babied by hostesses—the **Galaxy Restaurant and Night Club**, at 19 Rama IV Road, is the most renowned.

mixing it up in a bar

Go-go Bars

Found in three areas—Patpong, Soi Cowboy and Nana Plaza—go-go bars have girls clad in skimpy swimsuits or lingerie, or less, and high-volume music. Girls all have ID number badges pinned to their costumes. Most of the bars do not have a cover charge: beers cost around B40 during happy hour (usually up to 2100 or so), and B60-80 thereafter. Patpong bargirls pressure customers to buy them drinks (they get a commission on this lollywater) and take them out of the bar on payment of a "barfine." A barfine or buy-out fee is the amount that the customer pays to the bar to release the go-go dancer from the establishment before closing time. On Patpong, barfines are around B300-

400; on Soi Cowboy, B150. If a bargirl fails to turn over a certain number of drinks and barfines per month, an amount is deducted from her salary as a penalty. Bargirls get most of their income from customers, charging B500 for a "short time" or B750-1500 overnight, with "models" charging double that. Often bargirls are the main supporters of peasant families living in squalor in the north or northeast (others come from Cambodia and Laos). Complications include supporting a Thai boyfriend or an expensive drug habit (glue-sniffing, alcohol, heroin), or supporting children from a broken marriage. A Bangkok bargirl's dream is to rake in enough money to set up a small business, or buy a house up-country.

SAFE SEX?

Bangkok bargirls all have amulets, but there's only one amulet against AIDS: it's called a condom. Although attitudes are changing, very few Thai men use condoms with prostitutes, and foreigners tend not to use condoms either. Prostitution is ingrained in Thai society and brothels are used by all ages of Thai men as a show of manhood. A contributing factor to prostitution is the willingness of wives to overlook infidelities. To put this in perspective, short-term flings are tolerated, but longer-term liaisons are cause for crimes of passion: Bangkok is reputed to have the only clinic in the world devoted to reattaching the male member after an attack by a jealous female.

Many of Bangkok's bargirls are uneducated, but a feminist group called Empower has helped raise awareness about problems like AIDS. Although bargirls know about the use of condoms, and carry them, they may concede if a drunken customer refuses to use one. A Bangkok sex worker told an interviewer that she gave dirty-looking clients a shower in the belief that this would wash away AIDS and any other diseases.

In 1991, researcher Sheranne Dobinson talked to tourists of many nationalities in bars, and to Thai prostitutes, asking if they used condoms with partners, and if not, why. Dobinson was on an Australian government grant, as part of an anti-AIDS campaign. Few of the foreigners interviewed followed safe-sex practices, due to embarrassing loss of memory after

drinking, or because a condom would have spoiled their pleasure. Some customers stayed with one partner for the duration of their "sex holiday," hoping to minimize risks that way. According to Dobinson:

> The foreign sex tourists are asking for younger and younger girls, believing that they have slept with the fewest people and are less likely to have AIDS. Often they will choose the fattest prostitute reasoning if she is fat she must be healthy, or the ugliest because they think she is probably the one who has the least customers and is less likely to be infected.

Some bars display notices that their girls have weekly health checks. Even if this were true, and even if the checks were thorough, they have little significance: there is a time-lag of several months between contraction of the HIV virus and the growth of a sufficient level of antibodies to show up on a test. During that time, a patient's blood test would give negative results, but he or she could unknowingly spread the HIV virus. The risk is actually greater that bargirls may contract the virus from foreign partners during unsafe sex, since women are more likely to contract AIDS from men than the other way round. When interviewed about their last AIDS test, foreign male tourists invariably replied "never."

Escort Agencies

What's-On-type magazines distributed in Bangkok carry lots of advertising for escort agencies providing "services of every kind," with escorts being Thai, Western, movie stars, models, singers. . . . Agencies offer "professional beautiful lady guides for sightseeing—or for any occasion." Male escorts are advertised for men, and for women too. Tucked away in a discreet corner of the Manhattan Hotel is **Chippendale's**, a gigolo bar (male escorts for rich wives or bored mistresses are also reputed to hang around the Windsor Hotel and Indra Hotel areas).

Gay Bars

Identical in concept to the female go-go bars except that they're stocked with either male go-go dancers, musclemen or barboys. Other places have coffee-shops, restaurants, massage places, live shows; there are also health clubs and saunas in Bangkok for men only. Most of the gay bars are located in the Patpong 3 area (Silom 4), and around Silom and Surawong roads. About 40 bars in Bangkok cater to foreigners; another 200 exclusively to Thais. Some gay bars have transvestite revues: transvestites *(katoeys)* are part of Patpong both in the gay bars and in the regular go-go bars—many foreigners have trouble distinguishing between Thai females and *katoeys*. Homosexuality and bisexuality seem to be accepted in Thai society: there are no laws regarding homosexual acts.

Japanese Clubs

Sprinkled around nightlife areas and discreetly placed down back alleys are opulent Japanese member-only bars. The largest cluster of these is on Thaniya Road (Patpong 4). Japanese clubs have sushi, karaoke, teriyaki, Ginza-type neon—and if you don't resemble a Nippon businessman, no chance of getting in. Not that you'd really want to anyway—the beer is at least twice as expensive as in Western-patronized bars. After the Malaysians, the Japanese are the biggest tourist group visiting Thailand, with Taiwanese and Singaporeans as runners-up. The Japanese have sex-tour groups to Thailand; a bit more sophisticated are "golf tours." Golf is a very expensive sport in Japan, and members have to book up to a year ahead for a game there—golfing in Thailand is paradise compared to that. And the caddies are almost always female.

Thai Clubs

Entertainment catering to Thais is scattered along New Petchburi and Sri Ayuthaya roads: mainly massage-parlors, cabarets, and coffee-shops. Popular among Thai men are coffee-shops on the outskirts of Bangkok featuring "fashion shows": these involve groups of girls performing a protracted striptease, and soliciting garlands of flowers from customers (commissions are paid to the girls on the sale of garlands). After the show, the models will sit with the customers.

Massage Parlors

These are sometimes referred to as "fishtanks": rows of young women with numbers pinned to their blouses sit and watch TV in a brightly lit area, while Thai men lurk around in a darkened area and peruse them like sharks through glass windows. Some parlors are huge: the **Chao Phya** on Sri Ayuthaya Road and the **Mona Lisa** on New Petchburi Road each have over 500 girls on the books. Sex workers may be bonded to massage parlors (virtually sold by parents, or else abducted). The sidestreets off New Petchburi Road have many massage parlors for Thais; others are located in Thonburi and sprinkled around the city—sometimes attached to mid-range hotels. Some parlors welcome women and couples. Massage parlors or Turkish baths charge anywhere from B300 for a straight bath and massage ("extras" negotiable) to B1500 and up for an all-inclusive body-to-body massage (called a B-course: the masseuse uses her full body, covered with soap suds). High-class massage parlors charge a lot more, and foreigners are habitually charged more than locals. Other places, advertised as "Lady Barbers," have similar facilities and extras—usually upstairs and out of sight. If it's really a massage or a haircut you're after, forget about these places—go to a regular barber or a traditional massage place (these have licenced masseuses and no private rooms—see Health Services under "Bangkok Basics" for details).

Coffee-shops

Sometimes attached to massage parlors, these are after-hours "pick-up" bars, thronged with freelancers (no numbers, not attached to bar, and therefore not readily identifiable). The main foreign-patronized coffee-shop is the **Thermae**, on Sukhumvit. Thai-patronized places include **Siam Hotel Coffee-shop**, on New Petchburi Road, which is homing ground for masseuses from Mona Lisa Massage Parlour next door.

Short-time Hotels

Usually designated by letters or numbers (33 Hotel, or A-One Hotel), short-time and drive-in hotels cater to married Thai men who wish to be discreet, and to foreigners who have trouble taking a newly acquired partner back to their hotel. Rooms are rented for one to two hours. The major hotels in Bangkok do not allow overnight visits. This is not so much a question of morals as of security—the girls are notoriously light-fingered. In the mid-range hotels and budget hotels, the policies on overnight guests vary—at some, hotel staff don't bat an eye and will sign female visitors in at the front desk as a security measure (the hotel may seize the opportunity to charge more for an overnight guest). Signs in other hotels range from this odd disclaimer: "The management is not responsible for any dealings between the customers and the staff" (inference: there are dealings with the staff), to this abrupt sign: "This hotel is not a brothel: no guests allowed in the rooms."

Night Touring

Even when it does encompass the sleazy and the X-rated, nightlife in Bangkok is not intimidating. The bars have none of the pathos of a red-light district in the West—they're open, cheerful, unapologetic, and friendly. Along Patpong you'll see Western families with kids in tow doing some shopping in the night bazaar, and taking a peek through the bar doors. Women and couples are welcome in the bars. Taxis are freely available, so you can always get back to your hotel at any time. You're best advised to explore the nightlife of Bangkok with a friend. You can jump from one area to another using a taxi or *tuk-tuk*—never any shortage of those.

Although there is such a thing as a "night-tour" advertised by some hotels, it soon transpires that this is either a feeble attempt to poke into a few bars, or it's fronted by a tout trying to steer clients toward a massage parlour or worse. You don't need any assistance from touts or tour agents to sample Bangkok's nightlife: quite the contrary—steer clear of them, because they will lead you to the bars where you'll get into trouble.

NIGHTLIFE BY AREA

The following listing only takes in four nightlife areas that are frequented by foreigners. The four sketchmaps that go with this section match the sketchmaps in the food section of this book, making it easier to jump from restaurant to club, and to navigate the labyrinth of *sois*.

SILOM-PATPONG-SURAWONG

Restaurants With Classical Dance
Sala Rim Naam (on left bank of Chao Phraya, opposite Oriental Hotel), tel. 437-9417, *khon*

Noi, who landed the part of a bargirl in the movie,
The Deerhunter. *The bar scenes were filmed on Patpong Road, decorated to resemble a red-light district in Saigon.*

JOHN GIBSON

dance-drama nightly from 2030 to 2130—expensive. **Dusit Rimtarn**, in Suppakarn Shopping Center (on left bank of Chao Phraya, reached from Oriental pier), tel. 437-9671, has open-air setting with nightly shows from 2030 to 2115. **The Royal Orchid Sheraton**, tel. 234-5599, has a Rivernight Market with outdoor buffet and clasical dance; showtime 2015. **Ruen Thep**, Silom Village Trade Center, 286 Silom Road, tel. 233-9447, dance shows nightly from 2030 to 2130. **Sawasdee**, 66 Soi Pipat, tel. 237-6310, has nightly dinner/dance shows from 2030 to 2130. **Tawana Ramada Hotel**, 80 Surawong, tel.236-0361 has dinner/dance shows every Tues., Thurs., and Sat.

Hotel Venues
Bamboo Bar at the Oriental: chic cocktail bar with live piano music or jazz; dress code—jacket and tie for men. **Diana's** (disco) at Oriental Plaza, 3rd floor, close to Oriental Hotel—very expensive—open to 2400 weekdays and 0200 Fridays and Saturdays. Discos: at the Sheraton is the **Cavern**; at the Shangri-La Hotel is **Talk of the Town**; at the Montien Hotel is **Casablanca**. The Montien regularly stages Thai-language dramas in its own theater. Bars at the Dusit Thani Hotel: The **Basement** (bar with some entertainment, no cover); **Bubbles** (disco); and **Tiara** (top floor—aerial-view drinking and dining).

Pub-restaurants
At 173 Surawong Road is **All Gaengs**, a ritzy New York style piano bar (live piano, serves food, open 2100 to 0100 daily except Sundays). Buried in the carpark building (2nd floor) on Patpong 2 is an English pub-restaurant, **Bobby's Arms**—English food, live Dixieland jazz Sundays, starting 2030. The **Toby Jug**—on Silom opposite Robinson's, is a tiny, authentic replica of a British pub, complete with a collection of Toby jugs. Quiet place—you can actually hear yourself talk. **The Front Page**—on Soi Saladeng 1, just near Rama IV Road—is a pub with nice atmosphere, good food, live music.

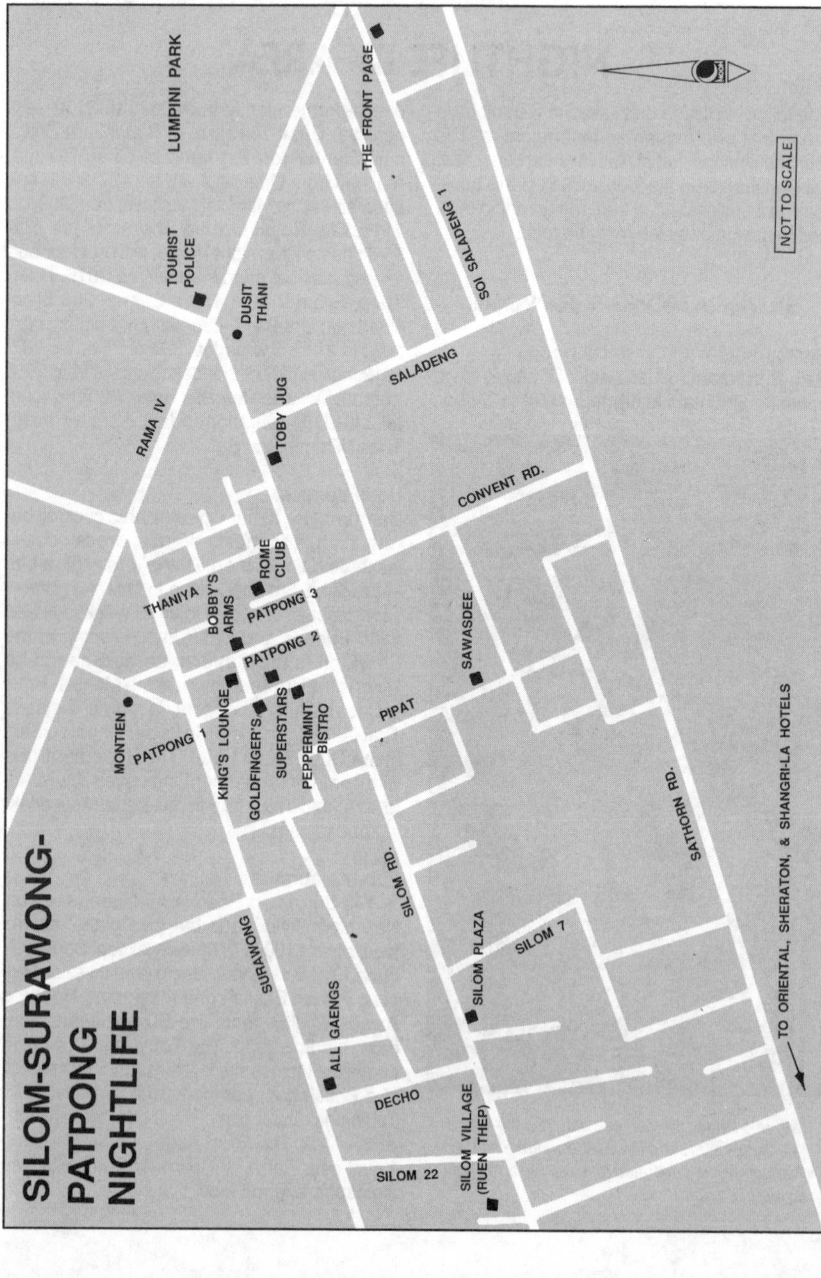

SILOM-SURAWONG-PATPONG NIGHTLIFE

LUMPINI PARK

THE FRONT PAGE

SOI SALADENG 1

NOT TO SCALE

TOURIST POLICE

DUSIT THANI

SALADENG

RAMA IV

TOBY JUG

CONVENT RD.

ROME CLUB

THANIYA

BOBBY'S ARMS

PATPONG 3

PATPONG 2

SAWASDEE

KING'S LOUNGE

GOLDFINGER'S

SUPERSTARS

PEPPERMINT BISTRO

PIPAT

MONTIEN

PATPONG 1

SILOM RD.

SATHORN RD.

SURAWONG

SILOM PLAZA

SILOM 7

ALL GAENGS

DECHO

SILOM VILLAGE (RUEN THEP)

SILOM 22

TO ORIENTAL, SHERATON, & SHANGRI-LA HOTELS

© MOON PUBLICATIONS

PATPONG

Patpong is the sleaze center of Bangkok, divided into four sois: Patpong 1 and 2 (mainly go-go bars); Patpong 3 (Silom 4: gay bars); and Patpong 4 (Thaniya: Japanese clubs). Running right through the middle of Patpong 1 is Patpong Night Bazaar, an overpriced market where foreigners haggle over everything from Burmese tapestries to pirated cassettes (gets under way about 1900). There are also beer-bars, massage parlors, a few pubs, short-time hotels, a few bookstores, drugstores, and a supermarket.

Patpong got its start in the 1960s, catering to U.S. troops on R&R. When the troops left in the '70s, it was thought that the place would collapse, but Patpong managed to establish itself with foreign tourists and with rich Thais. Downstairs Patpong bars have go-go dancers; upstairs bars on Patpong have live sex shows, with lots of touts advertising them. Never, ever, go into a bar on Patpong with a tout. Before going to any of the upstairs bars, live show or not, inquire closely as to whether there is a cover charge, and exactly how much the drinks are. Some bars have a sign in a dim corner somewhere that says drinks are B100 each—to avoid confusion, it is best to pay the tab regularly. Occasionally a newcomer gets stuck with a tab for B2000 (supposedly for girls' drinks): there is no point resisting in a country where the national sport is kickboxing. The best thing to do in this situation is to get a receipt, go and get the Tourist Police (stationed at both ends of Patpong at night), go back to the bar, and demand a refund. Another scam in bars is use of fake liquor—substituting local moonshine in brand-name bottles (there also seems to be an industry involving production of brand-name bottles with counterfeit labels).

Beer Bars

The Surawong end of Patpong 2 has a number of open-air bars. Scattered along Patpong 1 are sidewalk tables—ringside seating for observing mating rituals.

Discos

There are a few for young Thais on Patpong. Some popular western hangouts: **Superstars**, on Patpong 1—cover of B160 includes three drinks. **King's Lounge**, on an alley between Patpong 1 and 2—opens 2300, no cover; lively mixed crowd, loud rap music and videotheque effects. Busy around 0200 when bars from Patpong start closing down, and off-duty bargirls drift in.

The **Rome Club** on Patpong 3 (approached from Silom Road) is a videotheque with a huge screen and half a dozen monitors playing the latest rock videos. Mixed crowd: foreign, Thai, gay and transvestite. The Rome Club is a gay bar in the evening, but after 2200 it is a popular after-hours place for all (the Club welcomes women and couples), open till 0400. Women say it's a great place to go because they don't get bothered.

Peppermint Bistro on Patpong 1 is an after-hours place too, open to 0300, no cover. Along Silom Road is **Freak Out Disco**, in Silom Plaza shopping complex, which is between Soi Silom 7 and Silom 9.

Hostess Bars

For a break from the fray, there are several drinking spots with hostesses of the non-attack variety. There's the **Crown Royal** on Patpong 2; another "quiet" bar is the **Madrid** on Patpong 1, which serves food.

Go-go Bars

Every night is party night on Patpong. There are over 50 bars jammed along Patpong 1 and 2: with such names as Pussy Alive, Pussy Galore, Firecat, and Cleopatra's, the bars run the full spectrum from the presentable to the utterly depraved. Most of the depraved activity takes place in upstairs bars, with live shows from 2200 onward. A civilized go-go bar on Patpong 1 is **Goldfingers** (women customers are welcome). **Peppermint Bistro** is another civilized place (no go-go dancers). Or just take an outside seat at one of the bars and watch the world go by.

Gay Bars

On Patpong 3 (the sign on this cul-de-sac actually says Silom 4), and scattered through the *sois* bounded by Rama IV, Silom and Surawong. By day, Patpong 3 is thronged with office workers getting lunch from streetstalls, and hair-

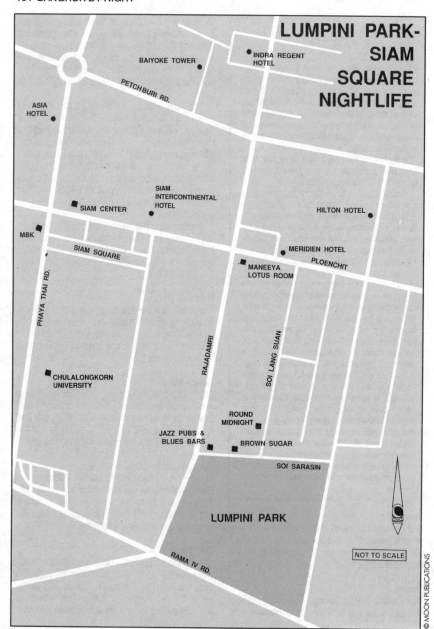

LUMPINI PARK-
SIAM
SQUARE
NIGHTLIFE

INDRA REGENT
HOTEL

BAIYOKE TOWER

PETCHBURI RD.

ASIA
HOTEL

SIAM
INTERCONTINENTAL
HOTEL

SIAM CENTER

HILTON HOTEL

MBK

MERIDIEN HOTEL

SIAM SQUARE

PLOENCHIT

MANEEYA
LOTUS ROOM

PHAYA THAI RD.

RAJADAMRI

SOI LANG SUAN

CHULALONGKORN
UNIVERSITY

ROUND
MIDNIGHT

JAZZ PUBS &
BLUES BARS

BROWN SUGAR

SOI SARASIN

LUMPINI PARK

NOT TO SCALE

RAMA IV RD.

© MOON PUBLICATIONS

dressers doing a brisk business; by night, it is transformed into a neon section of gay bars. The bars advertise live shows and handsome hosts and go-go dancers.

LUMPINI PARK-SIAM SQUARE

What's On
There's a large concentration of movie theaters around Siam Square: three cinemas on the 4th floor of Siam Center; three more across the street at Siam Square; and two mini-theaters on the ground floor of Mahboonkrong Shopping Center.

Restaurants With Classical Dance
Sala Thai, Indra Regent Hotel, Rajaprarop Road, tel. 251-1111, dance shows nightly from 2030 to 2115. **Maneeya Lotus Room**, 518 Ploenchit Road (close to Erawan Hotel), tel. 252-6312, nightly from 2015 to 2100.

Thai Boxing
Just east of Lumpini Park on Rama IV Road is **Lumpini Stadium**. Matches start at 1820—Tues., Fri., and Sat. Get there early as tickets go quickly.

Hotel Venues
Baiyoke Tower—go to the **Sky Lounge** on the 43rd floor for superb aerial views of the city (cocktails, no cover, B100 for a beer, no food after 1700, some live entertainment). **Juliana's** (disco) at the Hilton Hotel; bars at the Siam Intercontinental; Asia Hotel has a bar called **Entrepreneur**, with live jazz on Saturdays; Le Meridien President Hotel has a piano bar.

Jazz Pubs, Blues Bars
Round Midnight, at 106 Soi Lang Suan, is a large (two-floor) place with a crowd mainly from Chulalongkorn University—live jazz and rock. Around the corner, at the back of Lumpini Park on Soi Sarasin, is a string of small bars—**Shakin, Old West, Brown Sugar**—live music ranges from rock to progressive jazz. These places are lots of fun, with high-spirited university students getting hammered on bottles of Mekong whiskey. The action spills over onto the sidewalk, with tables outside if you like things a bit quieter. You can get food here too—from the bars, or from sidewalk vendors.

Near Le Meridien President Hotel (in the Keysorn Road area) is a pocket of clubs, bars, and restaurants, including **Blue Moon** (a jazz/blues place). In the Siam Square area is the **Hard Rock Café**.

SUKHUMVIT SOIS 1-21

Hotel Venues
At the Landmark is **The Huntsman**, an English pub; on the top floor is an exclusive restaurant and cocktail bar with aerial panoramas. The Ambassador Hotel has **Dickens Bar**, and the **Flamingo Disco**. The Manhattan Hotel has a discreet corner with **Chippendale's**, a gigolo bar.

Jazz Pubs
On Soi 11 is **The Glass**, open 1800 to 0100; live band after 2100 hours; serves food.

Beer-bars
Right under the expressway and around the railway tracks is **Buckskin Joe Village** with low-key beer bars and hostess bars. Maintain your sense of equilibrium after beer-consumption—if you cross the train tracks between bars, the odd freight train does come roaring through. There's a cluster of beer-bars downstairs at Nana Plaza on Soi 4. There are German beer gardens on Sois 3, 7, 15, and on Soi Asoke (Singha Bier Haus). For the weirdest beer-bar decor, go and check out **Cheap Charlie's** off Soi 11!

Go-go Bars
Off Soi 4, opposite the Nana Hotel, Nana Plaza has two stories of bars arranged around a courtyard, with beer-bars below and go-go bars above. The best of the upper-floor bars is **Asian Intrigue**, which has two shows nightly featuring lip-synch charades, finely dressed *katoeys*, candle-dancing (not the traditional kind) and other phenomena. The big spenders at Nana Plaza (and on Patpong) used to be Arabs and foreign oil workers flying in from the Middle East—they were in the habit of ringing the bar bell, which meant buying a round for the whole bar.

Coffee-shops

The main after-hours place on Sukhumvit is **Thermae Coffee-shop,** on Sukhumvit between Sois 13 and 15. Situated in the same building as the **Thermae Massage Parlour,** this basement bar is a tawdry affair, filled with the smell of smoke and cheap perfume—after 0130 the place fills up with girls from nearby Soi Cowboy, and by 0230 it is packed with freelance Thai women, paunchy Western men, and assorted lounge lizards. The atmosphere is something of a cross between bar, bordello, zoo, and

high-school prom: Fellini would feel right at home here. After 0100 the bar is officially closed, but unofficially it stays open till at least 0600—patrons are rerouted through the back door.

SUKHUMVIT SOIS 21 AND UP

Restaurants With Classical Dance
Baan Thai, 7 Soi 32, Sukhumvit Road (behind Rex Hotel), tel. 258-5403, dance shows nightly from 2100 to 2145—in traditional teak housing

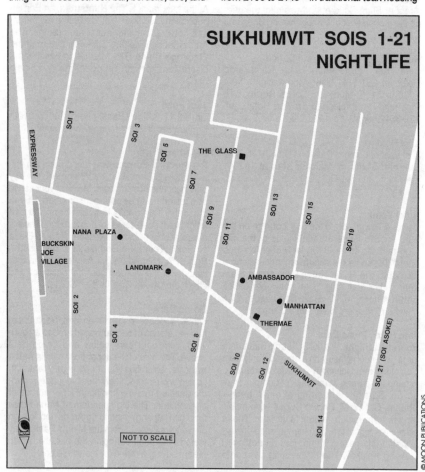

SUKHUMVIT SOIS 1-21 NIGHTLIFE

SUKHUMVIT—SOIS 21 UP NIGHTLIFE

with tropical gardens. **Piman Thai,** 46 Sukhumvit Soi 49, tel. 258-7866, nightly from 2030 to 2130, is a copy of a Sukothai-era house. Both recommended, although they are pricier than other places.

Calypso Cabaret

In a category all of its own is this transvestite revue—hilarious lip-synch numbers in a large theater at 688 Sukhumvit Road, between Sois 24 and 26, tel. 258-8987. Gay and straight clien-tele—families welcome. Show costs B300 a person; showtimes 2015 and 2215 hours. Calypso Cabaret is highly educational: men should take careful note of how easy it can be to tangle with the wrong gender. Go and see these ravishing beauties a little closer after the show, when they pose for photos. Also take note that female repli-cas *(katoeys,* or "ladymen") do operate around the Patpong scene and elsewhere in Bangkok, and are prevalent at Pattaya Beach. *Katoey* can mean a man impersonating a woman; somewhat more subtle, it can mean a person who has undergone a sex-change operation. These operations can be done in Hong Kong, Singapore, and in Bangkok. Some sex-change operations are such surgical masterpieces—and the "ladymen" play their roles so well—that only experts can tell. Ironically, females can detect the presence of the "third sex" far better than men. Some males, like the forlorn foreigner who was married to a female replica for eight months, find out the hard way. This story came to light in a *Bangkok Post* article, and the writer asked the pertinent question: why did the gentleman take so long to find out?

Pub-restaurants

At Washington Square off Soi 22 is **Bourbon Street**—a big place with restaurant, bar, darts, and friendly staff. Western, Thai, and Cajun Creole cuisine, and some live music (New Orleans jazz) on weekends.

Jazz Pubs, Blues Bars

On Soi 53, there's a large venue simply called **Blues/Jazz**. It features fusion jazz nightly except Sundays, jazz-rock on Fridays and Saturdays; drinks are expensive—B100 for a beer. **Witch's Tavern**, off Sukhumvit Soi 55 (Soi Thonglor), has live classical jazz (old standards), Victorian-style decor, English-style food.

Hostess Bars

On Soi 33 is **Renoir's**—a high-class hostess bar, with female bartenders in theme-night clothing (the idea here is the complete opposite of Soi Cowboy—bargirls dress up rather than down). Renoir's has a swank decor of glass-topped tables and thick carpet. Happy hour drinks are B45 (up to 2100); after that, drinks are B150 each, with girls' drinks at B100. Run by the same management is **Vincent Van Gogh** (next door to Renoir's), which caters to Thais, and over near Rama IV Road on Soi Saladeng is **P. Gaugain Club**, which has a Thai clientele and Thai music.

Another area with hostess bars and the odd go-go bar is Washington Square, on Soi 22: low-key nightlife with some bars and restaurants catering to foreign residents of Bangkok. One of these bars was so low-key it almost went out of business: it had a sign out front which read The Problem Bar. What the manager meant was the No Problem Bar (Mai Pen Rai).

Go-go Bars

Just north of Sukhumvit and running between Sois 21 and 23 is Soi Cowboy, a strip of go-go bars and beer-bars. It was named after a black American called "Cowboy," one of the first bar owners in the area—it's cheaper than Patpong and less sophisticated, but some prefer it that way. Patrons are not hassled to buy drinks, and since there are no live shows, there are no touts. For those interested in Ben Hur chariot-races, *tuk-tuk* drivers shuttling between Soi Cowboy and Nana Plaza often indulge in drag-racing along Sukhumvit.

EXCURSIONS FROM BANGKOK

INTRODUCTION

There's enough within a 200-kilometer radius of Bangkok to keep you busy for months, with activities as varied as diving in Pattaya, rafting in Kanchanaburi, hiking in Khao Yai National Park, bicycling in Ayuthaya, or just relaxing in Hua Hin. Some of the places can be visited on day-trips; others require overnight or two-day trips. Transport connections up-country are excellent—it's easy to get out of Bangkok and explore Central Thailand.

TOURS

If your time is short, there are numerous agencies around Bangkok that will squeeze four or five sights together in a single day. This can be useful if you don't want to deal with the logistics of getting around, and the agencies can save you considerable time and money (if you are going to several places where the entry fee is a hefty B180 for foreigners, an organized tour may pay for itself). Some tour operators use buses; others use air-con minibuses.

These agencies seem to have developed a special jargon for out-of-Bangkok touring. Elephant and Crocodile Wrestling? Floating Market Snake Farm? Death Railway Orchid Farm? Since there appear to be half a dozen snake farms out of Bangkok, and as many crocodile farms, you might inquire more closely about the schedule, as a lot of agencies don't give a hoot which reptiles you end up with, or how long you spend at a particular place. Watch out for floating market mix-ups, too—the one you want is Damnern Saduak (the other one, called Wat

a small car ferry on the Chao Phraya River

Sai, in Bangkok, is not worth the trip). And establish if all entry-fees for attractions are included. Some of these agencies are genuine, and others cater to the "instant tourist" who has to see everything Thailand has to offer in the space of a few hours.

There is no problem finding tour agencies. They're in and around all the hotels in Bangkok but they come and go; make sure the agency has a phone that is plugged in—it takes a good six months to get a phone installed in Bangkok. The agents in budget areas around the Khao San Road/Banglamphu area and the Malaysia Hotel offer some cheap tours; those agencies close to the Oriental Hotel naturally are more expensive. Worth keeping in mind are the tours organized by the Chao Phraya Express Boat company (to Bang Pa-In, on Sundays), and those run by the State Railways Department to the Kanchanaburi area and to Hua Hin (see "Kanchanaburi" and "Hua Hin").

GETTING OUT OF BANGKOK

By Plane

There are few air connections in Central Thailand—one is a Bangkok Airways flight to Hua Hin by light aircraft. Bangkok Airways is a domestic carrier that serves destinations not covered by the main domestic carrier, Thai Airways International. Bangkok Domestic Airport is just south of the International Airport; departure tax is B20.

By Bus

Air-conditioned buses (blue) are excellent—comfortable, fast, efficient, frequent, and very cheap. These are Mercedes buses equipped with reclining seats, reading lights, airjets, tinted windows, and curtains. Luggage can be stowed under the seat, in an overhead bin, or in the luggage compartment under the bus. Two problems: usually the air-conditioning is ferocious, so bring a sweater. And sometimes the video or cassette player at the front of the bus is rather loud—avoid the very front seats.

Ordinary buses (orange) are much slower (and cheaper) and have none of the facilities mentioned above (except, unfortunately, the video). These buses can be flagged down anywhere along the highway, so expect frequent stops and overcrowding. There is next-to-no suspension on some older models—don't sit right at the back.

Bus Terminals

Because the bus stations are on the fringes of town, you can sometimes consume an hour or more just getting across Bangkok from your hotel to the terminal. Usually with buses no advance ticketing is necessary—you front up and buy a ticket say 15 minutes before the bus departs. Departures vary in frequency from every 15 minutes to once an hour, depending on the destination; buses generally operate from 0600 to 1900 or later.

Eastern Bus Terminal (tel. 391-2504), just off Sukhumvit Road (opposite Soi 63 Ekamai), handles destinations to the Samut Prakarn, Pattaya, Rayong, and the east coast.

Southern Bus Terminal (tel. 411-4978) is actually at the northwest edge of Bangkok, just off Highway 338, at the corner of Pra Pinklao and Nakhon-Chaisri roads. This is the main a/c and regular bus terminal for destinations to the northwest (Kanchanaburi), the west (Nakhon Pathom, Damnern Saduak), and the southwest (Cha-Am, Hua Hin, Phuket). It's difficult to get to the station by public transport. Buses 124, 125, 127, and 128 run there, but these start in Thonburi.

North/Northeast Bus Terminal (tel. 279-4484), on Paholyothin Road in the direction of the airport, has regular and air-con buses sprawled over a large area with numbered platforms. The complex handles buses to Ayuthaya, Lopburi, Saraburi, and points north (Chiang Mai) and northeast (Sukothai, Udon, Nong Khai).

Private Buses: There are dozens of private bus and minibus operators around Bangkok, with bookings done via travel agencies or

---

CENTRAL THAILAND HIGHLIGHTS

East Coast
Crocodile Farm, at Samut Prakarn, 30 km south by bus—Thailand's largest, with 30,000 specimens and regular shows.

Pattaya, 132 km southeast by bus, train, or boat—raucous beach resort with water sports by day (diving, fishing, windsurfing), and a nightlife that rivals Bangkok's. Just south is **Jomtien,** with cleaner beaches than those at Pattaya; along the eastern seaboard are many other beach resorts—among them **Ko Samet.**

West Of Bangkok
Damnern Saduak, 110 km southwest by bus—Thailand's premier floating market area, in a skein of canals. Optimum time to visit is early morning.

Nakhon Pathom, 56 km west, reached by train or bus—famous for its giant pagoda with a standing Buddha. Nakhon Pathom is a frequent stopover en route to floating markets or to Kanchanaburi.

Rose Garden, 32 km west by bus—landscaped garden with a one-hour cultural show in the afternoons: short exhibitions of sword fighting, dancing, ceremonies.

Kanchanaburi, 130 km northwest, reached by bus or train (the historic River Kwai railway)—this town is the launching point for bamboo raft trips and jungle treks further inland. A minimum of two days is needed to explore the area; some travelers spend up to 10 days here swimming, cycling, and lazing around.

Hua Hin, 200 km southwest, reached by bus, train, plane, or boat—low-key beach resort. Minimum travel time is an overnight trip. The place is packed with Bangkokians from Friday to Sunday, so weekend reservations are advised. Hua Hin's beaches are polluted, as are the ones just north at Cha-Am; neither resort comes close to the fine beaches in Thailand's deep south.

North Of Bangkok
Bang Pa-In, 63 km north by bus, train, or boat—abandoned Summer Palace, which can be seen in a few hours. The boat trip from Bangkok to Bang Pa-In along the Chao Phraya is highly recommended.

Ayuthaya, 80 km north, reached by bus, train, or boat—the capital of Siam for over 400 years, Ayuthaya was sacked by the Burmese in 1767, resulting in piles of rubble, and ruins. To do this archeological site justice you need a full two days.

Khao Yai National Park, 160 km northeast by car or bus—overnight stop recommended for this park, which features hiking and swimming, and wildlife—particularly birds.

Lopburi, 155 km north, reached by train or bus—ruins from Khmer period. Little to see here, but Lopburi has a quiet charm and is used as a stopover on the route north. The town can easily be toured in a half-day excursion.

through hotels. Minibuses leave the Khao San Road area daily, charging up to double the price of those from the bus terminals, but they save you the time and trouble of getting to the terminal in the first place, and can arrange hotel pick-up.

By Car

It's very straightforward to rent a car in Bangkok and use it for out-of-town trips (for rental procedures, see "Getting Around Bangkok" section). Try to be on the road at the crack of dawn to clear the hurdles of Bangkok traffic and enable safe passage to the outside world. Two other tactics: get your rental at an agency on the fringes of the city; or, if leery about driving in Bangkok, get a man from the agency to drive you to the highway exit and pay his taxi fare back. You can hire a driver for your trip if you want, too: drivers charge around B300 a day, and will drive from 0800 to 1700 hours (overnight expenses are an extra B300 for the driver, or B600 for a 24-hour period).

Once you're out of Bangkok, driving is fairly easy. The roads are excellent, usually double highways. Keep in mind that slower vehicles must use the left-most lane. You'll find the usual array of gas stations—Esso, Shell, Caltex—sometimes you might get stuck with a smaller filling station which may have just a gas barrel with a hand-pump. If you get a flat tire, local

Thais will most likely help to change it and do not expect payment. Navigation is easy: the roads are well marked, highways are numbered, and outside of towns there are kilometer-posts tracking distances. If you have a decent map that shows the highway numbers, you shouldn't have any problems. On the highways there are international signs, or else Thai/English signs, but spellings are not consistent—you might see Ayuthaya, Ayuttaya, or Ayudhya.

Might is right in Thailand—bigger vehicles have the right of way, so motorcycles give way to cars, and cars give way to trucks. Watch out for farm vehicles; they can slow you down and create dangerous situations when you try to pass. Night driving should be avoided, especially near Bangkok, as the highway is dominated by trucks which often drive with their high-beams on, blinding you in the process.

Occasionally there is a sign that says Speed Limit, but it rarely tells you what the limit is. The speed limit is supposed to be 60 km/hr within city limits, and 80 km/hr on the highway. There are such things as speed checks and radar traps. Most highway police are quite helpful. If you are pulled over by highway patrol, you will most likely have been at fault. Do not *under any circumstances* argue with the officer. If you have been at fault, the officer may ask you to hand over your license or the car keys. To retrieve those items, a small "fine" (about B100-200) is levied—

Ayuthaya-style tuk-tuk

and this will be much less trouble (and less expensive) than paying the official fine at a police station, an exercise that may consume three hours of your time.

By Train

Trains out of Bangkok are not as frequent as buses and sometimes depart at inconvenient hours: it's best to get a timetable. Tickets can be purchased at the station, or through travel agents. There are four kinds of trains: diesel and ordinary trains stop at every station they can find; rapid and express trains go up to twice as fast, for a surcharge of B20 (rapid) or B30 (express). Express charges are levied regardless of distance, so these trains are expensive for short hauls. Going from Bangkok to Nakhon Pathom, for example, would cost B44 for third class on an express train, versus B24 for an air-con bus; from Bangkok to Hua Hin, third class on an express train (B74) costs the same as an air-con bus ride. First-class (air-con) and second-class sleepers are available on long-distance trains. Third-class seats are fine for short hauls, and on a lot of trains you may not have a choice anyway, since all the cars may be the same.

One good thing about the trains is that you avoid the Bangkok traffic jams that plague buses. Up-country, there are usually left-luggage offices at the railway stations, making it easier to tour. Food and drink are never a problem on the trains—there is a constant parade of strolling vendors armed to the teeth with skewered chicken, dried squid, packed lunches, beer, whiskey, iced drinks, and fruit.

Train Terminals And Tours

Hualampong (main station), off Rama IV Road, tel. 223-0341, handles the majority of the trains departing Bangkok. The station has 11 platforms, an advance booking office (tel. 223-7010), left-luggage office (open 0400 to 2230), information office with English schedules, a newsstand with English bestsellers, and a mini-mart for stocking up for the train.

Thonburi (Bangkok Noi) Station, tel. 411-3102, is right near the Chao Phraya River—the express boat landing nearby just says Railway Station. It has five platforms and only a handful of departures: ordinary (slow) trains to the west

and southwest (to Langsuan, Nakhon Pathom, Ratchaburi, and Sungai Kolok), as well as a few trains on the rail-spur to Suphanburi, and to Kanchanaburi (up to Namtok).

Railway Tours: The SRT (State Railways of Thailand) has several itineraries to the Kanchanaburi area, and one to Hua Hin (see "Kanchanaburi" and "Hua Hin"). Inquire at the advance booking office at Bangkok main station about current SRT tours.

By Boat

In the Ayuthaya period, boat travel was the main method of long-distance travel in Thailand, with a variety of boats used by kings and commoners. With the coming of road and rail, most of the boats are museum pieces. One classic boat trip you can take is from Bangkok to Bang Pa-In, in the direction of Ayuthaya (for more information, see Bang Pa-In under "North of Bangkok.")

Jet Cat: There's a new daily service to Pattaya by jet-powered catamaran, a Norwegian-made luxury passenger vessel that can seat up to 270 passengers. The twin-hulled vessel cruises at over 30 knots and takes just 90 minutes to get to Pattaya, or 2 1/2 hours to get to Hua Hin. Two trips a day to each destination are scheduled. Book through travel agents, or phone Seatran Travel at 249-1397 or 249-5656.

Hydrofoil: A 71-passenger hydrofoil called the *Thepsirinta* runs from its Bangkok/Menam Hotel terminal to Pattaya (takes 90 minutes, costs B350 one-way economy class); Pattaya to Hua Hin (two hours, costs B450); and occasionally from Hua Hin directly back to Bangkok (three hours, costs B450). It can be a bumpy trip on the open sea. The company concerned seems to be doing its best to drive customers away—the phone lines are always busy, the hydrofoil schedule changes overnight, and the staff never seem to know whether a craft is coming or going. For reservations, call 291-9613 or book through agents.

Longtailed Boats cost about B100-250 per hour, during which time you should be able to cover 25 km on a canal or river. If you're going one way on a longer trip, longtail operators will want a return subsidy. They'll probably ask the same amount, but you can usually bargain that figure down. Travel by longtailed boat on the rivers is a pleasant way of getting around Ayuthaya and Kanchanaburi—assemble a group and split the expenses.

GETTING AROUND THE TOWNS

The same transportation that's found in Bangkok is also found in the small towns of Central Thailand—*tuk-tuks,* taxis, motorcycle-taxis, *songtaos. Songtaos* are much more common; *tuk-tuks* and taxis are harder to find; and for short hauls there are trishaws—three-wheel bicycles that seat two passengers. These vehicles are cheap (B10 for short rides; B15-20 for longer ones) and the operators need the money, so patronize them if you're going from the bus or train station to your hotel. **Rentals:** In many places you can rent jeeps (around B400-1000 a day), motorcycles (ordinary and trail-bikes—around B150-300 a day) and chauffeur-driven

vehicles. **Warning:** unless you have the mechanical know-how to evaluate the condition of a rented motorcycle, and unless you have lots of riding experience, stay well away. You don't want to come home in a box. Too many travelers have been injured in accidents, usually due to faulty motorcycles (brakes or other critical parts were not properly maintained) or poor riding skills. Consider the consequences of an accident—do you have a proper motorcycle license? Are you covered by insurance that will fly you back home?

In some places (Hua Hin, Kanchanaburi, Ayuthaya) you can rent bicycles from guesthouses or small businesses. Bicycling is an excellent way of seeing what a place has to offer, at the right pace. Rentals are around B20-30 a day; some places require you to deposit B200 or your passport (do not leave a passport). Check that both brakes work and the tires are pumped up, and adjust the seat height to maximize leg power.

EAST COAST

Fun, sun, and sports are the main pursuits along the eastern seaboard—and in Pattaya the partying goes on all night. Buses to the following destinations run from the Eastern Bus Terminal off Sukhumvit Road.

CROCODILE FARM AND ANCIENT CITY

Because of high entry fees for these two attractions—B140 for the Croc Farm and B150 for the Ancient City—it is better to join a tour, costing maybe B400.

Samut Prakarn Crocodile Farm, 30 km south of Bangkok, is the largest in the world, with some 30,000 fresh and saltwater specimens. The emphasis here is on the word "farm"— the crocs are turned into wallets, shoes, and handbags, which are offered for sale. You can buy a bowl of croc soup, reputed to be an aphrodisiac. Crocodile wrestling is featured (man versus crocodile) several times a day; frenzied feeding time is 1630 to 1730. There's a mini-zoo with tigers, snakes, and elephants (elephant

shows are also put on). The farm is open daily 0800 to 1800; entry B140 for *farangs.*

The Ancient City (Muang Boran) is for those interested in Thai architecture, history, and monuments. It has large-scale models of such sites as Ayuthaya and Bangkok—resurrecting some palaces and temples that have long been destroyed. The Ancient City is a gift to the nation from the owner of the largest Mercedes-Benz dealership in Thailand. The place is laid out in the shape of Thailand on 200 acres of land, and models are linked by some 30 km of roadway; you can see most of the place in three hours by car. Open daily 0830 to 1800.

If driving yourself, take the Expressway to Samut Prakarn (Pak Nam), which has an interesting market; from here it's a short drive to the Croc Farm, and a half-dozen kilometers to the Ancient City. You can dine at Bang Poo, where there is an excellent seafood restaurant on a pier jutting into the Gulf of Thailand. Other transport options include hiring a longtail or other vessel to reach Samut Prakarn. This takes two or three hours and goes through Bangkok's bustling port section. The cheapest way of get-

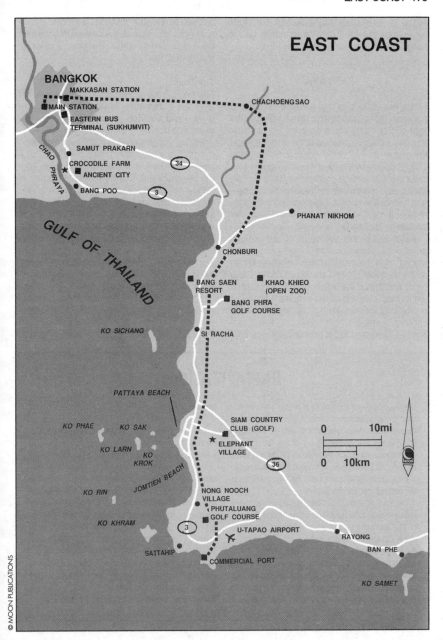

ting to Samut Prakarn is by a/c buses 8 or 11, or by ordinary bus 25. From the terminus, take a *songtao* for a few baht to the Croc Farm.

PATTAYA

There are visitors to this seaside resort who never set foot on the beach, who hardly see the light of day—they come here for the nightlife. If you're a party animal, raucous Pattaya is just the place—its nightlife rivals that of Bangkok. This "Patpong-by-the-Sea" has the largest concentration of foreign-patronized bars, discos, shows, and restaurants in Thailand. Not to mention hotels: the shores are carpeted with highrises and condominiums—the Miami Beach or Waikiki of Thailand.

Pattaya, 132 km southeast of Bangkok, is another of those fishing-village-turned-resort stories, with the transformers being American marines on R&R. When an aircraft-carrier battle group anchors off the beach, up to 5,000 marines are let loose: waiting on the sands are scores of nubile Thai women. With rapid construction of condominiums and high-rise hotels, little attention has been paid to the environment. The con-

dos and hotels have placed a large demand on resources: pipes send raw sewage into the sea; there is a chronic water shortage, and a surplus of garbage.

The Town
The beachfront at Pattaya is about three km long. It's a thin strip, not inspiring for swimmers—and polluted (most visitors use hotel swimming pools).

Pattaya roughly divides into three sections: in the north are expensive hotels catering to couples and groups. In the center, and away from the beach, is the Thai commercial section of Pattaya (Central Road) with the markets and cheaper budget accommodations. At the southern end of the beach is an area catering to rowdy single males, packed with cheaper hotels, bars, discos, and restaurants. Nobody in their right mind would swim here—the coliform count is so high that it's a health hazard. Those wanting to swim use hotel pools, or visit other beaches, or visit offshore islands.

South of Pattaya is **Jomtien Beach**, half of which is under the jurisdiction of Pattaya. Jomtien has very little nightlife and caters more to the sports-minded (windsurfing, sailing), to fam-

---

PATTAYIZATION

"Pattayization"—or the turning of virgin coastline into a monstrous collection of condos, hotels, and bars—threatens the east coast all the way to Cambodia. Bungalows are sprouting up along the Rayong Province coastline, and tour companies, having written off beaches like Pattaya as too polluted, are now eyeing the far-flung beaches near the Cambodian border around Trat and Ko Chang.

Destruction of coral reefs is a great concern. Some are destroyed to facilitate swimming, and in the south of Thailand coral reefs are being blasted with homemade bombs by fishermen bent on an easy catch. As the coastline becomes fished out, the local fishermen have turned into boatmen and tour guides. The towns, meanwhile, have to cope with serious garbage problems—the collection services cannot handle increased garbage output. What is not collected is

strewn around the communities, the beaches, or even in the water.

The setting up of national parks is seen as a possible solution to uncontrolled development, and that has perhaps saved the island of Ko Samet from being over-commercialized. This island is supposedly a national park with only camping allowed. In fact, the coastline is full of concrete and wooden bungalows, some with air-conditioning, TV, and fridge! Greedy operators and a deluge of tourists are trashing this island—garbage is strewn everywhere. Periodically there are raids. In 1990, the island was closed to tourists after Forestry officials and the Border Patrol Police arrested a number of operators for violating the National Park Act. However, the operators were eventually allowed to return and run their businesses by paying a monthly fine of B500 to the Forestry Department.

ilies, to group tours, and to those wanting a low-key approach. The beachfront here is cleaner (for the moment) and longer than Pattaya's. The southern end of Jomtien is okay for swimming.

Water Sports

Pattaya has a great array of sporting and recreational activities, particularly water sports. In Jomtien you can rent windsurfing and water-skiing equipment, Hobie Cats, Lasers, yachts (with or without crew), water scooters, or arrange to have yourself flown over all of the preceding in a parasailing outfit (high risk involved). Bargain, check equipment before rental, and do not sign liability forms. There seem to be few or no regulations governing activities like water-scooters, water-skiing, and parasailing, with the result that operators zip willy-nilly through swimming areas. A favorite water-scooter scam is to rent them out with almost no gas—a "rescue" fee is then charged.

Deep-sea fishing for marlin, barracuda, king mackerel, and sailfish can be arranged. **Pattaya Game Fishing Club**, operating out of **Jenny's Hotel** (tel. 429-645); and **Deutsches Haus** (tel. 423-626), both on Beach Road, run charters. At the northern end of Jomtien is **Pattaya Waterpark**, which has sets of slides ideal for kids.

Pattaya has half a dozen dive shops for scuba equipment rentals, supplies and instruction—most are found along or close to Beach Road. These include **Dave's Divers Den** near Soi 5; **International Divers Center** in the Siam Bayview; **Stevens Dive Shop** at 579 Beach Road; and **Seafari Sports Center** in the Royal Garden Resort. In Jomtien there's **Mermaid Sea-sport Center** at Mermaid's Beach Resort. Some offer instruction and certification for first-timers.

Popular diving and snorkeling destinations around Pattaya include **Ko Larn, Ko Sak**, and **Ko Krok** (an hour away by boat) with coral beds at depths of 6-30 meters. Water temperature is pleasant, but speedboat traffic is definitely not pleasant—to get away from the crowds, you have to go further afield to **Ko Phai** or **Ko Rin**, where visibility is better anyway. Dive shops have information on these places, and some run snorkeling and scuba tours.

Land Sports

On land there's tennis, bowling, snooker, badminton, horse riding (**Reo Ranch**, six km east), go-cart racing (80cc and 120cc carts available), shooting, motor racing (a spectator sport; the track is 20 km from Pattaya), and even bungee-jumping (from a crane). The **Pattaya Hash House Harriers** hold a mixed cross-country run on Monday afternoons at 1700, a good way of meeting people.

Golf: A 20-minute drive east of Pattaya is the **Siam Country Club**, tel. 428-002, which is a private golf club but visitors can play through arrangements with hotels (there are hotel rooms at the course, too). To the north, 45 km from Pattaya near Bang Saen, is the international-standard 18-hole **Bang Phra Golf Course**, tel. 321-332: rentals are available; visitors are welcome; and the course is open daily from 0600 to 1800 (phone ahead to make sure there are no tournaments going on). There is a deluxe 60-room hotel at Bang Phra. To the south is **Phutaluang** (Royal Thai Navy Golf Course, tel. 601-185), which is a 35-minute drive away—the course is regarded as Thailand's most difficult, with rolling hills, dense vegetation, winds, and water hazards. Right in Pattaya at **Asia Hotel**, tel. 428-602, is a nine-hole course.

Around Pattaya

On the headland to the south, near the Naval Radio Station, is a **viewpoint** with a small temple and a shaded eating area (food served), a pleasant place to sit and take in the scenery. Behind Jomtien Beach is **Wat Yannasang-wararam**, a delightful modern interpretation of classic Thai temple style, set in extensive landscaped gardens. Offshore from Pattaya are islands where the water is clear and the swimming is good—ideal for day-trips. You can join a group on one of the numerous excursion boats leaving south Pattaya piers. Vessels range from converted fishing trawlers to glass-bottom boats used for coral-sighting.

Elephant Village, five km east of Pattaya, has a daily two-hour show at 1430 (admission B160), with demonstrations of elephant-capturing, log-hauling, and other scenes of the pachyderms at work. At the end of the show, you are invited to mount an elephant and sit behind its

*Royal Cruise Hotel,
North Pattaya*

head for a ride—a rare thrill to be behind such a powerful but gentle creature, with your feet nuzzled behind its ears. If you're not up to that, you can also get on via a high ramp and sit in a backside box for a ride.

The announcer says the elephants here are on vacation from logging camps in the north, but they're more likely unemployed. Due to catastrophic soil erosion, the government banned teak logging in the early 1980s, and all domestic logging in 1989. With the teak forests all but wiped out, the survival of wild elephants in Thailand is questionable. As for the domesticated elephants, other employment has been found for them, particularly in tourism for such novelties as elephant soccer and reenactments of battles using elephants as "tanks." Another way that mahouts make a living is by going from village to village and selling charms: passing under an elephant is said to be good luck, especially for pregnant women, as it is said to ensure an easy birth.

Nong Nooch Village, 17 km south of Pattaya, has a 500-acre landscaped garden and cultural shows at 1000 and 1500 hours. There's an archery range at Nong Nooch, and accommodations available in Thai-style cottages.

Accommodations

Pattaya ain't cheap! Despite increasing vacancy rates, rooms in Pattaya are more expensive than in Bangkok. Cheapest accommodations are B100 and up per person; B300-700 for average double rooms; and B1000 and up for luxury accommodations; prices vary with the season (high season is Dec-Feb). There are hundreds of hotels in Pattaya, from guesthouses to multistory luxury hotels: over 21,000 rooms available at last count. Check with TAT in Pattaya for current prices, or go through travel agents.

North Pattaya: Super-luxury, luxury, and moderate hotels. Accommodations usually run from B1500 to more than B5000 in this area. In this range are the **Merlin**, tel. 428-755; **Montien**, tel. 428-155; and **Siam Bayview**, tel. 423-325. A startling landmark here is the **Royal Cruise Hotel**, tel. 424-242, which looks like a cruise liner. It offers "cabins" from B2000-5000 and up, and staff dresses as ship's crew. There are some moderately priced hotels (B400-600 d) tucked into north Pattaya, such as **Royal Night Bungalows**, tel. 428-038, and **Palm Garden**, tel. 429-386.

Central Pattaya: Budget hotels and guesthouses, with basic accommodations as low as B100 s and B200 d, are located back from the beach around Pattaya 2 Road, clustered near the strip between Soi Post Office and Soi 9. These are not places to recommend—the rooms are run-down; the area is noisy and seedy. **Summer Place Youth Hostel**, tel. 428-659, has basic B100 rooms in a quieter location.

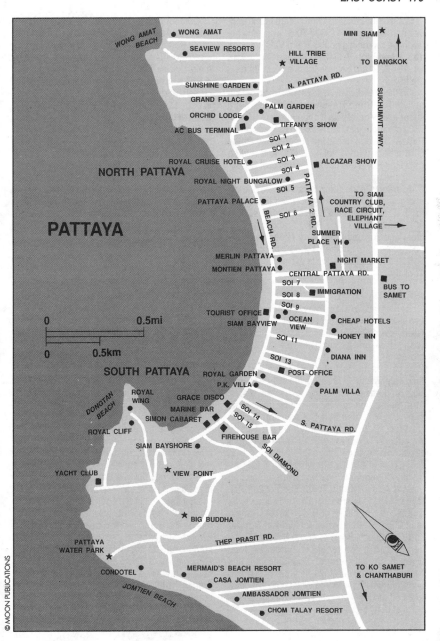

WONG AMAT BEACH

WONG AMAT

SEAVIEW RESORTS

MINI SIAM ★

HILL TRIBE ★ VILLAGE

TO BANGKOK

SUNSHINE GARDEN ●

GRAND PALACE ●

N. PATTAYA RD.

SUKHUMVIT HWY.

PALM GARDEN ■

ORCHID LODGE ●

TIFFANY'S SHOW ■

AC BUS TERMINAL ■

SOI 1

SOI 2

ROYAL CRUISE HOTEL ●

SOI 3

ALCAZAR SHOW ■

NORTH PATTAYA

SOI 4

ROYAL NIGHT BUNGALOW ●

SOI 5

PATTAYA PALACE ●

PATTAYA

SOI 6

TO SIAM COUNTRY CLUB, RACE CIRCUIT, ELEPHANT VILLAGE →

BEACH RD.

PATTAYA 2 RD.

SUMMER PLACE YH ●

MERLIN PATTAYA ●

NIGHT MARKET ■

MONTIEN PATTAYA ●

CENTRAL PATTAYA RD.

SOI 7

SOI 8

IMMIGRATION ■

BUS TO SAMET ■

0   0.5mi

TOURIST OFFICE ■

SOI 9

SIAM BAYVIEW ■

OCEAN VIEW ●

CHEAP HOTELS ●

0   0.5km

SOI 11

HONEY INN ●

SOUTH PATTAYA

SOI 13

DIANA INN ●

ROYAL GARDEN ●

POST OFFICE ■

P.K. VILLA ●

DONGTAN BEACH

ROYAL WING ●

GRACE DISCO ◆

PALM VILLA ●

MARINE BAR ◆

SOI 14

SIMON CABARET ◆

SOI 15

ROYAL CLIFF ●

S. PATTAYA RD.

FIREHOUSE BAR ◆

SIAM BAYSHORE ●

SOI DIAMOND

YACHT CLUB ●

★ VIEW POINT

★ BIG BUDDHA

PATTAYA WATER PARK

THEP PRASIT RD.

CONDOTEL ●

★

MERMAID'S BEACH RESORT ●

TO KO SAMET & CHANTHABURI

CASA JOMTIEN ●

JOMTIEN BEACH

AMBASSADOR JOMTIEN ●

CHOM TALAY RESORT ●

© MOON PUBLICATIONS

South Pattaya: Lots of moderate hotels popular with single males (B300-700 d a/c; some hotels have swimming pools). **Palm Villa**, tel. 428-153, **Honey Inn**, tel. 428-117, and **Diana Inn**, tel. 421-622, are decent; there are others near the beach.

On the Headland: At the southern tip of Pattaya is the **Siam Bayshore**, tel. 428-678, a super-luxury hotel with a price range of B2200-7000 per room. On the headland between south Pattaya and Jomtien is the super-luxury **Royal Cliff Beach Hotel**, tel. 421-421, and a wing called the Royal Cliff Grand. Rooms cost B3000-9000 and up.

Jomtien: Moderately priced smaller hotels and group-tour larger hotels. Down this way is the 100-room **Mermaid Beach Resort**, tel. 231-907, with prices in the B1200 range for doubles, and **Ambassador City Hotel**, tel. 231-501, with your choice of 2,500 rooms from B1500-9500 apiece—this is the largest hotel in Thailand.

Restaurants

Finding a place to eat in Pattaya is never a problem—signs crowd the southern section of Beach Road advertising pizza, tacos, Vienna Schnitzel, sushi, steak, and lobster. There are branches of top Bangkok restaurants here, hordes of seafood places, and lots of steakhouses and fast-food eateries. What is a problem is trying to find Thai food: restaurants cater to Western tastes. That means you can find Irish food (mince and mash at the **Poteen Still**, Soi Yamato), Scottish (at **Wee Andy's**, 19 Pattaya Beach Road), American (Texas-style BBQ at **Cattleman's Steakhouse**, 464 Pattaya 2 Road), Australian (meat pies at **Aussie Lifesavers** on Soi 2 Pattayaland; vegemite sandwiches, sardines on toast at **Aussie Ken's Toast Shop** at 205 Pattaya 2 Road), Mexican (burritos con salsa verde, and tacos con carne at **Blue Parrot**, Pattayland 2 Road), Polynesian (at **Mai Kai Supper Club** on Beach Road near the Novetel Tropicana), and a full range of European food (French, Swiss, German, Scandinavian, and Italian). Southern Pattaya has many "seafood supermarkets" where you pick your own creatures off the ice—payment is by weight, so beware of hefty tabs.

Outdoor dining is pleasant in Pattaya. **Ruen Thai Restaurant**, just off Pattaya 2 Road in south Pattaya, serves Thai and Western food in a setting of Thai pavilions and gardens—there is a nightly classical dance show. A similar venue is **PIC Kitchen**, on Soi 5, north Pattaya, with a classical dance show from 1930-2230 on Wednesdays, and recorded jazz during the week at the Jazz Pit.

For gourmets, two classic (read: expensive) restaurants are Dolf Riks, and the Orient Express. **Dolf Riks**, located behind the Regent Marina Hotel, north Pattaya, serves international cuisine, with the specialty of the house being Indonesian Rijsttafel (which is prepared by food columnist and artist Dolf Riks himself). The **Orient Express**, on Beach Road at the Nipa Lodge Hotel, consists of two converted Thai railway carriages, and serves French cuisine with premier wines.

Nightclubbing

By night, the southern section of Pattaya (called "The Strip") is ablaze with neon and popping lights, and there is a constant parade of freelance bargirls, transvestites, souvenir vendors, restaurant touts, and Western men with their Thai consorts. Go see this circus!

The emphasis in Pattaya is on open-air beer bars. There are hundreds of these in south Pattaya—some are open till 0500. There are few go-go bars—Soi 15 has a strip of them. Some of the open-air bars, such as the **Marine Bar**, feature Thai boxing with three-round slugfests. Occasionally a foreigner-in-training will show up in a fight—and if his legs don't get kicked in, he may even last the full three rounds. Upstairs at the Marine Bar is the disco hot spot of the area; another trendy place is **Disco Duck** in the Pattaya Resort Hotel on Central Road.

Gay Bars: Pattaya seems to be Thailand's unofficial gay capital. This is not advertised much—the word "gay" was banished from official English-language tourism advertising in Thailand in 1987 to counteract damaging associations with AIDS. There are several hotels in Pattaya that cater exclusively to gays (the **Ambiance Hotel**, tel. 424-099, being one), and a number of bars (with names like the **Cockpit**, and **Boys Town**) in South Pattaya along Pattayaland Sois 1, 2, and 3. Jomtien has a gay beach section, and there are gay cruises to the islands.

Cabarets: Pattaya is where Thailand's female impersonation cabarets got their start—there are lots of *katoeys* in town. Cabarets put on light and sound shows with lip-synch numbers, comedy routines, and elaborate costumery. Much of the showbiz hinges on the illusion of males masquerading as females. **Alcazar** and **Tiffany's**, at the north end of the beach, cater to group tours (the Japanese just love these shows!), with three shows nightly, 1930, 2030, and 2200, and a B300 entry charge. In the southern section is **Simon's Cabaret**, which has an entry-price of B160, including a drink.

Information And Communications

The **TAT office**, at 382 Beach Road, tel. 428-750, open 0830 to 1630, is very useful—bristling with brochures and maps. The **Tourist Police** are located next door. There are several free tourist magazines available, such as *Explore Pattaya,* with current information on hotel prices and events. Along Soi Post Office you can find the post office, postcards, stationery, packaging places, places to make long-distance phonecalls, DK Bookstore, legal consultation offices (for long-term visa extensions, work permits and so on), and small business centers (handling translations, copying, faxes).

Getting Around

Songtaos: These pick-up trucks with passenger seating in the back do an anticlockwise circuit of Pattaya (B5 for any distance), or else run to Jomtien (B30-40). You can hire a *songtao* the same way you would a taxi: negotiate the fee first. Traffic goes in a large circle around Pattaya: one way south on Beach Road; one way east on S. Pattaya Road; and one-way north on Pattaya 2 Road.

Vehicle Rentals: Jeeps, dirt-bikes, scooters, and other motorbikes are available. Most of the rentals are not legitimate rental agencies but extensions of shops doing other business.

They may have only one or two cars and a few motorcycles for rent, and not much in the way of insurance. Owners usually require a passport as deposit, but you should avoid leaving such a valuable document.

Driving in Pattaya is hazardous because there are so many maniacs on the road. There are Westerners who are riding high-powered motorbikes for the first time; there are lots of drinking drivers; there are jeep drivers showing off to their newly acquired girlfriends . . . you get the picture. The number of accidents involving tourists in Pattaya is frightening. Pattaya is small enough that you don't need your own vehicle to get around—you can either walk or use a *songtao.* A rented vehicle is best used during sober daylight hours when you want to get right out of town and find a clean, secluded beach.

Getting There

By Plane: The only connection at present is to Singapore, on Tradewinds Airlines. The airport, at U-Tapao, is a long way out of town.

By Bus: There are departures every half-hour from Eastern Bus Terminal. You arrive in North Pattaya two hours later. A number of private bus operators shuttle between Pattaya and Bangkok, and some will arrange hotel pick-up. There are also direct taxis and minibuses from Bangkok airport to Pattaya.

By Train: Slow train 239 from Bangkok's Main Station departs in the early morning and takes three hours to get to Pattaya. Train 240 returns in the late afternoon.

By Boat: There is a new Jet Cat service from Bangkok to Pattaya, taking 90 minutes for the run and scheduled twice a day—book through travel agents. There is also a hydrofoil service from Bangkok, taking 90 minutes (B350 one-way); it will drop you at the Ocean Marina Yacht Club 18 km to the south, in Jomtien, and a minibus transfers passengers to hotels. It's also possible to go from Pattaya to Hua Hin on the hydrofoil, a two-hour trip. Some private catamarans make the trip occasionally—make inquiries at bars along Soi Post Office.

WEST OF BANGKOK

Go west for low-key relaxation—whether at a jungle resort past Kanchanaburi, or in a national park, or at the fishing village of Hua Hin. Departures for the following destinations leave from Bangkok's Southern Bus Terminal. There are some slow trains running from Thonburi Station to Kanchanaburi. Trains for Hua Hin, Cha-Am, and fast trains west (to Nakhon Pathom, for example) leave from Hualampong (Bangkok Main Station).

DAMNERN SADUAK

Damnern Saduak, 110 km southwest of Bangkok, in Ratchaburi Province, is just another small town along the highway. Two kilometers to the west, however, is a junction of canals where farmers (mostly women) in boats converge around two fixed markets. There are boats loaded with coconuts and hands of bananas; boats piled high with cloves of garlic and spices; floating restaurant-boats; and boats stacked with straw hats for tourists. At the south end of the market is a large section full of gaudy souvenir shops. Once at the canal area, you can hire a small boat and be paddled around for an hour for about B10 a person (they seat 8 people, so B80 to use the entire boat). This usually includes a short trip to a coconut farm nearby, where you can see coconuts being boiled up in vats to enable sugar-extraction. The Damnern Saduak area is renowned for its fresh fruit—grapes in particular.

The floating market is best viewed between 0730 and 1000. After 1000 hours there are up to a thousand tourists wandering through, actually outnumbering the locals; in the afternoon there are hardly any boats left. To get there at the best viewing time, take the first bus out of the Southern Bus Station, at 0600, to arrive by 0800. The bus will drop you on the highway. From there, catch a small yellow *songtao* (two-seater minibus) running regularly into the canal area (costs B2). Or stay overnight at the town of Damnern Saduak at the Little Bird Hotel, tel. 241-315, which costs B120 for double room—nothing fancy. This hotel is a five-minute walk west of the bus station. Another early-bird game plan is to stay overnight at Nakhon Pathom, which is only 40 minutes away.

floating markets at Damnern Saduak

TAT

p-synch and dance routines at Calypso Cabaret (Bangkok) and Tiffany's (Pattaya): a host of high-kicking forms, nd there may even be a woman in there somewhere. Look again.

the naked, the naughty, and the neon—in Bangkok's bars

(clockwise from top) 1. noodle and tofu specialist, floating markets, Damnern Saduak; 2. fishing boat off Hua Hin; 3. vegetable-seller doing her accounting, Ratchaburi; 4. Mahout demonstrates how to get on board—using your knee hands—at Pattaya Elephant Village.

(top) an awesome Ayuthaya-style Buddha, cast in bronze and coated with gold leaf, at Wat Naphra Meru, Ayuth; (bottom left) wandering monk has his meal of the day under the canopy of his umbrella-tent; (bottom right) ruins the former Royal Palace, Ayuthaya

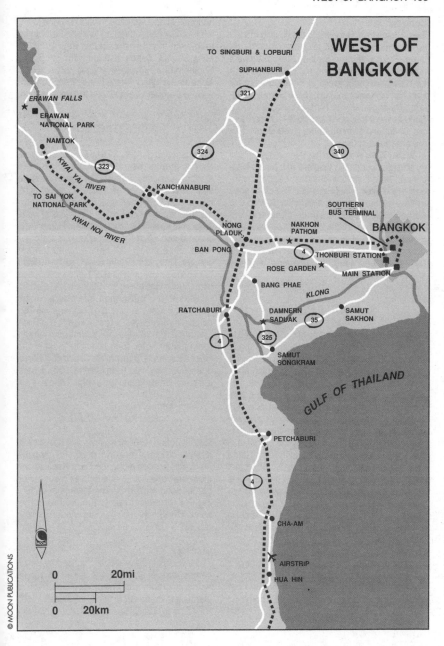

Connections

Bus: Buses from Bangkok to the floating market run every half-hour and take two hours to get there. From Damnern Saduak there are direct buses to Ratchaburi, to Nakhon Pathom (change for Kanchanaburi), to Bang Phae (change for Hua Hin or Kanchanaburi), or to Samut Songkram (change for Hua Hin). Leaving Damnern Saduak, most tour operators go to Nakhon Pathom Chedi and then on to the Rose Garden for the afternoon show.

Water Exit: A more adventurous option is to try and take commuter longtails or a rented longtail up Klong Damnern Saduak, headed northeast in the direction of Bangkok. The canal goes all the way into Bangkok, a distance estimated at 60 km, which takes between three and four hours to reach by longtailed boat. You can make it partway along this route using the commuter boats—try your luck! Fares are cheap enough (B10 for a long haul), and chances of getting lost are quite good.

NAKHON PATHOM

This area, 56 km west of Bangkok, is believed to be the earliest center of Buddhist learning in Thailand. The main sight here is the enormous (127-meter) **Pra Pathom Chedi,** which shelters an equally enormous standing Buddha. The Buddha is greatly revered, and there is a constant parade of worshippers placing offerings at the feet of the statue. Although the original site of this *chedi* had existed from the Dvaravati period, it was partially destroyed by the Burmese in the 11th century. In the 19th century, King Rama IV set about building a new *chedi;* the project was completed by King Rama V. The exterior is covered with golden glazed tiles imported from China, giving the impression of a shimmering tower of gold from a distance. The *chedi* is set in a park on a large terrace; there are four entrance chapels, located at the four compass points.

Though most consider Nakhon Pathom a stopover en route to other places, the town has several moderately priced hotels located between the train station and the *chedi*. There's no need to tell you where the *chedi* is—the colossal

handbell-shaped pagoda towers over the town. It takes 1 1/4 hours to get to Nakhon Pathom by train, with frequent departures from Hualampong Station. Buses also run from Bangkok's Southern Bus Terminal every half hour and stop close to the *chedi;* there are onward connections to Damnern Saduak and to Kanchanaburi.

ROSE GARDEN

A landscaped garden, 32 km west of Bangkok, with a theater where one-hour shows are staged—snippets of Thai culture and village life such as dances from the northeast, sword-fighting, a Buddhist ordination ceremony, a marriage ceremony, kick-boxing, elephants at work. A good-natured interaction between Homo Ektachromo and Siam Potted Culture Operators—most come away well pleased with the encounter. Entry to the grounds is B10; if you want to see the show, entry is B190 (price is included with tours). Showtime is 1500; a separate elephant show is performed elsewhere on the grounds. Buses run from the Southern Bus Terminal, or you can join a tour. Close to the Rose Garden is an 18-hole golf course and an 80-room luxury hotel. One kilometer east of the Rose Garden is **Samphran Crocodile Farm,** open 0900 to 1800 (admission B190), featuring croc-wrestling and an elephant show.

KANCHANABURI

Kanchanaburi, 130 km northwest of Bangkok, is a rather ordinary Thai town of 35,000 people—more picturesque along the River Kwai, where there are restaurants and houses mounted on bamboo-log platforms. The town is a launching-site for adventures to the northwest, but some find Kanchi itself relaxing enough to hang around.

Climate

The town is set in a valley surrounded by hills. It can be ferociously hot in the still air so bring a hat, sunscreen, and insect repellent if you're planning to camp out (a flashlight is useful, too). Best time to visit Kanchi is October and Novem-

riding between the rails, River Kwai Bridge, Kanchanaburi

ber, right after the rainy season—waters are higher for rafting, and weather is not scorching.

The Bridge

Better known than the town is the River Kwai Bridge, part of the infamous "Death Railway" undertaken by the Japanese from September 1942 to December 1943. Their plan was to forge a railway link with Burma—420 km of track, of which roughly one-third was in Burma and two-thirds in Thailand (the rails joined at Three Pagodas Pass). Construction exacted a terrible human toll; it is estimated that every railway-sleeper laid represents one dead soldier. Some 90,000 Asian conscripts and 16,000 Allied POWs died during the railroad's construction— of cholera, dysentery, malaria, starvation, heat, or exhaustion. The bridge was bombed in 1945 by Allied planes but the curved spans of the current bridge are the original ones.

After the war, the Thais ripped up the track from the Burmese border as far as Namtok, and upgraded the sections from Nong Pladuk (the beginning of the rail line) to Namtok in the 1950s. The bridge was made famous in a novel by Pierre Boulle, *The Bridge Over the River Kwai,* and in the movie that followed, directed by David Lean and starring a stiff-lipped Alec Guinness. The POWs tried their damnedest to make this bridge unsafe, so watch out when walking across it. Near the bridge are a couple of steam

locomotives, and a small, derelict monument built by the Japanese Army.

Allied War Cemeteries

There are 6,982 Allied war prisoners buried at **Kanchanaburi War Cemetery.** The headstones bear epitaphs charged with emotion. The land was donated by the Thai government, and the cemetery is maintained by the Commonwealth War Graves Commission. Survivors and relatives—Australian, New Zealand, British, and Dutch—come to pay homage. Across the river, to the southwest, is **Chung Kai War Cemetery,** which is similar in layout and has 1,750 graves. It occupies the site of a former POW camp.

JEATH Museum

To make sense of what you see in Kanchanaburi, visit this museum at the south end of the River Kwai. JEATH is an acronym for Japan-England-Australia-Thailand-Holland: there are artifacts, news clippings, photos, and memorabilia from the prison camps where the Allied POWs were kept. The small museum was set up and is maintained by dedicated Thai monks from the nearby *wat.* The monks will answer questions about the displays. Open daily 0830 to 1830.

Wat Tham Kao Poon

This peculiar *wat* has some deep caves; admission is by donation. The caves are lit by

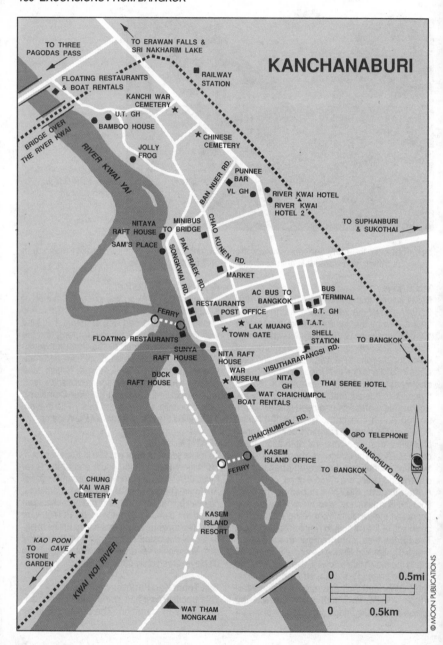

KANCHANABURI

TO THREE PAGODAS PASS

TO ERAWAN FALLS & SRI NAKHARIM LAKE

RAILWAY STATION

FLOATING RESTAURANTS & BOAT RENTALS

KANCHI WAR CEMETERY

U.T. GH

BAMBOO HOUSE

BRIDGE OVER THE RIVER KWAI

CHINESE CEMETERY

JOLLY FROG

RIVER KWAI YAI

BAN NUER RD.

PUNNEE BAR

VL GH

RIVER KWAI HOTEL

RIVER KWAI HOTEL 2

TO SUPHANBURI & SUKOTHAI

NITAYA RAFT HOUSE

SAM'S PLACE

MINIBUS TO BRIDGE

CHAO KUNEN RD.

PAK PRAEK RD.

SONGKWAI RD.

MARKET

BUS TERMINAL

AC BUS TO BANGKOK

RESTAURANTS

POST OFFICE

B.T. GH

FERRY

T.A.T.

LAK MUANG TOWN GATE

SHELL STATION

TO BANGKOK

FLOATING RESTAURANTS

SUNYA RAFT HOUSE

VISUTHARARANGSI RD.

NITA RAFT HOUSE

WAR MUSEUM

NITA GH

THAI SEREE HOTEL

DUCK RAFT HOUSE

WAT CHAICHUMPOL

BOAT RENTALS

CHAICHUMPOL RD.

GPO TELEPHONE

SANGCHUTO RD.

KASEM ISLAND OFFICE

FERRY

TO BANGKOK

CHUNG KAI WAR CEMETERY

KASEM ISLAND RESORT

KAO POON CAVE

TO STONE GARDEN

KWAI NOI RIVER

WAT THAM MONGKAM

0   0.5mi

0   0.5km

© MOON PUBLICATIONS

fluorescent tubes, but a flashlight would be useful. The front caves have every niche crowded with Buddha statues and animal statues. You thread your way through a series of caves with stalactites and stalagmites—and emerge into a larger cave with a seated Buddha.

Touring Kanchanaburi

By Bicycle: You can do a grand sweep around Kanchi in about five hours, including stops. It's best to start early to avoid the midday heat: a good starting point is the Town Gate. Wheel down to the "car ferry" nearby and cross the River Kwai to the left bank. This side has lush greenery and farmland, and it's very pleasant riding. Twenty minutes or so of pedal-pushing should bring you to Chung Kai War Cemetery. At the crest of a hill, further on, you'll come to Kao Poon cave. After visiting the caves, head back down the same hill, take the road north—pleasant countryside, light traffic. Cycle about half an hour till you see a wide dirt road on your right—this leads to the River Kwai Bridge. It is not advisable to try and cycle over the rickety bridge—so wheel your bike across. If there are oncoming motorcyclists (or a train!) use the pull-outs at the side of the bridge.

Once over the bridge, there are some floating restaurants where you can take a break. Or try some foodstall offerings like barbecued chicken, spicy papaya salad, or fried bananas sprinkled with sesame seeds and find a shady spot for a picnic. If you take the road closer to the river on the way back into town, you'll pass a series of streets named after all the nations involved in the forced labor for the River Kwai Bridge—the only reminder, it seems, of all the Asian conscripts who died here in WW II. If you want to continue touring, cycle all the way down past the markets to the JEATH War Museum.

By Motorcycle: Experienced motorcyclists can get further afield to Sai Yok Falls. Along the way, 35 km southwest of Kanchi, is **Ban Kao Museum**, featuring a Neolithic burial site; and eight km further are the ruins of **Muang Singh,** a sprawling 12th-century Khmer temple with recent renovations.

By Boat: There are six- to ten-man longtails for rent near the war museum and near the River Kwai Bridge. From the War Museum you can take the river over to Kao Poon Cave and Chung Kai War Memorial, then head north to the River Kwai Bridge. Boat rentals run around B300 for two to three hours. Try to assemble a small group.

Raft Trips

There are scores of rafting operators in Kanchanaburi, so shop around for prices if considering a trip of several days. Popular raft operators are located near the floating hotels just north of the war museum. A "raft" is virtually an open-air house sitting on bamboo logs, with a lower floor, upper sundeck, and diving platform—this assembly is towed upriver by a tugboat. The rafts are set up for different purposes. A few are laid out as floating restaurants for group tours taking in sunset near the River Kwai Bridge. Or you can take a day-trip on a raft; get a small group together.

Long-distance rafts have an on-board kitchen and sleeping mats. You can arrange to join a group of, say, ten people (up to 30 possible), and head off for a few days. Negotiate a rate that includes food. Highlights of the trip include sunbathing, drinking, deck games, and inane water sports. Another kind of raft, usually avoided by foreigners, is the infamous disco-raft. On weekends, hundreds of Thais descend on Kanchanaburi from Bangkok, board rafts, get thoroughly plastered, and boogie the night away to the same four hits that are played ad nauseam in Bangkok discos—and played at a similar volume here.

Where To Stay

Refer to the map for hotel locations. Popular in Kanchi are the rafthouses (floating bamboo-raft bungalows), and quiet jungle-style bungalows overlooking the river.

Luxury/Moderate: In the B300-700 d range (a/c) are **Duck Rafthouse**, tel. 512-046, down by the River Kwai, and **Kasem Island Resort**, tel. 513-359, with rafthouse bungalows. **River Kwai Hotel**, tel. 511-269, in town, is overpriced, with doubles B700-1000. Also overpriced is **River Kwai Resort**, tel. 511-313, which is by the bridge. Just north, and much better value, is **Prasopsuk Garden Resort**, tel. 513-215, with doubles B400 and up. Out of town, along Kwai

Noi River, are many luxury jungle-resort raft-hotels such as **River Kwai Family Camp** (seven kilometers from town), **River Kwai Farm** (38 km from town), and **River Kwai Village** (60 km north of town, at Namtok). They offer packages that include meals (B400-3000 range), and make good bases for local touring; book through agents.

Budget: Budget places run B70-200 for doubles, with singles as low as B50. Near the River Kwai Bridge is **The Jolly Frog**, tel. 514-579, which offers tropical hut-type accommodations; close by are **Bamboo House**, tel. 512-532, **UT Guesthouse**, tel. 513-339, and **PS Guesthouse**, tel. 513-039. Further south is **Sam's Place**, and **Nitaya Rafthouse**, tel. 513-541. Other recommended budget rafthouses include **Nita Rafthouse**, tel. 514-521, and **Sunya Rafthouse**, tel. 513-868. Along Sangchuto Road are some pricier places: **VL Guesthouse**, tel. 513-546, which has super-clean doubles with bath; just opposite is **River Kwai #2 Hotel**, tel. 512-696; and down the road is **Thai Seree Hotel**, tel. 511-128, with fan and a/c rooms.

Food

Nothing to write home about, but try the waterfront restaurants and floating cafes around Songkwai Road, near Fitness Park. There are some floating restaurants in the River Kwai Bridge area (and foodstalls in the evening); and there are a few restaurants close to River Kwai Hotel on Sangchuto Road, serving Thai and Chinese dishes. Otherwise, most dining takes place in hotels and guesthouses—the food is bland but adequate.

Travelers' Network

The TAT office, tel. 511-200, is just near the bus station. It has a good stock of brochures and is useful for planning or for advice about road conditions, current status of Burmese border crossing, and so on. Guesthouses often act as an informal travelers' network and will organize trips out of town. Try the Jolly Frog or Sam's Place. Punnee Bar is a good source of fresh info. The bar is foreign-owned, will organize trips, rents bicycles and motorcycles, sells books, acts as an info exchange point—and it does actually sell food and drink.

Getting Around

Bicycle rental is available from a number of guesthouses (BJ, Jolly Frog, Punnee Bar). Regular motorcycles and dirt-bikes go for B200-300 a day; jeeps can also be hired. Otherwise, use a trishaw for short distances. Trishaws can also can be rented by the hour, with driver, for about B80.

Getting There

Buses to Kanchi leave Bangkok's Southern Bus Terminal several times an hour and take three hours for the trip. From Kanchi there are lots of connections to the west—to Suphanburi (change for Lopburi or Ayuthaya), to Ratchaburi (change for Hua Hin) and to Nakhon Pathom (change for Damnern Saduak). Go to the bus station and they'll point you in the right direction.

The **Train** from Bangkok takes 2^{1}/2 hours. Railway buffs will enjoy the slow ride up to Namtok—trains leave from Bangkok's Thonburi Station several times a day on weekdays. The morning schedule departs Thonburi Station at 0800 (weekdays only), reaches Kanchi 1031, crosses River Kwai bridge at 1036, and arrives at Namtok by 1220. There's an immediate return trip, or you can stay at Namtok and catch the 1520 back to Kanchi. There are train connections on the Kanchanaburi line to other lines via an interchange at Nong Pladuk (where it's possible to change for Hua Hin).

SRT Tours: The State Railways of Thailand has several weekend packages to the Kanchanaburi area. Departures are from Bangkok Main Station. A possible one-day itinerary (Saturdays, Sundays, public holidays): depart Bangkok Main Station (Hualampong) at 0635, go to Nakhon Pathom, visit River Kwai Bridge, go rafting on River Kwai, visit JEATH Museum and Kao Poon Cave, and return to Bangkok at 1930 (cost B280 a person, including lunch). The SRT has other one- and two-day jaunts to the region—inquire.

UPSTREAM FROM KANCHANABURI

The main attractions out of town are the natural ones—jungle walks, river trips, bamboo rafting, rock climbing and visits to caves, waterfalls, and hot springs in the national parks to the northwest of Kanchi. This is a tonic after Bangkok—you get greenery, oxygen, birds, and peace and quiet. There are lots of tour agents in Kanchi who run treks and raft trips: accommodations once out of town vary from tents to elaborate raft-complex hotels. Several operators offer combination adventures—rail to Namtok, a pick-up truck to Sai Yok, a short jungle walk and overnight camp, and then a raft trip downriver to Kanchi the next day.

To the northwest of Kanchi there are four national parks, two of which are easily accessed. In Erawan National Park, **Erawan Falls**(60 km northwest) can be reached in a two-hour drive by hotel minibus—you are dropped off in the morning, hike up to the top falls, and are picked up again in the afternoon. The series of falls here is quite small—postcard material is taken in the rainy season when the flow is greater. Take your swim togs along—good bathing up there in natural pools, and a cool respite at 2,000 meters.

Further north are **Huay Khamin Falls,** which can only be reached by dirt bike or four-wheel-drive vehicle (about two hours from the Erawan area). Near the end of the rail line at Namtok is **Sai Yok,** with a waterfall and swimming area. The nearby River Kwai Village has air-con luxury rooms or raft bungalows.

It is possible to go from Kanchanaburi all the way up to the Burmese border, to Three Pagodas Pass, where you can make a visa-less crossing into a Burmese village for a couple of hours. Your first impressions of Burma may be somewhat skewed if you only take in this "village." In 1988 there was heavy fighting here between Karen and Mon insurgents for control of the strategic pass, where smuggled goods are subject to "tax"—the village was burnt to the ground. In early 1990 the Burmese Army attacked the pass and 15,000 Mon tribespeople fled into Thailand. The Burmese hastily erected another village at the pass and allowed tourists in. War between the Burmese Army and border tribespeople has been going on for decades—more recently intensified because Thai companies have struck a deal with the Burmese government to log teak forests on the Burmese side.

HUA HIN

Hua Hin, 200 km to the southwest of Bangkok, has the distinction of being Thailand's oldest beach resort, due to its association with Thai royalty. If you arrive at the railway station there is a Thai-style royal waiting room. Hua Hin got under way in the 1920s when King Rama VII built a summer palace called Klai Kangwon ("Far from Worries"), which is still in use by the royal family. Thailand's first golf course was built in the 1920s at Hua Hin. The main beachfront hotel was run by the Royal State Railways Department, and Hua Hin was a popular stopover for wealthy guests on the Penang-to-Bangkok route. It was described in a State Railways Guide as ". . . most popular with those longing for a round of golf. The Hua Hin Hotel carries in stock all golf requisites and loans are often made to visiting golfers. Swimming, shooting and fishing are among the popular sports . . ." After the heady '20s, the fortunes of Hua Hin took a nosedive, and it is only since the 1980s that the place has again come back into fashion.

The Town
The main beach is several kilometers due east of the railway station, at the Sofitel Hotel. Most tourist needs are catered to along Damnern Kasem Road, the one leading from the station to the Sofitel—with the GPO, a bevy of hotels, motorcycle and bicycle rentals, restaurants, and a souvenir bazaar. You can walk north from the Sofitel along the waterfront all the way to Hua Hin's fishing village, which is very active early in the morning and toward dusk.

What To Do
Most people do as little as possible—nothing more strenuous than reading a book or eating out. Sea water at Hua Hin is poor for swimming—pollutants include fishing waste and oil residue. You can use hotel swimming pools, go south to other beaches, or take a cheap local bus seven kilometers south to Suanson Beach. Various reports circulate of stinging creatures in the waters at Hua Hin—mainly jellyfish, but one more serious case that could be related to a

Sofitel Central Hotel,
Hua Hin

Portuguese man-of-war. There have also been sightings of sea snakes.

The 18-hole **Royal Hua Hin Golf Course**, next to the railway station, is under the operation of Boon Rawd Brewery, makers of Singha Beer. There is a clubhouse; rentals are available; visitors are welcome; open daily from 0600. About an hour south of Hua Hin by road is **Khao Sam Rot Yai,** a small national park with spectacular limestone hills and caves.

Where To Stay

Hua Hin has a couple of super-luxury hotels, a dozen mid-range hotels, and scores of cheaper guesthouses. Business is brisk on weekends—if you're going to Hua Hin then, try and reserve. Prices go up on weekends and during peak season (November to March); conversely, you can bargain rates down in the low season.

Sofitel Central: In a class of its own is the Sofitel Central Hotel, tel. 512-021—the original Railways Hotel, which was leased to the French Sofitel company and refurbished. It appeared as the Hotel Le Phnom in the movie, *The Killing Fields* (the town shots were filmed in Nakhon Pathom). This rambling Victorian-style hotel has a number of wings, several restaurants, two swimming pools, and extensive grounds, with hedges fancifully trimmed in the shape of elephants, giraffes, and other animals. The hotel is a classic—an attraction in itself—you can take a

look, but you probably won't be allowed in if you're wearing shorts. Room rates vary from B2300 for a one-bedroom villa or standard room up to B16,000 for a two-bedroom deluxe suite (taxes extra).

Super Luxury: Further south along the beach is the **Royal Garden Resort**, tel. 511-881, which has a sports center with windsurfers and catamarans. Prices range from B3000 up to B11,500 (deluxe suite). With a similar price range is **Royal Garden Village**, tel. 512-412, to the north of town.

Luxury/Moderate: A few notches down are hotels with air-con rooms in the B500-2000 range, including the **Hua Hin Highland Resort**, tel. 211-2579, popular with golfers; and **Sailom Hotel**, tel. 511-890. In the B200-500 range are the **Chat-Chai Hotel**, tel. 511-034; **Hua Hin Raluk**, tel. 511-940, and **Jed Pee Nong**, tel. 512-381.

Budget: The area around Naretdamri Road, a block from the beach and from the Sofitel, has loads of guesthouses for B100-200 a room.

Restaurants

Close to the fishing village there are some great seafood restaurants facing the water. **Sang Thai Seafood**, near the pier, is recommended. In the Naretdamri area, there are dozens of cafes, bistros, and restaurants—stroll along and take your pick. Hua Hin means "Hard Rock," but that refers to the natural kind. Restaurants double as bars and represent nightlife in Hua Hin—people gather to chat or drink, or make an evening out of watching a video. There is a night market close to the bus terminus at the northwest edge of Hua Hin.

Means Of Conveyance
It's easy to get around Hua Hin on foot. You can rent bicycles and motorcycles in the souvenir bazaar near the gates of the Sofitel Hotel. You can also rent jeeps, and boat tours and deep-sea fishing trips can be arranged.

Getting There
By Plane: Bangkok Airways flights on Dash-8 turboprop aircraft (37-seater or 56-seater) take 25 minutes, and cost B825 one way. Outbound and inbound flights on Friday and Sunday afternoons. The airstrip in Hua Hin is ten km north of town. In Bangkok phone 253-4014; in Hua Hin, 512-083.

Buses: Hourly departures from Bangkok; buses take four hours to reach Hua Hin.

By Train: Express trains take just over four hours to get to Hua Hin. The SRT has a two-day touring itinerary to Hua Hin for B660 a person, with departures every Saturday. The train departs Bangkok Main Station at 0635, stops at Nakhon Pathom for 30 minutes, and proceeds to Hua Hin, where guests are boarded at the Hua Hin Highland Resort Hotel (minibus excursions are possible from here to sights around Hua Hin). The tour arrives back in Bangkok at 1850 the following day.

By Boat: A new Jet Cat service from Bangkok takes 2½ hours to get to Hua Hin—book through travel agents. There is also a hydrofoil service running from Pattaya to Hua Hin, taking two hours.

CHA-AM

Cha-Am, 25 km north of Hua Hin, is a similar resort area with condos, high-rise hotels, restaurants, country clubs, golf course, and villas. It has more packaged tours, lots of development going on, and discos. Larger hotels: **Regent Cha-Am** and the **Beach Garden Cha-Am**. Water is not suitable for bathing here, either: pollution comes from raw sewage and untreated waste from a pineapple cannery.

NORTH OF BANGKOK

Upstream from Bangkok is the old Thai capital of Ayuthaya, with its crumbling fortresses and ruined temples; northeast of that is the ancient Khmer capital of Lopburi. This region is steeped in history, mystery, and legend—a trip back in time. Buses for the following destinations leave from the North/Northeast Bus Terminal.

BANG PA-IN

Wat Pailom and Bang Sai are usually included along the route to Bang Pa-In (which in turn is included in the route to Ayuthaya—but this is stretching it for a day-trip). Though you can go by road or rail, try and go at least one way by boat. It's a magnificent trip on the Chao Phraya in company with long lines of barges, tugboats and other river craft. This is the route that ambassadors to the court of Siam used to take in the 17th century.

Wat Pailom
About 40 km north of Bangkok on the Chao Phraya River, this *wat* and the surrounding forest on the banks of the Chao Phraya are home to thousands of rare open-billed storks which make their way from Bangladesh to winter here from December to May every year, courtesy of the abbot. The birds can be seen wheeling around in the skies close to the area; they nest high in the trees, and the whole area is coated with bird guano. If driving, take Highway 346 (left past the airport) to the town of **Pathum Thani,** and then hire a longtail for a 20-minute ride to the *wat.*

Bang Sai
A bit further north on the Chao Phraya is the **Royal Folk Arts and Handicraft Center,** under Her Majesty the Queen's patronage. Set in large gardens, the center provides training in traditional handicrafts like woodwork, silk-dyeing, bronze-casting, basketry, and leatherwork, which allows local farm families to develop skills for supplementary incomes. Entry B20; open daily 1000 to 1800.

Bang Pa-In
Bang Pa-In, 63 km north of Bangkok, is an abandoned Summer Palace, dating back to the Ayuthaya period. Set in pleasant gardens is a collection of pavilions—Thai, Italian, Greek, Chinese, Victorian. The site is strongly associated with King Rama V (Chulalongkorn, who reigned 1868-1910), as it was his favorite summer retreat: he used to travel from Bangkok in a fleet of up to 600 vessels. The outstanding pavilions now seen were built in his time.

In the middle of the lake is an exquisite Thai-style pavilion containing a statue of King Rama V. Close by is a white marble memorial to King Chulalongkorn's first queen, who drowned in full view of her entourage—at the time touching royalty was an offense punished by execution. Most striking of the structures is a Chinese-style pavilion that was shipped in sections from mainland China and presented to King Rama V by Chinese merchants from Bangkok in 1889. This is the only pavilion where you can tour the interior, full of priceless Chinese porcelain, bronze vessels, and carved screens. Bang Pa-In is open daily 0830 to 1530; entry B50 for *farangs.* Across the river, reached by a quaint gondola, is another startling piece of architecture—Wat Niwet Thamaprawat, a neo-Gothic church converted for use as a *wat,* with Buddhist interiors.

Boat Touring To Bang Pa-In
Large vessels on the Chao Phraya only run as far as Bang Pa-In. It is possible to go from Bang Pa-In to Ayuthaya by renting a longtail (costs about B150 plus return subsidy, so around B300). These are included with some tours.

Luxury Cruise: A number of hotels and cruise operators offer a one-day cruise package to Bang Pa-In and Ayuthaya for around B900, including lunch, a/c luxury, and tour guide. Daily departures. Cruisers include the *Oriental Queen* (operated by the Oriental Hotel), the

Ayutthaya Princess (operated by the Shangri-La Hotel), *Horizon I,* and *River Sun* (operating from River City). These vessels have a capacity of between 80 and 200 passengers. Bookings are made through hotels, travel agents, or at River City.

A combination of boat to Bang Pa-In, long-tailed boat or bus to Ayuthaya, and bus back to Bangkok is offered, or else the reverse trip. Transfers from major hotels by coach are usually included. A typical itinerary: hotel pickup at 0700 by coach; meet at River City and depart 0800; cruise to Bang Pa-In; buffet lunch at 1100; disembark at 1300 and tour Bang Pa-in; proceed by coach to Ayuthaya, then coach south, reaching Bangkok at 1700. The time spent in Ayuthaya is about 90 minutes, which is nowhere near enough time to see the place. Many prefer the return journey by boat because they can sit out the heat of the afternoon in a cool breeze and avoid rush-hour blues (and get a great sunset over the Grand Palace in Bangkok).

Overnight Ricebarge: The *Mekhala,* a converted ricebarge, does a slow run up to Bang Pa-In. The *Mekhala* is made of teak and has an onboard bar, canopied sundeck, and six spacious cabins with bathrooms. It departs from River City at 1500, moors overnight near Wat Pakret, north of Bangkok, and continues next day to Bang Pa-In. Guests can then transfer for a 45-minute ride by longtail up to Ayuthaya, and either take a bus back from there, or take the ricebarge back to Bangkok. Costs about B3000 a person; book through a travel agent or through Asia Voyages, tel. 235-4100.

Budget Cruise: The Chao Phraya Express Boat company has a full day's tour to Bang Pa-In and back on Sundays and national holidays. An express boat fitted with extra plastic seats on the top deck leaves Maharaj landing at 0800 on Sundays, stops at Tha Pra Arthit and Nonthaburi; reaches Bang Sai at 1010 (stops one hour); reaches Bang Pa-In at 1200 (stops two hours, allowing time for lunch); and drops in at Wat Pailom for half an hour on the return trip. The express boat reaches Bangkok at 1730. Cost is B180 a person (no food included); entry fees to Bang Sai and Bang Pa-In will run you another B70. Mostly Thais on the trip, and a few Westerners. Tickets can be bought from a num-

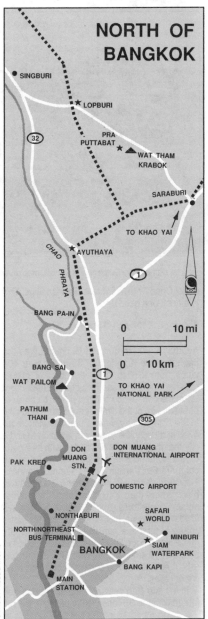

NORTH OF BANGKOK

© MOON PUBLICATIONS

a 17th-century Dutch impressionistic map of Ayuthaya

of Ayuthaya in 1569. The city was sacked, but the Thai forces rallied under King Naresuan and expelled the Burmese in 1584. Ayuthaya became a cosmopolitan city with enclaves of Chinese, Japanese, French, Dutch, Spanish, English, and Portuguese. Upon the death of King Narai in 1688, however, the Thais became suspicious of European designs and closed the country to foreign trade. In 1767, after a lengthy siege, Ayuthaya fell to the blood-thirsty Burmese, who went on a rampage—killing, demolishing, burning, and looting. Most of the citizens of Ayuthaya were either killed or taken off to Burma as slaves. The Thais retook Ayuthaya less than a year later, but it was subsequently abandoned and a new capital was built in Bangkok. The buildings at Ayuthaya suffered another demolition stage when building materials were shipped to Bangkok for construction projects there.

ber of Chao Phraya Express Boat landings. This is a heck of a good deal!

AYUTHAYA

Ayuthaya, 80 km north of Bangkok, was the capital of the Kingdom of Siam for over 400 years, from 1350 to 1767—the home of 33 successive kings. The site was chosen because it lay at the confluence of three rivers: a canal cut between two of the rivers formed an island-city. In the 17th century, when European visitors arrived at this capital, they were amazed to find a city that rivalled Paris or London with its wealth of luxurious houses and palaces—and which compared to Venice with its skeins of canals. Travelers described the dazzling island-city as having more than 400 gilt temples, three major palace complexes, and 50 km of waterways filled with vessels, including royal barges in the shape of fabulous *garudas* or *nagas*. The city measured 2.5 km by 4.4 km, and was bounded by a wall 12 km in length, with 17 forts and turrets. It had about 100 gates, 20 of which were water gates.

In the late 16th century, a series of wars was fought with the Burmese, culminating in the fall

Museums
Sam Phya Museum: The best statuary salvaged from the ruins is in this museum (and in Bangkok), so a stop at Sam Phya is a logical starting point as it helps you to mentally reconstruct Ayuthaya's grandeur. The museum has two floors, displaying large stone and metal Buddha heads, carved wooden door frames, architectural cornices and ornaments, statuary, pottery shards, even spittoons. Treasures from the crypts of *prangs* at Wat Rajaburana and Wat Mahathat were looted in the 1950s, but a few relics are preserved in the museum, including a magnificent royal sword, sheathed in a gold scabbard encrusted with precious stones. Some clay votive tablets found were sold to raise funds to build the museum. Closed Mondays, Tuesdays, holidays; otherwise open 0900 to 1600.

Chandra Kasem Museum: Very little to see here; more interesting than the exhibits are the buildings that house them—part of a 17th-century minor palace destroyed by the Burmese

Buddha head at ruins of Wat Mahathat, Ayuthaya

but reconstructed by King Rama IV. Closed Mondays and Tuesdays.

Ruins And Reconstructs

Taken individually, none of the sites in Ayuthaya rate as a major attraction, but taken collectively, the ruins are. The ruins are excellent for a quiet afternoon or a romantic picnic—with the atmosphere generated by all that grandeur reduced to rubble. This archeological garden has fallen arches, lopped-off pillars, stone torsos and limbs flung about the place, and defaced and hacked-up Buddhas that continue to shock Thai visitors. Unfortunately, the Fine Arts Department has not recognized that ruins are best left as ruins—they've patched up, reconstructed, and added brand-new concrete Buddhas, so you get a garish half-hashed mix of old red-bricked rubble and gray new concrete at some sites.

Most of the ruins are on the west side of town in an undeveloped area called **Ayuthaya Historical Park.** Sites are officially open from 0830 to 1630; individual sites charge B20 entry. Ruins being ruins, the walls are also ruined—so you can visit anytime and avoid the B20 entry fee. Actually, the best time to visit in terms of photography is before 0830 and after 1630 anyway. Too far to walk—hire a bicycle, or take *tuk-tuks.* You can also approach sites from a hired longtail.

The Ruins

Wat Mahathat is one of the oldest sites in Ayuthaya, dating back to the 14th century. Not much left here—a jumble of torsos and pieces of Buddha statuary. There's a peaceful Buddha head held in the embrace of the roots of a Banyan tree, clinging to the red-brick ruins—a striking image. **Wat Pra Si Sanpet** was once the royal chapel in the grounds of the palace. The site was completely razed by the Burmese, but three photogenic *chedis* (holding the ashes of Ayuthayan kings) remain in good condition. **Wat Pra Ram** was first constructed in the 14th century by Ramesuan, the second king of Ayuthaya; a lone *prang* next to a lake is all that's left standing. The 17th-century **Wat Chai Wattanaram** doesn't offer anything new to see in the way of buildings, but the superb location by a quiet riverbank makes it well worth the visit. An excellent place for a picnic, and it offers great silhouettes for sunset photography.

The Reconstructs

Lying out in an open field is a relaxed-looking **Reclining Buddha**—the building that once housed the massive statue burned down. The Buddha was restored in 1956. Close by is **Mongkol Bopit,** a large black Buddha statue with mother-of-pearl eyes. The statue, of uncertain origin, is boxed in by a modern prayer-hall, built 1951. This statue is popular with local

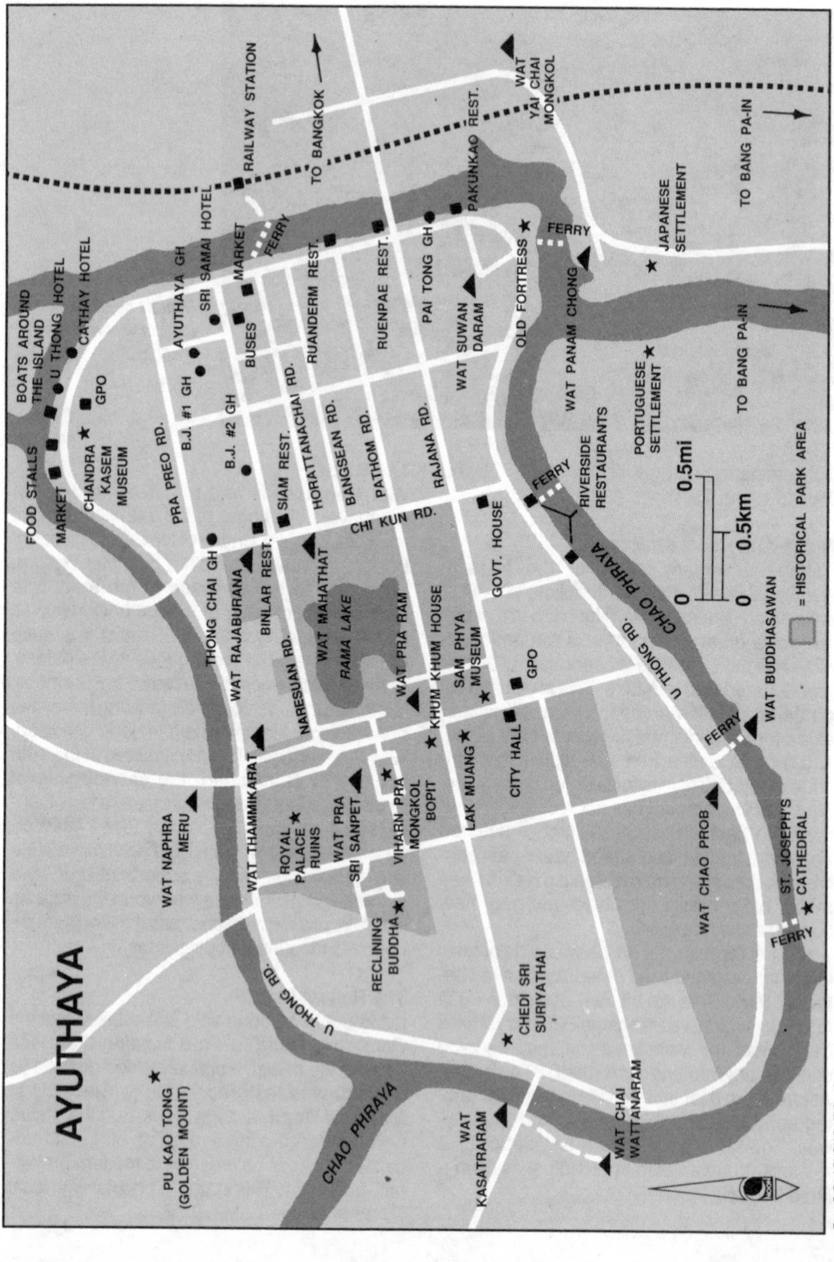

AYUTHAYA

PU KAO TONG (GOLDEN MOUNT) ★

WAT NAPHRA MERU ★

WAT KASATRARAM

WAT CHAI WATTANARAM

U THONG RD.

CHAO PHRAYA

CHEDI SRI SURIYATHAI

RECLINING BUDDHA ★

ROYAL PALACE RUINS ★

WAT PRA SRI SANPET ★

WAT THAMMIKARAT ★

VIHARN PRA MONGKOL BOPIT ★

LAK MUANG ★

CITY HALL

WAT CHAO PROB

ST. JOSEPH'S CATHEDRAL ★

FERRY

WAT RAJABURANA

WAT MAHATHAT

KHUM KHUM HOUSE

SAM PHYA MUSEUM

WAT PRA RAM

RAMA LAKE

NARESUAN RD.

BINLAR REST.

THONG CHAI GH

SIAM REST.

HORATTANACHAI RD.

BANGSEAN RD.

PATHOM RD.

RAJANA RD.

CHI KUN RD.

GOVT. HOUSE

GPO

WAT BUDDHASAWAN

FERRY

U THONG RD.

CHAO PHRAYA

RIVERSIDE RESTAURANTS

FERRY

PORTUGUESE SETTLEMENT ★

WAT PANAM CHONG ★

TO BANG PA-IN

JAPANESE SETTLEMENT ★

OLD FORTRESS ★

FERRY

WAT SUWAN DARAM ▲

PAI TONG GH

PAKUNKAO REST.

RUENPAE REST.

RUANDERM REST.

MARKET

BUSES

SRI SAMAI HOTEL

AYUTHAYA GH

B.J. #1 GH

B.J. #2 GH

PRA PREO RD.

CHANDRA KASEM MUSEUM ★

GPO

U THONG HOTEL

CATHAY HOTEL

BOATS AROUND THE ISLAND

FOOD STALLS

MARKET

FERRY

RAILWAY STATION

TO BANGKOK

WAT YAI CHAI MONGKOL ▲

TO BANG PA-IN

0.5mi

0.5km

0

☐ = HISTORICAL PARK AREA

© MOON PUBLICATIONS

worshippers and with group tours arriving by bus (prices in the stalls nearby are outrageous). North of the river is **Wat Naphra Meru,** which has been renovated many times over the centuries, and was rebuilt in 1987. It houses an awesome gold-plated Buddha, clothed (Ayuthaya-style) in king's regalia. In an adjacent chapel is a fine Dvaravati-style Buddha made of black stone.

At the southeast corner of Ayuthaya are two active temples. **Wat Suwan Daram** is one of the finest in Thailand—find a monk to open the two chapels. The first, the one with the peculiar Ayuthaya-style concave foundations, has intricate door frames, scenes from the *Ramakien,* and rows of murals that rival those in Bangkok's national museum. The second chapel has a huge fresco showing a clash on elephant-back. The original site dates to the 18th century—the temples miraculously escaped destruction by the Burmese, and were later restored by King Rama I and Rama III. A short distance away, across the river (take a ferry) is **Wat Panam Chong,** a Chinese-style temple with a 19-meter-high golden Buddha. The temple receives a steady stream of worshippers.

Two kilometers to the north of Ayuthaya, across the river, is **Pu Kao Tong,** a viewpoint with a soaring *chedi.* To the northeast of town is the **Elephant Kraal,** where wild elephants were once tamed and trained for battle in a teak stockade.

Places To Stay

Top End: Out of town to the east is U-Tong Inn, 210 Rojana Road, tel. 242-236, with a/c rooms for B500-600 d; in town the **Sri Samai Hotel,** tel. 245-228, has doubles from B350-700.

Moderate: To the northeast on U-Tong Road are two gloomy hotels: **Cathay Hotel,** tel. 251-562, and **U-Tong Hotel,** tel. 251-136, both charging B200-300 d. Another possibility is **Ruanderm Guesthouse,** tel. 241-978 (see "Dining Out").

Budget: Range is B50 for dorm accommodations or B60-80 for a room. **Ayuthaya Guesthouse,** tel. 251-468, is a pleasant place with an outdoor cafe where you run up your own tab. You can rent bikes from here at B30 a day.

The place is 150 meters north of the bus terminal and is operated by Mr. Hong. Also run by the Hong family is **BJ #1 Guesthouse,** a few doors west. **BJ #2,** at 19 Naresuan Road, tel. 251-512, has 20 rooms—and can be noisy. Cheap, but somewhat run-down, is **Pai Tong Guesthouse,** facing the river, with 10 rooms.

Dining Out

The cosiest places to eat Thai food are those facing the river—several at the southeast corner of Ayuthaya and also along the southern stretch of the river (see map). These include:

Pakunkao: This restaurant has a couple of boats moored out back which serve as breezy seating areas—a pleasant escape from the heat and dust, and it serves good Thai food.

Ruanderm: This funky restaurant, at the intersection of U-Tong and Thanon Pathom, is filled with rustic leftovers: a dilapidated sugarcane press, a wooden pig trough, dining tables made from old cart wheels, and traditional rowing boats used as seating nooks. The kitchen is in a barge on the riverside; dishes run about B80 each. Upstairs there are six double rooms (B200 a person) and an eight-person dorm (B150 a head).

Ranahan: At the south side of Ayuthaya (end of Chi Kun Road), overlooking the water, this place has no English sign, no English menu, but the food is good if you can get around all that.

Foodstalls: There are lots around the bus station and the nearby markets; also a big collection of open-air places near the boat landing to the northeast, in Ayuthaya's business district. Here at night you can enjoy the specialty of the region—barbecued rat. These are field rats from the rice-growing areas, which are skewered whole and barbecued on a stick. Mmmmm!

Getting Around

A bicycle is the best way to get around; there are *songtaos* everywhere or you can rent a *tuk-tuk.* In case you thought you had escaped the dreaded *tuk-tuks* of Bangkok, Ayuthaya has over a thousand of an older, beetle-shaped version—quite a lot for a population of 56,000. To get a historical perspective on Ayuthaya it's well worth hiring a longtail for an hour's cruise and visiting waterfront sites. Longtails cost B100-200 for an hour, or around B250 for 90 minutes—catch a boat from northeast side. A complete circuit is not possible since the north side is too shallow and narrow, so it's an out-and-back trip.

Getting There

Buses leave the Northern Bus Terminal every half hour from 0640 on. The ride takes about an hour—make sure you ride the bus to the very end. By train, it's 1¼ hours. From the station in Ayuthaya, walk west a short distance and take a ferry across to the main part of town. On the water: take a longtail from Bang Pa-In—a 45-minute trip up to Ayuthaya, costing B200 plus return subsidy. Longtail to Bangkok is estimated at four hours one way, so B800 plus return subsidy (totalling at least B1400). See Bang Pa-In for details of luxury river cruises to Bangkok.

KHAO YAI NATIONAL PARK

Khao Yai, 160 km to the northeast of Bangkok, is Thailand's oldest national park (established 1962), and has the best infrastructure for trail-walking. The park covers an area of 2,168 square km, with jungle and mountainous terrain, and over 50 km of hiking trails. There is an opportunity to view wildlife, with night tours from the visitor center—and though there are wild elephants and tigers in the rainforest, you probably won't spot much in the way of larger animals. You will see lots of birds, the most spectacular of which are hornbills. Picnicking and swimming in waterfall areas are popular. More information on trails and facilities is available at the park's visitor center.

Accommodations

There are accommodations in bungalows or at the **Khao Yai Motor Lodge**, which is busy on weekends; bookings can be made through TAT in Bangkok. A two-bedroom motel-unit with bath is B800; bungalows are over B1000. You can use campsites—a tent B10 a person, with B10 a person for a thin blanket rental; B20 to sleep in an open-air hut. Advance booking through TAT is advised. TAT operates a restaurant at Khao Yai, and an 18-hole golf course.

Transport

There are two park entrances—one at the north of the park, the other at the south. The fastest route from Bangkok is to take Highway 305 northeast to Nakhon Nayok, then Highway 33 toward Prachinburi. Before Prachinburi, there's a turnoff for Khao Yai. This route is 160 km long and takes about three hours. An alternate route is to take Highway 1 from Bangkok toward Saraburi, turn off onto Highway 2 (just before Saraburi), and follow this to a junction with Highway 2090, which is five km before the town of Pak Chong. Then drive south on 2090 for 40 km. This route is 205 km from Bangkok.

Buses from Bangkok run twice a day (at 0700 and 0900) from the Northern Bus Terminal, and take the longer route (four hours) via Highway 2. They only run as far as Pak Chong, which is 40 km short of the park. Tell the driver you're going to Khao Yai, get off the bus five km before Pak Chong, and then hitchhike or wait for a minibus or *songtao* into Khao Yai (TAT operates a sporadic Pak Chong to Khao Yai service which usually leaves Pak Chong at 1700 daily). The SRT runs weekend rail tours to Khao Yai—inquire at Hualampong Station.

LOPBURI

Lopburi, 155 km to the north of Bangkok, was once a Cambodian outpost, part of the far-flung Khmer Empire. As early as the 7th century, Lopburi was an important center of the Mon Empire. During the Khmer period (11th and 12th centuries), Lopburi was the regional capital, with the main capital at Angkor. After the Khmer period, Lopburi suffered a relapse, but stepped back into the limelight during the 17th century, when King Narai of Ayuthaya (who reigned 1656-88) declared it the second capital of Thailand. At this time it was called Louvo—there are a number of descriptions by European missions which came to establish links with Siam and curry favor with the king to set up trading ports.

Among the visitors was Chevalier de Chaumont, an ambassador of King Louis XIV, who arrived in 1685. The French became favorites of King Narai, who employed French architects, engineers, and military advisors sent by King Louis XIV. With them came Jesuit priests who ran a Catholic school in Lopburi. In the background was a Greek adventurer, Constantine Phaulkon, an employee of the East India Company who had been shipwrecked off the Malabar coast and somehow ended up being appointed Chief Minister by King Narai. In 1688, when Narai fell ill, there was a palace revolution: Phaulkon was captured and beheaded, the king died shortly thereafter, the French were expelled, and the new court moved back to Ayuthaya. And Lopburi went into decline.

The Town

Lopburi is a small town of about 50,000. West of the railway tracks is Old Lopburi, once a walled city. It has a smattering of ruins from the Khmer period: you can easily cover this place on foot in a few hours. To the east of the railway tracks is New Lopburi, with modern concrete structures and a number of army bases. To navigate in New Lopburi, take your bearings from prominent roundabouts on the road to the east. Leaving Old Lopburi there's the monkey shrine roundabout; two km to the east of that is a roundabout with a pond and a pagoda in the middle—the bus station is located on the southern

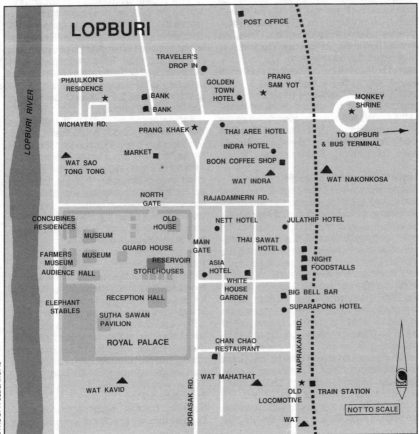

© MOON PUBLICATIONS

side of this circle. There is a third roundabout another two km east, with a statue of King Narai in the middle.

The Ruins

The ruins at Lopburi really *are* ruins—there's little to see here. Some of the ruins have ticket booths that charge B20 to enter, but you can see most of the ruins from the street. Opposite the train station is **Wat Mahathat**, a crumbled collection of walls of uncertain vintage with a *prang* from the 12th century Khmer period, and other additions from King Narai's reign. Stranded in a traffic circle in the center of town is **Prang Khaek,** a Hindu-Khmer ruin dating from the 11th century and later restored by King Narai. Just west of the monkey shrine is **Prang Sam Yot**—three pagodas dedicated to Brahma, Shiva, and Vishnu, built in the 13th century. This temple is featured on the 500-baht note. On the northeast side of town there is a compound where, if you try *very* hard, you might be able to make out the ruins of **Phaulkon's Residence** to the west, a Catholic church and Jesuit residence in the center, and buildings constructed for the French mission of 1685 to the east. **Wat Sao Tong Tong,** constructed during King Narai's reign, houses a large Buddha statue.

Lopburi Palace And Museum

The palace was built in the reign of King Narai and served as private residence as well as administrative and ceremonial center. After Narai's death, the court moved to Ayuthaya, and the buildings became dilapidated, although the site was used as an administrative center in the late 19th century by King Rama IV (who added some new buildings) and King Rama V. In 1924, a small museum was opened. Very little is left of the 17th-century palace, but the walls, gates, and garden are intact, which gives you enough to imagine what this place must have looked like. A small museum houses Lopburi-style Buddha statues on the ground floor and has a collection of European objects used by King Rama IV on the second floor. The museum is open Wed.-Sun., 0830 to 1200 and 1300 to 1600; closed Mondays, Tuesdays, and holidays.

In mid-February, a three-day fair celebrating the reign of King Narai is held in the grounds of the palace, and features ceremonies, processions, folk entertainment, and bazaars. Check with TAT in Bangkok for details.

Monkey Business

There is a monkey shrine dedicated to the Hindu god of time and death, Kala. It was probably first built when the Khmers were still in Lopburi, and reconstructed in Narai's reign; in 1953 a large new shrine was built: The place is home to hundreds of monkeys, which are not allowed into the inner shrine area, where offerings of fruit are placed.

In the early morning you will see troops of monkeys scampering across the railway tracks and on the road, returning home from raiding parties into town. Occasionally a monkey will succeed in electrocuting itself by touching the wrong overhead wires. And the odd monkey is run over and killed. The driver responsible for this must go off and purchase a new monkey to bring back to the shrine. Otherwise, it is said, he or she will have a run of bad luck because the god Kala will be furious.

Lopburi is so hard up for tourist attractions that it has attempted to create them. A noble effort sponsored by the Lopburi Inn at the end of November, 1990, was a monkey dinner for 500. At enormous expense, fruit, fried rice, nuts, and salad were delivered to the shrine, tables set up, 500 monkeys invited, and several thousand spectators gathered to witness the event. The monkeys passed up the fried rice, but otherwise it was, apparently, a howling success—and may become an annual event.

Fine Arts School

In the morning at the monkey shrine, you will sometimes see classical dancers performing (paid for as a merit-making procedure by a patron). The dancers come from the Fine Arts School, 1.5 km east of the railway station; a visit to the school where you can see training and rehearsals is recommended. Dress well. Closed for summer months (mid-March to beginning of June), as are most colleges and schools in Thailand.

Accommodations

Not a big choice in Lopburi. At the top end is **Lopburi Inn**, tel. 421-300, a luxury hotel four

MONK WITH A MISSION

Pra Chamroon Parnchand is the dynamic and unorthodox abbot of Tham Krabok. In his twenties, Pra Chamroon was a police officer with a family. His work involved highly dangerous detection and arrest cases, some involving narcotics operations. He had a powerful vision that involved saving people from suffering, so he turned his back on police work, left behind his wife and children, and disappeared into the jungle for a lengthy period. He decided to become a monk, but wasn't interested in following an established Buddhist school. His aunt, Luang Poh Yai, was his spiritual mentor. Tham Krabok means "Bamboo Cave"—in 1957, Luang Poh Yai, Pra Chamroon, and a few monks withdrew to a cave among the limestone crags behind the present monastery area to meditate.

In 1959 the Thai government outlawed the use of opium, and two addicts approached the caves and asked for treatment. The addicts were at first turned away, but Luang Poh Yai, an expert herbalist, recommended some medicines. From there, the word spread that addicts were being cured at Tham Krabok, and buildings were put up to house patients, with projects paid for by donations.

What has been created at Tham Krabok is not only a drug treatment center, but also a new order of monks. Unlike Theravada Buddhists, who confine themselves to study and meditation, and seek personal salvation, the monks at Tham Krabok are actively involved in all the building and farming projects around the monastery. These practices run contrary to the Vinaya, the 2,000-year-old code of conduct for Buddhists, which forbids heavy labor such as tilling the soil. Five percent of the addicts treated are female—the fact that monks at Tham Krabok deal directly with female addicts is another unorthodox procedure for Buddhism.

Highly unusual, too, are the vows the monks take. Among their vows, the monks swear never to use any kind of transport—including bicycles and horses. There are other Asian orders that take similar vows, wandering around from place to place to spread their teachings (pilgrimage is a form of merit-making, as taught by Buddha)—but at Tham Krabok the effect seems to be the opposite. The vow not to use transport has lead to a closer-knit community in that monks would have to think twice about taking a five-day hike to Bangkok. At other Thai monasteries, monk absenteeism is common—monks travel frequently to visit relatives, or to go to other schools for instruction.

In 1979 Pra Chamroon was awarded the prestigious Ramon Magsaysay Award for community services, but since he could not travel to collect it, another solution was arrived at: the Filipino ambassador traveled to Tham Krabok to give the award. Rather than the community at Tham Krabok going outside, the world comes to them. Any vehicles that are donated to the monastery are designated to lay operators by the abbot. If there is an accident, the injured monk would be rushed off in a stretcher by other monks to the nearest hospital—at Pra Puttabat, seven km away.

Once a year, in May or June, all the monks go off on a "walkabout," sometimes for a week, sometimes for three weeks. The entire band of 200 monks and retinue carry their own supplies. The monks each shoulder a 10-kilogram white umbrella that serves as a tent—the weight comes from the wooden staking pole in the center and from mosquito netting attached to the rim of the umbrella. At night the monks form a circle of umbrella-tents, light their lamps—and create their own village.

km to the east, close to the third traffic circle; prices range B300 single to B750 deluxe. Moderate hotels in Old Lopburi run about B100-200 double: these include **Asia Hotel**, tel. 411-892. Budget hotels can be found near the station and charge under B100 for basic rooms. These include **Suparapong, Nett, Julathip**, and **Thai Sawat** hotels. Some of the cheaper hotels operate as "short-time" places.

Hungry?

Strung out along the west side of the railway tracks at night are lots of foodstalls. Around here is **Boon Bakery** (see map), a favorite meeting spot for young people. It is a combination of bakery, coffee shop, and restaurant—and, wonder of wonders, they even have toast. A fancier location is the **White House Garden**, which, as the name suggests, has tables in a garden. This place is moderate to expensive (B80 a dish). In the same area, and expensive, is the **Chan-Chao** restaurant, with Western-style music and singing.

Slow Dancing

There are lots of army bases around Lopburi, so there is some nightlife catering to officers. There are a few hostess-type places with female disco singers, and dancing girls can be "rented" for dancing by the hour, for about B80. In fact, this rental is expected by the management: apparently a foreigner who arrives with a girlfriend or wife is charged B40 extra. These clubs are not cheap—Big Bell Bar charges B100 for a large beer. This kind of nightclub died out in Bangkok, but is still going up-country.

Meeting People

A good place to head for is the **Travelers' Drop-In Center**, an English school run by Richard, who hails from Lopburi and spent some time in Australia. His students are keen to meet real live Westerners: this can be a very fruitful exchange since they get to practice their English, and you get a free tour guide—and restaurant guide. Richard has maps and travel information; above the school are two rooms for B60 apiece—inquire.

Getting There

Lopburi is three hours from Bangkok by a/c bus—departures every 20 minutes. The bus terminus in Lopburi is two km east of old Lopburi—take a local green or blue bus going west for a few baht, or rent a trishaw for about B20. Rapid train takes 2 1/2 hours from Bangkok; ordinary train takes almost an hour longer; Lopburi to Ayuthaya is about an hour by train.

WAT THAM KRABOK

Wat Tham Krabok, 130 km to the northeast of Bangkok, is home to the most unusual community in Central Thailand. The monks at this monastery, under the direction of the abbot, Pra Chamroon, have been treating heroin and hard drug users in a detoxification program which has been operating since 1959. Since that time, over 60,000 addicts have passed through the rigorous ten-day cure, and the abbot claims a success rate of 70 percent, based on follow-up research. If this is so, the rate is exponentially higher than any rehabilitation program *anywhere*. Apparently the abbot has been so successful that opium barons in northern Thailand have threatened his life because of loss of "customers"—whole Hmong tribal villages from the north have arrived at Wat Tham Krabok for the detox program. Tham Krabok is an entire community, with about 200 monks, 20 nuns, 150 supporting lay people, and up to 150 patients in residence. Relatives of those undergoing treatment stay at the *wat;* there is also an out-patient section.

How do the abbot and his staff succeed where most Western programs have failed? It has been suggested that drug addiction is a spiritual thing—and requires a spiritual cure. Upon entering the monastery, addicts have to make a firm commitment that they will complete ten days of treatment, and that they will never again have anything to do with drugs. For the first five days, patients take herbal medicines, mainly a vile-tasting brown liquid that induces vomiting. For the next five days, they have regular steam baths, which ease aches and pains and lead to a feeling of cleanliness and well-being. They are given counseling to strengthen their resolve to abandon drug use. After this period patients can opt to stay on—joining work crews to cultivate the monastery's maize fields, or helping in other projects. This is intended to strengthen the body and develop confidence. Treatment is cheap—Thais pay B50-70 a day for basic expenses.

The abbot claims that his cure can be applied to any addiction—for treating alcoholics, for instance. One drug that seems to have been overlooked at the monastery is nicotine. Cigarettes are freely available to patients and to monks (who often smoke), although patients are not allowed regular tea or carbonated drinks during their treatment. The secret medicine used in the treatment is said to derive from scores of plants grown in the area—and it also appears to contain nicotine, which acts as an emetic.

Heroin addicts line up for a daily dose of vile-tasting herbal medicine at Wat Tham Krabok.

Visiting Tham Krabok

Due to a severe shortage of accommodations, not even patients are permitted to stay at the monastery (most are out-patients), so you cannot stay overnight unless you have a prior arrangement. On a day-trip you're welcome to wander around as long as you don't interfere with the work of the monastery. This means that the detox area (where the ten-day sessions are conducted) is off-limits to visitors—there is a warning sign outside.

What you will see are the patients who've completed the ten-day session and have elected to stay on—making furniture or helping in construction and farming around the *wat*. They're dressed in the faded pink clothing given to them on arrival. And you'll see brown-robed monks hard at work: among their ranks are former addicts and traffickers, and law and drugs enforcement officers. Some of the monks speak English. Two Western monks in residence are Pra Gordon, a black American from New York (a Vietnam war veteran), and Pra Peter, from Germany (a former addict). While the monks do not accept money themselves from any source, the monastery relies heavily on donations for its funding, so if you want to make a donation this will be greatly appreciated.

Set into the cliffs behind the monastery are the caves where the monastery was founded. The niches of the caves are being filled with large concrete Buddha statues—some 50 of them. There's a bizarre centerpiece at the monastery: a raised platform ringed by ten-meter-high seated figures representing the 25 disciples of Buddha. They face inward, gazing at another platform with three huge pillars on it and two giant wheels at either end. The three pillars represent Buddha, *dharma* (teachings), and *sangha* (brotherhood); the two wheels are a Buddhist symbol for the cycle of life and death. The shrine was built to honor Luang Poh Yai, the founding nun, who died in 1970. No doubt it will become a pilgrimage site, attracting merit-seekers from around the country.

Education is a very important part of the monastery's work. If your timing is right, you might see a group of schoolchildren listening to a lecture by one of the senior monks. As an example not to follow, the kids watch addicts throw up into buckets after being given doses of vile medicine. You can take part in the detox process yourself—well, the more pleasant side of it: you can take a 20-minute piping-hot herbal steam bath. There are two sets of saunas—one for the patients, and one for the monks. The patients' sauna functions from mid-afternoon onwards and has two small cubicles—one for women, one for men. Bring a sarong and a towel, and relax in the lemongrass steam-sauna.

Temple of the Footprint, Pra Puttabat

Men can enter the steam baths in shorts, but women should be conservative as this is a monastery (the lay women at Tham Krabok go into the steam baths fully dressed).

Basic food and drink are available at stands near the steam baths. You can buy herbal shampoo, conditioner, insect repellent paste, decongestant balm, as well as honey, rice, and foodstuffs—all produced at the monastery. The nearest accommodations are at Pra Puttabat, seven km away. Motorcycle riders around the monastery may be able to take you there for a fee.

Getting There

The *wat* lies midway between Lopburi and Saraburi, just off the highway (20 km from Lopburi). You can take a regular bus between Lopburi and Saraburi, but make sure the driver and conductor know where you want to get off, as the sign for the monastery is easy to miss. From the turnoff, you have to walk for a kilometer—the monastery is the only place in the valley.

You can reach Wat Tham Krabok directly from Bangkok by bus. The air-con bus to Lopburi goes via Saraburi: the trip takes about 2½ hours from Bangkok's Northern Bus Terminal.

PRA PUTTABAT

Pra Puttabat is about 15 km from Lopburi and 135 km northeast of Bangkok. There are several Chinese-style temples in the area: more important is an ornate Thai-style pavilion—the *mondop* that houses a sacred footprint of Buddha. The legend is that the Buddha's footprint was discovered here some 350 years ago when a deer-hunter stumbled across a pool of water in the shape of a huge human foot—and found it had miraculous curative powers. Stalls in the area around the temple sell spices, carved walking sticks, and sticks for whacking the temple bells.

Pra Puttabat lies between Lopburi and Saraburi (tell the driver where you want to go). It's about 1.5 km from the highway to the temple—you can take a *songtao* or a converted motorcycle for a few baht. The Temple of the Footprint is one of the most sacred sites in Thailand—every year, around Maha Puja (the full moon of the third lunar month), thousands of pilgrims head for the shrine, including wandering monks who camp in the fields below the temple. There is a week-long temple fair, with folk performances and a handicraft bazaar.

SUGGESTED READING

The books mentioned here may not be available outside Asia, particularly those published in Singapore or Bangkok.

Guides

Bangkok Guide. Bangkok: Australian-New Zealand Women's Group, 1990 (second edition). A spiral-bound 200-page manual designed for those living in Bangkok—tells you everything from how to hire a maid to where to take aerobics lessons.

Cooper, Robert, and Nanthapa Cooper. *Culture Shock! Thailand*. Singapore: Times Books, 1990. The third edition gives a crash course on cultural taboos, done in an anecdotal style.

Hoskin, John. *A Guide to Bangkok*. Bangkok: Asia Books, 1989. Concise and well-written guide to the city.

Van Beek, Steve. *Bangkok*. Singapore: Apa Insight Guides, 1988. Comprehensive coverage, but heavy to cart around. There is a 100-page version of this, called *Short Stay Bangkok* (1990), which has an innovative design.

Warren, William, and R. Ian Lloyd. *Bangkok's Waterways*. Bangkok: Asia Books, 1989. An entertaining account of sites along the Chao Phraya River, but it comes up short on the *klongs*.

History

Davis, Bonnie. *Postcards of Old Siam*. Singapore: Times Editions, 1987. Postcards capturing old Siam from 1880-1930, with lively caption-material.

Smithies, Michael. *Old Bangkok*. Singapore: OUP, 1986.

Wyatt, David. *Thailand: A Short History*. New Haven: Yale University Press, 1984. Best concise history, with a good outline of the Bangkok period.

Buddhism And Thai Culture

Hamilton-Merritt, Jane. *A Meditator's Diary*. London: Unwin, 1986. The subtitle is "a Western woman's unique experiences in Thailand monasteries."

Klausner, William. *Reflections on Thai Culture*. Siam Society, 1987. Hard to get—try the Siam Society on Asoke Road.

Roscoe, Gerald. *The Good Life*. Bangkok: Asia Books, 1989. A lucid introduction to Buddhism—short, but to the point.

Treasures from the National Museum. Bangkok: 1987. This 100-page book, put out by the National Museum Volunteers Group, is well illustrated and describes different periods in the fine arts.

Van Beek, Steve, and Luca Tettoni. *The Arts of Thailand*. Hong Kong: Travel Publishing Asia, 1988. Hardcover large-format book that makes a good introduction to the subject.

Warren, William, and Luca Tettoni. *Legendary Thailand*. Hong Kong: Travel Publishing Asia, 1986. Lavishly illustrated introduction to the land, the people, and the cultural heritage.

GLOSSARY

amulet—tiny sacred Buddha image carried on person

Ayuthaya—Thai capital from 14th to 18th centuries

bot—ordination hall in monastery, often used only by monks

Brahma—four-headed Hindu god of Creation

Brahmanism—classical precursor of Hinduism; in Thailand, sometimes mixed with Buddhism in ceremonial rites

chedi—pagoda or bell-shaped spire containing holy relics

Dvaravati—art style (and kingdom) from 7th to 11th centuries

Erawan—three-headed mythical elephant, mount of Brahma

Garuda—half human, half bird mythical figure, mount of Vishnu

Indra—Vedic god of war and thunder

Khmer—ancient race in Cambodia, based in Angkor Wat

mondop—ornate square library

mudra—pose of the Buddha

Naga—mythical snake, protector of Buddha

Pra—honorific title used for important Buddha images

prasat—royal or religious ceremonial building

prang—Khmer-style pagoda

Ramakien—Thai version of Ramayana legend

Ramayana—Indian cycle of legends, known all over Asia

Rattanakosin—18th- to 20th- century-era walled city of Bangkok

sanjao—shrine

Shiva—Hindu god—the Destroyer and Reproducer

Sukothai—Thai founding kingdom from 13th to 15th centuries

viharn—secondary prayer hall or sermon hall

Vishnu—Hindu god—the Preserver

wat—Thai temple or monastery

THAI LANGUAGE

Thai is a tonal language that shares a number of features with Chinese. Thai is thought to derive from Chinese, but has overlays of Indian influence. The Thai alphabet is of Sanskrit origin, and is similar to the Lao, Khmer, and Burmese alphabets. There are four regional dialects of Thai: Central, Northern, Northeastern, and Southern. Central Thai is compulsory for study in all schools and is the official dialect. The Thai alphabet has 44 consonants, 38 vowels and dipthongs, and five tonal indicators. Thai grammar is very simple, but pronunciation is complicated. Writing in Thai is very complex—vowels are written above, below, behind, or in front of consonants.

The tones carry the meaning in Thai—without them, words may not be understood, or may be misunderstood. For example, the word *sua* (pronounced as in the French word "sur") with a rising tone means "tiger"; with a falling tone it means "shirt"; and with a low tone it means "mat." English transcriptions of Thai are a nightmare: they cannot convey the language accurately. The sounds simply don't exist in English, and Thai tones are very different in concept from the emotional tones used in English. The best thing to do is to go over the following phrases with a Thai speaker to get the sounds right. Or get hold of a phrasebook with matching tape: you can listen to an English phrase first, then the Thai phrase. Constant repetition of tapes will attune your ear to the tones.

Two language packs on the market are the Language 30 series (Thai), produced by Educational Services Corp; Washington DC, U.S.A., with two audio cassettes and phrasebook; and the Hugo Thai Travel Pack, produced in Woodbridge, Suffolk, UK, with one cassette and a phrasebook. Another good pocket-sized version is Joe Cummings's *Thailand Phrasebook*, published by Lonely Planet. These phrasebooks are doubly useful in that Thai script is given next to the English phrase, so if all else fails, you can point to the Thai text for what you want. However mangled your attempts at Thai, the locals will be delighted that you're making the effort, and it will certainly help lower prices if you

know the Thai numbers. An American study in the 1970s found that American speakers were best able to pronounce Thai sentences after consuming one ounce of alcohol, which means that in Thailand, with a bottle of Mekong whiskey, you should have no trouble at all!

Tones: In transliterations, the five tones used in Thai are generally rendered: ^ falling tone; ∨ rising tone; ´ high tone; ` low tone. For a mid tone (normal voice pitch) no marker is used.

Particles: There are polite particles used in Thai that depend on whether the speaker is male or female. At the end of a statement or question, a male would frequently add the particle "kráp," while a female speaker would add the particle "kâ." Thus, "sawàtdee kráp" (hello) would be spoken by a male, and "sawàtdee kâ" would be spoken by a female (bear this in mind if listening to a tape as a male speaker will only use "kráp").

Negatives and Questions: To negate a statement, put a falling tone "mâi" before a verb or adjective, so that "sabai" means "well" and "mâi sabai" means "not well." To make a question, a rising tone "mǎi" at the end of a phrase is often used (similar to a tag question like "isn't it?"), so that "Kǒw dâi mǎi?" means "May I come in?"

Useful Expressions: Mâi Pen Rai: No problem, never mind, it's alright, it doesn't matter. If something goes wrong, Thais shrug it off with *mâi pen rai*—it's not the end of the world. Also used to shrug off praise, as in "don't mention it." **Sanùk:** Good fun, feeling good, having a good time. Food, drink, sex, sports, fairs, and festivals are all *sanùk*. Being caught in peak-hour traffic is not *sanùk*. **Pai Tiâo:** Hanging out, wandering around, taking a stroll to see what's up. Instead of asking about the weather, a Thai will open a conversation with "*pai nǎi?*" (Where are you going?), to which an acceptable answer is a cheerful "*pai tiâo*" (I'm going out for a stroll). **Sawàtdee:** An all-purpose opener or closer. Could be hello, how do you do, good morning, good afternoon, good evening, good night, or goodbye. Who said Thai was a difficult language?

Openers

Hello/goodbye, how do you do . . . *Sawàtdee (kráp/kâ)*
I'm pleased to meet you . . . *Yin dee tee dâi rúuchàk*
What's your name? . . . *Khun chêu arrai?*
My name is— . . . *Pŏm chêu—* (spoken by male) or *dichán chêu—* (female)
Mr., Miss, Mrs. . . . *Khun* (followed by first name)
How are you? . . . *Sabai dee rěu?*
Very well, thank you. . . . *Sabai dee, kòbkoon*
I only speak a little Thai. . . . *Puût pasǎ Thai nítnòy*
I don't understand . . . *Mâi khâw jai*
Do you understand? . . . *Khâw jai mǎi?*
Where are you from? . . . *Khun maa jàk nǎi?*
I'm from Canada/America . . . *Pŏm (dichán) maa jàk Kanadaah/Amehrikaa*
foreigner...*farang*
How old are you? . . . *Khun aayú taôrai?*

Flattery

good/very good . . . *dee/ dee maâk*
The food is great! . . . *Ahǎn arròi!*
terrific food! . . . *arròi maâk!*
very beautiful!...*suǎy maâk!*
very interesting! . . . *nâr son jai maâk!*
I had a great time! . . . *Dâi ráb kwam sanùk sabai!*

Negatives And Questions

yes/no/OK . . . *châi/mâi/oh-kay*
don't want/don't have . . . *mâi aò/mâi mee*
sorry, excuse me . . . *kǒr tôwt*
I don't know . . . *Mâi róo*
no good . . . *mâi dee*
Can I take a photo? . . . *Tai ruûp dâi mǎi?*
What's this called in Thai? . . . *Née pasǎ Thai riàk waâ arrai?*
where?/where is? . . . *tînǎi/yutînǎi?*
when?/who?/why?/how? . . . *meûa rai?/ krai?/tammǎi?/yang rai?*
how much/many? . . . *taôrai?*
how long/how far? . . . *nan taôrai?/klai taôrai?*

Asking/Giving Directions

I'm going to— . . . *Pai—*
How far is it to go to—? . . . *pai—taôrai?*
Turn right/turn left . . . *Leó kwǎ/ leó saí*
straight ahead . . . *trong pai*

Slow down . . . *Cha cha noi*
Stop here . . . *Yùd tî neê*
how many kilometers? . . . *gi kilomet?*
north/south . . . *neǔa/tâi*
east/west . . . *tawanòrk/tawantòk*

Transport

air-conditioned bus . . . *rót tooa*
ordinary bus . . . *rót tammadaa*
bus station . . . *sattǎni rót may*
Where is the bus station? . . . *sattǎni rót may yutînǎi?*
railway station . . . *sattǎni rót fai*
train . . . *rót fai*
boat . . . *rya*
longtail boat . . . *rya hang yao*
taxi . . . *teksî*
bicycle . . . *rót jàkrayan*
motorcycle . . . *rót motorsai*

Places

I want to go to—. . . *Pai—*
airport . . . *sanǎm bin*
embassy . . . *sathǎn tôot*
post office . . . *praisinee*
bank . . . *tanakan*
gas station . . . *pam namman*
hospital . . . *rong payabaan*
drugstore . . . *rǎhn kǎiyaa*
police station . . . *sattǎni tamrùat*

Restaurant (Rán ahǎn)

Please bring the menu . . . *Kǒr doo menu*
May I have—. . . *Kǒr—*
fried rice/steamed rice . . . *khâo pàd/khâo plao*
sticky rice . . . *khâo neěo*
water/cold water . . . *nám/nám yen*
no ice, thanks . . . *mâi sai nám khěng, kòbkoon*
hot tea/coffee . . . *nám cha ráwn/gafae ráwn*
fish sauce (salty) . . . *nám pla*
sweet/sour/spicy . . . *waǎn/prîo/phét*
not hot (spicy) . . . *mâi phét*
a little hot (spicy) . . . *phét nítnòy*
the bill please . . . *kǒr check bin*

Hotel (Rong Raem)

double room (two beds) . . . *hôrng kôo*
single room (one bed) . . . *hôrng deêo*
air-conditioned room . . . *hôrng air*

toilet . . . *hôrng nám*
May I see the room, please? . . . *Doo hôrng dâi mǎi?*
Can you give me a discount? . . . *Lòt raakah dâi mǎi?*

Bargaining
How much is this? . . . *Nee taôrai?*
do you have—? . . . *mee— mǎi?*
too big . . . *yài kern pai*
too small . . . *lék kern pai*
too expensive . . . *paeng pai*
Do you have anything cheaper? . . . *Toòk gwa née mee mǎi?*
Can you lower the price? . . . *Lòt rakaa dâi mǎi?*
thirty baht, okay? . . . *sǎm-sìp baht dâi mǎi?*

Time And Numbers
today/now . . . *wan née/ deeo née*
yesterday/tomorrow . . . *mya wan née/prung née*
morning/evening . . . *chaó/ yen*
1, 2, 3, 4, 5 . . . *neùng, sǒng, sǎm, sì, hâ*
6, 7, 8, 9, 10 . . . *hòk, jèt, baàt, gôw, sìp*
11, 12, 13 . . . *sìp-èt, sìp-sǒng, sìp-sǎm*
14, 15, 16 . . . *sìp-sì, sìp-hǎ, sìp-hòk*
17, 18, 19 . . . *sìp-jèt, sìp-baàt, sìp-gǒw*
20, 21, 22 . . . *yî-sìp, yî-sìp-èt, yî-sìp-sǒng*
30, 40, 50 . . . *sǎm-sìp, sì-sìp, hâ-sìp*
60, 70, 80 . . . *hòk-sìp, jèt-sìp, baàt-sìp*
90, 100 . . . *gôw-sìp, neùng rói*
500, 1000 . . . *hâ rói, neùng pan*

THAI CONSONANTS

ก ข ฃ ค ฅ ฆ
ง จ ฉ ช ซ ฌ
ญ ฎ ฏ ฐ ฑ ฒ
ณ ด ต ถ ท ธ
น บ ป ผ ฝ พ ฟ
ภ ม ย ร ล ว ศ
ษ ส ห ฬ อ ฮ

INDEX

Page numbers in **boldface** indicate the primary reference. *Italicized* page numbers indicate information in callouts, charts, illustrations, or maps.

ABOUT THE AUTHOR

Born in England and raised in Australia, Michael Buckley now calls Canada home. A self-taught writer and photographer, he spends part of each year on the road. He has traveled extensively throughout Asia, and has trekked and mountain-biked in the Himalayan and Karakoram ranges. In addition to *Bangkok Handbook,* Buckley has coauthored a guidebook to China, a guidebook to Tibet, and is author of *Cycling to Xian,* a travelogue about bicycling across China and Tibet.

One place he would never take a bicycle to is Bangkok, but he likes exploring large cities as a counterpoint to visiting remote places. As a photographer he is particularly drawn to Bangkok's dynamic nature, and to its "cultural feast"—a feast found in no other part of Thailand. He has visited Thailand many times, traveling throughout the country.

Buckley believes that travel is transformation. "Travel cuts across barriers of time and space. It gives you a special sense of being wide awake—everything is new and different and magical, and there's so much to be discovered, so much to learn. Real travel means encountering people whose way of life is very different from your own, and learning from them. That's easy to do in Thailand—the Thai people are outgoing, and take great pride in having visitors share their daily lifestyle."

THE METRIC SYSTEM

1 inch = 2.54 centimeters (cm)
1 foot = .304 meters (m)
1 mile = 1.6093 kilometers (km)
1 km = .6214 miles
1 fathom = 1.8288 m
1 chain = 20.1168 m
1 furlong = 201.168 m
1 acre = .4047 hectares (ha)
1 sq km = 100 ha
1 sq mile = 2.59 sq km
1 ounce = 28.35 grams
1 pound = .4536 kilograms (kg)
1 short ton = .90718 metric ton
1 short ton = 2000 pounds
1 long ton = 1.016 metric tons
1 long ton = 2240 pounds
1 metric ton = 1000 kg
1 quart = .94635 liters
1 US gallon = 3.7854 liters
1 Imperial gallon = 4.5459 liters
1 nautical mile = 1.852 km

To compute centigrade temperatures, subtract 32 from Fahrenheit and divide by 1.8. To go the other way, multiply centigrade by 1.8 and add 32.

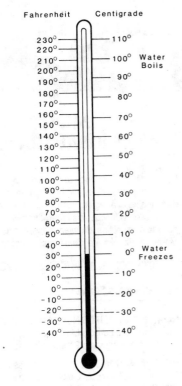

MOON HANDBOOKS
THE IDEAL TRAVELING COMPANIONS

Open a Moon Handbook and you're opening your eyes and heart to the world. Thoughtful, sensitive, provocative, and highly informative, Moon Handbooks encourage an intimate understanding of a region, from its culture and history to essential practicalities. Fun to read and packed with valuable information on accommodations, dining, recreation, plus indispensable travel tips, detailed maps, charts, illustrations, photos, glossaries, and indexes, Moon Handbooks are ideal traveling companions.

TO ORDER BY PHONE: (800) 345-5473 Monday-Friday 9 a.m.-5 p.m. PST

The Americas Series

NORTHERN CALIFORNIA HANDBOOK   by Kim Weir
An outstanding companion for imaginative travel in the territory north of the Tehachapis. Color and b/w photos, 69 maps, illustrations, booklist, index. 760 pages.   **$16.95**

NEVADA HANDBOOK   by Deke Castleman
Nevada Handbook puts the Silver State into perspective and makes it manageable and affordable. 34 b/w photos, 43 illustrations, 37 maps, 17 charts, booklist, index. 400 pages.   **$12.95**

NEW MEXICO HANDBOOK   by Stephen Metzger
A close-up and complete look at every aspect of this wondrous state. 8 color pages, 85 b/w photos, 63 illustrations, 50 maps, 10 charts, booklist, index. 375 pages.   **$13.95**

TEXAS HANDBOOK   by Joe Cummings
Seasoned travel writer Joe Cummings brings an insider's perspective to his home state. 12 color pages, b/w photos, maps, illustrations, charts, booklist, index. 482 pages.   **$11.95**

ARIZONA TRAVELER'S HANDBOOK   by Bill Weir
This meticulously researched guide contains everything necessary to make Arizona accessible and enjoyable. 8 color pages, 194 b/w photos, 74 illustrations, 53 maps, 6 charts, booklist, index. 505 pages.   **$13.95**

UTAH HANDBOOK   by Bill Weir
Weir gives you all the carefully researched facts and background to make your visit a success. 8 color pages, 102 b/w photos, 61 illustrations, 30 maps, 9 charts, booklist, index. 452 pages.   **$12.95**

WYOMING HANDBOOK   by Don Pitcher
All you need to know to open the doors to this wide and wild state. Color and b/w photos, illustrations, 66 maps, charts, booklist, index. 428 pages.   **$12.95**

ALASKA-YUKON HANDBOOK   by Deke Castleman, Don Pitcher, and David Stanley
Get the inside story, with plenty of well-seasoned advice to help you cover more miles on less money. 8 color pages, 26 b/w photos, 92 illustrations, 90 maps, 6 charts, booklist, glossary, index. 384 pages.   **$11.95**

WASHINGTON HANDBOOK   by Dianne J. Boulerice Lyons
Covers sights, shopping, services, transportation, and outdoor recreation, and has complete listings for restaurants and accommodations. 8 color pages, 92 b/w photos, 24 illustrations, 81 maps, 8 charts, booklist, index. 400 pages.   **$12.95**

OREGON HANDBOOK   by Stuart Warren and Ted Long Ishikawa
Brimming with travel practicalities and insider views on Oregon's history, culture, arts, and activities. Color and b/w photos, illustrations, 28 maps, charts, booklist, index. 422 pages.   **$12.95**

BRITISH COLUMBIA HANDBOOK   by Jane King
With an emphasis on outdoor adventures, this guide covers mainland British Columbia, Vancouver Island, the Queen Charlotte Islands, and the Canadian Rockies. 8 color pages, 56 b/w photos, 45 illustrations, 66 maps, 4 charts, booklist, index. 382 pages.   **$11.95**

GUIDE TO CATALINA AND CALIFORNIA'S CHANNEL ISLANDS   by Chicki Mallan
A complete guide to these remarkable islands, from the windy solitude of the Channel Islands National Marine Sanctuary to bustling Avalon. 8 color pages, 105 b/w photos, 65 illustrations, 40 maps, 32 charts, booklist, index. 262 pages.   **$9.95**

YUCATAN HANDBOOK   by Chicki Mallan
All the information you'll need to guide you into every corner of this exotic land. 8 color pages, 154 b/w photos, 55 illustrations, 57 maps, 70 charts, appendix, booklist, Mayan and Spanish glossaries, index. 391 pages.   **$12.95**

CANCUN HANDBOOK AND MEXICO'S CARIBBEAN COAST   by Chicki Mallan
Covers the city's luxury scene as well as more modest attractions, plus many side trips to unspoiled beaches and Mayan ruins. Color and b/w photos, illustrations, over 30 maps, Spanish glossary, booklist, index. 257 pages.   **$10.95**

BELIZE HANDBOOK   by Chicki Mallan
Complete with detailed maps, practical information, and an overview of the area's flamboyant history, culture, and geographical features. *Belize Handbook* is the only comprehensive guide of its kind to this spectacular region. Color and b/w photos, illustrations, maps, booklist, index. 212 pages.   **$11.95**

JAMAICA HANDBOOK   by Karl Luntta
From the sun and surf of Montego Bay and Ocho Rios to the cool slopes of the Blue Moun-
tains, author Karl Luntta offers island-seekers a perceptive, personal view of Jamaica.
Color and b/w photos, illustrations, maps, charts, index. 213 pages.   **$12.95**

BAJA HANDBOOK   by Joe Cummings
A comprehensive guide with all the travel information and background on the land, history,
and culture of this untamed thousand-mile-ling peninsula. Color and b/w photos, illustrations, maps, charts, booklist, index. 400 pages. **$13.95**

The Pacific/Asia Series

BALI HANDBOOK   by Bill Dalton
Detailed travel information on the most famous island in the world. 12 color pages, 29 b/w
photos, 68 illustrations, 42 maps, 7 charts, glossary, booklist, index. 428 pages.   **$12.95**

INDONESIA HANDBOOK   by Bill Dalton
This one-volume encyclopedia explores island by island the many facets of this sprawling,
kaleidoscopic island nation. 30 b/w photos, 143 illustrations, 250 maps, 17 charts, booklist,
extensive Indonesian vocabulary, index. 960 pages.   **$19.95**

PHILIPPINES HANDBOOK   by Peter Harper and Evelyn Peplow
Crammed with detailed information, *Philippines Handbook* equips the escapist, hedonist, or
business traveler with a thorough introduction to the Philippines's colorful history, landscapes,
and culture. Color and b/w photos, illustrations, maps, charts, index. 550 pages.   **$12.95**

SOUTH KOREA HANDBOOK   by Robert Nilsen
Whether you're visiting on business or searching for adventure, *South Korea Handbook* is
an invaluable companion. 8 color pages, 78 b/w photos, 93 illustrations, 109 maps, 10
charts, Korean glossary with useful notes on speaking and reading the language, booklist,
index. 548 pages.   **$14.95**

SOUTHEAST ASIA HANDBOOK   by Carl Parkes
Helps the enlightened traveler to discover the real Southeast Asia. 16 Color pages, 75 b/w
photos, 11 illustrations, 169 maps, 140 charts, vocabulary lists and suggested readings,
index. 874 pages.   **$16.95**

BANGKOK HANDBOOK   by Michael Buckley
Your tour guide through this exotic and dynamic city reveals the affordable and accessible
possibilities. Thai phrasebook, color and b/w photos, maps, illustrations, charts, booklist,
index. 214 pages.   **$10.95**

HAWAII HANDBOOK   by J.D. Bisignani
Winner of the 1989 Hawaii Visitors Bureau's Best Guide Book Award and the Grand Award
for Excellence in Travel Journalism, this guide takes you beyond the glitz and high-priced
hype and leads you to a genuine Hawaiian experience. 12 color pages, 86 b/w photos, 132
illustrations, 86 maps, 44 graphs and charts, Hawaiian and pidgin glossaries, appendix,
booklist, index. Approx. 880 pages.   **$15.95**

KAUAI HANDBOOK   by J.D. Bisignani
Kauai Handbook is the perfect antidote to the workaday world. 8 color pages, 36 b/w photos, 48 illustrations, 19 maps, 10 tables and charts, Hawaiian and pidgin glossaries, booklist, index. 236 pages.   **$9.95**

MAUI HANDBOOK: Including Molokai and Lanai by J.D. Bisignani
"No fool-'round" advice on accommodations, eateries, and recreation, plus a comprehensive introduction to island ways, geography, and history. 8 color pages, 60 b/w photos, 72 illustrations, 34 maps, 19 charts, booklist, glossary, index. 350 pages. **$11.95**

OAHU HANDBOOK by J.D. Bisignani
A handy guide to Honolulu, renowned surfing beaches, and Oahu's countless other diversions. Color and b/w photos, illustrations, 18 maps, charts, booklist, glossary, index. 354 pages. **$11.95**

BIG ISLAND OF HAWAII HANDBOOK by J.D. Bisignani
An entertaining yet informative text packed with insider tips on accommodations, dining, sports and outdoor activities, natural attractions, and must-see sights. Color and b/w photos, illustrations, 20 maps, charts, booklist, glossary, index. 347 pages. **$11.95**

SOUTH PACIFIC HANDBOOK by David Stanley
The original comprehensive guide to the 16 territories in the South Pacific. 20 color pages, 195 b/w photos, 121 illustrations, 35 charts, 138 maps, booklist, glossary, index. 740 pages. **$15.95**

MICRONESIA HANDBOOK:
Guide to the Caroline, Gilbert, Mariana, and Marshall Islands by David Stanley
Micronesia Handbook guides you on a real Pacific adventure all your own. 8 color pages, 77 b/w photos, 68 illustrations, 69 maps, 18 tables and charts, index. 288 pages. **$9.95**

FIJI ISLANDS HANDBOOK by David Stanley
The first and still the best source of information on travel around this 322-island archipelago. 8 color pages, 35 b/w photos, 78 illustrations, 26 maps, 3 charts, Fijian glossary, booklist, index. 198 pages. **$8.95**

TAHITI-POLYNESIA HANDBOOK by David Stanley
All five French-Polynesian archipelagoes are covered in this comprehensive guide by Oceania's best-known travel writer. 12 color pages, 45 b/w photos, 64 illustrations, 33 maps, 7 charts, booklist, glossary, index. 226 pages. **$9.95**

NEW ZEALAND HANDBOOK by Jane King
Introduces you to the people, places, history, and culture of this extraordinary land. 8 color pages, 99 b/w photos, 146 illustrations, 82 maps, booklist, index. 546 pages. **$14.95**

BLUEPRINT FOR PARADISE: How to Live on a Tropic Island by Ross Norgrove
This one-of-a-kind guide has everything you need to know about moving to and living comfortably on a tropical island. 8 color pages, 40 b/w photos, 3 maps, 14 charts, appendices, index. 212 pages. **$14.95**

The International Series

EGYPT HANDBOOK by Kathy Hansen
An invaluable resource for intelligent travel in Egypt. 8 color pages, 20 b/w photos, 150 illustrations, 80 detailed maps and plans to museums and archaeological sites, Arabic glossary, booklist, index. 510 pages. **$14.95**

PAKISTAN HANDBOOK   by Isobel Shaw
For armchair travelers and trekkers alike, the most detailed and authoritative guide to Pakistan ever published. 28 color pages, 86 maps, appendices, Urdu glossary, booklist, index. 478 pages. **$15.95**

MOSCOW-LENINGRAD HANDBOOK   by Masha Nordbye
Provides the visitor with an extensive introduction to the history, culture, and people of these two great cities, as well as practical information on where to stay, eat, and shop. 8 color pages, 36 b/w photos, 20 illustrations, 16 maps, 9 charts, booklist, index. 206 pages.   **$12.95**

NEPAL HANDBOOK   by Kerry Moran
Whether you're planning a week in Kathmandu or months out on the trail, *Nepal Handbook* will take you into the heart of this Himalayan jewel. Color and b/w pages, illustrations, 50 maps, 6 charts, glossary, index. 450 pages.   **$12.95**

NEPALI AAMA   by Broughton Coburn
A delightful photo-journey into the life of a Gurung tribeswoman of Central Nepal. Having lived with Aama (translated, "mother") for two years, first as an outsider and later as an adopted member of the family, Coburn presents an intimate glimpse into a culture alive with humor, folklore, religion, and ancient rituals. b /w photos. 165 pages.   **$13.95**

New travel handbooks may be available that are not on this list.
To find out more about current or upcoming titles,
call us toll-free at (800) 345-5473.

IMPORTANT ORDERING INFORMATION

TO ORDER BY PHONE: (800) 345-5473 Monday-Friday 9 a.m.-5 p.m. PST

PRICES: All prices are subject to change. We always ship the most current edition. We will let you know if there is a price increase on the book you ordered.

SHIPPING & HANDLING OPTIONS:
1) Domestic UPS or USPS 1st class (allow 10 working days for delivery):
   $3.50 for the 1st item, 50 cents for each additional item.
   Exceptions:
   Moonbelt shipping is $1.50 for one, 50 cents for each additional belt.
   Add $2.00 for same-day handling.
2) UPS 2nd Day Air or Printed Airmail requires a special quote.
3) International Surface Bookrate (8-12 weeks delivery):
   $3.00 for the 1st item, $1.00 for each additional item.

FOREIGN ORDERS: All orders which originate outside the U.S.A. must be paid for with either an International Money Order or a check in U.S. currency drawn on a major bank based in the U.S.

TELEPHONE ORDERS: We accept Visa or MasterCard payments. Minimum order is US$15.00. Call in your order: (800) 345-5473. 9 a.m.-5 p.m. Pacific Standard Time.

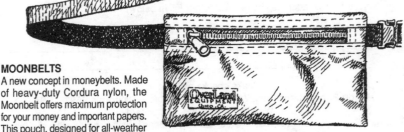

MOONBELTS
A new concept in moneybelts. Made of heavy-duty Cordura nylon, the Moonbelt offers maximum protection for your money and important papers. This pouch, designed for all-weather comfort, slips under your shirt or waistband, rendering it virtually undetectable and inaccessible to pickpockets. Many thoughtful features: one-inch-wide nylon webbing, heavy-duty zipper, and a one-inch high-test quick-release buckle. No more fumbling around for the strap or repeated adjustments, this handy plastic buckle opens and closes with a touch, but won't come undone until you want it to. Accommodates traveler's checks, passport, cash, photos. Size 5 x 9 inches. Available in black only.   **$8.95**

ORDER FORM

Name:_____ Date:_____

Street:_____

City:_____

State or Country:_____ Zip Code:_____

Daytime Phone:_____

Quantity	Title	Price

Taxable Total _____

Sales Tax (7.25%) for California Residents _____

Shipping & Handling _____

TOTAL _____

Ship to: ☐ address above   ☐ other (fill in below)

_____

_____

_____

Make checks payable to:
Moon Publications, Inc., 722 Wall Street, Chico, California 95928, USA
We accept Visa and MasterCard
To order: Call in your Visa or MasterCard number, or send a written order with your Visa or
MasterCard number and expiration date clearly written.

Card Number: ☐ Visa ☐ MasterCard

☐☐☐☐ ☐☐☐☐ ☐☐☐☐ ☐☐☐☐

expiration date:_____

Exact Name on Card: ☐ same as above   ☐ other (fill in below)

_____

signature_____